Why Any Woman

Why Any Woman

**FEMINISM AND POPULAR CULTURE IN
THE LATE TWENTIETH-CENTURY SOUTH**

Keira V. Williams

The University of Georgia Press
Athens

Published by the University of Georgia Press
Athens, Georgia 30602
www.ugapress.org
© 2023 by Keira V. Williams
All rights reserved
Designed by Kaelin Chappell Broaddus
Set in 9.5/13 Mencken Std Text Regular
by Kaelin Chappell Broaddus

Most University of Georgia Press titles are
available from popular e-book vendors.

Printed digitally

Library of Congress Cataloging-in-Publication Data

Names: Williams, Keira V., 1976– author.
Title: Why any woman : feminism and popular culture in the
   late twentieth-century South / Keira V. Williams.
Description: Athens : University of Georgia Press, [2023] |
   Includes bibliographical references and index.
Identifiers: LCCN 2023019356 | ISBN 9780820365565 (hardback) |
   ISBN 9780820365572 (paperback) | ISBN 9780820365589 (epub) |
   ISBN 9780820365596 (pdf)
Subjects: LCSH: Feminism and mass media—Southern States—
   History—20th century. | Women's mass media—Southern States—
   History—20th century. | Women in mass media. | Feminism—
   Southern States—Case studies.
Classification: LCC P96.F462 U695 2023 | DDC 305.420975—dc23/
   eng/20230630
LC record available at https://lccn.loc.gov/2023019356

CONTENTS

Acknowledgments vii

INTRODUCTION Wrestling with Scarlett
Southern Women, Feminism, and Popular Culture 1

CHAPTER 1 "Keep Living, Daughters"
Southern Sisters Ride the Wake of the "Second Wave" 15

CHAPTER 2 "You Get What You Settle For"
Staging Coups against Southern Patriarchy 52

CHAPTER 3 "The Business of Being a Woman"
Third-Way Southern Feminism 87

CHAPTER 4 "Change Your Life Television"
Oprah Winfrey's Southern, Neoliberal, Black Feminism 123

EPILOGUE "Just a Southern Girl in a Southern World"
Southern Feminist Pop Culture in the Early Twenty-First Century 159

Notes 173
Bibliography 199
Index 233

ACKNOWLEDGMENTS

Many thanks to all the usual and gracious suspects (friendly readers, letter writers, snack providers, etc.). I am especially grateful to Kimberly Chabot Davis and Cecilia Konchar Farr, who very kindly shared *Oprah* transcripts during lockdown when I had trouble accessing them from my home in Northern Ireland. Chapter 4 is heavily indebted to both of you.

I would also like to thank the British Association of American Studies and the School of History, Anthropology, Philosophy, and Politics at Queen's University Belfast, each of which provided funding for the research in this book.

This one is for Lolly. Everybody needs a twinkie.

Why Any Woman

INTRODUCTION

Wrestling with Scarlett

SOUTHERN WOMEN, FEMINISM,
AND POPULAR CULTURE

In 1976, the cable network HBO aired *Gone with the Wind* fourteen times in one week as part of the first television deal featuring the classic film. Twice a day for seven days, audiences tuned in; an estimated 382,500 viewers, or 85 percent of HBO subscribers, watched at least once during that week. A few months later, NBC got in the game, billing the first basic network telecast of *Gone with the Wind*, which took place over two nights, as "the most eagerly awaited event in television history." The hyperbole was warranted: Nielsen estimated that almost thirty-four million homes watched on both nights, making the film the "highest-rated television program ever presented on a single network."[1] That November, Carol Burnett's popular comedy show featured the now-classic sketch "Went with the Wind," which parodied the film not just by mocking Scarlett O'Hara's much-lauded ingenuity, but also by flipping the script to give the enslaved maid "Sissy" the upper hand in the end—literally, when she slaps "Starlett" and steals "Rat" Butler's famous line about not giving a damn. All told, the mid-1970s *Gone with the Wind* renaissance was a hit, and the film was a reliable ratings sweep, prompting CBS to acquire the rights in 1978 and air it throughout the following decade.[2]

With this able assist from Scarlett O'Hara, Lost Cause pop culture surged nationwide in the 1980s. The U.S. Postal Service issued a Margaret Mitchell stamp in 1986 to commemorate the fiftieth anniversary of the novel's publication, and the many media retrospectives of the novel and the film landed the former back onto the *New York Times* best-seller list for a few weeks. In 1988, native Atlantan Ted Turner, founder of CNN, launched the cable network Turner Network Television (TNT), which showed classic films acquired through his purchase of the back catalogs of Metro Goldwyn Mayer and United Artists. TNT debuted on October 3, 1988, with a performance of "The Star-Spangled Banner" followed by a showing of Turner's favorite movie, *Gone with the Wind*, programming he repeated a few years later for the unveiling of another of his cable channels, Turner Classic Movies.[3]

This network fare was an extension of Turner's offerings at the theater he owned at the CNN Center in downtown Atlanta, where, reportedly in response to tourist complaints about the city's lack of *Gone with the Wind*–themed attractions, he scheduled the film twice daily. To further satisfy this Old South craving, Turner held a premiere at the Fox Theater in Atlanta to celebrate the fiftieth anniversary of the film in 1989, part of what the *New York Times* called a "week-long promotional frenzy that included a costume ball, a parade, tours of antebellum homes, star-gazing and memorabilia-hawking."[4] As more American homes acquired VCRs, the popularity spread beyond Georgia, and *Gone with the Wind* joined the top-ten video rentals by the end of the decade. Others tried to cash in on this revival; plans to build a *Gone with the Wind* theme park in Atlanta sparked a bidding war in the early 1990s, although it was never built. In 1991, Charlestonian author Margaret Ripley was chosen by Mitchell's estate to write the sequel to *Gone with the Wind* because of her "very Southernness" and her record of writing best-selling, "gardenia-scented" novels about the genteel Old South. Critics generally panned Ripley's sequel, but like all things *Gone with the Wind* during this era, it sold well after a multimillion-dollar acquisition battle between publishers. Ripley's *Scarlett* stayed on the best-seller lists for weeks and was made into a televised miniseries a few years later.[5]

Even as Scarlett the rebellious belle continued her reign as the most famous southern character, "feminism" was a word one didn't hear often, at least not in a positive context, in the region in the 1980s. "Here in the South, we have a harder struggle," Sharron Hannon, editor of the *Southern Feminist*, the largest newspaper of its kind in the region, told the *New York Times* in 1986.[6] While it was more pronounced in the South, this "struggle" was nationwide. The rightward sociopolitical turn in the 1980s included what came to be known as the "backlash," a concerted effort to turn back the hard-won gains of the feminist movement through repressive policies, defunding, scapegoating, gaslighting, and a heavy-handed discourse regarding gender in American society. A corresponding culture of "postfeminism," or the idea that feminism succeeded in the 1960s and 1970s so much that by the 1980s it was hardly necessary, developed and similarly undermined the Women's Liberation Movement.[7] As a "discourse of containment" focused on the "'pastness' of feminism," postfeminism dovetailed easily with antifeminism, as scholars have noted, and the media heavily promoted these concepts.[8] In 1998, Erica Jong claimed that *Time* magazine alone had explored feminism's death over one hundred times in the preceding three decades. One memorable instance was in 1989, in a cover story in which the magazine declared that the feminist "superwoman" was "weary." "Is the feminist movement—one of the great social revolutions of contemporary history—truly dead?" *Time* asked. "Ask a woman under the age of 30 if she is a feminist, and chances are she will shoot back a decisive, and perhaps even a derisive, no."[9]

Time's preoccupation with the demise of feminism indicates popular culture's important role in the propagation of contemporary antifeminist ideas in the final few decades of the twentieth century, as documented by Susan Faludi, Bonnie J. Dow, and others. Some scholars argue that this postfeminist push was even more pronounced in films and television set in the American South. Deborah Barker and Kathryn McKee explain that films like *Steel Magnolias* "invoked the region's general resistance to politicized feminism and helped to establish the genre by facilitating the nonpolitical impulse" of contemporary postfeminism.[10] In the South especially, this neotraditional trend dovetailed with regional gender norms in which, as novelist Gail Godwin wrote in a 1975 issue of *Ms.*, girls found "image[s] of womanhood already cut out for" them and faced ostracization if they rebelled.[11] The Women's Liberation Movement, according to this line of thinking, either came too late to the South or bypassed the region altogether, leaving its social hierarchies intact and its culture particularly receptive to retrograde images of and ideas about gender.

Coming of age in the inhospitable climate of the 1980s South, then, it's little wonder that some of us latched onto the example of Scarlett O'Hara. Even though she was a half-century old by this time, Scarlett was a bootstraps belle well suited to this postfeminist backlash. Tara McPherson argues that the Reagan-era resurgence of representations of white southern women in popular culture served "to make new modes of southernness more difficult to envision."[12] But it is true that the older model of Scarlett was a liberated woman maneuvering in, and often ruthlessly trampling on, the strict norms of southern society. Scholars have long debated the feminist themes of *Gone with the Wind*, an argument I will not get into here. Rather, I am interested in the role popular media plays in "translating" feminism to a broad audience and in generating new forms of feminism. A related, relevant debate concerns audience reception, particularly the idea that readers and viewers are not passive consumers who wholeheartedly imbibe the intended messages of popular culture. Feminist scholars like bell hooks, Jacqueline Bobo, and Kimberly Chabot Davis counter that different demographic groups interpret texts in myriad ways, often offering oppositional, empathetic, and even activist readings of novels, television shows, and films that speak to intersectional experiences and feminist standpoints.[13]

I examine these kinds of claims in regard to specific texts in the subsequent chapters, but suffice it to say for now that while I find the academic debate about Scarlett's feminism to be robust and worthwhile, to many southern girls and women in the 1980s, the answer was clear. Scarlett was a clever belle who deftly managed men, was indifferent to marriage and motherhood, and ran her own successful businesses. She was, in Donna Tartt's estimation of the "belle" stereotype, "a Gatling gun dressed in a hoopskirt," with the "moral code" of a "soldier": "Divide and conquer. Feed off the enemy. Employ spies. Attack unexpectedly. Press an advantage. When surrounded, plot; when ambushed, fight. Always look good; never show fear, never show weakness—except, when necessary, to gain a secret advantage. On the parade ground, shoulders back and stomach in. Left, right. Smile to the grandstand; touch pearls, and wave."[14]

Scarlett upheld other white southern social standards as well: she was an enslaver, a keen exploiter of incarcerated Black labor, and a ruthless, pathologically self-centered capitalist. For her part, author Margaret Mitchell, who mocked the "lavender-and-old-lace-moonlight-on-the-magnolia" genre of southern popular culture, was shocked by the public's reaction to her most famous character, insisting that Scarlett was a "psychopath" and a "far from admirable woman about whom little that was good could be said."[15]

Yet Scarlett worship resurged in the 1970s and continued unabated—and not just among racists yearning for the Old South. In the 1980s, she could serve as a compelling counterpoint to other southern white women in popular culture, like *Steel Magnolia*'s blushing-and-bashful Shelby, the embodiment of the "fragile" angel who sacrificed her own health and life to be a mother for a few years. None of these women characters are uncomplicated, and they all feature variations of troubling regional tropes. The overt racism of *Gone with the Wind* morphed into the unremarked on but "unrelenting whiteness" of *Steel Magnolias* a half-century later. Riché Richardson notes the American tendency to anoint white southern actors like Julia Roberts, who played Shelby in *Steel Magnolias*, as "America's Sweetheart," a move which continually invigorates the long-standing "exaltation" of the region's white women.[16]

Its problematic racial politics notwithstanding, Steel Magnolias now lies atop many feminist film lists online, and subsequent generations of viewers have defended it as not reactionary but rather rebellious. As recently as 2017, a feminist blogger asserted that Steel Magnolias is not just a feminist film—it is "THE feminist film."[17] This retroactive designation decidedly ignores the historical contexts of both the popular antifeminism and the available types of feminism at the time that Steel Magnolias came out. Beyond the feminist novels, films, and television shows explored herein, Steel Magnolias was in theaters at the tail end of a decade in which Black feminism, especially in the work of southern scholars, flourished, and, indeed, the film debuted the same year that legal scholar Kimberlé Crenshaw coined the term "intersectionality." Much as the small-town nostalgia of Steel Magnolias calls on vague but familiar stereotypes of southernness, its allocation of the strength of "steel" to white women and silent servant status to Black women begs the question of what, exactly, fans mean when they deem the film "feminist." The simultaneous Gone with the Wind renaissance points to an active desire on the part of media consumers to fantasize in the present about past southern hierarchies.[18]

Yet to deem these films wholly un- or antifeminist flattens both the texts and viewers' experiences of them. Barker and McKee argue that the spate of "chick flicks" featuring southern white women at the end of the twentieth century—including Steel Magnolias, Fried Green Tomatoes (1991), Something to Talk About (1995), Hope Floats (1998), Where the Heart Is (2000), and The Divine Secrets of the Ya-Ya Sisterhood (2002)—offers a "traditional and often comic backdrop against which to examine the unresolved conflicts generated by the feminist movement."[19] The titular "Steel Magnolias" call on a specifically southern brand of ladylike feminism in which white women conduct their resistance to patriarchal dominance beneath the veneer of regional etiquette. The beauty parlor in which they frequently congregate is, according to Tara McPherson, a kind of "liminal space" between public and private, a "safe haven" for women in which they connect the personal and political.[20] They just happen to do so in folksy language, drawling accents, big hair, and sentimental scenes. Each can be viewed as a retrograde feminine stereotype of the southern white woman or, alternately, as a Trojan horse in which to smuggle quasi-feminism below the Mason-Dixon Line. Either way, their whiteness is a core component of their gender politics and their popular reception.

The public, critical, and scholarly debates over Gone with the Wind and

Steel Magnolias tap into several historical problems that *Why Any Woman* explores. What do these mixed reactions tell us about the ambivalence, contradictions, and complications of southern feminism in a region and during an era in which feminism was reportedly dead or was at least in a coma? What other forms of feminism did southern popular culture offer at the time, and how did these forms reflect or refract national gender politics? As feminist texts, what roles did this regional popular culture play as a bridge between "waves" and types of feminism in the final two decades of the twentieth century?

Like *Ms.* in its early years, the texts I explore herein were popular lifelines that connected viewers, readers, and consumers with feminist ideas across time, geography, culture, and politics in the 1980s and 1990s.[21] Through an examination of texts that represent various forms of contemporary southern feminism in the last two decades of the twentieth century, I find that pop culture by and about southern women offered often overlapping and sometimes contradicting feminist politics: liberal and radical, centrist and revolutionary, individualized and intersectional, capitalistic and communitarian. Indeed, I argue that pop culture by and about southern women was a—and when it comes to the media dominance of Oprah Winfrey in the late 1990s, it was perhaps *the* primary source of contemporary forms of feminism in this era.

Although historians have till recently tended to ignore southern popular culture as not quite meriting scholarly attention, the regional preoccupation with ideas about gender inevitably generates stereotypes that have, in each era, served as shorthand for understanding southern cultures. These stereotypes are powerful enough that one historian claims that the South is "as much an evolving set of images as an actual place."[22] The most well-known historical representations of the South are of the moonlight and magnolias variety, which was meant to redeem the antebellum South as part of the "Lost Cause" mythology around the turn of the twentieth century. As in *Gone with the Wind*, this fictional moonlight was both racialized and distinctly gendered: no figure looked better in it than the mythical southern white "lady." In the 1970s, writer Shirley Abbott deemed her "not so much a real person as a utilitarian device covering up ugly reality. What makes her powerful is not her own perfection but her ability to mask the imperfections of the world."[23]

The white lady thus offered a center of gravity for all manner of distasteful regional mythologies. This pale and perfect figure perhaps reached her height (and her death) in *Gone with the Wind* as the genteel plantation angels Ellen O'Hara and Melanie Wilkes. As the belle who judged her own bad behavior against these role models, Scarlett O'Hara was their foil. The film, which debuted in 1939 to much fanfare, deployed these women characters to help cement the entwined mythologies of the Old and New South anew for a Depression-era audience. *Gone with the Wind*, especially the film version (which reportedly made Margaret Mitchell "yelp with laughter"), looms large over all subsequent representations of the South.[24]

Yet, as the creator of the most famous female rebel in southern popular culture, Mitchell saw her epic novel as a challenge to southern traditions, even if readers have not. Mitchell mocked critics' praise of her unintended nostalgic symbolism, and scholars of southern women's literature have backed her up, arguing that *Gone with the Wind* is a complicated text featuring gender politics that "deromanticized" the Lost Cause and especially the stereotype of the southern lady, even as it upheld white supremacy.[25] Furthermore, they argue, Mitchell was part of a cohort of subversive southern authors. Linda Tate traces a "southern weave" of women's texts spanning the twentieth century that feature unsettling and often rebellious "secret selves" invisible to the hierarchies of the "white male world." In defiance of the "tight girdle" of regional gendered expectations, explains scholar Janet Gupton, "southern women writers have wrestled free to point out the ambiguities and discontentment that the role of the southern lady engenders."[26]

The various texts produced by southern women like Kate Chopin, Ellen Glasgow, Zora Neale Hurston, Gertrude Rainey, and Bessie Smith form an unbroken trajectory of resistance that leads from the 1890s directly to the more famous mid-century challenges to regional mythology posed by Carson McCullers, Flannery O'Connor, Lillian Smith, Eudora Welty, Nina Simone, Janis Joplin, and others who refused to traffic in the moonlight. Yet despite this pop cultural proto-feminism, as well as the vital activism of southern women in the social movements of the 1960s, they continue to play a negligible role in the historiography of the feminist movement.

As recently as 2017, sociologist Wanda Rushing targeted two lingering assumptions in scholarship on the region: "that southern feminists are rare or nonexistent" and that the "Problem South" still clings, desperately and ahistorically, to tradition.[27] Neither is accurate. This is not to say, of course, that the South has been a hotbed of feminist activism. Given its history as the bastion of traditional oppressive hierarchies in the United States, it's not surprising that antifeminism in the 1960s and 1970s was strong in the South. Yet recent scholarship indicates that a focus on events like the movement for an Equal Rights Amendment (ERA) skews the timeline of southern feminism toward its perceived failures. In fact, a closer look at changes in regional gender politics troubles the conventional trajectory and geography of feminist history, not just in the South but also throughout the rest of the nation.

For many years, much of the scholarship on the "second wave" of feminism in the South has emphasized that while white feminists were keen to seek expanded resources and opportunities for women, many of them still held tightly to certain historical elements of regional gender politics. One woman described this tightrope in *Mother Jones Gazette*, a publication of the Knoxville Lesbian Collective in Tennessee, explaining that she could "hold fast to the parts of traditional womanhood," such as nail polish, while still striving to be whomever and whatever she wanted to be.[28] Scholars of this ambivalent version of feminism argue that it was a kind of middle ground, a redefinition of white southern womanhood that combined both regional ideals and national feminist ideologies. In contrast to the hairy-legged, radical, national stereotype, scholars have developed a list of specific descriptors for southern feminists, including "velvet hammers" and "white-glove activists," and adjectives like "masked," "coded," and "stealth" have been frequently applied to movements for gender equality and liberation in the region. Evidence suggests that southern women were well aware of what they were doing when they donned these "disguises."[29]

Yet this ladylike feminism was not the only kind of southern feminist activism. Many scholars now emphasize the "contextual and contingent histories of women's liberation," which means, in this case, that southern women faced both a regional culture and historical challenges to a universal "sisterhood" that made their experiences quite different from those of other women in the nation. "Second-wave" southern feminism developed early, out of the specific context of Black and white activists' experiences with each other, not simply out of their experiences of misogyny, sexism, and oppressive gender norms and institutions. Evidence shows that the southern feminist movement predated the national Women's Liberation Movement and further offered a radical, regional critique of mainstream feminism throughout the 1960s. These experiences between women forged several southern variants of feminism and spawned some of the more famous forms of national feminism. Scholars have challenged ideas of easy southern sisterhood across race and class while showing how different groups nonetheless worked together in struggles for equality and liberation. Many southern activists, writers, and scholars—Toni Cade Bambara, Angela Davis, bell hooks, Akasha (Gloria T.) Hull, Joyce Ladner, Patricia Bell Scott, and Beverly Guy-Sheftall among them—have long offered intersectional analyses of the Civil Rights and Women's Liberation Movements, finding the tangled roots of both in the regional experiences of Black women.[30]

There is thus a growing consensus that southern women's activism was not just part of "second-wave" feminism—it was also a primary source of it. The South, in other words, was a veritable "incubator" for the coming "revolution in gender roles," and the women of the Civil Rights Movement were also the "founding mothers" of the Women's Liberation Movement.[31] Scholars have argued recently that the "flow" of feminist ideology and activism was often from south to north, contradicting the usual tale of the backward South in desperate need of external enlightenment.[32] Over the course of the Women's Liberation Movement, this flow continued to replicate itself through the movement of individual activists and organizations and the production and dissemination of feminist scholarship.

The social movements of the 1960s and 1970s, particularly the Civil Rights Movement, had the potential to cause a sea change in representations of southern women for mass consumption via popular culture. Despite years of challenges, however, gendered and racial stereotypes of the region remained potent at the end of the twentieth century. In 1985, sociologists Maxine P. Atkinson and Jacqueline Boles conducted surveys to determine the persistence of the mythology of the southern lady. The required traits, according to both historical and contemporary accounts, were described by these adjectives: "simple, good, passive, delicate, innocent, submissive, mannerly, economical, humble, sacrificing, sympathetic, kind, weak, generous, pious, shallow, nonintellectual, hospitable, rich, and calm" (not to mention "white"). Atkinson and Boles found that the image these terms described still abounded in the mid-1980s, albeit on a "shaky pedestal" and to the psychological detriment of the region's white women, who felt "ambivalent, torn between [their] desire to emulate the true Southern lady and [their] feelings of personal inadequacy for being unable to do so."[33] As Tara McPherson explains in her deconstruction of the lingering Dixie mythology, these were "ideologies with reality effects": "Whether or not women embraced these ideals, their popularity had material effects in women's lives, be they black or white, rich or poor."[34]

In the 1980s, then, even after the Civil Rights and Women's Liberation Movements, not to mention a long history of concerted literary and scholarly attacks on the historical myths of gender in the region, the moonlit lady still haunted white women in the South enough that they reported anxiety over their failure to live up to her angelic standards. The revival of *Gone with the Wind* and its frequent airing on cable television likely had something to do with this, although that is a bit of a chicken-or-egg question. Were viewers obsessed with the Old South because of the film, or did they consume the film because they were obsessed with the Old South? Either way, the Old South and its attendant gendered mythology performed considerable cultural work and sold increasingly well in the Reagan era.

Although the 1970s were known for political television shows like *All in the Family, The Mary Tyler Moore Show,* and *One Day at a Time,* most network fare was decidedly less controversial a decade later, and those shows that were set in the South, like *The Dukes of Hazzard* and *Dallas,* generally featured stereotypical gender and class roles in a decidedly whitewashed region. Just as the Lost Cause mythology at the turn of the twentieth century was popular for sociopolitical reasons that had little to do with antebellum historical reality, these representations of the South in the 1980s served a similar purpose: to keep traditional images at the forefront to both mask and forestall social changes in the region. Indeed, rather than proof of the nonexistence of the Women's Liberation Movement, the rising prevalence of southern gender stereotypes in 1980s popular culture can be seen as a reaction to it.[35]

At the same time, as the Reagan rollback and its attendant retrograde representations reigned, scholars have found that some southerners came to exercise "a much quieter but more effective 'feminism'" in the final two decades of the twentieth century, resulting in an "improving situation for women well below the Mason Dixon line."[36] This feminism took several forms: academic, via the formation of women's studies programs and departments in southern universities and the publication of works of feminist theory; activist, as southern women participated in actions as individual as escorting patients at abortion clinics and as collective as attending marches for reproductive and gay rights in Washington, D.C.; and political, as women lobbied at the state and federal levels for laws regarding equal protection, anti-discrimination, reproductive rights, violence against women, and LGBTQ rights. Despite its status as the birthplace of the Christian Coalition and the Moral Majority, studies of feminism in the South in the 1980s and 1990s increasingly complicate the overwhelming narrative of "backlash" and regional backwardness in the late twentieth century.[37]

Indeed, the study of southern feminisms over the course of the century challenges the ways we generally characterize feminist history. Traditionally, feminist history has been allocated into the first (1840s–1920), second (1960s and 1970s), and third (1990s) "waves" of organized feminism, divided by decades of ostensible lulls in activism. According to this linear narrative, each "wave" left "unfinished business" to its activist daughters, who took up the mantle and pushed the agenda forward in an ever-progressing trajectory, albeit at different paces in each era.[38] But for the past two decades, scholars have been filling in the gaps, challenging this "proclivity to periodization," arguing that it skews the historical understanding in favor of the movement's most recognizable leaders, "collapses the second wave into whiteness," and "obscures the laborers" behind an unbroken march of continuous, if sometimes conflicting, feminist challenges.[39]

Significantly, as Kimberly Springer argues, the "waves" model has the capacity to "drown" types of feminism that do not conform to this historical model.[40] Notably absent from the conventional narrative is the wide-ranging and intersectional activism of women—especially southern African American women—in the late 1950s and early 1960s. Feminist theory flourished in 1970s activism and in the 1980s through publications by southern Black women, and this timing also troubles the traditional trajectory of feminist history.[41] The waves model is thoroughly entrenched in scholarship and historical memory, but it is woefully inadequate, glossing over conflict as well as cooperation between different feminisms at any given time in U.S. history.

As even a brief review of southern feminisms in the second half of the twentieth century indicates, it is not just the presumed historical trajectory of feminism that does not seem to apply to the South but also its typology. Nancy Hewitt explains that the waves model posits "ever-more radical, all-encompassing, and ideologically sophisticated movements," a narrative that does not withstand scrutiny and ignores the variety of feminisms in each historical era.[42] Early feminist activities in the South, such as the women's strike at the SNCC headquarters in Atlanta led by Ruby Doris Smith Robinson, were not "white-gloved" campaigns of moral suasion. Rather, they featured radical tactics and critiques of the gender hierarchy in the ongoing Civil Rights Movement and labor movement. In a recent review, Carol Giardina—a prominent feminist who started the first Women's Liberation Movement group in the South in the 1960s—argues that the most radical elements of the movement were forged early in the region, primarily by Black women with experience in civil rights struggles.[43] Within a few years, multiple forms of feminism developed across the South.

Thus, the ever-more-radical trajectory and the liberal versus radical split in feminist historiography does not capture the complexities of feminisms in the region during the 1960s and 1970s, as local and statewide studies by Stephanie Gilmore, Janet Allured, Megan Shockley, and others have shown.[44] If national histories of the women's movement omit significant swaths of the United States in favor of urban, coastal cities, they also eclipse the varieties of feminism that have been and are in constant conversation with each other in marginalized regions like the South. Just as significantly, this omission ignores the influence of southern variants on national understandings of and developments in feminist ideology and activism.

Scholars are revisiting the history of feminist activism and organizations, mining it for a revisionist, grassroots gender politics in the South. The chapters that follow are intended to augment this historiography by focusing on one of the most productive sites of late twentieth-century southern feminisms: popular culture by and about southern women. Pop culture does significant "ideological work" that can uphold traditional ideals as well as challenge them. Popular media can be, in Amy Erdman Farrell's words, a "crucial site of intervention" for progressive and even radical politics.[45] And the nature of popular culture is such that the challenges it poses to the gendered and racial order, for instance, are likely to be consumed—privately, in theaters or at home, alone or with friends or family—by more people than would ever read a feminist manifesto, attend a civil rights demonstration, or lobby a legislator for change. Scholars of feminism in the twenty-first century unequivocally cite popular culture as a major site of feminist ideas and activism, and this applies to the previous century as well. In the "cultural desert" of the late century, pre-internet South, during a time in which there were fewer avenues of activism and organizing, other sources of feminism predominated, and pop culture is where we turned for guidance, for role models, and—whether or not we knew it—for consciousness-raising.[46]

Why Any Woman is not meant to be a comprehensive study of popular culture featuring the feminist South in this era; indeed, music is largely absent from this study, despite the radical 1990s feminism of southern artists like Missy Elliott and TLC or challenges to the traditional white working-class gender ideals of country music presented by southern women ranging from Loretta Lynn and Dolly Parton to the (Dixie) Chicks. Likewise, most of what I examine here would not be characterized as a part of "youth culture," although, to be sure, plenty of southern children and adolescents, myself included, consumed these texts at a young age. In the South, before the advent of the internet and the predominance of cable (and in rural areas like my hometown, long after cable predominated elsewhere but was still inaccessible to many of us), we all, regardless of age, watched television shows like *Designing Women* and *The Oprah Winfrey Show* that were marketed to middle-aged women.

Instead of a comprehensive analysis of all southern feminist pop culture during this era, I've chosen case studies of different forms of regional feminism during this era. These southern women authors explicitly and critically grappled with the changing contexts of feminism, eschewing the generational conflict model of feminist history and providing a crucial bridge between "waves" in the South. In their work, I've identified some familiar feminist concepts as well as the emergence of new ones during this cultural transition from the overlapping social movements of the 1960s and 1970s to the ascendance of neoconservative politics and neoliberal economics in the 1980s and 1990s.

For the cultural producers I examine, the southern context was crucial. "Place," Wanda Rushing argues, is "dynamic and agentic," and "it can be understood as being at the center of struggles of power and meaning."[47] As with the Old South of the Lost Cause, the Souths in the pop cultural texts in the chapters that follow are imagined spaces. While some of them are quite specific—the progressive, entrepreneurial city of Atlanta in *Designing Women*, for example—other settings could be almost anywhere in the rural Deep South, such as the small farming community of *The Color Purple* or Oprah Winfrey's grandmother's farm. Still others are a creative mix; the plantation porch from which Beyoncé gives the double middle fingers in "Formation" is actually in Pasadena, while much of the rest of the visual album *Lemonade* was filmed in Louisiana. Imagining different southern spaces, and thus different southern possibilities, past, present, and future, is a core part of the ideological work performed by these texts.

This is true of questions of gender too. Riché Richardson argues that "even in our time," ideas about and from the South are the source of "some of the prevailing representations of femininity in our cultural imagination."[48] When pop cultural texts envision new forms of southern womanhood and feminism, this also has implications beyond regional borders. While the multiethnic South has long hosted activism among Indigenous, Latinx, and immigrant women, the texts I examine center on white and Black women, as they have been the focus of mainstream popular culture emerging from the region in the past forty or so years.[49]

Why Any Woman examines texts by and about southern women—the play *Crimes of the Heart*, the novels *The Color Purple* and *Ugly Ways*, the films *Thelma & Louise* and *Beloved*, the television shows *Designing Women* and *The Oprah Winfrey Show*—as a means of understanding the role of regional popular culture in defining and redefining American feminisms as we approached the twenty-first century. Taken as a collective, these texts expand how we think about the whats, wheres, whens, and hows of feminisms in recent U.S. history.[50] "Why any woman give a shit what people think is a mystery to me," muses the blueswoman Shug Avery in Alice Walker's *The Color Purple*.[51] The following chapters feature southern women who decided not to "give a shit" by rejecting and reshaping gender norms, and their stories illustrate some of the ways southern women's pop culture has been and still is a crucial site of American feminisms.

CHAPTER 1

"Keep Living, Daughters"

SOUTHERN SISTERS RIDE THE WAKE
OF THE "SECOND WAVE"

Generational conflict is an enduring theme in understandings of the relationship between the second and third "waves" of feminism, or between the activists of the Women's Liberation Movement and their daughters' cohort in the 1980s and 1990s. Indeed, Astrid Henry wrote an entire book on the subject. In *Not My Mother's Sister*, Henry examines the centrality of the mother-daughter relationship, "with both its implied connection and aggression," to modern American feminism. Quoting Ruby Rich, Henry describes the "third wave" as a kind of "daughters' revolt," and she suggests that her cohort's "simultaneous identification with and rejection of second-wave feminism" is the source of their own identities as feminists. Sisterhood as a unifying metaphor was replaced, Henry suggests, by daughterhood as the personal standpoint from which "third-wavers" critiqued both society and the gender politics of their foremothers.[1] But in the South in the wake of the Women's Liberation Movement, feminist rebellion featured both daughterhood and sisterhood as a new generation of women writers started to come to terms with mothers in their fiction.[2]

A number of popular books by southern women during this era—including Dorothy Allison's *Bastard out of Carolina* (1992), Mary Karr's *The Liars' Club* (1995), and Rebecca Wells's *The Divine Secrets of the Ya-Ya Sisterhood* (1996)—center on daughters' individual conflicts with their mothers, whose struggles with womanhood, and especially with their roles as wives and mothers, wreaked trauma on their children.[3] In other works, however, southern authors foreground sisterhood in their feminist characters, offering sisterly support as a crucial tool for southern daughters who band together. These characters privilege their relationships with each other over the mother-daughter dyad in their regional rebellion. In particular, these dynamics played out in southern women's writing across multiple media formats in this era. Beth Henley's stage play and later screenplay *Crimes of the Heart* (1979) depicts daughters' resistance and sisters' strength through the lens of "second-wave" critiques as feminist politics slowly made inroads into the Deep South in the late 1970s, while Tina McElroy Ansa's popular novel *Ugly Ways* (1993) offers a regional take on the available types of feminism in the early 1990s through the story of three sisters grieving for their mother. These two texts serve as case studies of the generational tensions of southern gender politics that bridged the second and third "waves" of feminism and challenged the traditional regional prescriptions of wifehood and motherhood.

"Just a Real Bad Day"
Crimes of the Heart

As one of four sisters who came of age in the era when "sisterhood [was] powerful," Beth Henley was inspired by her sisters to write *Crimes of the Heart* in the late 1970s.[4] Born in Jackson, Mississippi, in the 1950s to a mother who acted in community theater and practiced her dialogue with her children, Henley was perhaps destined to become a playwright. Although she majored in theater in college, she was too shy to act (or even to send out headshots), but she took to writing, citing her family's quintessentially southern habit of storytelling as a major influence. In the mid-1970s, like so many other aspiring actors and screenwriters, Henley moved to Los Angeles to try to break into the film industry. But the stage was her milieu, and she endured several years of "destitution," as well as pressure from her father to go to "secretarial school," before she wrote a hit. Henley's first professionally produced play, *Crimes of the Heart* (1979), made her an "overnight sensation," and it eventually landed on Broadway after winning multiple major awards.[5]

In 1981, Henley won the Pulitzer Prize, despite mixed reviews from critics confused by the southern family drama. John Beaufort called *Crimes of the Heart* a "perversely antic stage piece that is part eccentric characterization, part Southern fried Gothic comedy, part soap opera, and part patchwork plotting."[6] But other critics praised Henley's work as part of a regional tradition, labeling her characters "eccentric" in the vein of Carson McCullers, Flannery O'Connor, Eudora Welty, and Tennessee Williams. Indeed, Henley has cited these authors as major inspirations, along with her mother's talent for storytelling. Early reviewers noted this aspect of Henley's work, applauding the authentic "vernacular, mannerisms, and ethos of the South" on the New York stage and her "penchant for 'whoppers,'" as well as her "keen southern sense of the grotesque and absurd experienced in daily existence."[7]

Henley has claimed that "vivid and violent" stories are likely just "inbred" from her upbringing. "Southerners always bring out the grisly details in any event," she explains, and *Crimes of the Heart* accordingly features a "shrunken ovary," a leg crushed during a hurricane, a horse struck dead by lightning, and a formidable patriarch reduced to a coma by "blood vessels popping in his brain."[8] But the primary wounds in this play are the multiple forms of psychological fallout—low self-esteem, depression, anxiety, psychotic breaks, suicidal ideation, and post-traumatic stress disorder—from the oppression inflicted by southern patriarchy on successive generations of women. Henley combines the "second-wave" emphasis on sisterhood with the rejection of the mother that later characterized "third-wave" feminism, reconfiguring the traditional regional focus on family values in the southern gothic vein.

Scholars note that the "mother-daughter connection" was often omitted from southern fiction prior to the 1970s, and, indeed, in some of the more famous women's texts like *To Kill a Mockingbird* and *The Member of the Wedding* the mothers are "simply missing."[9] But during the Women's Liberation Movement and in its wake, southern women's writing began to feature resistant women who struggle with their identities as daughters, enact these struggles in conflict with their families, and learn to resist regional patriarchy collectively with their sisters. Kathryn Lee Seidel points to mothers as the traditional "advocates who attempt to teach their daughters to conform to [southern] culture," yet the dysfunctional resistance of the mothers breeds the outright rebellion of their daughters in some southern women's texts in the 1980s and 1990s.[10] This rebellion is often directed at mothers, but Barbara Bennett has found that in regional women's fiction of the era, this kneejerk rejection is often followed by a reconciliation in which the daughters develop empathy for their mothers and, crucially, a feminist consciousness about their maternal histories and their futures as southern women.[11] In *Crimes of the Heart*, the development of a feminist consciousness is a painful intergenerational process mitigated and facilitated by collective action among sisters.

Although there is actual violence—attempted murder—at the center of the plot in *Crimes of the Heart*, the title refers to the more subtle injuries of patriarchal prerogative. The scene of these crimes is domestic: the "lived in, cluttered" kitchen of the old MaGrath family mansion in the small town of Hazlehurst, Mississippi, where the three MaGrath sisters were raised by their grandparents after their mother died.[12] The play opens in the fall of 1974, on the thirtieth birthday of Lenny, the eldest MaGrath sister. While the plot hinges on Babe, the youngest sister, shooting her husband and the subsequent return to Hazlehurst of Meg, the middle sister, this play is not so much about the present as it is about the past events, particularly their mother's suicide, that have determined the courses of each of the sister's lives.

Mama MaGrath's death predates the opening of the play, but she is in some ways an unseen character whose actions constantly haunt her adult daughters. Readers know almost nothing about Mama except that she committed suicide with her "old yellow cat" when her daughters were, respectively, fourteen, eleven, and eight years old. The macabre inclusion of the cat made her death a national news event, and the tragedy has followed her daughters into adulthood. It has broader reverberations throughout the town too: "all the skeletons in the MaGraths' closet" almost kept Chick, the sisters' first cousin, out of the Ladies' Social League, a scandal that Chick brings up as often as she can when scolding her embarrassing cousins. But even without Chick's shaming, the MaGrath sisters are not likely to forget their past for a moment, and they discuss their mother's death frequently.[13]

Although Meg concludes sadly that "she just had a real bad day," all three of the sisters link their mother's action to the men in her life. Like her daughters, Mama MaGrath had a domineering father, and, while Henley offers few details about the MaGrath marriage, it seems that she did not find a better model of southern masculinity in her husband. Lenny, the eldest daughter, says little about their father, but Meg remembers: "God, he was a bastard. Really, with his white teeth. Daddy was such a bastard." When Babe unexpectedly unearths a photograph of him—they thought their mother had burned them all—Meg recoils again: "Jesus, those white teeth—turn the page, will you; we can't do any worse than this!" Babe, who was too young to remember their father before he left, cites his abandonment as the cause of their mother's woes, "'cause it was after he left that she started spending whole days just sitting there and smoking on the back porch steps."[14]

After their mother's death, the MaGrath sisters became further entrapped in a dysfunctional patriarchal cycle when they moved in with their maternal grandfather. Although Old Granddaddy is confined to the hospital offstage throughout the play, cousin Chick serves as his constant "agent of acculturation," presenting herself as a model of southern decorum.[15] Chick is a former belle and carnival queen turned Junior Leaguer who judges, meddles, and worries constantly about appearances. "A brightly dressed matron with yellow hair and shiny red lips," Chick apparently has a cross to bear: the continuous craziness of the MaGrath women. "How I'm gonna continue holding my head up high in this community, I do not know," she laments in her first appearance in the play. Henley is very clear, however, that rather than a role model of femininity for the audience, Chick is garish, an embodied set of outdated regional norms that have failed to take root among the MaGrath sisters. The stage directions explain that "there should be something slightly grotesque about this woman" as Chick forces herself into too-small stockings in her cousins' kitchen, trying to make herself presentable to go retrieve Babe from jail. She loudly touts her own impeccable upbringing as she attempts to teach her cousins manners, scolding Meg for smoking, Babe for not cooperating with her lawyer, and Lenny for buying Chick's children inexpensive clothes that fall apart in the wash. "That's just the way I am; that's just the way I was brought up to be," she simpers immodestly when Lenny thanks her for her birthday present, a box of assorted chocolates. Later Meg notices the poinsettia wrapping on the box—Chick's thoughtful gift is both seasonally inappropriate and at least ten months old, which prompts the sisters to add "Cheap" to their list of unflattering nicknames for their cousin.[16]

That the sisters see straight through Chick is a prerequisite of their impending defiance of patriarchy, of which their cousin is the carefully crafted product. A "parlor fascist" according to pundit Florence King's hierarchy of southern types, Chick has painstakingly followed the rules laid out by Old Granddaddy and the small-town society of Hazlehurst, which rewards her with empty accolades and material wealth.[17] Of the four cousins, Chick is the only "success," although Old Granddaddy plays favorites and has clear plans for each of the girls, plans with which they struggle until the gunshots that set in motion the plot of the play. Susanne Auflitsch explains that Henley's early works are "marked by the disintegration of traditional southern values," and the juxtaposition of Chick's grotesque "ladyhood" with the psychological pain of the MaGrath sisters is an early indicator of this collapse.[18]

Sisterly trauma is evident from the very first scene. Readers meet Lenny as she furtively celebrates her birthday by sticking a candle in a cookie. Alone in Old Granddaddy's kitchen, she tries and fails repeatedly: the candle won't stay put and the cookie crumbles. Lenny's lonely failure is telling of her lack of selfhood. Often compared to Laura in *The Glass Menag-*

erie, whom Henley's mother played in their local theater when Henley was young, Lenny devotes her life to their overbearing grandfather, having setting up a cot in the kitchen to be closer to him while he was bedridden at home and visiting him daily in the hospital, where he has been fighting for his life for three months at the opening of the play. This life has taken a toll on her: she dresses frumpily, has a "round figure and face," and is nervous and prone to overreaction. "I try to do what's right!" she cries to Meg. "All this responsibility keeps falling on my shoulders, and I try to do what's right!"[19]

It is not just doing their grandfather's bidding that has worn Lenny out at a young age. The family patriarch has purposefully kept her close by gaslighting her about her so-called "shrunken ovary." This dubious diagnosis of "female trouble" devalued Lenny's femininity to the level of the Poor Thing stereotype, according to what Florence King called the "pelvic politics" of the South.[20] An "old maid," Lenny is unable to form relationships with men because she believes she is "deformed," and Old Granddaddy repeatedly, explicitly stokes her self-hatred, even convincing her to break up with a former suitor because of it. "I have this underdeveloped ovary and I can't have children and my hair is falling out in the comb—so what man can love me?" she complains to her sisters, revealing the depths of Old Granddaddy's indoctrination. She is a surrogate wife for her grandfather, and indeed, over time, she comes to resemble her grandmother. Her sisters notice that the years under their grandfather's thumb have turned Lenny into the spitting image of his wife, who gardened in an old sunhat and gloves that Lenny has taken to wearing in the yard. By the opening of the play, Lenny has almost fully succumbed to the "miserable, old, bossy man," so much so that she defends him to her sisters, saying that he only ever wanted "what was best" for them, to which Meg replies, "But sometimes I wonder what we wanted."[21]

Old Granddaddy's version of "what was best" differed for each of his granddaughters. His dream for Babe was for her to be the belle of Lost Cause mythology. Lenny explains that young Babe was "always the prettiest and most perfect of the three of us," their grandfather's "Dancing Sugar Plum." The old patriarch was pleased when Babe married well, predicting that she would "skyrocket to the heights of Hazlehurst society." "It was his finest hour," remembers Meg. But although Babe's husband Zackery is the "best lawyer in town" and a pillar of Hazlehurst, he is also a monster. As Babe's lawyer explains, with her medical record as evidence, her husband "brutalized and tormented this poor woman to such an extent that she had no recourse but to defend herself in the only way she knew how!" And so, Meg summarizes, after six years of abuse, "Babe shot Zackery Botrelle, the richest and most powerful man in all of Hazlehurst, slap in the gut." Babe explains simply that she was aiming to kill, going for his heart, but her shaking hands skewed her aim, so she shot him in the stomach and damaged his spine instead.[22]

Babe's first dialogue in the play is when Chick brings her home from jail. "Lenny!" she cries from offstage. "I'm home! I'm free!" This sets up a tension about how to read Babe: is she mentally unstable, or is she liberated? Henley writes that she is "exuberant," with "an angelic face and fierce, volatile eyes," and she does at first appear to be slightly mad, with her childish pink pocketbook, a new saxophone that she doesn't know how to play, and her refusal to explain her violent crime. When she is still behind bars, Lenny asks Babe why she shot her husband, and Babe replies that she "just didn't like his looks," which leads Lenny to wonder if Babe is "in-her-head ill." Meg, on the other hand, defends Babe, heartily agreeing that she never liked Zackery's looks either. Babe tells her sisters not to worry, her cheerful demeanor belying her grave situation: "Jail's gonna be a relief to me. I can learn to play my new saxophone. I won't have to live with Zackery anymore. . . . Jail will be a relief."[23]

When Babe's lawyer shows Meg her sister's medical records, it becomes clear why Babe might prefer jail to Zackery. Meg explodes: "Did he do this to her? I'll kill him; I will—I will fry his blood!" But Babe, still in shock, is almost bemused at the violent course of her marriage. She explains: "He started hating me, 'cause I couldn't laugh at his jokes. I just started finding it impossible to laugh at his jokes the way I used to. And then the sound of his voice got to where it tired me out awful bad to hear it. I'd fall asleep just listening to him at the dinner table. He'd say, 'Hand me some of that gravy!' Or, 'This roast beef is too damn bloody.' And suddenly I'd be out cold like a light." The southern feminist mystique exhausted Babe, an exhaustion compounded by her husband's abuse. If she, as Lenny worried, is "in-her-head ill," it is a traumatic response to violence at the hands of one of the town's most celebrated men. Unable to pretend any longer, Babe first dissociates like their mother, and then, to everyone's surprise, including her own, she fights back.[24]

While Lenny is baffled by this turn of events and concerned about Babe's mental health, their middle sister, Meg, is much more understanding. Summoned from California via a telegram from Lenny—"BABE'S IN TERRIBLE TROUBLE"—Meg returns promptly with her "sad, magic eyes" and "worn-out suitcase." Chick fills us in on Meg before her appearance in the play, citing her "loose reputation in high school" ("She was popular," Lenny protests feebly) and calling her "cheap Christmas trash" multiple times (a hypocritical insult, given Chick's regifting of ten-month-old Christmas candy as a birthday present to Lenny). Although she defends Meg to their preening cousin, Lenny resents her sister's need for self-gratification. She complains that Meg was allowed to "run wild," never making her bed, smoking and drinking at the age of fourteen, and crushing the dreams of local heartthrob Doc. Lest readers think that Lenny is just jealous, Meg confirms these accusations when she takes a bite out of each of her sister's birthday chocolates, looking in vain for the ones with nuts.[25]

Even in her apparent wildness, Meg too was fulfilling a fantasy for Old Granddaddy. She was known for her singing; Babe's young lawyer compliments Meg on the "sad and moving" songs she used to belt out at a local club, which he said she had sung like she had "some special sort of vision." Granddaddy loved her voice too, so much so that she lies to him when she returns to Hazlehurst, regaling him in the hospital with tall tales of her upcoming records, films, and television appearances. These lies are made possible by distance, particularly by the fact that Meg had run as far away from home as she could get after years of training herself not to feel the pain of their childhood. Lenny derides the "excuse" that Meg was the one to discover their mother's body as an explanation for her behavior, but Babe remembers their childhood differently, citing the "strange things" Meg started to do after their mother died in an attempt not to be a "weak person." When the young sisters would go to the library, Meg would force herself to spend the entire time poring over an old, graphically illustrated copy of *Diseases of the Skin*. She would do the same thing with images of polio-stricken children on March of Dimes posters, forcing herself to stare and stare. Then she would buy an ice cream cone and announce, "See, I can stand it. I can stand it. Just look how I'm gonna be able to stand it." This self-conditioning sustained Meg until she was able to flee Hazlehurst. To Doc, she explains that she left because she "felt choked," and she "didn't want to care."[26]

Once she fled town, however, Meg stopped this self-prescribed immersion therapy, refusing to read Lenny's long letters from home because they gave her "slicing pains" in her chest. She was unable to continue singing, and she ended up working an office job for a dog food company (a dismal occupation similar to one Henley held after college). Before her return to Hazlehurst, Meg "went nuts," landing in the Los Angeles County Psychiatric Ward after a nervous breakdown. She confesses to Doc: "I couldn't sing anymore, so I lost my job. And I had a bad toothache. I had this incredibly painful toothache. For days I had it, but I wouldn't do anything about it. I just stayed inside my apartment. All I could do was sit around in chairs, chewing on my fingers. Then one afternoon I ran screaming out of the apartment with all my money and jewelry and valuables, and tried to stuff it all into one of those March of Dimes collection boxes. That was when they nabbed me. Sad story. Meg goes mad." Back in Hazlehurst, Meg initially falls into old patterns of trying to please the patriarch. At Old Granddaddy's bedside, she hates herself for lying for him, not just "to" him, telling her sisters she feels "weak" playing the bon vivant belle role he has scripted for her.[27] But she is stuck in old patterns.

Each of the sisters has thus been trapped in self-destructive roles born of Old Granddaddy's fantasies for them, and their traumatic reactions—Lenny's depression, Meg's breakdown, and Babe's attempt at murder—unfold within the larger trap of Old Granddaddy's house, the setting of the entire play. In the family home, the sisters bicker, wonder, and worry as they discuss Babe's actions, their mother, their grandfather, and their relationships with each other. But subtle changes are afoot, symbolized by Lenny's eventual birthday candle success. After her futile attempts in the first scene, she succeeds in melting wax to make the candle stick to the broken cookie, and she lights it, makes a wish, and blows it out, repeating this cycle three times until she is interrupted by Chick. The candle is wobbly, but it holds, unlike the power the old patriarch has over his granddaughters. When Old Granddaddy has another stroke, Lenny reveals her birthday wish: all three times she wished that he would be put out of his misery.[28]

In the final scenes, Old Granddaddy slips into a coma, which prompts morbid laughter from the sisters. "We're just sick! We're just awful!" Lenny cries as they collapse into giggles over and over. In her analysis of the play, Alison Ruth Caviness explains that rather than being a "mournful" occasion, the loss of the old patriarch is "freeing," and, indeed, the sisters immediately begin to act out when Babe and Meg convince Lenny to call her former suitor Charlie, scared off by Old Granddaddy's talk of her "shrunken ovary."[29] "You're your own woman," Meg tells her. "Just take some sort of chance!" But they are interrupted when Chick comes over to share a bit of nasty gossip about Meg, whereupon Lenny finally reaches her breaking point. "Don't you ever talk that way about my sister again," she tells a shocked Chick, who begins anew to list the sisters' crimes against Hazlehurst society. Finally rejecting Old Granddaddy and claiming her space—in fact, claiming his domain as her own—Lenny shouts, "This is my home! This is my house!" Chasing Chick out of the kitchen with a broom and up into a mimosa tree in the yard, Lenny screams, "Get out!" She returns triumphant, and, after dancing around the kitchen with Babe, she calls Charlie, and they set a date for that very night.[30]

Meg's direct confrontation with southern patriarchy takes a different form. Although she came to Hazlehurst to "see about Babe," she ends up looking inward to address the family trauma. She was known for running from, rather than reckoning with, the past, but she is forced to confront it when Doc appears at their door. Meg and Doc have a troubled history; years before, she had convinced him to ride out a hurricane in Biloxi with her, but the roof caved in and crushed his leg. After medics evacuated them safely to a local shelter, Meg ran away to California. Heartbroken, Doc abandoned his dreams of medical school, moved away, and married a "Yankee," with whom he has a young daughter. He has only recently returned to Hazlehurst at the beginning of the play. He comes over the afternoon of Meg's arrival, and the bourbon they drink lubricates their conversation, which turns to the last time they saw each other in Biloxi. "I just kept wondering why," Doc said, and Meg cries, "I thought I was choking. I felt choked!" Finally dealing with these emotions, she tells Doc how she lost her voice, and temporarily her mind, in California. Doc is kind and forgiving, and they ride out to the country to "look at the moon." After her return at dawn with messy hair and a broken high heel, she tells her sisters that nothing happened, that Doc did not throw himself at her as expected, and that because of this turn of events, not in spite of them, she has found clarity: "Why aren't I miserable! Why aren't I morbid! I should be humiliated! Devastated! . . . I'm happy. I realized I could care about someone. I could want someone." This revelation has restored her voice, literally and symbolically. "And I sang!," she says wonderingly to her sisters the next morning. "I sang all night long! I sang right up in to the trees! But not for Old Granddaddy. None of it was to please Old Granddaddy!"[31]

Babe's gunshot heard 'round Hazlehurst is, of course, the most violent example of the sisters' clashes with patriarchy. As Babe tells her sisters, she gradually grew sick of Zackery's control and abuse, but later in the play it becomes apparent that there is a more immediate source of Babe's enlightenment about her miserable marriage. The precipitating event to Babe's resistance and eventually the attempted murder of her husband is her pedophilic relationship with her housekeeper's son, a Black teenager named Willie Jay. Babe presents her relationship with Willie Jay as frankly sexual, although she mentions that she adopted a dog of his that they also play with from time to time. Willie Jay gets no lines in the play; at only fifteen years old, he is a sexual object that Babe tries to protect by shooting Zackery when her husband finds them together. Shortly thereafter, Babe's lawyer arranges for Willie Jay to quietly board a bus headed out of town, and that is his entire role in the play.[32]

Beyond the power dynamics of age and race that make Willie Jay an obvious victim, this relationship is remarkable for a small southern town, but the MaGrath sisters hardly touch on it at all, even when photographs of the two together taken by a private investigator hired by Zackery surface. The closest anyone comes to acknowledging the extraordinariness of this relationship is when Meg exclaims, "I'm amazed, Babe. I'm really completely amazed. I didn't even know you were a liberal."[33] No one seems troubled by the age difference; it is not Babe's pedophilia that would ruin her reputation but rather her crossing of the color line. Henley has claimed that Willie Jay's role was a direct result of her initial inspiration for the play, a story she heard about Walter Cronkite:

> [He] was sitting up on the front porch of these rich people's house in the South, and this little black kid came up and said he wanted ice cream, and the man came down and socked him in the face and said "Don't you ever come around to this front door again." That made such an impression on him. I thought, "God, I'd like to kill somebody for just being cruel like that to an innocent person."... I thought it would be interesting to write about a character who tries to kill somebody, but you'd be in their corner rather than against them.[34]

In keeping with her sympathy for the child in this story, Henley presents Willie Jay as a victim of Zackery in the play, a move which completely eclipses the fact that Babe sexually exploits the teenager, enthusiastically and multiple times. Willie Jay is young enough to burst into tears when Zackery confronts him. Henley characterizes Babe as protective of Willie Jay, somehow sidestepping the fact that she is the one who put him in danger, thus mischaracterizing the perilous roles that white women have traditionally played in the sexual economy of southern white supremacy.[35]

First and foremost, Henley deploys Willie Jay as an expendable means to a white woman's enlightenment, a plot device with a nefarious history. At the time of the writing of this play, contemporary opposition to the Women's Liberation Movement often overlapped with white opposition to the Civil Rights Movement—one anti-ERA woman reportedly wrote to her senator, "Please don't desexigrate us!"[36] But southern white women have also historically used the gendered dynamics of white supremacy in the service of feminist politics. Some white suffragists in the South, for instance, relied on the image of the "black beast rapist" to justify their own bid for formal political participation, arguing that their votes were needed to protect Jim Crow.[37]

In *Crimes of the Heart*, Babe complicates this age-old dynamic by proclaiming her own desire in the statutory rape that she describes as consensual sex. Yet she does so privately, only to her sisters and her lawyer, a move indicating that she understood the danger involved. In *Crimes of the Heart*, then, Willie Jay is a sympathetic character, although for more reasons than Henley perhaps intended: he is a victim of white female sexual exploitation and of white male rage, a potent combination that often ended in lynching in the Deep South. Contemporary adults would remember that Emmett Till, one year Willie Jay's junior at the time of his own death, was brutally murdered for far more minimal contact with a white woman in 1955, just a few years before the fictional Willie Jay would have been born. But Willie Jay's mother Cora, Babe's housekeeper who had likely warned her son to mind his manners and watch his back around these powerful white folks, surely knew the danger, as well as the history of white women "crying rape" when Black men refused their sexual advances or when they got caught in consensual relationships.[38] Although Babe tries to protect Willie Jay from Zackery, none of the characters note that she is the one who has repeatedly harmed the boy and put him in Zackery's crosshairs. Because Willie Jay has already been surreptitiously bussed out of town by the beginning of the play, Henley essentially uses him as a set piece, a tool that Babe uses in her search for self.

And so it is Babe's sexual exploitation of Willie Jay that leads her to a cascade of feminist realizations about her marriage, her mother, and herself. When Zackery discovers them on the porch, he attacks Willie Jay, striking him in the face and shoving him into the yard. Babe tells Willie Jay to go home, and she runs for the gun in their living room. Her first instinct is to follow her mother's lead and escape through suicide. But then she pauses and thinks. She later says, "Then I—I brought [the gun] up to my ear. That's right. I put it right inside my ear. Why, I was gonna shoot off my own head. That's what I was gonna do. Then I heard the back door slamming and suddenly, for some reason, I thought of Mama . . . how she'd hung herself. And here I was about ready to shoot myself. Then I realized—that's right, I realized how I didn't want to kill myself! And she—she probably didn't want to kill herself. She wanted to kill him, and I wanted to kill him, too." Realizing that self-hatred was the misguided product of patriarchy and that Zackery was its facilitator, Babe repositions the gun and shoots her screeching husband. Afterward, she makes a pitcher of lemonade, drinks three glasses in quick succession, offers one to Zackery, and then calls the hospital. She is worried about landing in Parchman for her crime, despite the fact that few white ladies have ever ended up in the infamous prison modeled after a plantation. Even so, she does not regret her actions. When Zackery calls to harangue her from his hospital bed, she rails again about how she cannot stand to hear his voice.[39]

But Babe's resolve is tenuous, and she has not completed her reckoning with her mother's past once she pulls the trigger. Increasingly concerned that the news about Willie Jay will become public and ruin both of their lives, she attempts to hang herself, but the rope is too thin, so she trudges downstairs and sticks her head in the oven to try again. As she waits for the gas to come on, Babe makes a long-awaited but ill-timed psychological discovery; she speaks out loud to her mother, and then she realizes the answer to a question she has been asking the entire play. She pulls out of the oven to tell her sisters, but she bangs her head and falls back in. Fortunately, because the sisters are back together in the family home, Meg comes to her rescue. Gasping for air, Babe cries, "I know why she did it!" Their mother killed the cat too because, Babe explains, "she was afraid of dying all alone ... She needed him with her 'cause she felt so all alone." In the oven, Babe realizes that she is not her mother, and she is not alone. Crucially, she breaks the cycle of repeating her mother's actions. But she cannot do it by herself. Meg is there to revive her, and the sisters in turn save each other.[40]

Over the course of one full day, the MaGrath sisters—Lenny, exhausted from the years of patriarchal domination and caretaking; Meg, reeling from a breakdown; and Babe, suffering in an abusive marriage—come together, confronting their conflicts with their deceased mother, themselves, and the men in their lives. Their resentment transforms into support of each other as they break free of the patriarchal prescriptions of Old Granddaddy, of Hazlehurst, and of the pre-feminist small-town South. In the final act, Meg, distraught at Babe's suicide attempt, assures her little sister that she is not mentally ill: "Why, you're just as perfectly sane as anyone walking the streets of Hazlehurst, Mississippi!" Babe replaces Lenny's crumbly cookie with a birthday cake, and the sisters choose celebration instead of despair and emotional isolation. Together they light the candles as Meg advises that, in contrast to their mother, "we've just got to learn how to get through these real bad days here. I mean, this is getting to be a thing in our family." Babe agrees, finding strength in her sisters, assuring Meg that she's not "like Mama," not "so all alone." They sing "Happy Birthday" to Lenny, who blows out the candles and makes her wish, which is no longer centered on Old Granddaddy. Having confronted the past, Lenny looks with her sisters to the future, wishing "something about the three of us smiling and laughing together ... but it wasn't forever; it wasn't for every minute. Just this one moment and we were all laughing."[41] The delighted MaGrath sisters dine on birthday cake for breakfast, "laugh[ing] their heads off as they dig in."⁴² Saxophone music, such as the kind Babe might learn on her new instrument, plays as the lights dim and the curtain drops.

The very fact that the sisters happily consume Lenny's cake at the end of the New York productions of *Crimes of the Heart* represents the success of the play. Henley later explained that she was budget conscious when she wrote it. Assuming that she'd have to produce the play herself, she set the entire plot in one room, and she ended the first draft just before the sisters cut into Lenny's birthday cake, so that she would not have to buy a new cake each night of any production. But when a good friend of hers entered the play in the Actors Theatre of Louisville playwriting contest, it won, and its success launched *Crimes of the Heart* to New York. Critics unanimously loved it during its off-Broadway run, and soon thereafter Henley won a series of awards, including the Pulitzer, the New York Drama Critics Circle's Best New American Play, and the George Oppenheimer/*Newsday* Playwriting Award, and the play garnered several Tony nominations.⁴³

Of the prominent reviews of the play's Broadway run, Frank Rich's in the *New York Times* was by far the most appreciative. He recognized the Gothicism and dark humor as being in keeping with Henley's foremothers like Eudora Welty and Flannery O'Connor. The sisters' confrontations with the past are crucial, Rich wrote, to getting through the "bad days": "That can't happen for any of us until the corpses of a childhood are laid to rest."⁴⁴ Babe's gunshot helps the sisters confront, come to terms with, accept, and break—at least temporarily, "for this one moment," as Lenny explains of her birthday wish in the final scene—their ties to their dysfunctional family. In doing so, the sisters also break free of what scholars of regional gender roles call the "cage of southern patriarchy" or the "shackles of the pedestal."⁴⁵

This aspect of *Crimes of the Heart* has generated some discussion regarding Henley's feminist intent. Gene Plunka has tried to argue against this reading of the play, citing one interview from the mid-1990s in which Henley apparently "cringed" at the label "feminist," preferring to call hers a "human point of view."⁴⁶ However, except apparently for this one interview, Henley has consistently maintained a clear position on the gender politics of her work. When asked in 2004 about the statement that Plunka cites, Henley responded that she had no recollection of saying it, and she corrected the record:

> Perhaps I was just responding at someone's clichéd use of the term. I consider my plays adamantly feminist according to my understanding of the

word. To me "feminist" implies women are equal to men and also that women for many, many years have had their arms tied and their mouths bound. I think there is rage about that and some repercussions from that lack of freedom. Many of my women characters are in a rage about it or have some sort of self-loathing because of it. I think feminism is a very strong factor in much of my work.[47]

While it is certainly understandable that Henley might knowingly have avoided the label "feminist" in the backlash 1980s, perhaps her later embrace of the label is not a case of revisionism but rather of evolving clarity and self-awareness. She explained in an interview, "As a writer you don't always fully understand what you're writing. You sense things and know things in different ways and at different times."[48] In 2018, Henley acknowledged "in retrospect" her "incredible rage" as she wrote *Crimes of the Heart*: "I mean it was kind of sublimated.... There's something about growing up with misogyny, not to mention bigotry."[49]

Her first play reveals her struggles with being raised in this environment, and, indeed, although the plot did not come to her fully formed, one of her early inspirations was a story of a lost patriarch in her own family. Her paternal grandfather went missing in the woods for three days during Hurricane Camille in 1969, prompting a National Guard search and a governor's visit to Hazlehurst. Henley was inspired by this idea of a "family crisis bringing everybody back home," but, in her retelling, the story of the lost patriarch becomes an opportunity for the development of self among southern sisters.[50] The South is a crucial context for Henley and for her characters' feminist awakenings. In a later interview, Henley explained that it was important to be able to have a dual perspective, to be able to "see people that can swing really, really, really sad and horrible and terrible and really, really, really beautiful and funny." Growing up in the South, "there are these people who are feeding you, but they're chauvinist and racist. You kind of have to get a little perspective. You can't go with 'They're just evil,' and you can't go, 'Oh, I believe them, I love them.' You kind of have to go, 'This is a little more complicated.'"[51]

The timing of the play was significant both for Henley and for her characters' realization that "maybe this isn't the way things should be." When Babe shoots her husband, the Women's Liberation Movement hasn't yet reached Mississippi, but it is there, "subliminally," helping to influence the sisters.[52] *Crimes of the Heart*, Henley later realized, was her first experiment with a budding feminist consciousness, one that she does not regret: "I was touched that I was enraged … it's kind of a mark of who you were at the time if it's even vaguely honest—though you could never redo it. I couldn't recapture that sort of frivolous rage."[53] The MaGrath sisters "affront the notion of the southern lady," literally so when Lenny chases Chick out of the house.[54] Their ever-growing list of mean nicknames for their cousin makes explicit Henley's destabilization of the regional esteem usually afforded to former beauty queens—"You cannot call me Chicken!" Chick shrieks as Meg clucks at her in one scene.[55]

The fact that they have mocked Chick their entire lives indicates that theirs is not an unforeseen revolt. Unlike Chick, who has seamlessly conformed, the MaGrath sisters have struggled with southern gender norms from childhood as they watched their mother do the same. These failures to conform sowed the seeds of their resistance, which is both psychological and behavioral. The MaGrath sisters not only learn to actively defy the patriarchal roles prescribed for them by Old Granddaddy, Chick, and Hazlehurst society, they physically harm men, as Janet L. Gupton points out. Meg was at least partially responsible for Doc's debilitating leg injury, Babe statutorily rapes Willie Jay and then shoots Zackery, and Lenny fervently wishes for Old Granddaddy's death.[56]

Simultaneously, the sisters, especially Babe, learn to reinterpret their mother's self-directed violence. Their father's abandonment of the family drove Mama MaGrath to depression, but her final act was, in her daughters' estimation, not resignation but rather resistance. Susanne Auflitsch argues that Babe, in particular, even "seems to be impressed with her mother's heroism."[57] Babe adamantly defends her mother's actions when Chick tries to shame them, protesting, "Mama got national coverage! National!"[58] As the sisters finally confront their mother's desperate deed, one by one, they dispatch with the lingering representatives of traditional southern patriarchy, shooting the sexist scion of their small town, running the only "lady" in the play offstage and up a tree, and, in the most obvious metaphor for the destruction of patriarchy, celebrating after the death of Old Granddaddy. The sisters recognize and discard the tactics used to divide them, especially their grandfather's dysfunctional dreams for each of them, and they learn that they can take care of themselves and each other, a realization symbolized by their joyous sharing of the birthday cake in the final scene.

This is certainly a strong literal sisterhood in defiance of southern sexism, but is it feminist? If feminist definitions of "sisterhood" generally require not just shared struggle and mutual empathy but also "political solidarity," Henley's version is mixed. Henley has said of her feminism that it is apolitical and that, in general, she is "cynical about politics." "I don't really feel like changing the world," she explains. "I want to look at the world."⁵⁹ Yet *Crimes of the Heart* is not subtle in its attack on southern tradition when the sisters take direct aim at its gatekeepers, the patriarch and the lady. There is nothing "stealth" or "white-gloved" about their approach. When Babe makes lemonade like a good southern hostess, it is to quench her own insatiable thirst following an attempted murder, and, after offering it to her bleeding husband, she serves it only to herself, drinking an obscene amount that makes her stomach swell. But, despite its darkness, *Crimes of the Heart* is not a tragedy. Rather, in this gothic feminism, the sisters triumph together. In an interview, Henley confessed, "All these things that I feel inside are desperate and dark and unhappy." But in the process of writing through them, "they come out funny." She knew that Babe would attempt suicide, and she "had this horrible feeling that the play was going to be a tragedy."⁶⁰ But she surprised even herself with the final scene of the sisters eating birthday cake for breakfast.

Crimes of the Heart thus revises a well-worn genre—"gloomy postbellum family melodramas"—and offers southern women's gothic with a wicked sense of humor.⁶¹ Despite the mixed reviews, *Crimes of the Heart* packed theaters on Broadway and caught the interest of Hollywood, and Henley was hired to translate her play to the big screen. The "triple whammy" of powerhouse actors Diane Keaton, Jessica Lange, and Sissy Spacek played, respectively, Lenny, Meg, and Babe, but the film, like Henley's original play, to which the movie script was largely loyal, also got mixed reviews.⁶² Calling it a "felony," the *New York Times* panned it completely, opining that "a little bit of everything" was wrong with the "totally humorless" film.⁶³ By contrast, Roger Ebert applauded the palpable "love and warmth" with which the film addressed the dark themes of abuse, depression, and death, citing the "miracle of chemistry" between the actors playing the sisters. But even the positive reviewers seemed to miss its feminist messages. Although he recognized the southern tropes of Gothicism and family drama, Ebert lamented, "I am unable for the life of me to determine a theme in this material."⁶⁴

The mixed reviews did not prohibit Oscar buzz for the film, which grossed over $20 million and received several nominations, including of Henley for the screenplay, Sissy Spacek for Best Actress as Babe, and Tess Harper for Best Supporting Actress as Chick. Although the film did not win at the Academy Awards, it garnered other accolades, including a Golden Globe and a New York Drama Critics Circle Award for Best Actress for Spacek. Henley began to enjoy greater success, trading in her old car for a new Volkswagen and quitting her job in the parts department of an automotive company, and producers began to pick up her other screenplays. Even so, Henley had some issues with the film version of *Crimes of the Heart*. In the translation to the big screen, the timing was wrong. In 2019, she explained: "[The play] was written right when the feminist movement was starting. That's a really crucial element. That's why it wasn't quite right when they set the film in the '80's, because it wasn't on the cusp of the feminist movement like it's meant to be in '74. When people were just finding out that maybe this isn't the way things should be."[65] "These women are enraged," Henley said of the MaGrath sisters, citing "loneliness" and feminism as two of the play's primary themes—themes that got lost in critics' alternate delight in and derision of the southern gothic stereotypes in the play and completely buried in reviews of the mid-1980s film version.[66]

Still, *Crimes of the Heart* has over time come to enjoy a "mythic or iconic status" in American theater. Henley calls it a "memory play," indicating that the sisters' preoccupation with their mother was not merely some ghostly, gothic aspect. Rather, it is a crucial part of its gender politics that was lost in the displaced time frame of the film.[67] Susanne Auflitsch argues that in this and other plays, Henley's women characters are often in "constant mental contact with their mothers," and their resistance stems from making sense of their roles as daughters, as sisters, and as independent women.[68] Henley has affirmed this, explaining that her writing is "about overcoming ghosts of the past and letting go of what other people have said you are, what they have told you to be."[69] This struggle was a meaningful one in southern women's popular culture of her generation, and this tryptic dynamic of motherhood as haunting, daughterhood as traumatizing, and sisterhood as empowering was even more explicit in another such text, Tina McElroy Ansa's *Ugly Ways*.

"Tried My Best to Make Them Free"
Ugly Ways

Growing up in Macon, Georgia, which serves as the fictional setting of Mulberry in her novels, Tina McElroy Ansa recalls that stories were core parts of her upbringing as the baby of five siblings. Her mother was an avid reader, and she remembers listening to her grandfather's stories on the family porch and in the juke joint her father owned. Ansa has referred to herself as being "part of a writing tradition, one of those little Southern girls who always knew she wanted to be a writer."[70] A graduate of Spelman College, Ansa got her start as a journalist, writing for the *Atlanta Journal-Constitution*, the *Charlotte Observer*, and *CBS Sunday Morning*, for which she contributed a series of essays, "Postcards from Georgia." After becoming a freelancer in the early 1980s, Ansa started writing fiction, and her first novel, *Baby of the Family* (1989), was well reviewed. In her second, *Ugly Ways* (1993), Ansa takes an overtly feminist stance by focusing on the relationships between Black mothers, daughters, and sisters.[71]

Ugly Ways follows the three Lovejoy sisters, Betty, Emily, and Annie Ruth, as they come together to grieve and plan the funeral of their mother, Esther Lovejoy, known to them as Mudear. "[T]he kind of mother they had touched them all the way through their lives," Ansa writes of the sisters. "Not just when they lived with her, not just when they spent time visiting her, but all through their lives."[72] But, unlike Mama in *Crimes of the Heart*, Mudear is not just a preoccupying memory in her family; she actually haunts her daughters, watching and judging their behavior following her death in her own point-of-view chapters. By providing Mudear's beyond-the-grave narration, Ansa is able to juxtapose generational perspectives as the sisters come to terms with their maternally induced post-traumatic stress disorder. In doing so, Ansa's feminist fictional exploration of southern sisterhood goes beyond Henley's as it mines multiple types of mother-daughter relationships and intergenerational resistance to patriarchy.

The novel opens with a feeble Annie Ruth, the youngest sister at thirty-five, calling from the small local airport asking her sisters to come pick her up. She has just arrived in Mulberry, "The Big Little Town in the Heart of Georgia," from Los Angeles following the death of Mudear (a derivative of "Mother Dear"). While the plot follows the sisters during a few days of funeral preparations, the real action is their sisterly dynamic and, most significantly, how this dynamic has been mediated by their relationships with their mother. Each sister explores the trauma of the peculiar maternal bonds that developed in the Lovejoy household after Mudear underwent what they call "the change." This phrase is not a euphemism for menopause. Rather, through the voice of Mudear from her coffin in the funeral home, Ansa reveals that, years before, Mudear had a kind of feminist breakthrough that completely altered her behavior and thus her relationship with her family.[73]

Some three decades prior to the events of the novel, Esther abruptly stopped performing her expected duties as a wife and a mother, withdrawing from local society and delegating all household chores to her daughters, the eldest of whom was eleven at the time. After "the change," Mudear was fearsome even as she was more or less prostrate, spending her days "lounging around" in "freshly laundered" pajamas, making "everyone's life miserable in the house." She slept late every day, arising in time to make herself a nice lunch and have a long bath before her husband and daughters came home from work and school to do her bidding. The remote control to her television, she maintained, "was one of the world's best inventions." Her only activity beyond watching television and thumbing through mail-order catalogs was working in her beautiful garden, which she did exclusively at night. In interviews, Ansa has called this Mudear's "kiss-her-butt time."[74]

From outside of the Lovejoy home, Esther's transformation looked very strange indeed, and Mulberry's gossip mill spent years "discussing and dissecting" the family. Rumors abounded that Mudear had become an agoraphobic and murderous alcoholic whose garden was actually a graveyard in which she buried her victims. Local wags claimed faulty genetics were at work and that "it was only a matter of time before all the Lovejoys were seen running up and down the streets of Sherwood Forest half-naked with their hair standing on top of their heads." Others agreed that it was a disease Mudear would pass down, that "the whole family had 'walking insanity' like other folks had 'walking pneumonia.'" As far as people in Mulberry were concerned, all the Lovejoys were "walking-, talking-, working-, shopping-crazy."[75]

But within the home, Mudear's withdrawal was not simply strange—it was traumatic. Although the novel takes place in the present, largely through discussions between the sisters as they work through the shock of Mudear's passing, much of it centers on their memories of growing up in their mother's orbit. To her grief-stricken daughters, Mudear is a terrifying figure. Esther Lovejoy's small stature belied her post-change status in her family's eyes as a "mighty goddess" who issued orders from her throne-like bed, surrounded by catalogs and clad in any number of lovely bed jackets. As she contentedly gardened alone in the dark, her daughters saw her as something of a "strange, exotic plant herself" or a "jungle plant that had reversed the natural order."[76]

After "the change," Mudear did not leave the house except to work in the garden, even refusing to attend her own mother's funeral and Emily's wedding. She relied on her daughters to connect her to the outside world, picking their brains meticulously for gossip, which the girls eagerly fed her "like royal honey for the queen bee," hoping to inspire Mudear's roaring laugh. They took up the domestic slack, especially Betty, the eldest. Mudear explained to them that while she expected men to be lazy, "there's nothing worse than a trifling, slouchy woman." She repeated this adage even as she delegated tasks from a prime position on the living room couch, having had the door to the kitchen removed so that she might oversee all chores. And so her daughters, whom she treated like women rather than children, scrubbed the kitchen, cleaned the house, and paid the bills, while her husband Ernest handled the heavier tasks, like planting trees in Mudear's garden. Their mother, her daughters maintain, studied "the religion of Mudear," of which "selfishness" was the only tenet.[77]

This strict instruction in Mudear's "religion" took its toll on each daughter. With a distant father and a formidable mother, the Lovejoy sisters banded together, supporting and protecting each other from the time of "the change" through Mudear's death. They share dark and dirty jokes, clothes, and traumas, although the psychological damage that characterizes each sister's relationship with their mother is distinct. Betty, the eldest at forty-two, is considered by all to be the most capable of the sisters, and it is she who stays in Mulberry to be close to their aging parents as she oversees her two successful beauty salons. Since taking over the care and feeding of her sisters at the age of eleven, Betty's work ethic is unrivaled. Even when she develops a mysterious rash—likely a traumatic response—she continues to do "what Mudear expected of her." Growing up, she liked school, but her responsibilities at home kept her from making good grades or going to college, so she concentrated on making her sisters do well academically. Mudear's default response to problems—"Betty will handle it"—haunts her and keeps her in constant maternal mode. Betty is very protective of her sisters; she wants to take them into her lap as they gather on Mudear's porch after their mother's death, remembering how they would huddle there while their parents fought. Despite her strong maternal instincts and her financial success, Betty is unable to form her own sense of self in her mother's looming shadow.[78]

Yet Betty, the only daughter with memories of Mudear pre-change, is emotionally and psychologically the strongest of the sisters. Some of Mudear's more severe lessons for her daughters perhaps frightened Emily, thirty-eight, the middle and "craziest Lovejoy" sister, the most. Citing her "wild eyes and lip biting," town gossip held that she was the most volatile of the daughters. Emily developed lifelong insomnia after years of listening for her father so that she would know that Mudear had not made good on her "implied threat" to murder him in his sleep. To deal with her sleeplessness, Emily consults a litany of doctors and healers, drives aimlessly at night, and smokes "enough marijuana to keep a small country's economy going." During her frequent trips to Mulberry to Betty's beauty shop and to see her parents, Emily often stops under an overpass at the Ocawatchee River "to see if the river was deep enough now to jump in and drown," a practice she had begun as a teenager. Emily has obsessive-compulsive tendencies—"checking," she calls them—which Betty sees as her sister's desperate attempts "to be whatever was asked of her," fallout from years of being at Mudear's beck and call.[79]

Despite Emily's suicidal thoughts and obsessive-compulsive behaviors, Annie Ruth, thirty-five, is the most fragile of the sisters, having suffered a nervous breakdown that landed her in a Virginia hospital two years prior, and she is working on a second at the outset of the novel. When Betty and Emily retrieve her from the tiny Mulberry airport the day after Mudear's death, Annie Ruth is a "perfumed wreck," slumped in a wheelchair, weeping, smelling of vomit, face "still streaked with traces of some expensive European makeup." Beyond the shock and grief which has taken a clear toll on her, Annie Ruth is harboring secrets: she is pregnant, and she has been hallucinating cats in strange places for several weeks since Betty told her over the phone that "Mudear didn't seem herself."[80]

The trauma that governs each of the sisters is also the source of their bond. Although Betty is particularly maternal to her sisters, speaking to each of them on the phone frequently and arranging a three-way conference call once a week, they are all protective, and they are so close that they can read each other with just a glance. Together they feel like "survivors of a war" who have physically supported each other on the battlefield, "stepping over the dead bodies" to keep going. Mudear had high expectations of each of them, and so they learned to play their prescribed roles both in her household and in the wider world as they became adults.[81]

As grown women, however, they begin to passively resist. They defy Mudear's beloved gardening by hating plants and her dictates against school by loving books. In her work on Beth Henley, Susanne Auflitsch writes of southern women's fiction that some daughters of dysfunctional mothers choose not to become mothers, "possibly because they are afraid to leave their children with the same emotional scars they themselves have suffered." In *Crimes of the Heart*, this choice is implicit, but it plays out starkly in *Ugly Ways*: the sisters' firmest form of resistance to Mudear is a secret pact that they made as teenagers, as soon as Annie Ruth, the youngest, got her period. "As women," the three sisters vowed together that "they would never get pregnant and have children just to abandon them the way Mudear had done with them." For decades, they kept the pact. After Emily became pregnant during her second marriage, she got an abortion, and Annie Ruth traveled to Atlanta to be with her through the surgery, helping her to concoct the lie that presaged the end of that troubled marriage.[82]

Annie Ruth's pregnancy at the time of Mudear's death is therefore a shock to her sisters, and Betty and Emily assume she must be planning to have an abortion. But Annie Ruth has decided to keep her baby, and this violation of the sacred sisterly pact, combined with their mother's sudden death, serves as a catalyst for painful conversations about the wreckage Mudear made of her daughters. Annie Ruth claims, "She's all we ever talk about really," yet the discussions they have in the hours following Mudear's death are something different. By the end of the novel, these discussions have become a deep consideration, rather than a bitter rehashing, of maternal trauma. As they plan Mudear's funeral, the sisters talk openly about their mother, alternately breaking each other's hearts as they express enduring pain and sparking sad laughter as they imitate Mudear's many memorable one-liners.[83]

But confronting the past is not something the Lovejoy sisters do alone in *Ugly Ways*. Unlike Mama in *Crimes of the Heart*, about whose experiences and motives readers, theatergoers, and movie audiences can only speculate, Ansa gives Mudear a voice as she narrates chapters from her coffin in the funeral home. This narrative device allows a different perspective not just of Esther's own experiences but also of her relationship with her daughters. Although she complains about her children from her casket—"Them girls got ugly ways about them sometimes," she whines, appalled that they plan to bury her in an expensive but unattractive dress—Mudear's post-death monologues reveal that, despite her daughters' experiences to the contrary, she loves them fiercely. In her study of "ugliness" in women's fiction, Monica Carol Miller argues that the concept has a "specifically southern definition" that denotes "rude[ness], rebellio[n], or other inappropriate behavior."[84] Ansa plays with this definition; even as Mudear calls her girls "ugly," she applauds their independence, and she also takes credit for it. "The change," according to Mudear, was not just to save her own life but also those of her daughters.[85]

Only Ernest and Betty, and of course Mudear herself, have memories of their lives before the change. It was not a happy time. Ernest reminisces about how he had once ruled his household so thoroughly that he only had to use gestures for Mudear to do his bidding, and he further controlled her with physical abuse. Betty recalls that Ernest beat Esther badly enough that she feared he might kill her mother, and Mudear recounts him throwing clean clothing at her and demanding that she wash it again. He also slapped her, slept around with women he met at the local bar, called her a whore, came home drunk, and threw his wife and daughters out of the house so that they had to seek refuge with family members and neighbors many times. Esther, who was at the time emulating her own meek Mudear, endured the indignities and abuse for the first several years of their marriage as she tried to placate Ernest and raise her three young girls.[86]

But, over time, Esther began to practice passive resistance, burning Ernest's okra every night for dinner and calling him "Mr. Bastard" when he was not around. Mudear explains that just before the change, food began to taste bad, "like wet cardboard." But she slowly realized, "It wasn't my cooking, it was my life." Although "the change" seemed quite sudden to her daughters, her husband, and her community, Mudear had carefully waited many years for the appropriate "kiss-my-ass time." According to her daughters, "It all added to Mudear's mystique that she could know just when she could safely change." The breaking point was one winter when Ernest "overextended" himself and was unable to pay the power bill. Babies Emily and Annie Ruth both became gravely ill from the cold, and Mudear, after years of secretly collecting loose change, astonished Ernest by paying the bill herself. From beyond the grave, she laughs, considering how she might have "gone for years and years like I was if it hadn't gotten so cold that winter," citing that "cold, no-heat-and-no-lights-in-that-freezing-assed-house day" on which she paid the bill as the final straw. From that day forward, Mudear began to recede from her duties. It was a gradual but deliberate shift: "At first, when I made up my mind it was gonna be different, I had thought about just walking away. Leaving that house and that kitchen and everything and walking away free and clear of it all. But then, I thought, why should I leave something that was mine? A nice comfortable house where I had three girls—two of them—and soon all of them—big enough to help with everything, the cooking and cleaning and sewing, and a man that I knew inside who had a steady enough job."[87] "The change" began, then, as self-liberation—at the expense of her daughters.

Ernest too recalls the day Esther paid the power bill as the initial date of her "change," and as a result he also changed. But he did not relinquish his authority immediately or easily, provoking long fights overheard by his daughters as he tried to regain his former "authority." After Mudear made it clear that she "didn't give a damn what he did," Ernest gave up, emasculated. He felt as if "someone had pulled his pants down in public," and he started leaving Mudear alone, eating less, and working more to avoid being at home.[88]

Mudear explains that rather than abandoning her family, a tactic she did consider, she "stay[ed] in body" but left "in spirit," with no regrets. Although the sisters see Mudear's actions as essentially selfish, Ansa's approach of allowing Mudear to tell her own story after death reveals that she relied heavily on them not just as servants, as the girls thought, but as core companions, and, in her internal monologues, Mudear expresses quite a bit of love for them, in her own harsh way. She frequently described the girls to

Ernest as "the hand I fan with," and, beyond her own liberation, Mudear cites one of the reasons for "the change" as protecting her daughters from the potential emotional and physical abuse of Ernest and other men. She explains that she constantly imparted vital life lessons to her girls. From a very young age, Mudear taught her daughters that men were incompetent and duplicitous, wondering aloud why "more men aren't found murdered in their beds"—the musing that gave rise to Emily's frequent nightmares about her father's untimely demise. She raised her daughters with a warning, "a man don't give a damn about you," which Emily began to repeat as a baby and all the sisters ruefully recite throughout the novel. Although the sisters see this form of instruction as part of their trauma—all three are single, with varying degrees of dysfunctional relationships with men in their past—Mudear tells readers that railing about uncaring men was meant to liberate her daughters from dependence, to help them escape the cage in which she had formerly been trapped.[89]

Some of her lessons, then, had hard edges. Tara Green calls Mudear "the medicine forced down the throats of her daughters that consequently causes ailments or side effects," but independence, Mudear claims, became her goal not just for herself but also for her girls.[90] Ansa explains that the novel is an exploration of the tension inherent in how mothers "try to shape us and make us strong, and the ways that we interpret that."[91] Mudear taught her daughters not just how to do basic tasks like cleaning, cooking, and sewing but also how to survive as Black women whom the world would use and abuse in whatever ways it could. Mudear believes that she showed them "how to keep that part of themselves that was just for themselves so nobody could take it and walk on it," an edict that Green says she modeled for her daughters in her garden. "I tried my best to make them free ... as free as I could teach them and still be free myself," Mudear claims in her first internal monologue. She deliberately did not "coddle" or "cuddle" her daughters, instead opting to "push 'em out there to find out what they was best in," so that they could learn and know themselves. "They know things ... about life," she explains, taking credit for "making them the women that they are." "Keep living, daughter," she told each of them constantly.[92]

Even in their pain, her daughters acknowledge that Mudear frequently "said something so true, so insightful" that it shocked them, "even when it cut to the quick." Emily explains to her therapist, "Mudear would stroll into the room and say, 'You cannot build a chimney from the top. You cannot drive a car from the rear.' Or something like that. And I know it sounds crazy, but most times it would really help. She could be wise that way, sometimes." Mudear gave her daughters unvarnished, blunt, and often cruel truths, "little pieces of wisdom without any of the flavoring to make it taste better." "I guess that's what we all wanted so bad," Emily concludes sadly. "We wanted that seasoning from Mudear." But Mudear believes she gave her daughters something much more valuable: self-sufficiency.[93]

Ansa intersperses the different narrators so that a fuller picture emerges, not of maternal neglect but rather of generational misunderstanding, successive trauma, and good intentions that did not quite succeed. The final scenes involve the sisters confronting each other and Mudear, coming to terms with the past and coming together anew. At the end of the novel, the Lovejoy sisters' grief-stricken rehashing of some of their most painful memories reaches a crescendo at Mudear and Ernest's home, where Annie Ruth grows angry, stating unequivocally that she is going to keep and love her baby and that she is ready to "turn loose some of this crazy shit." Shouting, she exhorts her sisters to fight past the trauma, to relinquish their fear of Mudear, to stop thinking of their mother as "some kind of powerful goddess who can strike us mute or dead for some minor transgression." "When we gon' start making a change? ... I'm sick of being a product of Mudear, sick of it," she proclaims, and then she rushes out of the house to confront her mother's corpse. Her sisters, appalled and alarmed, follow closely behind and attempt to restrain Annie Ruth in the funeral home. In a darkly funny and moving scene, their struggle results in the toppling of Mudear's casket. Their mother's body lands just before them, forcing the conversation that Annie Ruth has been seeking: "For the first time in their lives since the change, they all looked Mudear directly in the face, and because she didn't insult them or shoo them off, they talked to her. They all spoke from the hurt in their hearts." Betty tells Mudear that they are going to "work on happy and peaceful and appreciative and joyful ... we want to move on." The sisters hold each other, keening on the floor, their tears falling onto their mother's body "like baptismal water."[94]

This scene seems like a natural conclusion to the sisters' emotional journey, but it's not the end of the novel. Instead, Ansa gives Mudear the last word. In the final chapter, she observes her own funeral, admiring her daughters (because, after all, "pulling herself together was what each of the Lovejoy sisters did best") and admonishing slyly that they will never be free of her, especially now that Annie Ruth is about to have a baby girl. "Now they think they free women 'cause they think they got me told," she harrumphs. "Getting mad is just the first step." Ansa makes it clear that their therapeutic confrontation did not vanquish Mudear. Rather, she will stay with them as they evolve, grow, and exercise the independence that she so brutally taught them.[95]

Ugly Ways received mixed reviews, but it sold well and remained on the BlackBoard list of African American bestsellers for years. While some critics were less than appreciative—Kirkus Reviews called it "repetitive" and "episodic," and Publishers Weekly deemed it "static"—Ugly Ways was lauded by others, earning an NAACP Image Award nomination and later a spot on the Georgia Center for the Book's "Top 25 Reading List."[96] Some reviewers and scholars have derisively deemed it "chick lit" or lumped Ansa in with other contemporary Black authors who focus on the middle class and whose novels are critiqued as being "'whitewashed' in the interest of assimilation."[97] This is, as Tara Green points out, an unfair characterization of Ansa's body of work that is apparently based on the assumption that African American writers are better suited to write "racial protest literature." In fact, the middle-class status of the Lovejoys is important to the gender politics of the novel. In a psychological analysis of Ansa's work, Melissa Sue Romweber Whitney argues that the socioeconomic settings of her novels are a "device" that gives her "characters the leisure time necessary for reflection and contemplation that enables readers to see inside the characters in order to better analyze them."[98]

Veronica Chambers, in her Los Angeles Times review of Ugly Ways, "The Things That Drive You Crazy Make You Whole," understands the novel as being about confronting the psychological fallout of both patriarchy and of "sort[ing] through the past." The titular "ugly ways," she writes, are both Mudear's "good intentions" and the sisters' defiance of them.[99] Indeed, the mother-daughter dynamics of the novel are the crux of Ansa's feminism. Black feminist theory positions motherhood as empowering for both the mother and her children, who are the subjects of maternal training that helps them to avoid, navigate, and/or resist systems of oppression—especially, for daughters, sexism and racism—in a process Patricia Hill Collins calls "socialization for survival."[100] But Ansa's feminism in the novel is a kind of hybrid version, featuring elements of women's liberation more closely associated with the 1960s and 1970s, aspects of Black feminism as expressed by theorists in the 1980s, and hints of what would come to be known as neoliberal feminism in the 1990s. All of this takes place firmly in the context of the small-town Deep South at the end of the twentieth century, which Ansa depicts as a setting of promise, progress, and prosperity for Black women. As such, Ugly Ways offers a new kind of southern feminism.

Mudear after "the change" can be viewed as a Black woman who summarily decides to define herself rather than allowing herself to be defined by others. In *Black Feminist Thought*, Patricia Hill Collins argues that "change can ... occur in the private, personal space in an individual woman's consciousness."[101] Mudear raises her own consciousness, and, in her rejection of patriarchal domesticity, including child-rearing, she in some ways exemplifies the Women's Liberation Movement critiques of motherhood as a major site of gendered oppression. This concept drew criticism from Black feminist theorists in the 1980s. In 1984, bell hooks argued that it was based on the experiences of white, middle-class feminists: "Had black women voiced their views on motherhood, it would not have been named a serious obstacle to our freedom as women. Racism, availability of jobs, lack of skills or education ... would have been at the top of the list—but not motherhood."[102] Collins notes three major ways in which African American mothering is largely different from the dominant social model targeted by white feminists: racial and economic discrimination made the nuclear-family ideal unattainable; "strict sex-role segregation" is "less commonly found" in marriages and parenting; and full-time, stay-at-home motherhood is "uncharacteristic" of Black families.[103]

Ansa's depiction of Mudear, however, adheres more closely to the white, middle-class feminist characterization of marriage, even though she was an economically struggling Black woman. Instead, Mudear's experiences as a wife and mother are lonely, occurring within the private, male-dominated, nuclear family. Mudear's "change," then, conforms to the white, middle-class, "second-wave" critique of the institutions of wifehood and motherhood, hinging as it did on a "click moment" of feminist consciousness—in Mudear's case, that fateful winter day when she paid the power bill.[104] Ansa contradicts Black feminist theories of motherhood in other ways as well: Mudear's withdrawal from her family and society is a direct rejection of the value that Black communities place on mothers. The Lovejoy sisters are, they feel unanimously, essentially unmothered after the change. Mudear's behavior isolates her girls, who endure gossip and ostracism and are no longer invited to parties, so that the African American tradition of "othermothering" or community mothering, a practice that Black feminists argue is vital to the development of self-reliance, resilience, and resistance to oppression, is unavailable to them.[105]

However, there are some elements of Black feminist maternal theory in Ansa's characterization of Mudear. Perhaps the most obvious representation is Mudear's brilliant garden. In *In Search of Our Mothers' Gardens* (1983), Black feminist author Alice Walker writes of "mothers and grandmothers [who] have, more often than not anonymously, handed on the creative spark, the seed of the flower they themselves never hoped to see: or like a sealed letter they could not plainly read."[106] Walker's discussion of her mother's garden is part of her foundational text on womanism, which I will examine in more detail when we get to her novel *The Color Purple* in the following chapter. As depicted by Walker, the garden as a space of liberation has been an essential metaphor for Black feminists since the 1980s. Walker's own mother, when she was not caring for her children or working in the Georgia fields, "planted ambitious gardens" with dozens of different types of flowers that she would use to decorate "whatever shabby house we were forced to live in." Walker explains, "Whatever she planted grew as if by magic, and her fame as a grower of flowers spread over three counties. Because of her creativity with her flowers, even my memories of poverty are seen through a screen of blooms—sunflowers, petunias, roses, dahlias, forsythia, spirea, delphiniums, verbena." Her mother became "legendary" for her flowers, which she gave away freely, explaining, "A house without flowers is like a face without a smile."[107]

For Walker's mother, gardening was her soul's work, her art, her resistant joy, her form of creative expression in an oppressive society that denied Black women's humanity. Walker's essay on the subject is a major work of Black feminism, and her gardens metaphor is well known and oft-used. In *Ugly Ways*, Mudear's carefully tended flowers—angel trumpets, petunias, lilies, all in white so that they are visible at night—make up a "paradise" that only she enjoys. Her "prodigious" garden is a symbol of Mudear's liberation. "I did so love to dig in the dirt," she muses, citing waking up with dirty fingernails as "some of the happiest moments" of her life. It is her flowers, she claims from the coffin, that she will miss the most.[108]

In one of the few references to her foremothers, Mudear says she got her "love for gardening" from her mother, who "grew collards and turnips winter and summer." Esther's own Mudear "was a woman who always had a smile on her face"; she was "the kind of woman who hummed while she did her housework." Growing up, Esther assumed she also had these qualities: "You know, like mother, like daughter." But after marrying Ernest and finding "out how the world really was," Esther rejected this maternal model, and the only remnant of her mother's teaching was her beautiful garden. This generational link serves as a connection between the two Mudears and a crucial component of Esther's self-actualization, much like Walker's mother's garden. But her flowers, Mudear insists, are also for her girls, despite their rejection of them. She planted the multiple white blooms in her garden expressly for them to enjoy so that they could even see it at night—perhaps her clearest gesture of love, as she had "extraordinary night vision" and thus had no use herself for an all-white garden.[109]

As in Walker's formulation, Mudear's garden was a physical manifestation of the creativity of and connections between generations of Black women. But Ansa complicates the metaphor; Betty, Emily, and Annie Ruth's rejection of Mudear's garden thus symbolizes the break between the second and third "waves" of feminism, represented as a conflict between mothers and their daughters.[110] Well into adulthood, none of them will "abide a growing plant in their homes," and Ansa lists "their hatred of plants" as one of the "few things" all three sisters have in common.[111] This denial of their mother and her misguided motives sets up a generational conflict in the feminist politics of *Ugly Ways* that was in keeping with the generational tensions plaguing "third-wave" feminism in its infancy in the early 1990s. The garden is a symbol of the Black mother's creativity and artistic identity, but it also represents, in the love-starved eyes of the Lovejoy sisters, their mother's neglect. Mudear speaks to the reader, not to the other characters, offering a personal explanation for her behavior that is also a historical one, situating her experiences as limited choices that she made in the pre–Women's Liberation Movement South. So readers know from Mudear's monologues that her garden was meant to be a space of liberation for her and for her girls, but, crucially, her daughters do not. While Mama MaGrath dominates her daughters' psyches in *Crimes of the Heart*, Mudear haunts her daughters in *Ugly Ways*, but her presence is of little use to them: they cannot hear her. Expressing oneself is crucial to consciousness-raising, but so too is listening. This, then, is failed intergenerational communication both during Mudear's life and after her death.[112]

Ansa's Black feminism is thus riddled with ambivalence. It is also not especially radical. In keeping with the tenets of neoliberal feminism that were developing in the early 1990s (and that I explore in depth in chapter 4), Ansa promotes the individual gendered liberation of her characters rather than direct challenges to systems of oppression. Growing up in Macon, Ansa was exposed to activist influences; her father went to school with John Oliver Killens, a famed civil rights activist and writer from Macon best known for his Pulitzer Prize–nominated protest novel *Youngblood* (1954), and Ansa took a writing workshop with him as she drafted her first novel. But while her role model Killens famously targeted Jim Crow in his writing, Ansa is more interested in internal revolutions: her characters undergo psychological epiphanies that change their own behavior rather than threatening systemic gender inequality.[113]

This kind of private rebellion is in keeping with the solution Mudear prescribes for her daughters. For the Lovejoy sisters, liberation is achieved through financial success, and Ansa offers distractingly detailed descriptions of material objects to make this point, using multiple adjectives to indicate their costs and symbolic value as trappings of the middle and upper classes. The sisters wear cashmere, suede, and fancy foreign makeup, and Betty's "elegant" home in Mulberry is full of expensive furniture. Indeed, the depiction of Betty's house is one of the only sections of the novel in which Ansa explicitly discusses race. Betty's historic colonial house, "once home to old white southern Mulberry belles having afternoon teas prepared and served by women like Betty who had to wear black and white starched uniforms," now smells like lemon oil due to the ministrations of Mrs. Andrews, the older woman who cleans for Betty each week. As Betty considers giving her a raise, she realizes: "Mrs. Andrews, who wasn't that much younger than Mudear, looked like her, too." This realization causes "a bout of fatigue," but Betty moves on to other things quickly, refusing to dwell on the reversal of the traditional regional hierarchies that has placed her in a position of power over a woman who could be her mother. Other than noting Betty's "fatigue" at the thought, Ansa does not explore the intergenerational, intraracial, socioeconomic power dynamics of this scene or of the sisters' status. Nor does white supremacy seem to determine or influence the characters' lives, despite the fact that they live in the Deep South. In general, in contrast to the vicious gossip about everything else, Mulberry comes across as a color-blind town, and in her description of the Lovejoy sisters, especially Betty and Annie Ruth, Ansa does not indicate racism as an obstacle to any of their financial successes.[114]

The seemingly racially homogeneous society of Mulberry is based on Pleasant Hill, the neighborhood in Macon formed by freedpeople after the Civil War that became the historic center of the city's Black community. Ansa grew up in Pleasant Hill, and, although she protests that her books are fiction, she finds that readers from Macon insist that they know her characters. She remembers Pleasant Hill as a "safe place," a culturally rich and close-knit community of Black-owned businesses, churches, and caring neighbors. It was segregated but self-sufficient, so much so that she never felt "bereft" or "isolated" growing up. Her world was a complete and fulfilling one that functioned, in her childhood memories of the 1960s, independently of white supremacy. Growing up in Pleasant Hill offered a kind of "armor" and "confidence" that Ansa took with her when she attended a newly desegregated high school in the mid-1960s. Pleasant Hill taught its children their self-worth during this volatile decade in the Deep South, and

Ansa recalls implicit lessons about gender, class, and the politics of respectability as well. She cites numerous role models among the women of Pleasant Hill whose manners, dress, and diction she emulated.[115]

Yet Ansa's fond memories of Pleasant Hill, which feature prominently in some of her other novels, are missing from *Ugly Ways*. She describes feeling a "globe of protection" growing up in Pleasant Hill, but the Lovejoys are shunned by their neighbors, Mudear becomes the favorite subject of local rumors after "the change," and no one steps in to help her bewildered young daughters during their many years of need. While Black feminists emphasize the significance of the support of a community of women and "othermothers" for building resilience, this missing element is a major component of the Lovejoy women's traumas.[116] This type of ostracization allows Ansa to isolate her characters in order to explore the depth of Mudear's helplessness early in her marriage and her daughters' enduring neuroses as adults.

Although Ansa does not posit race or racism as major factors in her characters' experiences, she does offer some commentary on working-class motherhood. Mudear's early experiences as a poor Black woman are what drove her to "change," and it is significant that she bides her time as an abused wife for years until the lights get cut off. This palpable manifestation of poverty intersects with her desperation as a mother—both of her younger girls were sick, and they only got sicker in the cold, dark house—to spur her to the action that Ernest interprets as a frontal assault on his masculinity. A gender- and class-based understanding of Mudear's actions does not, however, lead Ansa to a radical or politicized feminist analysis. From this experience, Mudear imparts two lessons to her daughters—do not rely on men and make your own wealth—both of which are individualized. In their study of Black and white motherhood, Gloria Joseph and Jill Lewis argue that Black mothers emphasize teaching their daughters skills that "enable them to survive, exist, succeed, and be important to and for the Black communities," so much so that "Black daughters are actually 'taught' to hold the Black community together."[117] However, Mudear's concerns, born of her experiences as a poor Black mother and known solely through her post-death monologues, are only for her daughters' survival and success. Although she encourages her girls to share as much gossip as they can gather from school and errands, she does not appear to care about community at all, neither her daughters' roles in it nor improving it.

This inward, individualized focus is in keeping with the development of neoliberal, "lifestyle feminism" in the 1990s. Mudear is not interested in challenging the systems of oppression so much as avoiding them herself—

by not leaving the house, rejecting Ernest's patriarchal priority, and teaching her daughters how to support themselves despite these systems. Perhaps because their lives are so circumscribed within her orbit, Mudear's monologues mention very little about teaching her daughters to deal with racism. One exception is her pride in Betty's ability to "handle those white bastards down at the gas company" and her recounting of telling the "old cracker" at the department store to "kiss her black ass" after the lobby clerk "called her names once too often." But Ansa does offer a few glimpses into the fruits of Mudear's teachings via her daughters' memories. Revealing the reason for Betty's "fatigue" as she thought about her housekeeper, Emily told her psychiatrist that her mother vehemently opposed any of her daughters working in the homes of "white folks." Mudear's commentary on the racist class system of domestic labor in the South was succinct: "Humph, let them wash their own drawers. I wash my own. The world would be a better place if everyone, no matter how rich and no matter how many servants, if everyone had to wash their own drawers."[118] It's clear that even though Mudear's lessons seem to focus on her daughters learning to be independent from men, she also made them aware of the various oppressive systems at work in the lives of Black women.

Over the years, Annie Ruth thinks, their mother "had made it impossible for any of her girls to truly float through life acting as if they didn't understand what was really going on in just about any situation." In her own strange and damaging way, Mudear maintained an explicit focus on patriarchy, teaching her daughters self-sufficiency from men in order to opt out of the sexist trap in which she found herself early in her marriage. Her mantra "a man don't give a damn about you" rings in their heads, and each grows up to be financially independent. The Lovejoy sisters are also sexually independent—Betty and Annie Ruth both enjoy a variety of love affairs—although, except for Emily and Betty's brief marriages, none of them are involved in long-term, romantic relationships.[119]

But even in her teachings about patriarchy, Mudear is no radical, and she is certainly not revolutionary. She does not mean for her daughters to overthrow sexism or facilitate new, more equitable systems, even for themselves. In fact, she traffics in sexual-economic stereotypes, telling her daughters that "only whores" wear certain hairstyles and ankle bracelets and teaching them "how to be ladies" (Mudear had a "long litany of things that Lovejoys did and did not do"). Her solution, then, is in line with what scholars have called "southern feminists' decisions about comportment as a political strategy," a tactic that many Black women have deployed as an explicitly "political rejection of racism and sexism."[120] The basis for liberation for her girls is, according to Mudear, buying into respectability politics to succeed economically. "Shit, you make your own luck in this world," Mudear mutters as she teaches her daughters to escape the gendered, racial, and class-based oppression that she herself experienced.[121]

Although her daughters enjoy their own successes, they see Mudear's life lessons as alternately comical and oppressive. Patricia Hill Collins notes that some Black "mothers may have ensured their daughters' physical survival at the high cost of their emotional destruction."[122] Esther's own trauma is intertwined with the lessons she imparts to her daughters, and what they see as her "meanness" is, according to Barbara Bennett, really her "undeniable" anger "at the southern and black patriarchal society that dominates and subjugates women like her." Rather than abandonment of her daughters, Bennett argues, Mudear's hard lessons have "forced all of them to succeed."[123] Mudear gave her children, in her own estimation, "the one thing in life that they could always look to with pride, a mother who set an example of being her own woman." Esther calls her daughters out when they sneer at her lectures on "The Lovejoy Women," retorting with a smirk, "Well, there must be something to it. 'Cause married or not, I notice all y'all still go by 'Lovejoy.'" They begrudgingly agree that this is true, and that despite their resentment and resistance, they have learned a lot from their mother.[124]

In her study of mothers in contemporary southern women's literature, Bennett argues that Ansa "transcend[s] stereotypes" with the character of Mudear. She is not a passive victim, a self-sacrificing mammy, or a ball-breaking matriarch, nor is she simply the "destroying mother," as her daughters initially see her.[125] Rather, she is free, but that freedom comes with a cost. Ansa explained in an interview in 1993:

> It's about what happens in our society when a woman decides she's gonna be free, when a black woman decides she's gonna be free, when a black mother decides she's gonna be free. And I think black motherhood in our society and our culture resonates with us, you know. The epitome of the black mother is one who self-sacrifices and who does everything for her children, who is always there, who is always going to make the sacrifice. And I was very interested in exploring other kinds of mothers. Black mothers have become icons in our society, you know. They aren't even humans anymore. They are able to do everything.... And I wanted very much to create a mother who did not fall into that stereotype.[126]

Ansa's exploration of this type of maternal freedom is ambivalent, as Mudear's revolt leaves bodies in her wake and unreconciled questions about, as Anthony Grooms put it, "the more poignant tensions of personal freedom."[127] But Ansa is not interested in tidy answers so much as complicated questions with multiple perspectives, and Mudear's narration is strategic, as it indicates that readers "cannot completely trust the criticism Mudear's daughters heap upon their mother."[128] Mudear is a "puzzling" character to her daughters and to readers. "Withdrawal," Bennett contends, is her "only outlet and escape," but unlike the ultimate withdrawal of suicide enacted by Mama MaGrath, Mudear does not escape so much as transcend her abusive situation, forcing a dysfunctional revolution in the mother-daughter dynamic.[129] But Mudear is not the Medea that her daughters think she is. Instead, she is a woman who had limited choices and uses them to both liberate herself and teach her girls some painful lessons so that they too will be free. And the next generation, through the pregnant character of Annie Ruth, has both learned these difficult lessons and reconfigured Black motherhood as a site of empowerment. Even though Mudear gets the last word in the novel, readers are left with new images of the southern mother.

Empowerment, in Ansa's fictional formulation, is apolitical and individualized; it does not have the goals of social consciousness, community solidarity, or activism as defined by Black feminists. But the internal revolutions in *Ugly Ways* are important to understandings of feminism in this era. Mothering, both for Mudear and for Annie Ruth at the end of the novel, is a powerful force through which to affirm the selfhood of Black women. Thinking of how Mudear cautioned her daughters not to let anyone "steal their joy" is what led Annie Ruth to decide to keep her baby:

> You know what, I want to get big as a house and have this baby and love her and sit and rock her and brag on her and bore people to death talking about her and making them look at pictures. Before she's even born, I want to think about her and worry about her and name her, name her Betty Jean or Emily or even Esther, no, not Esther. But name her something that has some meaning for me and will for her. So when I look into her face I think of something I love, when I call her name I remember tenderness. I don't care if I call her "Turnip Green," at least when I say it, I'll remember how good and sweet turnips are when Betty cooks 'em down with a little fatback and long red hot pepper.[130]

Having come to terms with her mother, she only needs her sisters, and together they will lovingly raise her daughter. Even as they bury their Mother Dear, the Lovejoy sisters look to the future together.

In her study of Beth Henley's early plays, Susanne Auflitsch notes that maternal "dysfunctionality" so thoroughly colors many southern daughter characters' lives that they are unable to create their own families.[131] Certainly this is true of *Crimes of the Heart*, in which none of the sisters have found any kind of lasting love beyond each other, and none have, or even apparently considered having, children. With the solemn pact between Betty, Emily, and Annie Ruth, *Ugly Ways* is more explicit on this front, yet Annie Ruth's pregnancy makes them revisit their pact, just as their mother's death makes them confront her "ugly ways." In the end, the sisters have come to terms with their mother and with each other, and Annie Ruth swears that, with her sisters' support, she "sure as hell [is] gonna be a mother."[132]

In some southern fiction of the 1980s and 1990s, then, victimized mothers traumatized their daughters, but the cycle could be broken. *Crimes of the Heart* and *Ugly Ways* both feature oppressive patriarchy and damaging mother-daughter relationships, but, with the inclusion of some feminist tenets of motherhood, Ansa's characters succeed in transcending these traumas, not just for themselves but also for their daughters. *Ugly Ways* ends with an affirmation of sisterhood but also a promise of a next generation even further removed from the corruption of traditional southern patriarchy.[133]

Thus, as southern women writers came of age with the Women's Liberation Movement and with Black feminism, their texts began to exhibit these influences, and the mother-daughter relationship became a primary means of making sense of intergenerational gender politics. Bennett argues that this "thread" in southern women's fiction, particularly the "reconciliation and acceptance of old traditions with new choices" as told through the perspectives of adult daughters, is a "crucial" step toward healing, growth, and the achievement of female agency.[134] Employing the critiques of the gendered institutions of motherhood, daughterhood, sisterhood, and womanhood offered by the Women's Liberation Movement, Henley and Ansa depict mothers victimized by southern patriarchy, and daughters who suffer, confront, and then reject oppressive regional norms. Henley's white, middle-class characters are less successful; Mama MaGrath only escapes via suicide, while her daughters struggle mightily in all aspects of their lives. Their strength only becomes apparent when they come together in collective rejection of southern patriarchy. Ansa's middle- and upper-class Black characters, however, succeed more clearly, a function of her combination of "second-wave" critiques of patriarchal marriage, Black feminist concepts of mothering, and the neoliberal feminist emphases on individual wealth and self-sufficiency.

Neither *Crimes of the Heart* nor *Ugly Ways* exhibits radical feminist tendencies, and they are not political in the sense that they do not depict or encourage collective activism. But they explicitly grapple with questions of gendered oppression, maternal pedagogy, and the solution of strong sisterhood, during an era and in a region in which feminist ideology was thought to be virtually nonexistent. American readers, filmgoers, and theater audiences engaged with contemporary southern feminism through these complicated configurations of mother-daughter dyads and trios of sisters. At the same time, however, other southern women writers were producing major feminist texts that deployed more radical critiques of the problem of patriarchy, as well as strategies for addressing it and solutions to it. Instead of fighting with each other or with their mothers, some southern women characters came together in fictive sisterhood to fight back against the men who harmed them, as we will see in the next chapter.

CHAPTER 2

"You Get What You Settle For"

STAGING COUPS AGAINST SOUTHERN PATRIARCHY

In the summer of 1991, a national debate about gender and violence graced front pages, think pieces, and nightly television news for several weeks, causing a broader referendum on the backlash against feminism that had characterized the previous decade. Alarmed critics explained that "male-bashing" and "toxic feminism" were both the causes and consequences of the abandonment of the family by American women.[1] What was the trigger for all this hand-wringing? The film *Thelma & Louise*, in which two Arkansas women flee the men in their lives, shoot a rapist, confront a serial sexual harasser, and defy the feds, with heavy doses of feminist consciousness-raising, sexual awakening, armed robbery, and female bonding in between.

Thelma & Louise was just one in a series of southern stories in the 1980s and 1990s which featured women fleeing from and fighting back against repressive regional norms of gender. These stories were rooted in southern landscapes and told with southern accents, but they were writ large as mythical tales featuring ordinary women as heroines, and they were enormously popular with national audiences. While the women of the feminist texts in chapter 1 mostly offered internalized, psychological forms of resistance, their compatriots in this chapter practice active forms of rebellion as they physically evade and violently fight against patriarchy. In doing so, they offer radical models of southern feminist sisterhood.

Chapter 1 featured biological sisters supporting each other, but, as a feminist concept, "sisterhood," while "powerful," can be complicated.[2] Gloria

Steinem characterized it in *Ms.* in 1972 as the "deep personal connection of women" that bridges "barriers of age, economics, worldly experience, race, and culture."[3] Historian Nancy A. Hewitt defines "sisterhood" as "the sharing of essential emotional and economic resources among females," and she deems it a central historical fact of most American women's lives.[4] During the Women's Liberation Movement, the term "sisterhood" was used to bring women together, ideally across race, ethnicity, and class lines, but in practice it often served to eclipse those differences in favor of a universal critique of sexism that ignored intersectionality.

Black feminist theorists have both criticized and deepened the concept of sisterhood as one that erases difference but also has the potential to build coalitions and go beyond mere sympathy, support, and/or recognition of shared experiences to real solidarity between women. Specifically, bell hooks writes of the distinction between traumatized sisterhood, which is "rooted in shared victimization," and empowered sisterhood that is bound by "political solidarity" in collective action against systems of oppression.[5] Connected by their childhood traumas, the MaGrath and Lovejoy sisters of chapter 1 represent the former. Linked by common enemies and active strategies of resistance, the women characters examined in this chapter—friends, lovers, and chosen sisters—represent the latter. In an era that feminist critics have called the "age of ambivalence," the characters in Alice Walker's National Book Award– and Pulitzer Prize–winning novel *The Color Purple* (1982) and Callie Khouri's Oscar-winning film *Thelma & Louise* (1991) offered politicized models of loving sisterhood that were difficult to find elsewhere in popular culture at the time. Both texts explore women's varied reactions to daily misogyny, feature liberating relationships between women, and sparked national conversations about feminist popular culture that were divided along gendered lines.

The southern authors of each of these texts privilege women's relationships over heterosexual ones and position these bonds as crucial prerequisites to resistance to patriarchy. Friendships between women in these texts are not simply support networks, and they are more than mere foundations for resistance. Rather, they have revolutionary potential for interpersonal liberation as it is defined in each text. In *In the Company of Women*, Karen Hollinger argues that "female friendship films" serve multiple purposes. Beyond offering representation, these films also resist patriarchal prerogative and "provide women with support in thinking through some of the changes stimulated by the women's movement."[6] Hollinger's findings apply equally to literature during this era. Indeed, the women's relationships at the heart of *The Color Purple* and *Thelma & Louise* were highly emotional, sometimes erotic, and fundamentally political in their challenges to regional patriarchy. If the mantra of the Women's Liberation Movement in the 1970s was "the personal is political," we might say about the 1980s and 1990s that the pop cultural was both personal and political.

These fictional feminist sisterhoods were radical for both the South and the neoconservative nation in the era of the backlash. They overturned the literary and cinematic male gaze that privileges male supremacy, objectification of women, and violence against women, and on the concept of southern violence itself. Rather than repeat the indiscriminate white male supremacist aggression traditionally associated with the region, these texts feature women characters with violent thoughts and behaviors that are depicted as self-defensive and justifiable reactions to patriarchal abuse. Anyone who doubts the relative regional radicalism of *The Color Purple* and *Thelma & Louise* needs only to read the reactionary criticism of each, which will be discussed herein. In this chapter, I explore how novelist Alice Walker and screenwriter Callie Khouri offered visions of radical sisterhood through their depictions of southern women fighting against, fleeing from, reconfiguring, and ultimately defying patriarchy.

"You've Got to Fight"
The Color Purple

In *Ugly Ways*, Ansa offers the color lavender as an enduring metaphor for Mudear's liberation after "the change." She misses her variegated lavender plants in her garden from beyond the grave and wishes her daughters would bring her a few sprigs for her casket. Mudear longs for both the sight and the smell, as she used the plants and petals to create potpourris that she scattered around her bedroom and personal bathroom, which was painted lavender. When Annie Ruth enters that sacred room, which Mudear had prohibited anyone else from using while she was alive, for the first time after her mother's death, the smell of the herbs—"Essence of Mudear"—is so overpowering that Annie Ruth thinks she has "opened Pandora's box."[7]

By choosing this color and scent, both of which were linked to her precious garden, to be Mudear's signature, Ansa nodded to the feminist tradition developed by southern author Alice Walker. In *In Search of Our Mothers' Gardens*, Walker offers several poetic definitions of "womanism," concluding: "Womanist is to feminist as purple is to lavender."[8] Mudear's preoccupation with the latter, then, indicates her feminist tendencies do not quite reach the level of womanist praxis, as seen in her rough raising of her daughters. By the time Ansa published *Ugly Ways*, purple had long served as a metaphor for Black women's liberation, inspired by Walker's work, most famously her novel *The Color Purple* (1982).

Walker, a civil rights and feminist activist from Eatonton, Georgia, gave her heroine Celie what she herself could not have in the South: a happy ending. Set in rural Georgia in the first few decades of the twentieth century, *The Color Purple* is an epistolary novel that follows Celie as she endures multiple abuses from the men in her life and, over time and with the crucial aid of other Black women, develops a feminist consciousness. While, as a Black southern woman, Celie is "trapped in the whole range of possible oppressions," Walker characterizes sex oppression as the most brutal and enduring source of her abuse.[9] Through Celie and her community of women, Walker makes clear which types of antisexist strategies work toward liberation, and which ones lead to more misery, as Celie submits, fights, flees, and finally rebuilds her family and community around womanist tenets.

The Color Purple won a Pulitzer and a National Book Award in 1983, six months before Walker's *In Search of Our Mothers' Gardens*, a collection of her writings between 1966 and 1982, was published. At the beginning of this collection, Walker defines "womanism," offering her readers prose explorations of the type of feminism espoused in *The Color Purple*. Womanists, Walker explains, love other women first and foremost, "sexually and/or nonsexually," preferring "women's culture, women's emotional flexibility ... and women's strength." That said, womanists are not anti-men; rather, they are, Walker writes, "committed to survival and wholeness of entire people, male and female."[10] Most importantly, as a means of counteracting the dangerous blind spots of white feminist "sisterhood," Walker's womanism offers a form of "love politics" to address interlocking oppressions, especially of gender, race, class, religion, and sexual orientation, a concept that predated Kimberlé Crenshaw's term "intersectionality" by several years.[11] Walker's womanism is a form of southern Black feminism that is radical in its vision of new possibilities for social, political, economic, interpersonal, and spiritual liberation. While *In Search of Our Mothers' Gardens* is more explicit regarding the theoretical and historical underpinnings of womanism, *The Color Purple*, as popular fiction, became the more widely known conduit of womanist ideas to the media-consuming public.

In the first line of *The Color Purple*, Celie quotes her stepfather, whom she believes is her biological father, warning her not to tell anyone about his repeated rapes of her: "You better not never tell nobody but God. It'd kill your mammy." This "paternal injunction of silence" immediately challenges southern rape mythology by placing a Black girl at its brutal center.[12] Unlike a white victim, who could mobilize the entire power structure of white supremacist patriarchy with a claim that she had been sexually assaulted, Celie is forced by this same system and by her father to remain mute, silenced except for her secret letters to "God." The initial reference to her feeble "mammy" immediately establishes that, like Mama MaGrath in *Crimes of the Heart*, Celie's mother has been victimized to the point of shutting down, and she cannot protect herself, much less her daughter. When Celie inevitably becomes pregnant by her rapist father, her mother gets "sicker and sicker" as she blames her eldest daughter, unaware of the violent incest occurring in the home. By Celie's second letter, her mother is dead, and Celie has had two children by her father. Unable to protect herself or her children, whom her father sells to a local family, Celie resolves to protect her younger sister Nettie, asking her father to "take [her] instead" and warning Nettie to "keep at her books" so that she has an escape route through education. Their father, however, trades Celie like a mule to Mr. _____, a local man who has his eye on Nettie. Celie goes from one abusive patriarch to another, constantly worrying about how to save her sister from their father.[13]

But Nettie has a more proactive solution: she runs away from their father to live with Celie. "You got to fight," she urges her older sister. But, fed up with Mr. _____, who sexually harasses her and beats Celie, Nettie keeps moving. Resolving to write Celie, she goes to live with a missionary family as their nanny, unaware that the children for whom she cares are Celie's, given away by their father years ago. Nettie joins the family first as a domestic servant and then as a missionary herself in Africa. For years, however, Celie does not know Nettie's whereabouts. When she receives no letters from her sister, Celie assumes the worst: "I think bout Nettie, dead. She right, she run away. What good it do? I don't fight, I stay where I'm told. But I'm alive."[14]

For Celie, then, submission is survival, and resistance appears to be fatal. But after Nettie's disappearance, Celie finds another model of rebellion in Sofia, the bold wife of Mr. _____'s son Harpo. A "big strong girl"—"if she sit down on something, it be mash," Celie marvels—Sofia believes in an equal division of labor in her marriage. However, in discussions with his father, who models toxic masculinity for Harpo in his violent treatment of his wife, Harpo attempts to control Sofia and to "make her mind." Mr. _____'s prescription for Harpo's "problem" with Sofia is, of course, a "good sound beating," which he prompts Celie to support as an effective tool of control. Celie complies, telling Harpo, "Beat her," in a line that, more so even than her strategic passivity in the first half of the novel, reveals the true depths of her internalization of patriarchal prerogative.[15]

But Sofia is not Celie, nor is she Nettie. When Harpo tries to assert control over her, she does not submit, and she does not flee. Rather, she lashes out, and Celie finds Harpo and Sofia "fighting like two mens." Sofia wins this first round, and she later confronts Celie, who is guilt ridden and sleepless after telling Harpo to beat Sofia. "I say it cause you do what I can't," she confesses to Sofia, whose anger dissolves into pity as she explains her defensive position to Celie. "All my life I had to fight.... But I never thought I'd have to fight in my own house.... I loves Harpo, God knows I do. But I'll kill him dead before I let him beat me. Now if you want a dead son-in-law you just keep on advising him like you doing.... I used to hunt game with a bow and arrow."[16] As they make up and begin sewing a quilt together, Celie and Sofia realize that although they practice different forms of resistance, they have the same enemy.

Sofia's fight continues throughout the first half of the novel. Every time Harpo tries to dominate her, she responds by beating him up and leaving. This latter form of resistance is enabled by her own community of women when her sisters—"big strong healthy girls, look like amazons"—come to collect Sofia, and she leaves with her children. She reappears six months later at Harpo's juke joint on the arm of a prizefighter, drinking white lightning and looking like "her usual stout and bouncy self." In the meantime, Harpo has taken up with the aptly named Squeak, a meek and submissive woman. The diametrically opposed personalities of these two women are obvious in their relationships with Harpo and with each other—Sofia knocks Squeak's teeth out in their first encounter—as well as to the white power structure in town. Shortly after her appearance at the juke joint, Sofia lands in jail after "sassing" the mayor by refusing to be his wife's maid. Wisely switching resistance strategies, Sofia begins to channel Celie while behind bars: "Every time they ast me to do something, Miss Celie, I act like I'm you. I jump right up and do just what they say ... I'm a good prisoner, she say. Best convict they ever see." But the longstanding survival tactic of "wearing a mask" does not come naturally to Sofia, and she has a "wild" look as she says this. She confides quietly: "Nothing less than sliding on your belly with your tongue on they boots can even git they attention. I dream of murder ... I dream of murder sleep or wake."[17]

The family scheme to get Sofia out before her homicidal dreams become reality does not quite go as planned; she is released from jail but ends up as the mayor's wife's maid—the very suggestion of which had prompted her fight with the mayor in the first place. This turn of events indicates that the strategy of trying to negotiate with white supremacist patriarchy results in further violent intrusion of the state into the private lives of women, including the mayor's wife, who is terrified of Sofia. While this move may have saved Sofia's life, it does not restore her spirit. Sofia contemplates murder just as frequently outside of prison as she did inside as she very half-heartedly cares for the mayor's children. Although she still shows sparks of humor and never bows down to men, she is a shell of her former self. Her own children begin to treat her as if she is "not there," and when the other women finally leave the abusive household of Mr. _____ for good, they do not even consider taking Sofia with them: "One look at this big stout graying, wildeyed woman and you know not even to ast." The most potentially "revolutionary" character in the novel, the only woman who aggressively resists both racism and sexism, is reduced to a "tragic figure," a "wildeyed" store clerk in the end.[18] Fighting back, then, is at the very least an exhausting model of resistance in *The Color Purple*.

But Walker offers another alternative. When Celie first sees a photograph of Shug Avery, her husband's longtime mistress, she is in awe of her beauty, her makeup, her furs, and her grin. As Sofia dreams of murder, Celie dreams of Shug, and she hopes that Mr. _____ will bring her into their home. When Shug becomes ill, he does just that, and Shug arrives barely able to walk but "dress to kill" in a red dress and a feathered hat. Upon first sight, Celie wants to shout: "Come on in. With God help, Celie going to make you well." Shug looks her up and down, confirms to Mr. _____, whom she calls by his given name Albert, that Celie "is ugly," and then she laughs like a "death rattle." Despite this comment, Shug's "mean" eyes, and her smile "like a razor opening," Celie is smitten. She bathes Shug like a child, feeds her by hand, and combs her hair "like she a doll" until her health is restored.[19]

As she nurses Shug, Celie and Sofia work on a quilt that includes one of Shug's yellow dresses based on the Sister's Choice pattern—another callback to Walker's mother, who, in addition to gardening, was an avid quilter.[20] Quilting has long served as a primary means of Black women's expression, self-care, and community support, and in the novel it serves as a metaphor of Celie's psychological development.[21] With these women, Celie opens up to sisterhood, solidarity, and the kind of liberation that Shug represents. Despite her nearly lifeless condition when she arrives on Celie's doorstep, Shug does what she wants: she sings and dances, says "whatever come to mind," takes up with any man she chooses, and leaves her own children with her mother to travel the country as a blueswoman (and what's more, she tells Celie she doesn't miss them at all).[22] Many scholars pinpoint the beginning of Celie's liberation during the moments in which Shug teaches her the location of her clitoris or during their first sexual encounter. Based on Audre Lorde's premise that lesbianism is a "reclamation" of the erotic and "assertion of the life force of women," Michael Bibler argues that homosexuality is a priori resistant to the social hierarchies of the South because "it joins two people as equals in a system where equality is rare indeed."[23] Walker's definition of womanism includes women's sexual and "nonsexual" love for each other, a claim which has become axiomatic to Black feminism. Brittney Cooper says bluntly, "[O]ne can't truly be a feminist if you don't really love other women."[24] Celie and Shug's sexual relationship thus offers what Farrah Jasmine Griffin calls "textual healing," which helps to transform Celie's body from one in pain to a site of both pleasure and resistance.[25]

At the same time, there are glimmers of Celie's developing consciousness throughout their time together that indicate that her breakthrough is more than a sexual awakening, although it is also certainly that. When she is well enough to perform again, Shug sings a song for Celie, and Celie, in a revelatory act of selfhood, recognizes and loves her own tune. When Shug learns that Mr. _____ beats Celie when she's not there, she promises not to leave until he stops for good, protecting Celie in a way her mother could not and replicating the sisterly act of protection that Celie tried to extend to Nettie. Even though she travels and takes up with other men, Shug's true love, the one to whom she always returns, is Celie.[26]

Before Shug, survival is all Celie can contemplate. She tells Sofia early on that she "can't remember the last time" she felt angry; following the biblical command to "honor thy father and mother," she could not be mad at her father or later at her husband for their pervasive and persistent abuses. They made her feel "sick" for a while, she explains, and then she started "to feel nothing at all," using emotional repression as a survival strategy. Isolation reinforced her numbness, but Shug's appearance on their doorstep upends Celie's strategy of inward withdrawal. For Celie, the love and tutelage of Shug are nothing short of revolutionary, and her resolve strengthens when she learns that Nettie, who fled decades before, is still alive. Shug's discovery of a cache of letters from Nettie, hidden by Mr. _____, awakens the dormant anger in Celie. After years of numbness, this discovery enrages her, and she finds herself "standing hind his chair with his razor open" and "stumbl[ing] about the house crazy for Mr. _____ blood." Shug, who knows a thing or two about successful resistance, intercedes, putting Celie to bed with a "fever" and talking to her until she calms down enough that they can steal the hidden letters.[27]

Nettie's letters become a crucial part of Celie's developing feminist consciousness, as she begins to picture the world beyond Mr. _____'s dysfunctional household. The first letter is all about resistance. "You've got to fight to get away from Albert," Nettie writes to Celie, repeating her desperate plea to her sister in their last meeting years before. Celie is, for the first time, ready for this message. Nettie's potential return gives Celie something to live for, and she is murderously angry at Albert. "How I'm gon keep from killing him?" she asks Shug, who keeps Celie calm and busy by putting her to work making pants. As Shug reads the letters, Celie sews and listens to her sister's descriptions of her travels in Europe and Africa.[28]

For years, Celie believed that Nettie was dead and therefore that fleeing patriarchy was a futile strategy. The knowledge of Nettie's successful flight liberates Celie, and this is compounded by the secret her sister shares about their father. "Once upon a time," Nettie wrote, a "well-to-do," property-owning farmer opened a store with his brothers, and they did quite well. So well, in fact, that "white merchants" responded with Jim Crow justice: they burned the store down and hanged the three men, one of whom was Celie and Nettie's biological father. The violence drove their mother mad, and she was soon manipulated into marrying a second man, Celie's rapist stepfather. In other words, Nettie explained in her letter, "Pa is not our Pa!," and Celie's children were safe in Africa with a family that loved them.[29]

As she digests this information, Celie feels "daze," as if she is dreaming. Once she pulls herself together, she starts getting rid of the shoddy men in her life. First she abandons God, who she says "act just like all the other mens I know"—"trifling, forgetful, and lowdown." "What god do for me?" she asks, explicitly denouncing Christian patriarchal authority. In redirecting her correspondence to Nettie even though she does not know if her sister will ever receive her letters, Celie breaks out of her lonely relationship with an oppressive God and strengthens her ties to a "broader female community."[30]

As Celie starts to fight back ideologically, Shug decides that they should flee. "That's it," Shug proclaims when they read Nettie's letter about their father. "Pack your stuff. You coming back to Tennessee with me." When she tells Mr. _____ that she is leaving and taking Celie with her, he retorts that it will have to be over his dead body. Celie definitively derails his impending tantrum: "You a lowdown dog is what's wrong, I say. It's time to leave you and enter into the Creation. And your dead body just the welcome mat I need." When he reaches to slap her, she stabs him in the hand with a knife, and the women begin to "laugh and laugh." As they settle into the car to drive away, Celie curses Mr. _____, telling him, "The jail you plan for me is the one in which you will rot."[31]

But Walker is not done with Mr. _____, and *The Color Purple* is not a simple fairy tale, contrary to some criticism. Rather than merely defeating her enemy, Celie transforms herself and returns to share the revolution. Celie moves from male-dominated rural Georgia to feminine-infused urban Memphis, into Shug's enormous pink house, where she starts a cottage industry in the dining room that they name Folkpants, Unlimited. As she sews and perfects the pattern, Celie learns to be "happy," and her business grows. Walker thus genders and challenges the nostalgic concept of the South as the nation's pastoral ideal. Celie's hard labor in the fields is associated with violence and exploitation by men, while women's entrepreneurship is the path to liberation.[32]

Celie's choice of products is significant, not just as a rejection of the gender norms of clothing but also as a marker of her ownership of her body. Wendy Wall notes that gendered power in *The Color Purple* is frequently enforced through bodily harm; the repeated rapes and physical abuse enacted on the women are painful evidence of patriarchal supremacy in Black communities. But "folkpants" allow Celie, and those for whom she lovingly creates special pairs, to build community and "reinscribe the imprints and the contours of her body in such a way as to allow self-expression."[33] It is not just Celie who transforms. When she returns to Georgia for a visit, she learns that Mr. _____ has also changed, and he is clean, hardworking, and even "scared" of Celie. The old bogeyman has been defanged, especially after Celie's stepfather dies. After his death, Celie learns that his house is really hers; the house and the land belonged to her biological father and mother, who left it to Celie and Nettie. Although Celie's flight to Memphis enables her self-actualization, the moral is not that Black women must flee the rural South to survive, heal, and thrive. Rather, Celie packs up her business in the city and returns home for good to run a pants factory and store. She and Shug burn sage in the old house, and Celie makes it her own, complete with a purple and red bedroom for herself.[34]

While Shug is on the road singing the blues one last time, Celie begins to spend more time with Mr. _____. Just as Celie had to unlearn patriarchal norms, so too does Mr. _____, and it is a process with which she helps him. Walker opens the novel with lyrics from Stevie Wonder: "Show me how to do like you / Show me how to do it." Just as Shug showed Celie "how to do," Celie does the same for Mr. _____. In what amounts to porch therapy lessons, Mr. _____ talks about his own abusive father, and he tells

Celie sheepishly how he loved to sew with his mother as a boy, but "everybody laughed" at him, so he stopped. "Well, nobody gon laugh at you now," she tells him, and she hands him a needle.[35] With Celie's thread, he stitches a new life together, letting go of the brutal masculine socialization of Jim Crow.

Reconciliation is essential to the liberation of Black women, bell hooks argues.[36] The rehabilitation of Mr. _____ into the thoughtful Albert on Celie's porch is not simply part of Walker's concluding utopia. It is also crucial to the "love politics" of Walker's womanism, in which love is the foundation of personal salvation, protest, and community transformation.[37] Celie and Mr. _____, whom she calls by his name Albert in the last letter, sew together and talk about how much they love Shug, who retires from singing and returns to sit on the porch with them. A white woman's maid no more, Sofia clerks in the pants store, and Nettie, now married to the missionary after his wife's death, returns with Celie's grown children and their partners for a family reunion at Celie's, where they "spend the day celebrating each other."[38]

Dinitia Smith writes that *The Color Purple* is "about the struggle between redemption and revenge," and to this I would add that Walker offers a third option as a solution: reconstruction of the gendered system altogether, at least on a community scale.[39] The novel's ending conforms to Jack Halberstam's theory of "the production of counterrealities as a powerful strategy of revolt," and, more specifically, Walker offers a vision of southern womanist strategies of resistance and reconfiguration, as *The Color Purple* centers a loving Black sisterhood that collectively liberates both women and men.[40] According to Mae Henderson, the "predatory," heterosexual, patriarchal family is replaced by "a variation on the eternal triangle in which women complement rather than compete with each other, and at the same time, share an equal status with men." The new family, headed by Celie and Shug, "decentralizes the patriarch and calls for a more democratic distribution of kinship ties."[41]

And it is an explicitly southern reconfiguration. "Because I'm black and I'm a woman and because I was brought up poor and because I'm a Southerner," Walker explained in an interview, "the way I see the world is quite different from the way many people see it."[42] The answer in the novel is not fighting, given what happens to Sofia, but it's also not simply the geographical solution of fleeing—Shug, Celie, and even far-flung Nettie all happily return to the scene of some of their most harrowing experiences. Thadious Davis writes of "southscapes," the matrix of society, culture, economics, politics, and environment that influences, and can even determine, lived experiences.⁴³ In *The Color Purple*, the grim landscape of cotton fields representing exploited labor and the small town representing white supremacy and class exclusion become, by the end, a reformed southscape full of hope, color, and feminine spirit, in both Celie's transformed home and in town, where the Folkpants store is located. Walker's systemic critique is based on growing up in the South, but her proposed fictional solution takes place there too.

The Color Purple was incredibly radical for southern feminist popular culture in the early 1980s, but, more than that, it was radical for Reagan's America. Black lesbian activist and scholar Barbara Smith deemed it "without question ... the most radically brilliant book I'd ever read."⁴⁴ Some scholars have read Celie's sexual orientation, and in particular her relationship with Shug, as "politically charged," along the continuum of sexuality that includes both lesbianism and "the spectrum of women's friendships and sisterly solidarity."⁴⁵ Other scholars posit it as a primary example of "black lesbian shamelessness," a "celebration of the fact that same-sex relationships sustain and nurture the lives of countless black women." Rather than maintaining the traditional silence about sexual experiences between women, Walker "questions the salvation assumed to be inherent in silence and respectability" and affirms the centrality of lesbianism to Black feminism.⁴⁶ Lesbianism for Celie is a personal and ideological standpoint from which she challenges the sexual, racial, and economic hierarchies in her community, in keeping with Walker's womanism. This standpoint calls back to a specifically southern feminist tradition as well: lesbian activists in the region were early to community organizing as vital local arms of the blossoming LGBTQ civil rights movement in the 1970s, and these groups spanned the South.⁴⁷

But at the same time, as bell hooks points out, the positioning of same-sex desire as noncontroversial in *The Color Purple* frames it as apolitical even as Celie's lesbian relationship with Shug facilitates her rebellion against other systems of domination. When the women in the novel challenge patriarchy or white supremacy, they are severely punished, but when they resist compulsory heterosexuality, it does not warrant a mention from the ruling men. This critique by hooks relies on Mariana Valverde's claims that same-sex desire is "robbed of its radical potential" when "it is portrayed as compatible with heterosexuality, or rather as part of heterosexuality itself."⁴⁸ Although he is jealous of Shug's other men, Mr. ____ has no apparent problem with Celie and Shug's relationship, and more broadly, hooks points out, homophobia is completely absent in the novel. On the other hand, E. Patrick Johnson's recent work on Black lesbian communities in the

South shows that gendered expectations of Black women could be more fluid in small towns, particularly when it came to working-class women, who were, he argues, "freer to transgress" certain gender norms like dress codes. Moreover, Johnson's interviews with queer Black southern women show how the heteronormative stereotypes through which southern men, among others, view Black women have always framed them as "sexually available to men," a blind spot which has perhaps tempered homophobic reactions (although it has also, at times, exacerbated misogynist reactions).[49] As a blueswoman, Shug knowingly plays with raunchy hetero- and homosexual images, cultural production that Angela Davis reminds us is a primary means of historical resistance, protest, and even liberatory politics for African American women.[50] Thus, regional and even local culture matter in any sexual analysis of *The Color Purple*.

Of course, class matters to any analysis of the feminist politics of the novel too. hooks has also challenged the economics of *The Color Purple*, arguing that its characters conform to middle-class aspirations even as they resist the heterosexual mandate inherent in bourgeois propriety. Walker clearly condemns capitalist exploitation in the novel, particularly through descriptions of Celie's agricultural labor and Sofia's experiences as a domestic servant in the mayor's household. The violence of racialized capitalism in the rural South of *The Color Purple* harms all Black people: Celie's father was lynched for his economic success, and both her stepfather and her husband enact their brutality on her through forced labor from which they profit. But, as hooks points out, this theme does not translate into an indictment of capitalism itself, and thus Walker's fictional womanism eschews the radical position of Black feminist socialism. For hooks, the fullness of Celie's transformation is tempered by her wholehearted embrace of entrepreneurial capitalism. Lauren Berlant likewise explains that Celie's "utopian" ending is based on a "partnership of capitalism and sisterhood," and that the feminist community in the end is intricately intertwined with—and indeed enabled by—Celie's business.[51] Walker said of Celie, "I wanted her to be happy," and so she "liberated [Celie] from her own history."[52] But, as hooks argues, "happiness," rather than being subjected to "re-vision" and "radicalization," is rather conventionally defined here according to the economics of the American dream.[53] Even as Celie and Shug create the new possibility of a Black matriarchal utopian community, they use some of the "master's tools"—entrepreneurial capitalism and private landownership—to achieve it.[54]

Yet for Celie, even if her transformation is in accordance with national "bootstraps" mythology, this is a rebellious act and even, in Jacqueline Jones's estimation, a "political statement," as she is, in the end, dependent on neither Black men nor, crucially, white people. White supremacy is a controlling subtext in *The Color Purple*. Although Celie does not directly challenge the racial order in the manner of, say, Sofia, like her father before her, she creates a local industry that serves and employs her community, "free from white control."[55] Black economic success necessarily defied Jim Crow in the rural South, and Folkpants additionally flouted the gendered logic of popular images of the region as a "corrupted Eden" with a defining attachment to the land. Walker offers a reworked "black women's geography" by rewriting the agricultural land on which Celie is forced to work as a space dominated by Black men, which Celie, after an empowering stint in Shug's Memphis "pink palace," reconfigures as a matriarchal site of family and community.[56] In contrast to the nostalgia offered by the white male Agrarians, who mythologized the "natural," rural South and made their "stand" against industrialization in the region during the era in which *The Color Purple* is set, Celie, as part of her rebellion, embraces industry, and hers is powered by and for women.[57] She likewise transforms the nearby town from one in which Black women are abused in the streets into one featuring their entrepreneurship and fair labor practices, offering a kind of "third perspective," a space of "new forms of life that assert new geographic formulations."[58]

But this kind of rebellion, always dangerous in the Jim Crow South, was especially so in the dire economic context of the Depression in the region President Franklin D. Roosevelt deemed "the nation's number one economic problem" in 1938.[59] Black people in agricultural and domestic services, like the characters in Walker's novel and her own parents, found themselves excluded from many contemporary public relief programs. Black economic success was thus rare in this context, and middle-class status did not afford protection from white supremacy; indeed, it may have garnered increased white scrutiny. Celie's father was lynched decades before for his success, and while this particular brand of terrorism had declined overall by the 1930s, other forms of violent, racist social control, such as the rape of Black women by white men, were ever-present forms of terrorism across the South in the 1930s.[60] Yet this danger does not appear to overly trouble Celie, Shug, or the members of their beloved community at the end of the novel. Perhaps their lack of concern about white backlash was itself a form of resistance. As Jacqueline Jones argues, the timing of the novel's ending places it as perhaps a "lyrical prelude to the civil rights movement" in which the main characters have "prepared themselves to launch an all-out attack on the twin pillars of racist southern society, disfranchisement and segregation."[61]

Walker's *The Color Purple*, then, was utopian in its womanist vision, if not unimpeachably revolutionary in its avoidance of the additionally oppressive realities of homophobia, capitalism, and how white supremacy has intersected with both. However, the novel is explicitly radical compared to the film version, which went to theaters nationwide in 1985. Walker's original script foregrounded the context of white supremacy, as it opened in 1903 when Celie was a "happy baby," just before her father was lynched by "envious whites" for his entrepreneurial success. Walker also emphasized Shug's bisexuality and Celie's lesbianism for the big screen, as fundamental parts of the latter's development of womanism. She wrote a full screenplay, but after she refused to sign what she called a "chain-resembling contract," director Steven Spielberg decided to use the script of another writer, a Dutch man, and to hire Walker as a "consultant" entitled to 3 percent of the film's profits.[62]

Walker's initial apprehension about the film continued as she consulted on location in North Carolina, and she offered detailed character notes and suggestions in memos and letters to producer Quincy Jones and director Steven Spielberg. While some of her fears, like her vivid dread that the set for Harpo's juke joint would look like a McDonald's, did not come to pass, Walker expressed clear disappointment and even confusion at some of the creative choices made in the film. The movie "avoided entirely" Walker's insistence in the novel on what she called "Shug's completely unapologetic self-acceptance as an outlaw, renegade, rebel, and pagan; her zest in loving both women and men, younger and older." She later wrote, "I knew the passion of Celie and Shug's relationship would be sacrificed when, on the day 'the kiss' was shot, Quincy reassured me that Steven had shot it 'five or six' different ways, all of them 'tasteful.'" Although she came to accept the film as a different perspective of her original text, Walker felt "terrible" on first viewing of the completed product. She wrote in her journal, "It looks slick, sanitized, and apolitical to me.... The film looks like a cartoon."[63]

Some critics agreed with Walker's negative assessment. Writing for the *Village Voice*, Michele Wallace detailed the film's many "little white patriarchal interventions."[64] In spite of an outstanding performance from Whoopi Goldberg, Celie's wit is missing from the film, and even Shug is denuded of much of her resistance to gender norms. Unless she is singing in sequins, Shug is dressed demurely on screen, and her anti-patriarchal folk theology is replaced by a fabricated side plot in which she desperately seeks the approval of her preacher father. In addition to the reduction of Celie and Shug's relationship, Mr. ____ remains unredeemed, and he is seen skulking away alone with his horse in the final scene. With the possible exception of Sofia's physical resistance to both sexism and racism, the radical potential of the novel is completely absent from the film.[65]

But the big-screen version of *The Color Purple* nevertheless caused quite a stir, provoking protests and outrage, primarily from male critics regarding its portrayal of Black men. On an episode of talk show *Tony Brown's Journal*, titled "Purple Rage," host Brown called the film "the most racist depiction of black men since *The Birth of a Nation*," while filmmaker Spike Lee dismissed it by saying, "The quickest way for a Black playwright, novelist, or poet to get published has been to say that Black men are shit."[66] Others, however, countered that this critique of Walker as a "racial turncoat for her portrayals of black men" was yet another stereotype of Black women, in keeping with the "black nationalist aesthetic" that privileged the experiences of men and punished women who spoke out against sexism.[67] Rather than attacking Black men, Walker's true crime, according to her defenders, was disrupting the "family romance" of the "Black Family cum Black Community headed by a Black Male who does battle with an oppressive White world."[68] Instead, she shattered the silence around violence against women in Black families. Henry Louis Gates summed this up: "Lamentably, its very success exposed its author to charges of male-bashing by those who would prefer that the varied forms of violence against women be discreetly ignored by the Black literary record."[69]

Despite their differences, the novel and the film *The Color Purple* both performed crucial cultural work for readers and audiences. In the afterword, Walker signs *The Color Purple* as "author and medium," suggesting that she is giving voice to women who have been silenced.[70] Indeed, Celie's story was inspired by the experiences of Walker's own enslaved grandmother, who was raped by her enslaver at the age of twelve, and of her mother, who worked in white family's homes. As Terrence Musanga points out, the various traumas in the novel—rape, removal of children from the mother, and forced marriage—recall women's experiences of slavery.[71] The reunion of Celie with her children and Nettie at the end similarly calls on family reunification post-Emancipation. In her collection *Revolutionary Petunias*, Walker writes of the importance of thinking back through her foremothers: "To acknowledge our ancestors means we are aware that we did not make ourselves, that the line stretches all the way back. . . . We remember them because it is an easy thing to forget: that we are not the first to suffer, rebel, fight, love and die. The grace with which we embrace life, in spite of the pain, the sorrows, is always a measure of what has gone before."[72] In *Reel to Real*, bell hooks argues that this kind of collective thinking back informs how Black women consume popular culture, a "process whereby we see our history as countermemory, using it as a way to know the present and invent the future."[73]

While thinking back through matrilineal heritage can, some researchers argue, further traumatize Black women and lead to a state of "normalized chaos" in which they begin to view their experiences of racism, sexism, and classism as "normal," Shawn Arango Ricks argues that womanist ideology can be a mitigating factor by instilling "self-love" and a sense of community among women.[74] Before she developed this ideology, Walker herself benefited from this kind of community. She has said that her mother "gave her permission to write" when she was growing up, allowing her time off from chores to read uninterrupted and buying her a typewriter.[75] Other women facilitated her success too. Just before she headed off to Spelman on a scholarship, the women of her family's Methodist church in Eatonton gathered donations to send with her. She wrote of them in her poem "Women," describing her "mama's generation" as "headragged generals" who "led armies" over minefields to discover "Books / Desks / A place for us."[76] Walker used the creative space and resources carved out for her by her mother's cohort and her sisterhood with other women active in the Civil Rights and Women's Liberation Movements to write and develop her form of radical Black feminism. And she hoped that the novel and film versions of *The Color Purple* might offer this liberating vision, and teach this ethic of loving activism, to different audiences.[77]

The lofty goals of the novel were bound to be compromised by its Hollywood translation, and, on first viewing, Walker despaired that she had "failed the ancestors." But, over time, her reactions to the film evolved. Her fears were put to rest when her ailing mother enjoyed *The Color Purple* at a hometown premiere organized by her older sister in purple-swathed downtown Eatonton.[78] Walker gave Nettie, the "most longed for" character, the name of her maternal grandmother, a woman who was "battered unmercifully" by her husband, and during the filming Walker wrote in her journal that Ghanaian actor Akosua Bosia looked "so much like my grandmother (when young) it makes me wonder." And after her second viewing at the New York premiere, Walker grew to "love" the film: "I was finally able to see it, and to let go of the scenes that were not there." She later explained that she "writes for a lot of people who don't read," and thus visual "ways of reaching them" were perhaps more important than staying true to her original "vision." From the process, she learned "an old idea": "you really cannot step into the same river twice. Each time it is different, and so are you." Even with the many changes, Walker hoped that the story was "progressive enough for people to see some necessary reflections of themselves."[79]

Walker thus came to recognize the potential value of using different forms of media to promote womanism, and she pushed back against feminist critics who trashed the film as a way of defending the novel. After scholar Barbara Christian concluded that Spielberg made "the purple pink," substituting "sentimentality" for the radical "passion for living" in the novel, Walker asked her to "let it go" and to learn to "love it for its own sake," suggesting that a wholly womanist film would have enjoyed a smaller distribution and "would probably never make it to my hometown."[80] When Walker wrote in her journal that movies "are the most powerful medium for change on earth" because of their wide reach, she endorsed bell hooks's conclusion that the "pedagogical role" of films is confirmed by research on exposure to difference via popular culture.[81] Some critics agreed. On *The Phil Donahue Show*, historian Donald Bogle argued that the basic fact of representation in the film was significant: "When you see Whoopi Goldberg in close-up, a loving close-up, you look at this woman, you know that in American films in the past, in the 1930s, 1940s, she would have played a maid. She would have been a comic maid. Suddenly, the camera is focusing on her and we say I've seen this woman some place, I know her."[82]

This was enough to explain the film's popularity for some reviewers. One wrote wearily that protesters were "naïve" to expect a radical or liberating narrative from Hollywood, of all places. According to bell hooks's extensive work on the subject, feminist film critics are generally informed by a women's movement that privileges whiteness and ignores "black female spectatorship." For Black viewers, hooks writes, the gaze is never "passive," and movies are "not a place of escape" but rather of "confrontation and encounter." Thus, this "on guard" gaze is the "starting point" for many Black women rather than a state of critical spectatorship arrived at later via a deliberate interrogation of gender ideology.[83] In her multiple studies of how Black women viewers practice "different viewing strategies" to salvage "progressive and useful" messages and images from commercial films, Jacqueline Bobo has shown how women of color read through and between popular texts differently from other audiences "because of their low expectations of the media." Although the pressure to walk away with the dominant, "encoded" reading of a text is very high, viewers can also "make their own meanings." This is especially true of marginalized groups in their consumption of popular culture, as they are more likely to approach it with an "oppositional stance" due to their constant experiences of misrepresentation and maltreatment. Bobo found that this is precisely what Black women did with *The Color Purple*, even those viewers who had not also read the novel and thus were not familiar with the more radical elements of the narrative.[84]

According to Bobo, many Black women viewers, "through a complex process of negotiation," offered more "subversive readings" of the film, latching onto the images of the female characters as "cultural workers" in a story based on "black women's constructions, history, and real-life experiences." This was especially true of the depiction of Black men's violence against Black women, and the responses in Bobo's study mirrored those of Black women in the media coverage of the controversy surrounding the film. One respondent offered a feminist insight in Bobo's group interview about the film: "Listening to us talk here I'm beginning to see that [the controversy over the film] is a sexist thing."[85] "There is no healing in silence," hooks argues, and she cites *The Color Purple* as a "collective unmasking" that is "an important act of resistance."[86] Angela Davis hailed the novel and the film as significant exposés of "issues about which we had learned to remain silent," a sentiment echoed by Black women across the country.[87] Disagreeing with the all-male panel on Tony Brown's "Purple Rage" episode, one audience member argued that her work with teenagers and senior citizens confirmed the prevalence of incest, and the enforced silence surrounding it, in Black families.[88] The *New York Times* quoted a woman from Sunflower County, Mississippi, who confessed that the film "lifted a burden" of silence on intimate partner violence in Black communities, which she and the women of her family had experienced firsthand. "Black women should not be sacrificed for Black men's pride," she said. "Let the film roll."[89]

Critical responses to *The Color Purple* took on a life of their own, and Walker was encouraged by the public discussions that began with the novel but were "opened up more widely by the film."[90] Protests of the film, including a picket of the Oscars by the Coalition Against Black Exploitation, served to keep these conversations going, and this continuing controversy shattered the silence around the issue of violence against Black women. Responses to *The Color Purple*—not just the novel or the film—could thus serve a radicalizing function. Walker received countless letters from fans disclosing their reactions to *The Color Purple* and to the criticism of the film. Black women wrote about seeing themselves and their foremothers in the characters. Lesbians wrote about the significance of "the kiss," "chaste" as it was. And some Black men reassured the author that, despite the criticisms of the film, they understood her portrayal of the damages to Black masculinity resulting from white supremacist patriarchy.[91] Reactions like these indicate a kind of multilayered consciousness-raising: in the first instance, of intimate partner violence and incest in the text as social, not simply personal, problems in Black families, and, in the second, of the patriarchal prerogative inherent in reactions to popular culture.

The "oppositional gaze" of Black female viewers, then, is, according to hooks, "political" when it "emerges as a site of resistance" that challenges "the imposition of dominant ways of knowing and looking," a process that continued to play out as these readers and viewers went on to challenge the criticism of the film.[92] As Walker had hoped, the engagement with her womanist ideas was intertextual, as many fans consumed both versions of the text in addition to the reviews of the novel and film. And this intertextuality had an enduring life span; although the film had wider reach and impact from both its time in theaters and its popularity as a video rental, it reinvigorated the sales of the novel some three years after it won the Pulitzer and the National Book Award, making it, according to the publisher, "the fastest-selling paperback in a long time."[93] Walker's *The Color Purple*, in its various versions, both described the evolution of womanist consciousness and facilitated its development among some readers, viewers, and critics.

Criticism of *The Color Purple* centered on its depictions of male violence, but from at least the moment Sofia enters the story, women's violence, particularly women's reactive violence against men, becomes a possibility in a way that is rarely featured in regional narratives. And this theme is not just centered around Sofia's battles with Harpo. Before Celie learns how to reconfigure her world, Shug has to stop her from slitting Mr. _____'s throat when he commands her to shave him. While no fan of Celie's would want her to endure the repercussions of murdering her husband, most surely understood the impulse. And this understanding endures, Farrah Jasmine Griffin claims: "If you hear one sister saying to another, 'Don't do it, Miss Celie,' you better move out the way, 'cause somebody is liable to get cut."[94] As she wrote her letters and developed a feminist consciousness, with able assistance from Shug, Celie staged a coup against southern patriarchy, but in the end, despite her silent rage, she did so nonviolently. This contrasts sharply with another famous pop cultural representation of southern feminist rebellion in this era, the film *Thelma & Louise*.

"Deep Shit, Arkansas"
Thelma & Louise

Like Celie and Shug when they laughed in Mr. _____'s face and packed the car for Memphis, Thelma and Louise initially just want to get away from southern sexism, even if only for a weekend. But they find no refuge like Shug's pink palace in Memphis or entrepreneurial alternative like Folkpants once their weekend vacation turns into an outlaw flight. This fictional feminist coup started simply enough, when wannabe screenwriter Callie Khouri jotted down an idea—"Two women go on a crime spree"—in her notebook. Khouri is a self-described "army brat," the daughter of a "southern belle" and a doctor, who grew up in Texas and Kentucky.[95] After a few post-college years in Nashville, Khouri made her way to Los Angeles, where she landed a job at a music video production company. In 1988, Khouri was struck with "an idea that landed on [her] like a ton of bricks." Explaining years later that she had been "called to it," she started with just the characters and the conclusion: "I knew it was two average women who were not criminals, who were only outlaws in that the society that we were asked to live in was so insane that you could not help but break that law if you were yourself."[96]

Khouri took six months to think deeply about her characters, and then she began to write their story, scene by scene, by hand in a notebook. She later said that the "southern sensibility," which she defined as "the acceptance of eccentricity as normal, you know, as just part of people's daily life," was key to her writing. It could be "colorful and entertaining," but there is also "kind of a dark side to the South. . . . It's known for hospitality and lynching, you know."[97] In the age of *Steel Magnolias*, Khouri mined that dark side.

As a newcomer to the industry, Khouri entered a film-making landscape fraught with "ambivalence" over feminism.[98] Khouri's idea capitalized on the popularity of the contemporary female friendship films, but she did not restrict herself to the rules of genre. She later explained: "There is a certain stigma, I think that there is a set of expectations that women write a certain type of picture, so you don't look for an action movie that's written by a woman. You don't look for a thriller. . . . People still call things 'women's pictures.' If it has a female audience then there is always a somewhat derogatory connotation to a so-called woman's picture."[99] In defiance of these unwritten rules, Khouri combined many genres in her screenplay: road movie, western, comedy, female friendship film, even horror, as Thelma implies when she packs a gun at the last minute in case of "psycho killers." In a description Khouri endorses, her then-husband deemed it "*9 to 5* meets *Easy Rider*."[100]

Khouri had never written a screenplay before, and she hoped to also direct it, but her "genre-melding" script was not an easy sell, especially during the decade in which the industry would come to be dominated by Miramax, the company run by Harvey Weinstein, the sexual predator of #MeToo infamy.[101] Khouri joked, "[I]f this thing ever sees the light of day and the title hasn't been changed to *Tits and Bullets*, it's going to be a miracle."[102] Ridley Scott was an early backer, and finally, fed up with directors who wanted to rewrite the characters, the ending, or both, he agreed to direct. Scott was known for "revisionist" popular films like *Alien* and *Blade Runner*, so Khouri signed on, with the firm caveat that Scott would not change the ending in her original script.[103] The result was cinematic gold. *Thelma & Louise* was a pop cultural Trojan horse that offered a form of regional feminism never before seen on screen: a friendship forged into sisterhood through shared sexist oppression, a sisterhood that becomes radical, furious, and, yes, vengeful. The titular characters deploy all of the forms of resistance available to them: dissemblance, violent self-defense against misogyny, and abandonment of the South in search of a better society.

Although the film is often compared to classic westerns, and its majestic scenes of Monument Valley and the finale in a Grand Canyon–like setting certainly invite this comparison, the roots of the characters' repression and rebellion are in Arkansas, where Thelma is a naïve housewife with what one critic described as "a twitchy-eyed, sexist jerk of a husband."[104] When the film opens, Thelma and Louise plan to temporarily escape the daily sexism in their lives by going to a friend's lake house for the weekend. In their first on-screen conversation, Louise acknowledges Thelma's dismal domestic plight when she jokingly addresses her friend as "little housewife" and asks whether Darryl is her husband or her father. Khouri explains that she envisioned Thelma as a woman with few options: "You were expected to be less than you were, and you were expected to be happy about it. Like that was supposed to somehow be success. She was doing her job, what was expected of her, which was that she would get married, and probably have kids, and for whatever reason they hadn't gotten around to that, and her husband was the king of his tiny little castle, and you know she went about her day trying to figure out what it was he wanted, you know, without ever really thinking of herself very much."[105] In the first scene, Thelma, played by Geena Davis, gamely attempts what pundit Florence King, in her investigation of southern "types," called "pertness"—feigned cheerfulness combined with "playing dumb" to bolster her husband's fragile ego—yet she is clearly failing at being an ideal housewife.[106] The kitchen is overflowing with dirty dishes, and her husband berates and belittles her as he gets ready for work.[107]

Louise, played by Susan Sarandon, is in a different kind of messy situation, with an emotionally distant, bedroom-eyed, musician boyfriend and, at the diner where she works, a boss who harasses Thelma when she calls, teenaged customers who roll their eyes at her, and an impending "nervous breakdown" that she laughingly cites as their reason for leaving town. Khouri describes Louise as wearing "the woman mask," hiding herself, donning "these faces that go on over [her face] that completely change [her]" as a means of survival. Khouri wanted to write characters that she could "love" and that she knew from growing up in the South. "Given that I was prepared to do nothing with my life that would bring me any money," she explained, "these were the people I was going to be working with unless I married somebody rich."[108]

The Arkansas town that Thelma and Louise flee is a dingy place of strip malls and diners. While industry, symbolized by the long-haul trucks along the highways and the oil rigs that dot the landscape as they flee westward, forms the backdrop, none of the characters appear to have benefited from the much-touted prosperity of the Sunbelt South, where the "price of progress," as historian James C. Cobb put it, was a polluted landscape and an exploited working class.[109] On-screen, this industrial landscape visibly constricts Thelma and Louise. Critics have noted the tightly framed shots that enclose the pair in Arkansas; indeed, they are nearly forced off the road and out of a shot by a massive truck just as they begin their journey. Leo Braudy writes that "the camera continues to stress the choking inevitability of the world they are trying to escape, not just the massive machinery, oil drilling equipment, and trucks that constantly threaten to squeeze them out of our vision."[110] Like patriarchy itself, the gritty landscape of the upper South at the beginning of the film cages the women as they try to push against its boundaries.

The pair's acts of resistance begin on a small scale. Carmen Eraso argues that a prerequisite for the development of female "easy riders" in a road movie is the "breakdown of the family unit," which happens almost immediately in *Thelma & Louise*.[111] Thelma is scared to get Darryl's permission to go on vacation, and so she doesn't ask; after he leaves for work, she haphazardly packs her things, including a gun, and piles in the car with Louise. "He never lets me do one goddam thing that's any fun," she complains to Louise. "Well, you get what you settle for," her friend replies, exhaling cigarette smoke as she offers this pre–feminist consciousness line, one Khouri said often to a friend when they worked at the music production company. Thelma brightens, realizing that, at least this weekend, she's not settling. "I left him a note," she cackles as they pull off in Louise's Thunderbird convertible. "I left him stuff to microwave."[112]

Their short-term escape from sexist reality, however, almost immediately becomes a nightmarish confrontation with violent misogyny. During a stop on the road, at a honky-tonk called the Silver Bullet where they have a few drinks, Thelma and Louise encounter a rapist who derails their vacation plans and changes the course of their lives. Harlan, a creepy local, comes on to Thelma as soon as the pair sits down and orders drinks. Once she is drunk and disheveled from dancing, he walks her outside, intent on raping her in the parking lot. Louise, a survivor herself from an unnamed assault in Texas, interrupts, pointing Thelma's gun at Harlan. Thelma, bruised and bloody, collects herself as Louise holds Harlan at gunpoint, his hands in the air. The two women turn to walk away, but Harlan, desperate to get the last word, calls obscenities to them. Ann Putnam pinpoints this moment as a pivotal one in the film, a "pause between the real danger" of the rape and "the pulling of the trigger."[113] In this moment, Thelma and Louise are free of Harlan, and they could just jump in the car and drive away. Instead, Louise confronts Harlan, eyes wild and determined, and she shoots to kill. Thelma gets the car, and they peel out of the parking lot before their crime is discovered.[114]

Country music from the Silver Bullet plays throughout the entire scene, offering a southern soundtrack to both sexual assault and the women's unexpectedly violent defense of themselves. Putnam notes that this is not "acceptable" women's violence: it is "not in defense of husband or child," but rather it is meant to "avenge not just this outrage but all of the little rapes, the everyday usurpations of female autonomy that all women know."[115] The pair's subsequent decision not to alert the authorities is both a strategic move and a systemic critique, as it positions them against not just Harlan but also against the misogynist system that would prosecute Louise for the murder of her friend's rapist. Louise says as much when Thelma suggests that they call the police, knowing that when she pulled the trigger it was not self-defense and that no rape shield law would protect Thelma from blame. "We don't live in that kind of world, Thelma!" Louise cries as they flee the scene. The kind of world they live in, according to one reviewer, is not simply one in which rape victims are condemned as "asking for it" but also one in which "they can hold a gun to a man and still he fails to take them seriously."[116] So the shooting is a turning point. "This time," Louise tells Thelma, "things have changed. Everything has changed."[117] After just one stop on the road, without ever reaching their intended destination, Thelma and Louise decide to fight their way out of the South in search of a better society.

Although their experiences are those of American women writ large, the two are also specifically running from southern misogyny. In fact, "Deep Shit, Arkansas" is Louise's metaphor for the trouble they're in: for the cultural norms that argue that Thelma was "asking for it" in that parking lot because she had been drinking and dancing with Harlan, for the society that is unable to see their actions as self-defense, and for the legal system that will hold them accountable for murder. Louise adamantly identifies this dangerous patriarchal system as a regional problem.[118] This becomes clear as they make their plans to flee to Mexico: Louise insists they must get out of the South, and in fact go westward, around every part of the South, before they head to the border, despite the fact that, as Thelma rightly points out on the map, Texas is pretty much the only thing between the two outlaws and Mexico. As sites of gendered violence, Texas and Arkansas are one and the same to Louise. Although the script does not explicitly state that Louise was raped in Texas before she moved to Arkansas, it heavily implies this fact, and Khouri later confirmed it. Violence against women is clearly correlated with geography in Louise's mind. And so, even though time is of the essence, especially after the FBI joins the Arkansas State Police in the hunt for the two women, Louise simply will not go through Texas. It is imperative to her that they get out of, and stay out of, the U.S. South.[119]

With much of the film spent speeding out of and away from the region in Louise's Thunderbird, *Thelma & Louise* rewrites the gendered script of the masculine southern car chase seen in popular television shows like *The Dukes of Hazzard* and films like *Smokey and the Bandit*. As they drive hard westward, like Celie and Shug, Thelma and Louise come to share power equally and alternate taking care of each other. Initially, the older Louise is firmly in charge of the childlike Thelma, telling her friend after Harlan's assault that she will "get it together, and figure out what to do." Louise maintains this authority along the dusty backroads until the smooth-talking hitchhiker J. D. steals their getaway money from a motel room, whereupon she loses all semblance of control. While she sobs, a newly authoritative Thelma drags her out of the motel, gets behind the wheel, starts smoking—formerly something she had only pretended to do in an imitation of her friend—and dons Louise's sunglasses. While Louise herself is essentially catatonic in the passenger seat, Thelma, using the tactics charmingly described by the veteran thief J. D., robs a store to replenish their cash. Each woman, then, is able to take charge when needed, "need" being defined not just by the circumstances of their flight but also by her best friend's mental health status. Even as the danger of state violence against them grows, their give and take is a loving partnership, and Louise recovers as Thelma sips mini-bottles of Wild Turkey behind the wheel and the roadside oil rigs give way to red canyons. Both women start to shed the trappings of femininity as they leave the southern landscape of interchangeable roadside towns and flee into the wide, wild West. As the terrain becomes iconically western, they rip their shirts up to make them more breathable, their skin burns in the hot desert sun, and Louise exchanges her jewelry for an old man's cowboy hat outside a desolate gas station.[120]

After she recovers from losing her savings and both women embrace their roles as fugitives, Louise still refuses to discuss her own rape, even as they log hundreds of miles trying to bypass Texas for this very reason. Thelma pressures her, but Louise will not talk about it. It was director Ridley Scott's decision to cut a scene from Khouri's script in which Louise discussed her past, a move some critics saw as a kind of enforced silencing. But other viewers applauded Louise's choice to remain unknowable, her refusal to render the violence scrutable, a move which also subtly underscores the lack of voice the women would have in court should they go to trial for Harlan's murder. "If this were the TV rape-movie-of-the-month," Richard Schickel wrote in a cover story for *Time*, "a hysterical revelation of the exact nature of the abuse—especially if it were, say, gang rape or years of incest—would be obligatory in order to balance the moral scales." Inclusion of this information would, he rightly noted, help to quell the "'male-bashing' criticism" of the film, but it would also have "cheapened" it: "By leaving Louise's mystery intact, the film implies that all forms of sexual exploitation, great or small, are consequential and damaging."[121] Film scholar Karen Hollinger agrees: "By not discussing her experiences as a rape victim, Louise refuses to engage in the kind of intimate self-disclosure that would render her a powerless victim of male violence."[122] Louise refuses to even consider engagement with the patriarchal state, preferring their chances on the run instead.

As they put as many miles between themselves and Arkansas as possible without going through Texas, Thelma and Louise resist victim status and instead create their own feminist outlaw counterculture. When they get pulled over by a state trooper and lock him in his own trunk to escape detection, this action is not just about the fear of getting caught. Thelma tells this agent of the sexist state to be good to his wife, explaining, "My husband wasn't sweet to me—look how I turned out." All the way across the Midwest, from Arkansas to Monument Valley, fueled by Wild Turkey and raised consciousness—"I don't remember ever feeling this awake," proclaims Thelma—the women fight back, confronting multiple men along the way, most memorably a long-haul trucker who sexually harasses them at various points on the road. It's worth noting that the two are not on some man-hating free-for-all, as the critics who descried the film's "toxic feminism" would have it. This charge was often based on the ultimate trucker scene, but in the film all the women want from the trucker is an apology (although when they don't get it they shoot gleefully until his big rig explodes).[123] As the trucker rages at them, screaming that they are "bitches from hell!" while his truck burns in the background, they circle him in Louise's iconic 1966 Thunderbird. As a parting insult, Thelma plucks his hat from the dust as they drive off, pairing it with the sunglasses she stole from the state trooper.[124]

Their consciousness ignited, Thelma and Louise cannot live in the South, the United States, or any other male-dominated society. "Something's crossed over in me, and I can't go back," Thelma explains. "I mean, I just couldn't live." Thelma is not simply citing the very real possibility of prison sentences, for armed robbery for herself and for murder for Louise. Rather, the pair are no longer able to even contemplate a return to sexist subordination. Unlike in *The Color Purple*, in which Celie and Shug return to the scene of their oppression and modify it to their own ends, when Thelma and Louise deploy flight as resistance, it is a permanent position. Despite the pleas to the contrary by one sympathetic FBI agent, Hal Slocumb, they cannot return to, reconfigure, or revolutionize their former lives. There is no justice and certainly no liberation for them in Arkansas or anywhere else, as they learn once they've left the South only to find even more male agents of the state hunting them. The farther west they flee, the more the landscape opens up, but the false sense of freedom offered by these wide-open spaces is belied by the many phallic images along their route: oil rigs give way to the soaring buttes of Monument Valley as the system closes in on the two outlaws.[125]

In an obvious metaphor, the final scene features the two being trailed by dozens of male officers—police, state troopers, and the FBI. There is a moment in which it seems like Thelma and Louise have outrun their pursuers and might actually get away, but as they pause to shakily share a cigarette after a harrowing chase, a helicopter rises out of the canyon and the dust clears, revealing that they are surrounded. "Omigod, it looks like the army!" Thelma exclaims as Louise loads her gun. The camera shows the Thunderbird through gun sights in an attempt to reassert the traditional cinematic male gaze and position the women as targets of not just the individual men who have abused them but also the state that relies on and maintains male supremacy. "Any failure to obey that command will be considered an act of aggression against us," says one of the men through his bullhorn, effectively reciting the requirements of the patriarchal system and informing the women that, although they sought freedom in their westward flight like so many Americans before them, "manifest destiny" is clearly gendered here. "How many times are they going to be fucked over?" pleads Slocumb, the sympathetic agent, just as the pair decides that they won't be, not this time. "Let's keep going," Thelma says softly, nodding toward the canyon, and the women kiss each other goodbye. The two clasp hands as Louise hits the gas, launching the car into the canyon.[126]

The final frame shows the Thunderbird in the air, either flying over or about to crash into the canyon, and this ambiguity became the source of much debate. True to this revision of the typical, male "buddy" script, Thelma and Louise did not "go out in a blaze of testosteronic glory" per the formula of western and action films, "rejecting the shoot-out" that is the traditional ending of these genres and choosing instead their own sisterhood.[127] But the freeze-frame of the outlaws' final flight left many wondering. While some audience members read this as self-destruction and a statement that women essentially had to commit suicide to be free of patriarchy, no "literal death" graces the screen: the car is shown flying, with a fadeout to a blank white screen.[128] It is crucial that they choose this conclusion, together. Scott filmed an alternate ending in which Louise saves Thelma by ejecting her from the car just before they reach the cliff's edge. But Khouri fought for her original ending, which actor Susan Sarandon deemed "the least compromising": "You built this whole film to have these people not settle anymore, and then you'd toss them back into the system?"[129] Feminist novelist Alix Kates Shulman agrees, arguing bluntly, "It's better to die on your feet than live on your knees."[130] But others expressed concern about the muddled feminist message. "When death is your only choice, how free are you?" asked film scholar Annette Insdorf.[131]

Yet those critics of *Thelma & Louise* who argue that the film takes a dismal or confusing view of the progress of feminism perhaps ignore the more immediate context of the Reagan-era backlash. The problem was not so much that the Women's Liberation Movement had failed but rather that it had done pretty well, actually, only to be pummeled to a shadow of its former self throughout the 1980s. Media studies scholar Elayne Rapping argues: "The assault on this film must be read as part of a much larger political backlash against the real gains of feminism fueled by those for whom changes in gender power relations mean a serious loss of privilege and power." She continues: "That they are so nervous proves to me that feminism has had a greater impact on this society than it sometimes seems in these politically dark days."[132] In other words, the controversial nature of *Thelma & Louise* was proof positive of the power of its feminism—why else would it cause such public consternation? Moreover, no matter how one reads that ambiguous ending, feminists scholars argue that questions of agency in women's suicidality are more complicated than the simplistic interpretation that they must die to escape dominance might indicate.[133]

At any rate, Callie Khouri dismissed this aspect of the controversy outright, arguing that suicide was a misreading of the ending. "Read a book," Khouri sarcastically told critics, suggesting that they did not understand symbolism. "[Thelma and Louise] flew away, out of this world and into the mass unconscious," she explained. "Women who are completely free from all of the shackles that restrain them have no place in this world.... After all they went through I didn't want anybody to be able to touch them."[134] Lauren Berlant argues that "sometimes a person doesn't want to seek the dignity of an always-already-violated body, and wants to cast hers off, either for nothingness, or in a trade for some other, better model."[135] Having already traded their "violated bodies" for powerful outlaw identities, Thelma and Louise, in their own words, "can't go back." As one critic put it, "they can no longer tolerate a deepshit status in a man-made American universe," and the fact that they choose their own ending by hitting the gas at the canyon's edge is crucial to the message.[136] "Patriarchy would have them live," writes Linda Rohrer Paige of the pairs' ultimate act of resistance, and Lynda Hart agrees, noting the significance of their successful elusion of the pursuing men as well as their choice of departure "together," a final "fuck-you" to the heterosexual mandate (although, as Hart points out, the pair's heterosexuality is firmly, "insistently" established throughout the film).[137]

Their final flight into the canyon, hands clasped, indicates, as Hollinger argues, that their relationship is no mere "refuge" from patriarchy. Rather, their sisterhood is their resistance, their own outlaw "social structure," writ "forever unrepentant" when Louise steps on the gas pedal.[138] Marsha Kinder deems this ending a "grand suicidal leap into that great vaginal wonder of the world."[139] In a 1992 poem celebrating the film as both revising and in keeping with western exploration, Diane Glancy wrote, "It's just a matter of deciding, Fuck yourself, Darryl. Get in your ship and go. You have to make your own way." She concluded, "Thelma and Louise carry on where men have failed / And actually discover the end of the end. / Landlessness. /

And sail off."[140] Rather than the public death of women's resistance, Khouri's ending was a middle finger to the backlash.

At its theatrical release on Memorial Day weekend in 1991, *Thelma & Louise* "hit like a brick through a window."[141] The film was a financial success, although *Time* noted that its earnings in its first month were along the lines of what "muscular big-boy" movies might make in one weekend.[142] Dubbed an "instant classic," *Thelma & Louise* sparked immediate "table-pounding discussions between men and women" featuring conservative consternation about "violent rebellion" and progressive applause for its feminist depictions of "female discontent."[143] As with *The Color Purple*, reactions to *Thelma & Louise* were generally divided along gendered lines. "I've talked with enough people to be convinced that when men and women see *Thelma and Louise*, they see two different movies," wrote one reviewer.[144] Predictably, it was less the male "buddy" movie genre-bending and more the "gender bending" violence that worried some viewers. Kyle Smith, writing in the *New York Post*, called it a "date-rape revenge saga" and the "story of two idiotic hysterics": "Stupidity and hot tempers, not entrenched sexism, are the causes of their problems."[145] According to John Leo in the *U.S. News and World Report*, the film was "very disturbing," "toxic," and "a paean to transformative violence" based on "an explicit fascist theme."[146] Richard Johnson of the *New York Daily News* added that it was "degrading to men" and "justif[ied] armed robbery, manslaughter, and chronic drunk driving as exercises in consciousness raising."[147]

Others complained that Thelma and Louise acted like "shoot-first-and-talk-later action heroes," living out "a male fantasy of life on the road" and even acting like men by "behaving, in the time-honored tradition of most American heroes, violently and without reflection."[148] As Hart points out, these critiques indicate both incoherent fears and an inability to see the characters "as women within the buddy-film conventions."[149] Violence and disposal of the "visual signs of their femininity" do not equate to Thelma and Louise becoming, or fantasizing about becoming, men. Scholar Peter Chumo notes that while Thelma imitates J. D.'s "robbery speech" to the letter, she puts her own spin on it, and, of course, the goal of the robbery is not personal gain, as with J. D., but rather flight from the patriarchal state.[150] The pair knows exactly what they are doing, and their violence, rather than being "spectacle" or "nihilistic" as in other contemporary road films like *Kalifornia* and *Natural Born Killers*, has one premise: resistance to misogyny.[151] Khouri has addressed this, observing wryly, "Bad guys get killed in every goddamn movie that gets made," but when Harlan the rapist was shot, "it was only because a woman did it that there was any controversy at all."[152] Star Susan Sarandon agreed, retorting in an interview, "This kind of scrutiny does not happen to *Raiders of the Lost Ark* or that Schwarzenegger thing where he shoots a woman in the head and says, 'Consider that a divorce.'"[153]

Although it is depicted as a form of feminist resistance in the film, it is worth noting that violence is generally one of the "master's tools" of enforcing status quo hierarchies. Yet, as with Celie's embrace of entrepreneurial capitalism, the co-optation of these tools by women can be transgressive. Jack Halberstam argues that "represented violence" perpetrated by marginalized people has "an unpredictable power" that can produce change, noting the "unprecedented wave of discussions" about violence against women that accompanied *Thelma & Louise*. Rage and violence from marginalized individuals or groups thus have significant functions in representational politics.[154] In his study of violence in the film, David Russell deems the women's acts "the necessary first step for being heard and acknowledged."[155] Scholars note the "fine line" between resistance and rage, and Halberstam laments the disappearance of rage from "the vocabulary of organized political activism." According to Halberstam, "role reversal," as in the gender-bending violence in *Thelma & Louise*, "never simply replicates the terms of an equation." Rather, "[w]omen with guns confronting rapists has the potential to intervene in pop imaginings of violence and gender by resisting the moral imperative to not fight violence with violence. Films like *Thelma & Louise* suggest, therefore, not that we all pick up guns, but that we allow ourselves to imagine the possibilities of fighting violence with violence."[156] As the embodiment of Celie's fantasies of slitting Mr. _____'s throat, Thelma and Louise's strategic deployment of violence is a revisionist use of the "master's tools."

This revision caused not just outrage but also confusion. A related theme in criticism of violence in the film is the consistent referencing of Harlan's attack on Thelma as an "attempted" sexual assault. Legal scholar Ann Althouse rightfully notes that there is nothing in the film to suggest that this was not a full-fledged rape.[157] The scene itself looks like rape, and Thelma later says that Harlan "was raping" her when she and Louise discuss going to the police. Yet even many reviewers who loved the film, applauded its feminist themes, and had no interest in defending Harlan "downgraded" him to a would-be rapist. Ignoring filmic evidence to the contrary, others even refused to acknowledge Harlan as a clearly signified predator before the assault and blamed Thelma for flirting, drinking, and dancing with him, behaviors which allegedly "prove" the anti-male tenor of the film.[158]

Khouri summarily dismissed these as "hysterical" reactions: "All I could say was that if you're a man and were threatened by that when you saw it, well, now you know how women feel every time they walk into the movie theater." She continued, "If men feel uncomfortable in the audience it is because they are identifying with the wrong character."[159]

Yet another patronizing line of criticism was that the darkness—the essential southern Gothicism of the film—was unintentional. Although Khouri described her ending as a radical, transcendent feminist moment, some critics, especially Richard Schickel in his cover story for *Time*, refused to give her credit for its message, arguing that the film was one "in the honorable line of movies whose makers, without quite knowing what they were doing, sank a drill into what appeared to be familiar American soil and found that they had somehow tapped into a wild-rushing subterranean stream of inchoate outrage and deranged violence." Schickel asserted that while Khouri's mission was to "vary and freshen traditional generic themes," she and director Ridley Scott "ended up" taking the audience "on trips much deeper, darker, more disturbing that anyone imagined." Thus, the role of *Thelma & Louise* as an "expression of the values or confusions jangling around in" society was potentially coincidental or at least subconscious, rather than a well-timed, carefully calibrated feminist statement, according to Schickel.[160] Yet Khouri's deliberateness about these themes is evident in interviews at the time of the film and ever since. And it was in keeping with regional genres; perhaps Khouri was following the logic underlying southern Gothicism, famously explained by Flannery O'Connor: "[T]o the hard of hearing you shout and for the almost blind you draw large and startling figures."[161]

Startling the film certainly was, and many viewers immediately noted the cultural significance of *Thelma & Louise*. Film critic Peter Keough argued that it would "be seen as a turning point," and many female viewers agreed. A lesbian activist in Los Angeles called it "the first movie I've ever seen which told the downright truth," a sentiment echoed by a Houston woman who said it was "like seeing my life played before my eyes."[162] Even those fans who condemned the film's violent solutions generally applauded the relationship at its core as a transformative one for depictions of women in Hollywood. Manohla Dargis wrote that *Thelma & Louise* "reinvented sisterhood for the American screen."[163] As with *The Color Purple*, the controversy surrounding the film after its release through Oscar season served to keep discussions of gendered violence going and, as Hollinger argues, "added significantly to its social impact."[164]

Thelma and Louise's initial crime against patriarchy is committed in secret—at least, when Louise shoots Harlan, Thelma is the only witness. But as soon as they peel out of the Silver Bullet parking lot and decide not to turn themselves in, and especially once they cross state lines and start robbing stores to fund their flight, Thelma and Louise are public enemies. When they kiss, clasp hands, and openly defy federal orders at gunpoint, it is an explosive moment of southern feminist rebellion, even if their next move is to go over a cliff. In doing so, they became part of a public discussion of feminism, specifically of direct confrontations with patriarchal abuses.

Thelma & Louise was thus part of the "genderquake" of the early 1990s in which events, experiences, and representations of women converged to force feminism back into public consciousness.[165] The film came out just a few months before the Clarence Thomas Supreme Court nomination hearings, in which Anita Hill testified about his repeated sexual harassment. The public nature of these accusations and the ensuing discussion is significant here. Celie's confrontation with misogyny in *The Color Purple* is private; it happens within the family, but it is successful, and she liberates herself. In *Thelma & Louise*, and in the case of Anita Hill, the opposite happened. During the Thomas hearings, the state circled the wagons around the offending man, targeting Hill according to age-old racist and sexist stereotypes of Black women and even questioning the very existence of sexual harassment. Thomas was, of course, confirmed as Hill was dragged through the mud.

But as with the ensuing commentary on both *The Color Purple* and *Thelma & Louise*, Hill's public actions—her televised confrontation with patriarchy—had reverberating effects, even if they did not achieve the immediate desired result of preventing Thomas from being seated. According to Lauren Berlant, "[d]espite her failure to convince the Senate about Thomas and his alleged proclivities, Hill's testimony turned into an act of national pedagogy that still generates commentary, controversy, and political struggle."[166] The very fact that these conversations—about sexual harassment, sexual assault, and women's "appropriate" responses to sexism—were happening publicly and daily, on the big screen, in the headlines, in the televised confirmation hearings and accompanying news coverage, represents a change. The same year that audiences debated whether or not Thelma and Louise's rebellion represented "toxic feminism," the phrase "sexual harassment" reentered American media consumers' daily lexicon via Hill's testimony, and those conversations continued long past Thomas's confirmation.

Even as it can be viewed as complementary to contemporary pop cultural feminism, Hill's testimony also helped to spark a new form of feminism with regional roots. In early 1992, Alice Walker's daughter Rebecca Walker was so enraged by Thomas's confirmation that she took to the pages of *Ms.* to declare a new era of "third-wave" feminism. The Thomas hearings, she wrote, "unleashed more repressed anger than I thought possible," and she pleaded with American women to channel their rage into a new movement.[167] This was a timely clarion call from a feminist born in the South and with an impressive activist and artistic genealogy from the region. Walker's rage and "thoughts of separatism" echo Celie, Thelma, and Louise's visceral responses to misogyny. But Walker urged her audience to channel that rage: "Let this dismissal of a woman's experience move you to anger. Turn that outrage into political power."[168]

Two months after the publication of Walker's groundbreaking call to arms, Callie Khouri won the Oscar for Best Original Screenplay for *Thelma & Louise*. As she accepted the award, Khouri thanked the actors, stating that Geena Davis and Susan Sarandon "made the world a better place with these performances," and she concluded, brandishing the statue: "Well, for everybody who wanted to see a happy ending for *Thelma & Louise*, to me this is it." Like Alice Walker, for whom writing was a necessary act of resistance, Khouri wrote for women who went to the movies and left feeling "dirty and worthless."[169] And she did so at a time when a new generation of southern women like Walker's daughter Rebecca came of age ready to take on the backlash. Together these texts offered models of sisterhood and resistance, giving voice to and channeling the rage that many southern and other American women felt during this era when organized feminism languished and neoconservatism took over national politics. The ongoing national discussions of these popular texts, as well as their misreading—in reviews, on talk shows, in interviews with the authors and actors, and in scholarship ever since—brought questions of gendered violence, southern sisterhood, and differing strategies of resistance firmly out of the private and into the public sphere.

At the same time, however, an alternative form of southern feminism was developing on television, one that tapped into regional ideas about gender and race while promoting a progressive brand of politics associated with shifts in the contemporary Democratic Party. And, in fact, this new feminism had roots in Walker's Georgia and Thelma and Louise's Arkansas. Its primary medium was a tempered version of liberal feminism created by a powerful television production team from Arkansas, but it was set in the New South metropolis of Atlanta. Despite this shared geography, the middle-class politics of this new southern feminism were a world away from the Jim Crow–era exploitation of *The Color Purple*'s Georgia and backlash-era misogyny of *Thelma & Louise*. Instead, on *Designing Women*, a prime-time sitcom that ran on CBS for seven years, viewers were exposed to a "third way" of southern feminism that carefully navigated a middle ground between "second-wave" liberal feminism, neoconservatism, and regional ideals of white womanhood.

CHAPTER 3

"The Business of Being a Woman"
THIRD-WAY SOUTHERN FEMINISM

The year that Callie Khouri won an Oscar for *Thelma & Louise* and southern daughter Rebecca Walker declared an era of "third-wave" feminism, 1992, also became known as the "Year of the Woman." Inspired by Anita Hill, women began to speak out in unprecedented numbers: the Equal Employment Opportunity Commission reported a 153 percent rise in the number of sexual harassment complaints, membership in the women's political group EMILY's List grew by 600 percent, and funding for this and similar organizations reportedly doubled in the months following the Thomas hearings.[1] This windfall of recruits prompted more women to run for office than ever before in the 1992 elections. That year was a liminal moment in which it seemed that the antifeminist backlash was on its hind foot, and that perhaps some of the successes of the Women's Liberation Movement could be regained, with its priorities retooled intersectionally according to Rebecca Walker's proclamation of the imminent third "wave." Southern popular culture, as we saw in the last chapter, was a vital source of feminism during this era, as Celie, Shug, Thelma, and Louise showed readers and viewers how to survive, fight against, flee from, reconfigure, and/or ultimately deny patriarchal power. These types of southern sisterhood had radical implications, but, as with radical feminism in the 1970s, they did not develop into a broader movement.

Instead, the type of progressive southern feminism that came to dominate popular culture and feminism in general in the early 1990s emphasized practical compromises between feminist and regional politics. From

1986 to 1993, prime-time television audiences tuned in to a popular sitcom featuring four southern yuppies—female interior designers with their own Atlanta firm, their own complicated family dynamics, and, most memorably, their own opinions. *Designing Women* was overtly feminist, and it was sharply funny, featuring laugh tracks targeting characters with retrograde gender politics. Like the texts examined in the preceding chapters, *Designing Women* offered American audiences in the late 1980s and early 1990s a distinct, regionally specific, historically contingent brand of feminism.

Although neoliberal feminism, or the kind of "market feminism" that encourages strategic individual behavior rather than structural change to address gender inequality, is more commonly associated with the early twenty-first century, *Designing Women* reflects an early version that tracked closely with the tortured permutation of progressive national politics at the end of the Reagan-Bush era.[2] As Clyde Woods points out, American neoliberalism is southern in origin, with clear roots in racist reactions targeting the state, such as anti-unionism and the dismantling of the welfare system, following the Civil Rights Movement.[3] In the 1980s, Democratic politicians were swept rightward as neoconservatism rose—or rather, they chose to reposition themselves to remain competitive. After the 1984 election in which Reagan trounced Walter Mondale, the Democratic Party strategically developed moderate positions just slightly left of the Republican Party on many major issues. This became known as "Third Way" centrism, and the poster boy of these New Democratic politics by the end of the decade was southerner Bill Clinton, who served as governor of Arkansas for most of the 1980s and as U.S. president for most of the 1990s.[4]

As he rose to national prominence, Clinton had ample help crafting his image and message via popular culture from none other than Linda Bloodworth-Thomason and Harry Thomason, the powerhouse production team behind *Designing Women*. The Thomasons were very close friends of the Clintons, so much so that they served as informal media advisors during Clinton's gubernatorial and presidential campaigns and administrations, producing commercials, booking television appearances, engineering a makeover of Hillary Clinton, and writing, directing, and producing Clinton's 1992 campaign film, *The Man from Hope*.

Crafting a nonthreatening form of progressive gender politics in the context of the backlash was an important part of this endeavor. Linda Bloodworth-Thomason, known for the *Designing Women* version of southern, white, middle-class, "prime-time feminism" that contrasted with both postfeminism in the 1980s and "third-wave" feminism in the 1990s, was a self-taught expert in charting this middle ground. While recent theorists have criticized the Third Way as a kind of "politics for women without feminism," this was not the intent in the late 1980s and 1990s, when cultural producers like Bloodworth-Thomason and politicians like Bill Clinton and especially his wife actively sought a place for feminism in the New Democratic movement.[5] Bloodworth-Thomason's Third Way—white, middle-class, pro-business, feminine, and southern—represented a deliberate compromise between "second-wave" ideology, regional neoconservatism, and shifting Democratic politics. Even as Celie and Shug reconfigured their small-town South into a womanist community, and Thelma and Louise shot to kill when faced with toxic southern masculinity, the *Designing Women* maneuvered within the existing system to maximize their own race- and class-based power without toppling white male supremacy, carving a powerful place for themselves in southern patriarchy rather than threatening it. For seven years, *Designing Women* offered "twinkling fantasies of the New South" that promoted a new form of feminism that carefully navigated the post-movement context of the late 1980s and early 1990s.[6]

"Honest Propaganda"
Designing Women

By the time she created *Designing Women*, Linda Bloodworth had been writing for television for over a decade. A native of small-town Poplar Bluff, Missouri, "Gateway to the Ozarks," Bloodworth grew up in a family with a history of activism, but, despite these influences, young Linda did not totally defy regional gender roles for white women—she was a cheerleader in high school, where she was also voted "Most Popular." Later profiles described her as a "small town Southern belle" who was "raised to be both a traditional southern woman and much more than that."[7] After college in Missouri, Bloodworth followed some friends to Los Angeles, where she taught English in Watts, worked as a journalist, and wrote for television. This last occupation proved to be her calling, as she and her friend Mary Kay Place became the first women writers for M*A*S*H*, and their very first script was nominated for an Emmy. Bloodworth also wrote the pilot script for *One Day at a Time* as she freelanced throughout the 1970s. Through her early work in television, Bloodworth met producer Harry Thomason, and, as part of the small southern diaspora in Hollywood, the two bonded immediately over their roots (Harry was from tiny Hampton, Arkansas, a few hours south of Bloodworth's hometown). The pair married in 1983, and shortly thereafter they formed Mozark Productions (a derivation of Missouri and Arkansas, their two home states). According to the *Washington*

Post, "Together they made a winning combination, he with the ingenious concepts and pitches, she with the spot-on scripts."[8]

As she continued to write, Bloodworth-Thomason became a vocal advocate of the ideological potential of the small screen. She knew from her mentor, Larry Gelbart, the creator of *M*A*S*H*, that television could be a powerful medium, not just through quality but also through quantity. "The first thing he taught me," she later explained, was "that more people would see a single [television show] episode than would ever view *Gone with the Wind*."[9] Television, because of its simultaneously private and ubiquitous nature as a staple in most American homes, is a mediator that "facilitates relationships between spaces and places," and, more specifically for our purposes, the medium is a daily site for both the maintenance and contestation of regional mythologies.[10] Linda Bloodworth-Thomason was well aware of this, and, with expert skill, she used television to convey her concern with the rise of the New Right and its ill effects on women.

The mid-1980s, scholar Bonnie J. Dow explains, were a "key moment in the 'posting' of feminism," and Reagan's resounding reelection in 1984 confirmed the popularity of reactionary neoconservatism, of which antifeminism was part and parcel.[11] As Susan Faludi has documented, popular myths of the negative effects of progressive gender politics facilitated a dismal context for organized feminism. In 1986, anchor Peter Jennings presided over a three-hour "ABC Special Report," *After the Sexual Revolution*, which recounted the changed status of women and rising rates of divorce, single-parent households, "latchkey children," and day care populations. The overwhelming message was that gender equality was a double-edged sword, as feminism's success heaped "postrevolution problems" on women.[12] Television was just one of the many areas of popular culture offering at best a mixed review of the Women's Liberation Movement and, at worst, an account of its failures and continuing fallout.

This inhospitable climate was the context for Bloodworth-Thomason's new prime-time brainchild. In the mid-1980s, she negotiated with CBS to let her create a series for four of her actor friends. As part of the network's strategy to garner viewers who felt "disenfranchised" by ABC's Monday Night Football, Bloodworth-Thomason's plan for *Designing Women* was simple: "Get four women together and listen to them talk."[13] She found the idea that televised entertainment wasn't serious to be "amusing," and she dedicated herself to changing minds: "I hear people say sitcom the way they used to say Arkansas."[14] To rescue both the genre and the South from such uninformed opinions, Bloodworth-Thomason created *Designing Women* as "a forum for the opinions of the former Swamp-east Missouri river rat."[15]

Bloodworth-Thomason claimed that the characters were based on her father's friends, "big-mouthed intellectuals who knew something about everything and didn't mind sharing it."[16] But on her show, the big-mouthed intellectuals were women. One of its stars explained that the characters were "all facets of Linda's personality," a claim later echoed by Bloodworth-Thomason's longtime best friend.[17] The titular designing women—Delta Burke as Suzanne Sugarbaker, Dixie Carter as Julia Sugarbaker, Annie Potts as Mary Jo Shively, and Jean Smart as Charlene Frazier—all had thick southern accents, big hair, and strong opinions. By putting this group together, Bloodworth-Thomason was trying to "stir things up" on prime-time television: "The show is preachy by design. The women are southern, and being southern is being preachy."[18]

Pitched as a show that was "not just about women business" but also "about the business of being a woman," *Designing Women* was an in-depth exploration of the tensions of middle-class, white feminism during the backlash, and it became an enormously popular commentary on the gender politics of its time, all in easily digestible, half-hour increments.[19] Bloodworth-Thomason wrote the initial thirty-five episodes of the series herself—the first American television writer to do such a thing—and she set the series in Atlanta, the capital of the New South. Yet the primary exterior setting shown at the beginning of each episode as home of Sugarbaker & Associates was the Villa Marre mansion in Little Rock, while the exterior images of Suzanne Sugarbaker's enormous house pictured the Arkansas Governor's Mansion, where Bill and Hillary Clinton resided at the time.[20] The choice of these Arkansan mansions was no accident. Bloodworth-Thomason's production would be a primary means of promoting the New Democrat–style politics that the Clintons represented via prime-time television.

Designing Women is not simply set in the South; the region is a character in the show. Or rather, it is two: the Old South is a figure of ambivalent nostalgia and ridicule, while the New South is one of prosperity, harmony, and hope. No city has embodied this New South ethos like Atlanta, euphemistically deemed the "City Too Busy to Hate" by its mayor at the height of the Civil Rights Movement. But if Atlanta has a lasting brand, it is as a city that is constantly trying to reinvent itself. James Cobb writes that "no residents of the South seem to struggle more consistently to make sense of their place than the movers and shakers of Atlanta," and those struggles resulted in the "favorite local pastime" of constantly reimagining and "reimaging" the city.[21] Atlantans' self-images of their city consistently gloss over uglier realities. Maurice J. Hobson charts how "Black empowerment became intricately linked to white business" in post-movement Atlanta as the city's leaders capitalized on the Black electorate to build a political machine that maintained the traditional intraracial class divide and even exacerbated poverty.[22]

In his 1985 essay on a series of murders of twenty-nine African American children, teenagers, and young adults in Atlanta between 1979 and 1981, James Baldwin cites the contemporary local "leitmotif" of the "Black Administration," a power structure meant to "prove" that "the 'city too busy (making money) to hate'" could not possibly be administering justice for its African American children.[23] At the same time as "the Terror" of the child murders, the city promoting simultaneous "economic progress and racial progressivism" was also home to massive white flight, which resulted in further inner-city poverty and blight, as historian Kevin Kruse points out. This "suburban secession," the "most successful segregationist response" to the Civil Rights Movement in the area, proceeded in tandem with the growth of a new kind of grassroots conservatism. Neoconservatism abandoned the overt racism of the past for a seemingly race-neutral language of "rights, freedoms, and individualism" that sparked nothing less than a massive political realignment in the last quarter of the twentieth century.[24] Each of these trends played out on *Designing Women* as both text and subtext.

Much ink has been spilled on the evolution from Nixon's Southern Strategy to neoconservatism as it existed by the 1990s, a transformation centered in the South, specifically in Atlanta and its suburban environs as a sort of microcosm of the national shift.[25] The choice, then, of the so-called "Empire City of the South" as a setting for a feminist show like *Designing Women*, debuting as it did amid the rapid ascendance of the New Right, was crucial. Through *Designing Women*, Bloodworth-Thomason waded into what would become known as the culture wars, offering a gendered brand of progressive New South boosterism set in the region's most aggressively marketed metropolis.

Later explaining that she believes in "honest propaganda," Bloodworth-Thomason defused the danger of her show's feminist dialogue by placing it in a genteel antebellum home, which also serves as the interior design firm where the primary characters work.[26] The outspoken women are safely ensconced in a feminine space and in a feminine industry—indeed, in an almost all-female world. In a 1992 profile, one reporter praised this as "Bloodworth-Thomason's cleverest device, this understanding that full-chintz femininity would demilitarize things for those who might not agree with her on the issues."[27] Scholars have referred to "stealth feminism" in regional history, a sort of "Southern lady" activism that cloaks "defiance in respectability and decorum."²⁸ *Designing Women*'s feminized setting is that "cloak," or, to use a more apt southern metaphor, its televisual white gloves, a safe vehicle for feminist critiques, discussions, debates, and rants. While most scenes take place in the design firm headquarters, the women are rarely shown working, and the hybrid work-home setting enables these women to get together for daily discussions, resulting in what Bonnie J. Dow calls "a variation on consciousness-raising." While positioning these feminist discussions in a domestic space might render them nonthreatening, Dow also argues that this setting has "subversive potential," as it challenges the patriarchal boundaries of public and private, work and home.²⁹

In keeping with the femininity of the setting, the characters conform to contemporary standards of southern beauty. They are perfectly and fully made up at all times, with permed halos of hair and jewel-toned, era-appropriate women's professional wear. As Tara McPherson argues, there is little ambivalence about the "deployment" of southern femininity on the show, and this deliberate deployment was rewarded: while *Designing Women* was nominated for multiple Emmys over its seven-year run, its only win was in the category of Outstanding Achievement in Hairstyling. Bloodworth-Thomason explained that, despite its enduring popularity with American audiences, for a Television Academy made up of men, *Designing Women* was "too Southern. Too loud. Too opinionated. I think the way we're not too much is with our hair."³⁰

From the initial episode, which aired in September 1986, *Designing Women* positioned itself as a collective safe space for women. The first of Julia Sugarbaker's memorable monologues sets these boundaries when a man interrupts the women as they dine on sushi (a notably bourgeois cuisine for the South in the 1980s). Julia stops him, telling him that most women just want to be left alone. "There's no need for introductions," she tells him.

> We know who you are.... You're the guy who's always wherever women gather or try to be alone. You want to eat with us when we're dining in hotels, you want to know if the book we're reading is any good, or if you can keep us company on the plane. And I want to thank you, Ray Don, on behalf of all the women in the world for your unfailing attention and concern. But read my lips, and remember, as hard as it is to believe, sometimes we like talking just to each other. And sometimes we like just being alone.

The episode ends with a toast to Julia, "the best of the big-shouldered broads."³¹ From its inception, then, *Designing Women* featured women claiming space, talking back to men, and supporting each other.

Crucially, these "big-shouldered broads" have a southern accent, and the show knowingly plays with gendered regional stereotypes, as did its stars. During a publicity blitz during the first season, Dixie Carter (Julia) and Annie Potts (Mary Jo) joked with the *Washington Post* about needing to "get out of [their] hoopskirts," "get off the rockin' chair on the front porch," and get rid of their "bourbon breath." The interview ended with Potts pretending to stab Carter in the back with a table knife, saying "Southerners can be so sweet."[32] These kinds of jokes work in specific ways: white, middle-class femininity was the necessary vehicle for the feminist politics of the show, and southernness made its transgressive message both palatable and popular. As Tara McPherson writes, when the women of Sugarbaker's "break with the southern code of etiquette and politeness," they "get away with" it because they "look like ladies." McPherson argues that *Designing Women* is "less overtly about the South" than other contemporary texts like *Steel Magnolias*. Instead, she explains, the show "mediates the region for a wider sphere within the conventions of broadcast, but the South and its women are still important tropes for the sitcom."[33] I think, however, that the show doesn't so much "mediate the region" as regional conventions mediate the feminist message of the show. If the white southern woman has traditionally been the "discursive symbol for the region," then the designing women were a cleverly disguised introduction to the New Democrats in feminine form. This was a new weapon in the battle against Reagan-era neoconservatism, and it was a geographically specific form of feminism—white, middle-class, and firmly inscribed in the New South.[34]

Class status is an important part of the *Designing Women*'s role as New Southern feminists. The design firm itself is the product of Julia and Suzanne's investment of "old money, antebellum money," and the sisters' upper-class status is never in question. As a divorcee and single mother, Mary Jo is firmly middle-class, and Charlene, the office manager who hails from Bloodworth-Thomason's hometown of Poplar Bluff, serves as the prototype of the poor southern girl who made good. The youngest of eleven siblings, Charlene, through a combination of earnest wit and hard work, has climbed her way into the middle class. While sometimes the poverty of Charlene's past is portrayed empathetically, her memories of growing up poor, as well as her lingering low-brow tastes, are played for laughs over the course of the series. Her occasional "hillbilly" sensibilities are represented as funny relics of her hardscrabble Ozark past, left behind when she fled to join the prosperous, progressive, racially harmonious New South of Atlanta boosters' dreams.[35]

This South does not have room in it for working-class politics, and the show rarely acknowledges its own class ethos. Suzanne Sugarbaker serves as the series' exaggeration of both wealth and retrograde beliefs, such as when she is excited about the theme "Hobo Heaven" at a country club ball: "Yeah! We're all gonna dress up like poor people!" A running theme involves Suzanne's jokes about her housekeeper Consuela, who is presented in the third episode as being "from one of those little countries where they're always having trouble." Consuela, who is frequently heard yelling off-screen but hardly seen throughout the series, is described as frightening and violent; she delights in scaring Suzanne, threatens her with knives, wields curses, pins voodoo dolls, and "slaughters live animals in the kitchen." Even as Suzanne is often the butt of the other designing women's jokes, the laugh track encourages identification with her classism and racism as she relays these kinds of details about her domestic "help."[36]

A rare episode featuring explicit commentary on working-class politics is the third season's "But They're Really Great Curtains," which features textile workers on strike outside Sugarbaker's, a major wholesale customer for the curtains produced by the exploited workers. Charlene has compassion, but Julia is angry at the effects of the work stoppage on their bottom line. The situation is a reflection of the New South's so-called "favorable business climate" that was a successful bid to bring manufacturing to the region. Overtly hostile to unions and heavily featuring individualist, bootstraps economic rhetoric, these efforts succeeded in both industrializing parts of the South and making it, in Peter Applebome's words, "the bad-job capital of America."[37] In keeping with this anti-union, pro-business regional stance, the designing women cross the textile workers' picket line to finish the curtains themselves. But after an encounter with one factory worker, the story diverts from the initial controversy over fair pay into a Julia rant about illegal piecework, deftly derailing the episode from the issue of the low wages and long hours that caused the strike in the first place. The end result is not justice or even a modest pay raise for the textile workers but rather the theft of their union strategy by the middle-class women. The episode closes with a newly emboldened Mary Jo, who goes with her colleagues to picket the sexist mechanic who tried to cheat her over car repairs. As the end credits roll, the women march out chanting, "Free the Shively Volvo!," thus appropriating working-class activist tactics for a decidedly yuppie goal.[38] As a maneuver to protect the class interests of white women, the solidarity on display here embodies "second-wave" concepts of sisterhood as exclusive, bourgeois, and ultimately blind to its role in maintaining hierarchies of race and class. This, then, is Third Way feminism: these privileged women empower and enrich themselves by exploiting, dismissing, and ultimately co-opting both the labor and the activism of the textile workers.

Designing Women tends to combine its class politics with its urban bias, generally referring to anywhere outside the Atlanta metropolitan area as the dangerous backwoods. This was in keeping with Atlanta's own self-image as a bustling haven in the middle of the backward South; one contemporary advertisement assured visitors to the city, "Hillbillies? You won't find them dining in a revolving restaurant-lounge atop the breathtaking Atlanta Skyline."[39] In a 1985 essay on Atlanta, James Baldwin questions the "stubborn and stunning delusion" of people who protested, "I'm from Atlanta, I'm not from Georgia," as if the mere proclamation protected them from association with the region's hinterlands—and its history.[40]

On *Designing Women*, the safe, modern, urban New South is most clearly contrasted to the backward rural South in "Nightmare from *Hee Haw*." The women and their male partners head off for a canoe trip, making *Deliverance* jokes about "Ned Beatty in his underwear" all the way. In a local bar, they are approached by a monosyllabic family of men, who force the women to slow dance, which, after some discussion of how intimidated the city men are by their more rustic competitors, predictably ends in a bar fight.[41] The rural South, according to *Designing Women*, is treacherous territory peopled by the volatile working class. Historian Zachary J. Lechner deems the latter the "ass-kicking, Masculine South," a frequent representation in post-1960s popular culture that featured violent, rural white masculinity as a means of addressing the perceived loss of the old hierarchies of gender and race.[42] On *Designing Women*, the erstwhile forays into this Masculine South are contrasted with both the progressively feminine urban world of Atlanta and the comic paternalism of the male characters on the show.

Despite some clearly classist episodes, Bloodworth-Thomason rarely foregrounded socioeconomic politics on *Designing Women*. In keeping with the transition from liberal to neoliberal feminism and the attendant shift in focus from economic inequality to "cultural struggles," the show's weekly commentaries on "women's issues" were its primary form of overt politics.[43] Because of these politics, the network was apparently not sure what to do with its own hit, as it shifted the show's time slot around, prompting an outcry from fans. Likewise, critics did not initially know what to make of this new brand of southern feminist comedy. Near the end of its first season, *People* explained the dilemma:

> *Designing Women* set itself up as a bawdy tour of the New South. Its heroines weren't Scarlett O'Hara or Blanche DuBois but raucous women specializing in earthy humor. Within weeks the show had attracted a devoted

audience that cherished such lines as, "If sex were fast food, there'd be an arch over your bed." Or, "Of course men still appreciate virginity. All of my husbands did." But *Designing Women* also had its share of detractors, people just as passionately put off by its Introduction to Gynecology approach.[44]

This last line was not just a passing reference; *People* also described the show as a "gyne-com with female locker-room humor," indicating the multivalent discomfort with women's comedy and their bodies on television. Often compared to The *Golden Girls*, a popular contemporary sitcom featuring four older women, *Designing Women* was by no means the only female-oriented show on prime-time television. But star Annie Potts explained the crucial differences: "We're not living together, and we're out there working. And we're more dangerous: We're still in our reproductive years. We could go out there and reproduce ourselves. When [the women of *Golden Girls*] do it, everyone says, 'Oh, that's so cute.' But when we do it, everyone says, 'You hussies.'"[45] Although it might seem tame now, *Designing Women* could be potent stuff in the context of the Reagan era and on the inherently conservative medium of 1980s network television.

While much of the feminist ideology put forth by the characters was fairly explicit, *Designing Women* does play it safe by refusing to tackle the more controversial aspects of most issues. In "Killing All the Right People," Bloodworth-Thomason addressed the AIDS crisis. She was inspired by her mother, who contracted HIV from a blood transfusion after heart surgery in 1983 and died in 1986, just as Bloodworth-Thomason was furiously writing the first few dozen scripts for *Designing Women*. While her mother was in the hospital, Bloodworth-Thomason witnessed the "bigotry and mistreatment" of "all the young men on her hospital floor."[46] She channeled this into an episode early in the second season featuring an HIV-positive young gay man, Kendall, who asks Sugarbaker's to design his funeral. Kendall appears only briefly in the episode, and, when he describes his treatment at the hospital, the women condemn sexual and medical discrimination. But the episode quickly shifts from the stigma Kendall endures to a broader discussion of safe sex, which Mary Jo brings up at a PTA meeting, earning herself the nickname "Condom Queen." *Designing Women* thus deftly positions HIV as the sole problem to be solved, rather than homophobia and its devastating effects—a sanitized approach that won "Killing All the Right People" an Emmy nod the following year.[47]

This episode is also typical of the show's treatment of sexuality. While the women accept and love Kendall, they are at best skeptical when it comes to lesbians, and Suzanne is downright homophobic. And despite the "gyne-com" fears expressed in reviews, the *Designing Women* are timid in general when it comes to heterosexual practices too. While they make some jokes, especially "slut" jokes aimed at frequent target Suzanne, sex itself is rarely the subject of their conversations, and racier feminist topics like the female orgasm or even basic female pleasure are completely off-limits.[48] This avoidance was at least partly a function of the fundamentally conservative nature of television as a medium, especially in this era and in contrast to the overtly feminist television shows of the 1970s like *Mary Tyler Moore* and *One Day at a Time* (for which Bloodworth-Thomason wrote some scripts).[49] The fundamental goal of television networks is, of course, to expose consumers to advertisements more so than ideas. Nevertheless, the ideas that Bloodworth-Thomason embedded in *Designing Women* were very much in keeping with contemporary liberal feminism as it developed over the course of the show's run.

In a direct reference to the backlash against the Women's Liberation Movement, *Designing Women* prefers to talk about dating rather than sex or even marriage, repeatedly referencing the "man shortage" myth that was one of the core cultural "bulletins of despair" meant to blame American women's woes on the successes of the feminist movement. In the fifth episode of the show, Charlene reads aloud from the infamous *Newsweek* article about the "man shortage" study, informing her coworkers, "According to this, your age group stands a better chance of being killed by a terrorist" than of getting married. Julia replies drily, "Yes, well, I think the fella who wrote that stands a pretty good chance of being killed by a feminist." Three seasons later, Mary Jo complains that these dubious statistics are "etched on the brain of every single woman." If this were not true because of the ubiquity of these statistics in the news media in the late 1980s, it was certainly true for *Designing Women* viewers, who heard them referenced in multiple episodes, even after Julia presents Mary Jo with the *New York Times* article debunking the study.[50]

The "battle of the sexes" narrative is frequently played for laughs, but *Designing Women* takes a strong stand when it comes to sexual harassment and assault, addressing the issue each season. The women are frequently harassed by male characters, including a rival designer who refers to them as "the eight finest breasts in Georgia" and construction workers who hiss at Mary Jo and Julia from across the street. Entire episodes are devoted to sexual harassment, most memorably "The Strange Case of Clarence and Anita," in which Mary Jo wears a T-shirt that says "HE DID IT" as they all watch the Thomas confirmation hearings on television. The episode is clearly addressed to the "I'm not a feminist, but . . ." crowd, as Mary Jo warns her friends not to trust reports that women believed Thomas's claim that he did not sexually harass Anita Hill. "Oh, come on," she retorts. "The polls say too that most women aren't feminists. But if you ask women about individual feminist issues, the majority of them are for them. They just don't want to call themselves feminist because George Bush and Phyllis Schlafly want to make people believe that feminists are all these big-mouthed, bleeding heart, man-hating women who don't shave their legs. . . . If believing in equal pay and mandated child care make me a feminist, then I am damn proud to be one!"[51] Mary Jo's breathless monologue is followed by applause and affirmation from other characters. But the episode simultaneously caricatures Mary Jo and Julia as out of control, even insane, much like the antifeminist stereotypes Mary Jo mentions. A side plot involves the two women in a local production of *Whatever Happened to Baby Jane*, so when Mary Jo gives her interview to a local television station about the Thomas hearings, it is in full, grotesque Baby Jane makeup. Locking eyes with the camera, she shouts about wanting "to be treated with equality and respect." When she yells, "I don't give a damn anymore if people think I'm a feminist or a fruitcake," in her thick white face powder and smeared lipstick, it seems that she might be both.[52]

The episode concludes with a montage of news clips of white male senators trashing Anita Hill, suggesting that she was fantasizing, and questioning the very existence of sexual harassment. The final shot is a still closeup of Hill testifying as the credits roll. Bloodworth-Thomason described this episode as her "valentine to all the women who felt Anita Hill was treated unfairly" by the "old-boy network sending us women packing," a line she gives to Julia in the episode.[53] But the construction of the show itself offers a different message. The voice of feminism here is Mary Jo in ghastly stage makeup, a problematic position made explicit when she describes herself as "berserk" after the interview just before she and Julia slow dance together in the final scene.[54] Together, the two most feminist characters represent stereotypical "unruliness" for the audience and enact, with comic effect, the backlash-promoted link between feminism and female "pathology."[55]

Moreover, an authoritative monologue about how Thomas is "barely qualified" to serve on the Supreme Court, combined with Julia's comments about the "old boys' network" making "a lot of women in this country madder tonight than they've ever been," indicates that the issue is sexual harassment alone, thus completely silencing discussion of the racial dynamics of the hearings and of Hill's experiences of discrimination. Ultimately the white male senators are given the last word, while viewers only see, but do not hear, Hill in the final news clip montage, effectively allowing the white female characters to be her only voice.[56] Bloodworth-Thomason's overt form of regional feminism thus talks back in prime time but in a way that often falters and sometimes fails in its consideration of the many factors at work in contemporary battles like the Thomas confirmation, most obviously and consistently in the silencing of the voices of Black women and the suppression of any inkling of an intersectional feminist response to the hearings.[57] Cloaked in Baby Jane makeup, white femininity, and class privilege, Designing Women avoids the radical potential of southern sisterhood seen in The Color Purple or Thelma & Louise.

Instead of revolt, reconfiguration, or revolution, Designing Women's apparent solution to dealing with the "old boys' network" is self-defense. In an episode in season 2, after repeated harassment and attempted assaults, Mary Jo hits a client with a vase just as she is about to be raped in the bedroom she is renovating for him. When the rest of the cast bursts into the room, they knock the man out, and Julia leaves a triumphant note saying that "Sugarbaker's always finishes the job."[58] Unlike in Thelma & Louise, there is no talk of reporting the crime or of the pitfalls for women who choose to do so. Instead, in "Stand and Fight," the women learn physical self-defense as a means of protecting themselves from male violence. As Bonnie J. Dow points out in an analysis of this episode, this solution "disregard[s] the larger question of modifying men's behavior or questioning the cultural acceptance of violence against women," endorsing instead the "individual, self-help perspective" of later neoliberal feminism.[59] While Designing Women never endorses wholly individual solutions—the four women always work together and support each other—their collective is quite exclusive, and they never seek systemic remedies.

Designing Women's feminist politics are intertwined with its racial politics, although not explicitly—that is, the text does not indicate that this is a conscious combination. For example, a domestic abuse episode involves the women entering a lip sync contest as the Supremes, featuring Suzanne's donning of blackface. Suzanne's get-up is meant to be embarrassing and prompts eye-rolling from the other characters, a clumsy juxtaposition that perhaps most clearly illustrates the show's failures when it comes to concepts of race and especially white women's roles in historical and contemporary regional hierarchies.[60] These problematic racial politics are part and parcel of the show's Third Way, centrist feminism. Seemingly unaware of its overwhelming whiteness, the show only addresses race explicitly in the context of the character of Anthony, a Black male employee and later partner at Sugarbaker's.

Tara McPherson points out that white feminists in the region have historically used images of Black men for their own devices, for example by offering their own enfranchisement as a counterweight to African American votes, a pattern "that should leave us wary of playing the southern lady for feminism."[61] As the primary recurring male and the only major Black character on *Designing Women*, Anthony serves as "proof" of southern progress on racial issues in general and as evidence of the white women's liberal politics in particular. A formerly incarcerated student who initially serves as the design firm's delivery driver, Anthony refers frequently to his "unfortunate incarceration" (for a crime he did not commit), and he gamely plays the role of ambassador from Atlanta's Black community to the designing women. He rarely challenges racism, instead walking a thin line between acknowledging and dismissing it. He defends Suzanne's use of blackface, arguing that it is no different from Lawrence Olivier's makeup in *Othello*, yet, in other episodes, he parodies minstrel characters and Black stereotypes, singing spirituals in response to a suggestion from Julia that he get back to work. A running joke relies on Anthony's "white" voice; he imitates his parole officer, an attorney, and a businessman in a Mercedes ("Uh, yeah, Phil, would you go into my office immediately and staple everything on my desk together?"). His white voice is a caricature of the 1980s yuppie, a figure that also happens to be his primary aspiration. "All I want now is to go to junior college, get one of those sweaters that button down the front, and join the pep club," Anthony proclaims in the first season.[62]

Despite his appropriately middle-class ambitions, work ethic, and eventual promotion to partner, Anthony is always more sidekick than equal. The idea that he could be a love interest for any of the main characters is a near-constant comic subtext, usually via the character of Bernice, an older friend of Julia and Suzanne's mother whose cheerful dementia and aggressive attraction to Anthony is a frequent theme. His friendship with Suzanne also provides fodder for the series-long joke that *Designing Women* makes of interracial relationships. In one episode, Suzanne, who has accidentally purchased Anthony at a bachelor auction, wears an unattractive bathrobe on their date to deter any sexual inclinations. After a fun evening together, she tells him he's her "best friend," to which he responds, "Why, thank you, Miss Daisy," jokingly restoring their relationship to one of the southern lady and her "help." In another episode, Anthony and Suzanne are stranded by a snowstorm and pretend to be a couple to get the last available room at a motel. Any unease about a potential tryst is placated by their costumes: because of the storm, there is no heat in the motel, so Suzanne is wearing several layers of heavy clothing, while Anthony is trussed up in whatever she is not wearing, including pantyhose, with the effect that she looks impenetrable and he looks like a haphazard version of winter drag. Indeed, dressing Anthony in feminine clothing was a recurring comedic trope on *Designing Women*. It is simply unimaginable on this show that he might be a suitable partner for one of the white women, despite their similar interests, ages, and occupations. And to deter those viewers who might dare to consider it, Anthony is frequently coded as gay or sexless. The one character allowed to explore this possibility is Bernice; her inappropriate and cheerfully racist harassment of Anthony is played for laughs, as part of her dementia and general kookiness.[63]

Even as Anthony works his way up from delivery man to law student and eventually partner in the design firm, his inferior class and racial status are constantly underscored. In group photographs advertising the early seasons of the show, the women characters have Anthony firmly, and physically, under control. In one magazine ad, they encircle him, smiling, and Suzanne is holding her hands on either side of his face. In a different ad, they flank him, again smiling, and Julia has him by the tie, while in another from the same shoot, Suzanne has him in a hot-pink headlock, while Julia and Mary Jo are pulling his tie in two different directions. The women have turned him loose in later ads, after he becomes a partner in the fifth season, although he is invariably positioned behind them, not on equal footing, and he never got comparable screen time.[64]

Even as Anthony is sometimes coded as gay throughout the series, he at times has love interests that serve as commentary on his upward mobility. Over the seven seasons, Anthony's few girlfriends are of two types: conniving yuppies or dumb dancers. The latter tend to be recurring characters, particularly Vanessa, who first appears as Anthony's New Year's date during the fourth season. Clad in a purple fur coat and gold lamé, Vanessa looks like a young Tina Turner and acts like a hypersexual stereotype. She returns in "Nightmare on Harlot Street" a few episodes later—in the same outfit, no less—to cause trouble, until the designing women take her under their tutelage and give her a middle-class makeover. Applauding their efforts, Anthony explains that Vanessa is "everything [he's] worked to get away from," and he instructs her that if she wants to continue dating him, "there are going to be some changes," including getting an education, landing a real job, and "being responsible." While the makeover of Vanessa has mixed results and Anthony's relationship with her is short lived, this dynamic is replicated when Anthony later marries a Vegas showgirl on a mission of self-improvement whom the Sugarbaker's women again help to make more "respectable."[65]

Although Anthony's love interests are not main characters, their roles are important to the white feminism of the show. The idea that these designers can help Anthony make over his love interests and advance his economic prospects is the crux of *Designing Women*'s Third Way politics. On a global scale, by the turn of the twenty-first century, neoliberal feminism came to rely on a process of "empowerment" that was "associated with individual self-improvement and donor interventions rather than collective struggle."[66] On a regional scale, in Bloodworth-Thomason's southern version, the designing women's investment in and development of the working-class white woman Charlene, the formerly incarcerated Black man Anthony, and, to a lesser extent, his sexualized African American girlfriends is part of the project of improving their prospects in a purportedly equal social playing field and a market that serves those who play by the rules. "Empowerment" thus trumps structural solutions and assumes a universal goal to be achieved individually, a kind of updated American dream for the Reagan-Bush era. *Designing Women* subtly deploys this socioeconomic rhetoric, which was increasingly heavily gendered, especially in the language around welfare, "personal responsibility," and women's competitiveness in the workplace.

But *Designing Women* was not simply the voice of New Democratic feminism; it was a specifically southern version of it, and regional identity is fundamental to this message. In 1970, historian Paul Gaston deconstructed the "New South Creed," a "propaganda device" for development in the South after the Civil War. The New South mythology, spun most famously by *Atlanta Constitution* editor Henry W. Grady in the 1880s, sought to smooth over sectional differences and racial conflict through the promotion of a newly industrialized southern economy. Thereafter, "New South" became a malleable but remarkably durable concept. Gaston notes that each generation since Grady's time has purportedly come of age in a slightly different New South, although he agrees with Wilbur Cash regarding the "vastly exaggerated" dimensions of the break from the Old South.[67] Gaston did not include gender in his analysis of the development of this creed, but scholars have since demonstrated the key role that women, particularly elite white women, have historically played in its making.[68] The New South of *Designing Women* features a largely white world of racial harmony, a prosperous white middle class, and unimpeded development as Sugarbaker's renovates and designs the interiors of different businesses and wealthy homes across Atlanta in each episode. Crucially, this southern success was undergirded by hardworking, business-savvy white women.

It is thus an updated version of the creed that the show promotes, and accordingly the characters defend the South against spurious stereotypes that are not in keeping with its Third Way feminist fantasy. The Sugarbaker's women constantly remind viewers that they are not the regional stereotypes of lore. In the third episode of the series, Mary Jo complains about how "TV and movies always show southerners to be so stupid," especially the women, who "are always these oversexed loons, sitting around in a satin slip and no air conditioning." Charlene has a rejoinder: "That reminds me of the story of the southern woman who goes to this la-di-da cocktail party in New York City. She turns to a northern woman and says, 'Where y'all from?' The northern woman looks at her and says, 'We're from where we don't end our sentences with a preposition.' So the southern woman looks at her and says, 'Oh, well then, where y'all from, bitch?'"[69]

Despite these kinds of jokes and the women's frequent verbal defensiveness, the show nevertheless falls back on stereotypes of the South as needed. When Mary Jo writes a statement for the Southern Style Expo, she defines "southern style" as featuring "warmth," "flowers," "food," and familiar things.[70] This stereotypical home could be set in the Old South or New South, and, of course, this beautiful setting was created and maintained by the "ladies" of the region.

Many scholars of the new southern studies of recent decades understand "the South" as a commodified set of images, and *Designing Women* offers its own version. A major part of the show's ideological project was to integrate some of the age-old media stereotypes of the region with an updated form of middle-class, white feminism. As in Charlene's "where y'all from" joke, when the designing women get defensive about the South, their anger is provoked by stereotypes of the region as low class or pathological (or both). "Getting Married and Eating Dirt" opens with Julia ranting about how "every few years" the *New York Times,* lazily relying on stereotypes, "feels compelled to run a story about how people still practice dirt-eating in the South." Despite Mary Jo's caution that "they'll think you're some loony drunken debutante left over from the Civil War," Julia calls the *Times* to complain. Clad in a frilly pink bridesmaid dress that looks much like the wedding outfits in *Steel Magnolias* (which would air in theaters less than a year later), Julia gives the reporter a piece of her mind: "But speaking for myself and hundreds of thousands of my southern ancestors who have evolved through the many decades of poverty, strife, and turmoil, I would like for Mr. Weeks to know that we have surely eaten many things in the past, and we will surely eat many things in the future, but, as God is my witness, we have never—I repeat, never—eaten dirt."[71] De-

signing Women clearly attempts to rescue what's good about the South—or what Bloodworth-Thomason's team perceived to be good about the South—a project that involves dismissing regional realities like the structural inequality, poverty, malnutrition, and/or cultural traditions that have led some southerners to eat dirt, as explained in the actual *New York Times* article that prompted Julia's outrage.[72]

These economic realities applied to the rural South that was so frequently a topic of ridicule on the show and to the urban South just outside the front door of Sugarbaker's. During *Designing Women*'s run, white flight from Atlanta to its suburbs continued unabated, and the number of poverty-stricken Black families almost doubled, reaching over one-third of all households, while over half of Atlanta's children lived below the poverty threshold. In his work on Atlanta, Maurice J. Hobson describes a "tale of two cities" in which the booming metropolis that won the bid for the 1996 Olympics was also an increasingly sprawling urban area where the conditions for poor African Americans had changed little since the 1960s. The New South of *Designing Women* was a middle-class fantasy centered on progressive white people and upwardly mobile African Americans like Anthony. In this sense, perhaps the show is an accurate depiction of the "South's crown jewel" in which post–Civil Rights Movement developments "reward[ed] its elite while punishing its poor."[73]

Prime-time viewers thus saw a shiny South that was not perfect but was in a state of constant improvement through the uplifting, centrist progressivism of the show's characters. In a review of images of southern women in the 1980s, Tara McPherson asks, "Is the southern lady locked in her old masquerades, or can she be mobilized differently?" *Designing Women* suggests that she can be alternately deployed, offering viewers the "belle with a briefcase, newly out of therapy and interested in 'women's issues,' including equal pay."[74] Yet this new mobilization is very clearly tethered to the past. Like guidebooks luring conventioneers to the city, *Designing Women* "exuded thick gobs of syrupy Atlanta Spirit, knitting the same old familiar yarns about the city's magic marriage of Northern bustle and Southern charm."[75]

Indeed, the show often referenced perhaps the most "familiar yarn" about the South. While much talk on one episode centers around the characters' plan to go see *Steel Magnolias* in the theater, the film and the historical reference point that really undergirds this series is *Gone with the Wind*. The novel was written by Atlanta native Margaret Mitchell, and the heroine's love of her adopted city neatly encapsulates *Designing Women*'s relationship with regional identity: "Like [Scarlett O'Hara], the town was a mixture of old and new in Georgia, in which the old often came off second best in its conflicts with the self-willed and vigorous new."[76] The film enjoyed a revival during the third season of *Designing Women*, when Ted Turner, the "worthy heir to Henry Grady," bought the rights to it, aired it repeatedly on his new cable network, and sponsored a premiere in downtown Atlanta for its fiftieth anniversary.[77] On *Designing Women*, references abound to the romance between Rhett and Scarlett, and multiple characters discuss the film, which Charlene claims to have seen twenty-seven times.[78]

Gone with the Wind is the "ur-text" of the region's white women, and it has traditionally been read by gender scholars as "the struggle of one individual against the confines of southern womanhood."[79] But, of course, it was a product of its time and place and thus reveals not just Mitchell's own conflict with gender norms but also her deeply held racial prejudices as well as Atlanta's near-constant attempts at stable identity formation. Scarlett O'Hara can be read as the "living embodiment of the Atlanta Spirit, a Henry Grady ... in hoop skirts."[80] As such, she has done heavy lifting as a symbol of the South ever since, and the designing women gamely follow in her footsteps. Tara McPherson writes: "If *Gone with the Wind* sought to reconcile Scarlett and the New Woman, various Sun Belt versions of the late twentieth-century lady also explore how southern manners and women's rights might be woven together, proposing various strategies of performance and outlining different possibilities."[81]

To explore the "different possibilities" presented by changing gender roles in the South, *Designing Women* opted to make its revision of Scarlett O'Hara explicit in the two-part series finale in March 1993. "Gone with a Whim" opens with the designing women touring a house that is, according to its owner, an "exact replica" of Tara from *Gone with the Wind*, prompting each character to fantasize about attending an antebellum ball there. Julia's vision of her Old South self reflects her New South persona, as she retorts to Rhett Butler that she will never be "anybody's little woman," while Mary Jo's fantasy is of being the alluring belle of Lost Cause dreams. Anthony's features his wife Etienne, a former Vegas showgirl, as Scarlett, who berates Prissy, played by Charlene's cousin Carlene, about delivering Melanie's baby. Carlene gives the famed "I don't know nothin' 'bout birthin' babies" speech, whereupon Etienne/Scarlett slaps the white woman (Prissy), and then she slaps her again just for "fun." Rather than destruction of the old ways, then, Julia and Mary Jo fit right in as updated Scarletts, and Anthony's reverie is a racial role reversal of slavery, with his wife as the plantation mistress enacting violence on the enslaved.[82]

The episode then turns to B. J., a new addition to the cast in the final season. A wildly wealthy, irreverent Texan modeled after Governor Ann Richards and columnist Molly Ivins, B. J. is the epitome of southern Third Way feminism: white, feminine, middle aged, socially liberal, entrepreneurial, and enormously rich. In the final episode, she tells Julia to "wake up and smell the magnolias": "Forget *Gone with the Wind*. You want southern pride? Don't we have Ann Richards? Don't we have Rosalynn Carter?" Her fantasy begins with the men going off to war, Anthony and the other enslaved characters fleeing, and "Yankees" invading Tara. Firing her rifle out the front door, B. J. as Scarlett says ruefully, "Well, isn't that just always the way. The women end up doing the work. Stand back, ladies, I'll show these Yankees what us southern women are really made of. You'll regret the day you ever tangled with Scarlett O'Hara and the Georgia peaches!"[83]

Scott Romine argues that the "opposition between the real and the fake" in representations of the South "performs crucial narrative work."[84] In B. J.'s fantasy, the well-to-do white women take care of business, and the audience applauds them for it (perhaps without realizing that, in addition to a gutsy feminine South, this applause endorses the Confederacy and the struggle to maintain slavery, as B. J. and the "Georgia peaches" are shooting at Union soldiers to protect the plantation). This racist conclusion would have been a fitting enough finale to the series, yet the episode continues, ending rather strangely with Bernice's Old South vision. In it, she is alone, pleading for Rhett Butler. Anthony/Rhett appears in a tux and a mustache, and he picks her up and sweeps her up the stairs in homage to the rape scene from the film. "It's 1865 and people will talk," he says. "I'm Black and you're white. Frankly my dear, I don't give a damn." Bernice chortles her famous (and exceedingly cringeworthy) line—"Black man, Black man, where did you come from?"—and the final credits roll to the tune of the *Gone with the Wind* theme music.[85] In the end, after years of applause for the strong women of the New South, the studio audience cheers for the sexist-slapping, gun-toting, white ladies of the Confederacy, with the final applause and laugh track reserved for the one character of the Jim Crow generation and her sexual fetishization of the one major Black character on the show.

Designing Women thus offers a southern feminism that both mocks and uses Old South nostalgia, and its New Democratic South is one of white female empowerment, middle-class aspirations, and selective racial and class uplift. This was a brand of southern feminism that was in contrast to other contemporary forms, such as the more radical feminist rage of *Thelma & Louise*, in interesting and sometimes explicit ways. For instance, angered by the Clarence Thomas hearings, Mary Jo, in full Baby Jane makeup, says she wants to "get in [her] car and drive to the center of the U.S." and yell "Who do you men think you are?" This could be an allusion to Thelma and Louise's epic, sexism-defying outlaw flight (this episode aired just a few months after the film was in theaters), but it's also just talk—it is clear that Mary Jo is not going to go on a feminist road trip and rampage, and in fact she calls herself "berserk" shortly thereafter for even suggesting it.[86]

A more direct contrast between these kinds of southern feminisms is set up in "On the Road Again," in which the women make several *Thelma & Louise* jokes. After a canceled date spurs a disappointed Julia to plan an impromptu drive to Nashville, B. J. urges her to "jump in the car like Thelma or Louise and pick up a hitchhiker and have your way with him." They don't do this, but Bernice is inspired by the reference, and on the short road trip with Julia and Mary Jo she begs them to help her enact another scene from the film by "entic[ing]" a trucker "into a field and blow[ing] up his truck." Of course, they don't do this either, but while they are on their way back to the office, a truck driver tailgates their car and blows his horn, terrifying the women. Calling him a "homicidal hillbilly," Mary Jo handles the wheel like a "professional stunt car driver" and gets them home quickly, but the trucker follows them into Sugarbaker's—to return a credit card that Julia left at a diner. This episode not only denies the designing women the escape of *Thelma & Louise*—their disappointing journey was merely to a highway diner, the kind of place where Louise worked before hitting the road—it also rewrites female fears and feminist anger as unwarranted. There is no system of male supremacy here, just a few paranoid women and a nice man returning their lost card. The radical revolt of *Thelma & Louise*, according to *Designing Women*, is perhaps even a bit ridiculous.[87]

But Bloodworth-Thomason's brand of feminism was increasingly popular, and by the early 1990s, she had become a force beyond the television industry. By 1991, CBS effectively put its prime-time fate in the Thomasons' hands when they inked a $45 million deal for five more series over the following eight years in "the network's biggest bankroll ever of a production team."[88] The final season of *Designing Women* aired during a banner year for Bloodworth-Thomason, as CBS's nightly lineup led the ratings in 1991–1992 and one of her closest friends decided to run for the nation's highest office. A few months later, the powerhouse production team stood on the banks of the Arkansas River with Bill Clinton before a bevy of reporters as he kicked off his campaign for the presidency. The intertextuality of Bloodworth-Thomason's media work with Clinton and her pop cultural productions like *Designing Women* demonstrate the reach of her vision of Third Way feminism in the 1990s.[89]

Designing New Democrats
A Place Called Hope

The Thomasons met the Clintons in Little Rock in the early 1980s through Harry's younger brother Danny, and they remained very close throughout the decade. When Bill Clinton announced on a clear October day in 1991 that he was running for president, Harry Thomason, known for his "aw-shucks folksiness," delivered a tear-jerking speech, written hastily by his wife, about the Arkansas River, which bound southern voters to their ancestors and to the nation's future. In a later interview, Bloodworth-Thomason recalled her pride as they stood beside Clinton and "the river that runs through all of us who share the DNA of that special place."[90]

Leaning heavily on that DNA in his presidential campaign, Clinton positioned himself as a son of the South who was proud of his roots. But he was also a harbinger of something new. As the golden boy of the Democratic Leadership Council—he became chair of the organization in 1990 and helped to found over twenty state chapters—Clinton was the epitome of a New Democrat, a pragmatic, if sometimes slippery, centrist who aimed to reinvigorate the party. But Clinton's significance as a new kind of politician was not simply due to his age, the timing, or his centrist appeal. It was also distinctly regional. For one thing, the Democratic Party wanted desperately to recapture the white southern voters who had been flocking to the GOP since the passage of the Civil Rights Act in 1964. Clinton was a new breed of southern politician charting a "Third Way" through the growing ideological divide between the two major parties, with rhetoric aimed first at white middle-class voters in Arkansas and eventually across the South and the whole nation. This centrism, which explicitly avoided the label "liberal" in favor of "progressive," had major appeal in a state like Arkansas. Perhaps this son of the South could stop the bleeding and bring the region back to the Democratic fold.[91]

Much like the characters in *Designing Women*, Clinton had bona fide southern roots. In fact, under the headline "Seen as White Trash," a North Carolina paper wondered if maybe Clinton was "too Southern."[92] But he was also carefully packaged, melding traditional trappings of the region with updated centrist politics of race, class, and gender. Monica Carol Miller compares Clinton to Bloodworth-Thomason's sitcom, arguing that his election was "certainly an event that exemplified the strategic deployment of southern style and charm to implement a more progressive political agenda."[93] Mickey Kantor, Clinton's 1992 campaign chair, explained: "A lot of politics is not so much ideological as it's cultural—Do you get it? Are you one of us?"[94] Clinton's ability to speak in regional dialects—not just his accent or his use of local lingo but also his uncanny ability to get regular, local people talking to him—played beautifully on the campaign trail in Arkansas, where he won the governorship in 1978, 1982, 1984, 1986, and 1990. Nicknamed "Bubba" by his younger brother Roger, Clinton was equally at home with corporate party donors and their golf buddies at country clubs as with "country boys" and their bird dogs in rural Arkansas.[95]

Like so many of his constituents in his home state and white voters across the South, Clinton was a devout Baptist. But his deep religion was only the second-most southern thing about Clinton; the first thing Danny Thomason, Linda Bloodworth-Thomason's brother-in-law, listed when asked about this for PBS was Clinton's love of catfish. Other stereotypical tastes also topped the list: singing in church on Sundays, watermelon, "go[ing] down to the creek," "smell[ing] magnolia blossoms," and "courtesy."[96] But despite this reputed love of magnolias, Bill Clinton was not of the Old South, nor was his religiosity reminiscent of the rapidly ascending neoconservative variety in the region. In his autobiography, Clinton claims to have thought "a lot about the past and [his] roots" and to have used the sins of the past as a springboard to progressive politics.[97] As governor, Clinton appointed African Americans to many powerful positions, supported a statewide civil rights bill (which failed), and generally positioned himself as a politician who bridged racial divides. It was an effect he had on his friends as well: Danny Thomason credits Clinton for enlightening him about racism and structural inequality.[98]

Despite the many rumors of sexual harassment and infidelity during his time as governor of Arkansas, Clinton also positioned himself as progressive on policy issues of gender and sex. His friends have credited this to the presence of strong women in his life. Clinton's mother Virginia Kelley was an "immensely powerful figure" to her son, and she was as southern as they come, with her Arkansas drawl, big hair, heavy makeup, and jewel-toned wardrobe. But she was also not a traditional southern mother. She "didn't bake pies," and she loved to gamble, smoke, drink, and play the horses in Hot Springs, a mountain resort town in the Ozarks. From her son's first run for office in 1974 onward, Kelley campaigned tirelessly, going door-to-door in small Arkansas towns with a "whole carload of ladies."[99]

The interplay of "larger than life" Virginia Kelley's down-home southernness and the liberal feminism of Clinton's Chicago wife, Hillary Rodham Clinton, and their complementary influences on the candidate, was exactly the kind of dynamic Bloodworth-Thomason explored on *Designing Women*; Kelley was Charlene to Rodham Clinton's Julia. As the southern politician's wife, Rodham Clinton was controversial from the outset, despite the fact that in early 1974 she gave up opportunities to join big law firms in New York and Washington, choosing instead to follow Clinton back to Arkansas. Once there, however, her refusal to play the role of the passive and pretty political wife, and her reputation as a "Yankee liberal"—"hard-edged even by Northern standards," according to one profile—apparently "rankled voters" and played something of a role in Clinton's defeat as the incumbent running for reelection as Arkansas governor in 1980.[100] Even from this early date, then, Rodham Clinton was a target of the "sexual politics of the New Right," and her status as a working mother—their daughter Chelsea was born in the winter of 1980—was perceived as a problematic indication of the nontraditional gender roles in the Clinton family.[101]

In the early 1980s, neoconservatives had yet to truly hone their antifeminist "family values" rhetoric, but the alleged slippery slope from paid labor outside the home to challenging sexism in the public sphere, and then to the overturning of hierarchies and the wholesale transformation of society, made Rodham Clinton suspect. Critics homed in on her use of her maiden name, with Clinton's gubernatorial opponent in 1980, Frank White, exclaiming that that sort of thing was acceptable "in some parts of the world, New York, perhaps California," but "the South was not ready for that!" Making fun of the South's reputation as a bastion of patriarchy, Rodham Clinton told the story of a friend's suggestion of "staging an elaborate ceremony on the steps of the capitol": "Bill would put his foot on my throat, yank me by my hair and say something like, 'Woman, you're going to take my last name and that's that!', at which point flags would wave, hymns would be sung and the name would change."[102] Jokes aside, the Clintons were savvy political animals, and they knew a makeover was in order after his 1980 loss. Rodham Clinton repackaged herself in time for the 1982 gubernatorial election, hiring a fashion consultant, bobbing her hair, going blonde, wearing makeup, trading her thick glasses for contact lenses, and switching her "unremarkable" clothes for more feminine outfits. On the day that Clinton announced his candidacy, she officially dropped her maiden name.[103]

By 1982, the new, "southernized" Hillary Clinton was complete: "mute, smiling, fixing on Bill what Ellen Brantley describes as 'the Nancy Reagan gaze.'"[104] Clinton was reinstated as governor in 1983, a position he would hold until 1992. Journalist Barbara Matusow recounts Rodham Clinton's performance on returning to the Arkansas Governor's Mansion, claiming, "She even acted perky, as if she'd been away at cheerleader camp for two years."[105] This was a carefully crafted façade behind which Hillary Clinton's laser focus on reforming education in Arkansas during her husband's time as governor bolstered his gubernatorial power and her own nascent political career. She continued to work and became known as one of the top litigators in the state, yet she also did her duty as a politician's wife at social events, fielding inanely gendered questions about her favorite foods and flowers. Arkansas's women were paying attention. Mirroring the gender gap that developed in voting behavior nationwide in the 1980s, women in the state seemed to prefer "candidates that their husbands, brothers, and fathers clearly rejected," repeatedly voting in majorities for Clinton.[106]

The Clintons' New Democrat approach in Arkansas was thus also a New South strategy that exhibited distinct elements of the kind of "stealth feminism" associated with the region. Going national with a presidential run required expert help from the Thomasons, who were by that point pros at this kind of packaging. Although Clinton is known for his charisma and for his ability to connect with average Americans, his first major national appearance, the nominating speech at the 1988 Democratic National Convention in Atlanta, in which he went seventeen minutes over his allotted time and endured resounding boos, was, by all accounts, a disaster that had the potential to tank his broader political ambitions. Linda Bloodworth-Thomason tossed and turned over it, finally waking her husband up in the middle of the night with her Hail Mary plan: get Clinton on *The Tonight Show* with Johnny Carson to "make this right."[107] Clinton was an early convert among politicians in the 1980s to the power of the medium of television, and he eagerly got ready to apologize, ingratiate, and reintroduce himself to the American public. On Carson's show, Clinton was relaxed, self-deprecating, and funny. When the host asked Clinton about his political ambitions beyond the Arkansas Governor's Mansion, he replied slyly, "Depends on how I do on this show tonight."[108] It turns out that this was no idle joke. The Associated Press reported that he went from "the media doghouse to media darling in one short week," and scholars have credited his *Tonight Show* appearance with saving Clinton's national career.[109]

Clinton's appearance on the Carson show was a signal of the important uses of popular culture in his quest for national office, but he also campaigned the traditional way, working the sidewalks, local businesses, and town halls of his home state. Over the next few years, Clinton claimed to have "shaken hands with half the voters in Arkansas," and he continued to position himself as a moderate Democrat, an alternative to the rising neoconservatism that itself had regional roots.[110] By the early 1990s, this neoconservatism had both southern suburban origins and a southern figurehead: Newt Gingrich, who mastered the coded language of racism, sexism, and classism, overlaid with a heavy nostalgia for the pre–Civil Rights

Movement era. Gingrich represented suburban Cobb County, just outside of Atlanta, in the U.S. House of Representatives. He capitalized on the grassroots secessionist ideology in the rapidly expanding white suburb—the "fastest-growing county in the nation" during the 1980s—and helped it to evolve into a welcoming home for far-right politics masked by a veneer of "middle-class rhetoric of rights and responsibilities."[111] In contrast to both the reality of the Black majority in Atlanta and the fantasy of the white progressive South on *Designing Women*, the newly gerrymandered Cobb County was "a Republican pollster's dream, a sprawl of affluent suburbs as far as the eye [could] see, a Lexus in every driveway and a Lean Cuisine in every microwave."[112]

Neoconservatism blended this new demographic reality and traditional ideas, offering white voters diatribes against "big government" to disguise racist and classist appeals. Gingrich, who told voters that the ideal year for the nation was 1955, depicted his district as a sort of "Norman Rockwell world with fiber-optic computers and jet airplanes."[113] This suburban utopia relied not just on traditional hierarchies of race and class but also on clearly delineated gender roles. Marjorie Spruill argues that although the rise of neoconservatism was not simply a southern phenomenon, "the region presented special opportunities and tremendous rewards" at least partly due to its "profoundly conservative views about women."[114] Gingrich frequently used sexism as a tool to promote retrograde policy. In one of his famed televised lectures, "Renewing American Civilization," Gingrich explained that women were unfit for combat because they liked to shower frequently, disliked "grubby field work," and were prone to "infections," while men were "biologically driven to go out and hunt giraffes."[115] Part of Gingrich's appeal, or what one *Atlanta Journal-Constitution* reporter deemed "Cobbservatism," was his barely disguised code of gender, class, and race that juxtaposed "the pristine work ethic of Cobb versus the 'welfare state' values of Atlanta, a pitch as old as the South."[116] The Right's "regional utopia" was the white, suburban South, a fantasy that was heavy on both "neo-Confederate" nostalgia and traditional American values, especially individual liberty. If *Designing Women* sought to offer southerners a genteel urban alternative to the backwoods, Gingrich's vision offered a third option, safely removed from the city in gated communities "just across the Chattahoochee."[117]

As part of what political scientists Angie Maxwell and Todd Shields call the "Long Southern Strategy," harking back to when the GOP acknowledged in the 1960s that it would never get substantial Black votes and decided instead to "go hunting where the ducks are," Gingrichian Republicans and Clintonian Democrats in the 1990s set their sights on the same demographic: white southern voters. Regional roots aside, Clinton was vulnerable in the conservative South, and not just because of his liberal views on race. Maxwell and Shields have charted how "gender-role angst" has motivated conservative southern voting at least as much as white supremacy.[118] Accordingly, Clinton's gender politics were perceived in terms of those of his wife, who was derided as "an out-of-the-mainstream radical" by the New Right.[119]

Although candidates' wives are always under a microscope, this was no mere sexist sideshow in the 1992 presidential contest. That year Rebecca Walker declared a new era of "third-wave" feminism, and new women's political organizations proliferated after the Thomas confirmation. Fundraising increased dramatically, as did political participation and voter registration drives in the South conducted by "freedom riders" organized by the Third Wave Direct Action Corporation, a group Walker cofounded.[120] As more women ran for office in 1992 than ever before, the press promoted the "Year of the Woman," and Clinton joked at rallies that voters would be getting "two for the price of one" in reference to Hillary, a line that confirmed neoconservative nightmares.[121] Although he toned down his "buy one, get one free" references to his wife on the campaign trail by late spring in response to media scrutiny, Clinton continued to proudly present himself as the "grandson of a working woman, the son of a single mother, the husband of a working wife," who had learned through these experiences that "building up women does not diminish men."[122]

But opposition to Rodham Clinton increased in tandem with women's activism, and, at the same time, problems of sex famously plagued the Clinton campaign and later administration.[123] When the *Star* tabloid dropped a bombshell of an interview with Gennifer Flowers, an Arkansas woman who claimed to have had a twelve-year affair with Bill Clinton, and CNN subsequently broadcast Flowers's live press conference featuring tapes of her conversations with the governor, the Clintons worked with seasoned campaign staff to craft a televised defense. Two days later, the couple appeared on *60 Minutes* to do some damage control. On air, the two spoke openly of their marital problems, about which Rodham Clinton famously proclaimed, in a "pronounced" southern accent, "You know, I'm not sittin' here, some little woman standin' by my man like Tammy Wynette." Maintaining the accent for a beat longer, she concluded, "If that's not enough for people, then heck, don't vote for him."[124] Rodham Clinton's performance in this interview, watched by some fifty million people, has been credited with helping to save her husband's campaign. Steve Kroft, the *60 Minutes* correspondent who conducted the interview, concluded bluntly, "She saved his bacon."[125] The interview garnered overwhelming support from viewers, unprecedented media attention for Bill Clinton, and a national lead that the campaign maintained through the election.

Yet while this careful performance co-opted the headlines, increased Clinton's name recognition, and helped to save the campaign, it also combined with some of Rodham Clinton's other interactions with the press—including her famous exasperated retort about staying home and baking cookies, which prompted the *Washington Post* to describe her as caught between "Tammy Wynette and Betty Crocker"—to do little for her likeability.[126] Concern expressed in focus groups that she was "going for the power" herself led the campaign to decide it was time for another makeover. Rodham Clinton was, according to *Advertising Age*, a "product with an image problem."[127]

Of course, the Clintons knew whom to call to address this "problem." While presidents' wives traditionally worked to embody the "ideal woman-citizen through volunteerism," Bloodworth-Thomason understood the gendered fears of Rodham Clinton: she was promoting politics on her husband's behalf as someone who was equally as qualified for public office.[128] Bloodworth-Thomason explained to *Vanity Fair*: "Hillary doesn't have to stay with Bill Clinton. She could get to the Senate or possibly the White House on her own, and she knows it."[129] So Bloodworth-Thomason engineered a solution that was shallow but effective, a stopgap measure to defuse the "Hillary factor" until the election: "Offer up a cosmetically reassuring version of 'Hillary' while resolving thereafter to reveal as little of Hillary as possible."[130] Bloodworth-Thomason hired three consultants—one for makeup, one for hair, one for wardrobe—to corral the candidate's wife's image. Gone were the reliable headbands that had served Rodham Clinton well after her previous makeover a decade earlier. Bloodworth-Thomason's famed Hollywood hairstylist Christophe lightened, fluffed, and softened her hair. The stylists from *Designing Women* updated her makeup and wardrobe. And Rodham Clinton retreated from the spotlight for a few months, relegated to smaller campaign stops with less press coverage and a message that focused more on family than policy. In a historically ironic comment, she privately claimed at the time to "hate this Ivana look," in reference to Donald Trump's wife at the time.[131]

As the Democratic National Convention (DNC) in July approached, the Thomasons organized a media blitz, booking Bill Clinton on all the major morning shows as well as on MTV and *The Arsenio Hall Show*, so that he might reach younger viewers. Because 60 percent of the voting public claimed that television was their primary source of news, the campaign relied heavily on their producer powerhouse friends' expertise with the medium. Months earlier, Clinton surprised Bloodworth-Thomason when he asked her to make his campaign film for the convention. While Harry Thomason could call back to distant experience (he had produced campaign commercials for politicians in Arkansas), his wife and business partner had no filmmaking credits. When Clinton's political consultants deemed Bloodworth-Thomason an "inappropriate" choice, the candidate was adamant: "She knows me. She knows what to do. Everybody just needs to leave her alone."[132]

And so, eschewing political advice and focus groups, Bloodworth-Thomason began working eighteen-hour days during the seasonal hiatus of *Designing Women*. Although in ensuing years other directors have taken, or been given, credit for Clinton's campaign film, Bloodworth-Thomason had complete creative control over every aspect of it: title, concept, script, crew, photographs, interviews, music, and editing. She amassed a transcript of one thousand pages, most of which were discarded. Bloodworth-Thomason knew her audience was no longer just the millions of women who tuned in to her hit shows each week. Rather, the Democratic Party had its eye on male voters generally, and working-class, southern, white, male voters in particular. She culled from her massive transcript accordingly, carefully crafting seventeen minutes of New Democrat biography. Bill Clinton reportedly wept when he saw the final cut.[133]

Introduced by Governor Ann Richards of Texas, the well-known southern feminist and chair of the Democratic National Committee, as a "truly American story," *The Man from Hope* aired on the final night of the 1992 convention. In "A Special Personal Message from Bill Clinton," which precedes the film, the future president explains that the "film doesn't deal with important issues." Rather, "it's about the kind of values [running mate] Al Gore and I have growing up in small towns." Accordingly, the film transforms images of Bill Clinton from the Ivy League, draft-dodging, "Slick Willie" politician portrayed by Republicans to a working-class kid from rural Arkansas. Clinton's first recollection in the film is of the "old, two-story house" where he lived with his grandparents. Of the black-and-white images of the house, Rodham Clinton explains: "Some people think that Bill must've been born wealthy and raised wealthy, you know, that he had all of the privileges that you could ever imagine ... [but] instead of being born with a silver spoon in his mouth, he was born in a house that had an outhouse in the back yard." The film returns to this theme time and again. In the only anecdote in which Clinton isn't in the South—the couple's description of their first meeting at Yale Law Library—he is talking about the

South, protesting as classmates tried to convince him to join the *Yale Law Journal*. "I'm going home to Arkansas," Clinton recalls saying to them at the time. "I'm not going to get a big Wall Street job. I'm not going to go clerk on the Supreme Court. I'm going to go home and be a country lawyer."[134]

In the film, his return to Arkansas after law school morphs from a narrative of class into one of race. In a voiceover accompanying black-and-white photos of the town, Clinton explains that the Hope of his childhood was "segregated, like all southern towns were then," but his grandparents supported integration and opposed the infamous closing of Central High School in Little Rock. The film then moves on to Roger Clinton's claim that "one of his earliest memories" is of his big brother reciting Martin Luther King Jr.'s "Dream" speech. Bill Clinton calls it "the greatest political speech of my lifetime" as he describes his devastation at King's assassination. This is followed by footage of Robert F. Kennedy, to whom the Democratic National Convention had paid an evening of tribute the night before, and Clinton vaguely muses about what would have happened if King and Kennedy had lived: "I think the last twenty years would have been a lot different for America, and much better."[135]

But this is as far as the film delves into race relations, and the Kennedys are both political symbol and narrative bridge in *The Man from Hope*. The reference to Robert Kennedy is subtle compared to the film's emphasis on Clinton's own fleeting connection to John F. Kennedy, which serves as the cipher for his racial politics. In July 1963, as a part of Boys Nation, an organization for boys who were interested in politics, Clinton traveled to Washington, D.C., to meet the president. All Democratic presidential candidates since the 1960s have posited "some kind of connection to the Kennedy persona," but this brief meeting served as "an especially powerful version of torch passing," one that Bloodworth-Thomason worked hard to emphasize. Her production team scoured the John F. Kennedy Presidential Library for footage of that meeting to serve as the "crowning jewel" of the film. The video slows to show young Clinton, in a white Boys Nation polo shirt just like the sea of other boys around him, shaking hands with the president, an expression of "awe and excitement" on his face. This moment, viewers are led to believe, cemented the young Clinton's political ideologies and ambitions. The film uses the image twice, as Clinton and his mother tell the story of the meeting and again at the end, during the candidate's final pitch.[136]

The positioning of Clinton as the heir to Kennedy, a connection initiated in an all-male institution—Boys Nation—that would ideally also end in one—the presidency—was an essential part of the tone of the film and the portrayal of the Clintons as a potential First Family. Unlike other Bloodworth-Thomason productions, the overarching theme of *The Man from Hope* is progressive paternal authority. Aside from his brother Roger and Bill Clinton himself, the interviewees are women in his family, and these women play supportive roles as mothers, wives, and daughters who fulfill the traditionally feminine task of "substantiat[ing] and authenticat[ing]" the candidate's moral character, implicitly countering his image as a "womanizer."[137] The paternal theme is set from the beginning, as Clinton references his father's death and his grandfather's influence over a montage of black-and-white photos of Hope. Clinton's lifelong quest to be a good father becomes clear as Virginia Kelley describes when teenaged Bill stood up to his alcoholic stepfather's violence against his mother. Her description of young Bill's role as the masculine protector of the family drew applause from the crowd at the convention, and it was underscored by Roger's memories of Bill taking "the leadership role" in the family, evidenced by old photographs of Bill with a protective arm around his brother.[138]

Virginia Kelley and Roger Clinton both describe Bill as the man of the house even at a young age, and women have a clear corresponding role in *The Man from Hope* as well. As on *Designing Women*, that role is both feminine and professional. Rodham Clinton is interviewed on a porch with a tree-lined, trimmed lawn out of focus behind her. Flattered by the soft, natural light and a pastel sweater, her makeover-mandated, shoulder-length bob ruffles in a light breeze, and she alternates smiling and tearing up as she recounts stories of her husband. Perhaps as atonement to those she put off with her famous "cookie blunder," her lines keep her clearly in the domestic sphere. She talks lovingly about Bill and Chelsea, and that's it. Over a soundtrack of hopeful piano music, Rodham Clinton recalls her first meeting with Bill, outside the Yale Law Library. Indicating his control over their relationship, Clinton then takes over the story, laughing, explaining how he bought a house in Arkansas that she liked and surprised her with it. "So you better marry me because I can't live in this big house by myself," he says as the video shows an image of the newlyweds. He acknowledges the struggles in their marriage, and he pivots to the pain of exposing their daughter to the media coverage of these problems. His frank conversations with his daughter as well as his concern for her wellbeing during periods of intense media scrutiny underscores that Clinton is a new kind of southern father, a role he emphasized on the campaign trail.[139]

In *The Man from Hope*, Bill Clinton enacts the paternal power that his own father did not get to experience and that his alcoholic stepfather abused, but, like his role as a husband, his hands-on fatherhood is a different kind of authority. Twinkly eyed, beaming, and slightly tearful, he describes his "gratitude" when his daughter was born, and Rodham Clinton, also with tears in her eyes, reiterates that Clinton's father "never got to see his own child." Footage shot for the film shows the father and daughter playing softball together, as Chelsea explains how embarrassingly enthusiastic Clinton could be as a fan at her games, while a montage of old photos and home movies show that this closeness has been characteristic of their relationship for years. The future president is a gently updated model of fatherhood, both the protector and the softie, and Chelsea is shown alternately playing ball, skipping rocks in the river, curtsying in a pink dress in a home movie, and dancing with her dad. Clinton twirls Chelsea as the video fades into a shot of him surrounded by U.S. flags at a campaign rally, making the personal political and completing the paternal-presidential metaphor. If, as scholars contend, campaign films define presidential character and justify voters' choices, then *The Man from Hope* defined Clinton as a good southern son, a loving husband with a smart but feminine partner, and a caring father who hoped to extend his New Democrat values, and those of the small-town South, to the nation. He was the ideal southern man to pair with any one of Sugarbaker's designing women.[140]

The Man from Hope earned Bloodworth-Thomason the title "the woman who introduced Bill Clinton to America," but when the major networks declined to air the full footage of the film that night, claiming that Clinton's personal life was "not news," she was furious.[141] As the end drew near and polls showed a tight race, Clinton bought airtime on all major networks the night before the election to show *The Man from Hope*. Like *Designing Women*, *The Man from Hope* was Bloodworth-Thomason's pop cultural vehicle in which she smuggled Third Way progressivism into the homes of millions of viewers. And it worked: Clinton won, and *The Man from Hope* was critically acclaimed at the time and has served as a model for campaign films ever since.[142]

Bloodworth-Thomason refused to take credit for Clinton's victory, demurring that Clinton "was going to bring a kind of inclusive feeling to this country that we haven't had for a long, long time."[143] She celebrated this feeling on *Designing Women* as the inauguration approached. In an episode that aired on CBS on January 15, 1993, five days before the real-life event, the designing women ready themselves to attend Clinton's inauguration. The entire cast cheers when Julia cries, "Our man is going to the White House, and we're going to be there to see it!" When they are stranded by travel delays, however, Julia blows up at an airport gate agent, yelling about the "extremely expensive ballgown" she has been "waiting for twelve long years to wear." They do not make it to Washington, and so they dress in their finery to view the inauguration on television in an airport lounge. Julia laments, "I was supposed to be there. I had this fantasy of standing right next to the president and just sort of gently suggesting that his first appointment to the Supreme Court be Anita Hill." Their enthusiasm returns as they watch, and B. J. applauds both Clinton's politics and his provenance: "For the first time in twelve years, we have a president who understands the correct usage of the word 'y'all'. That's a man I can get behind."[144] Two months later, the popular series ended with its two-part, New South homage to *Gone with the Wind*.

Bloodworth-Thomason, then, was able to adapt her tactics to a variety of successful media productions, carefully cloaking her brand of southern gender politics in contemporary women's professional wear and Third Way centrism. Although the Thomasons rejected the label "back-porch advisers," they remained close to the Clintons throughout their time in Washington, helping to plan and film the inauguration, attending state dinners, and spending some holidays together.[145] In a 1993 *New York Times* profile of the Thomasons, Maureen Dowd joked that the "confessional talk-show sensibility and Hollywood production values" of contemporary politics "resemble[d] a situation comedy that might be called 'Designing Presidents.'"[146] The Thomasons continued to help with spin in times of crisis, as when Hillary Clinton called them in to "work the phones and buck up morale" during the Monica Lewinsky scandal.[147] And they remained the go-to producers when it was time to repackage Clinton each election season: Bloodworth-Thomason made the 1996 Democratic National Convention film *A Place Called America* for Clinton's reelection bid, and *Legacy*, his "final farewell to the nation," which aired at the 2000 DNC. Bloodworth-Thomason refused payment for these films, saying that "it seemed as if I had already been paid." She does not know why the Clintons chose her, but she suspects their shared roots played a role: "Maybe it has something to do with that 'river that runs through us' thing."[148]

As she served in an informal advisory capacity at the White House, Bloodworth-Thomason's television productions grew more overtly political. In 1995, *Designing Women* fan favorite Suzanne Sugarbaker returned to the small screen, this time as a southern politician. In *Women of the House*, Suzanne's husband dies in office and she heads to Washington to "keep his seat warm" until he can be replaced in a special election. Although her character was known for retro beliefs on *Designing Women*, Suzanne does not have a formal political affiliation in her new iteration as a temporary member of Congress. Rather, she "just sort of decides on each issue as it comes along," she explains, like "they do in Miss America [pageants]." Suzanne cops to being "big-mouthed, southern, and rich," but she is also depicted as a breath of fresh air in Washington. She proclaims on the House floor: "This is our capital, not just yours. And these monuments here belong to all of us.... And by all Americans, I mean sheep farmers, little people, movie stars, and hicks!" Despite her reputation for ditziness and her deceased husband's conservatism, Suzanne ably bridges the partisan divide, spending hours on the phone with Bill Clinton and, in a nod to Bloodworth-Thomason's role in the campaign, planning a makeover for his wife ("I got big plans for her. Now, I like her hair long, but I think she's got to keep the bangs, because you know it softens her entire face").[149] True to the Bloodworth-Thomason formula, in their discussions in *Women of the House*, the main characters air different views and arrive together at feminist conclusions, especially about representations of violence against women in the media. But Suzanne and her new team of working sisters did not have time to delve into other issues: the show was canceled before the end of its first season.

Women of the House debuted in January 1995, just as George W. Bush replaced Ann Richards as governor of Texas and a wave of newly elected Republicans swept into Washington. Riding the tide of the "angry white male" vote, the GOP took control of both houses of Congress for the first time since 1953, and, beyond the so-called Southern Strategy of coded racism and sexist nostalgia, the "Republican Revolution" had a noticeably regional flavor. The most powerful members of the party in the House were all southern white men—Gingrich of Georgia, and Dick Armey and Tom Delay of Texas—who "represented white, suburban, middle-class districts in key southern metropolitan areas (Atlanta, Dallas, and Houston)."[150] In response, Bill Clinton moved ever more to the political center over the course of the 1990s, and Bloodworth-Thomason continued to champion him and Third Way feminism. This brand of southern feminism represented a compromise, a means of bridging the vast divide between neoconservatism and what remained of the liberal center of the social movements of the 1960s. In doing so, this Third Way sacrificed some of the more potentially radical elements of feminism in the region to make a broader appeal to the so-called Silent Majority, the mass of white voters and media consumers.

Women like Shug who refused to conform; women like Celie who developed an intersectional feminist consciousness and reconfigured the existing system to create a loving, female-centered community; women like Thelma and Louise who acted on their righteous anger against misogyny and chose an ambiguous flight into the Grand Canyon over capitulation to patriarchy: none of these character types appear in Bloodworth-Thomason's southern feminist productions. The sisterhood of *Designing Women* was exclusive, limited to liberal, middle-class, white women who endorsed individual uplift rather than revolution. By the end of the decade, this brand of sisterhood had a wider distribution and a name: neoliberal feminism. As a "lifestyle" rather than a political venture, this form of feminism offered gendered micropolitics that focused on individual struggles and prescribed mutual support among groups of women, rather than sociopolitical change, as the solution to sexist oppression. And, as with Bloodworth-Thomason's Third Way feminism, this brand could be found on television, reaching a national audience. Instead of a weekly prime-time sitcom, however, this lifestyle feminism was disseminated daily to millions of viewers by the most famous southern woman in the world: Oprah Winfrey, the subject of the next chapter.

CHAPTER 4

"Change Your Life Television"
OPRAH WINFREY'S SOUTHERN, NEOLIBERAL, BLACK FEMINISM

In 1999, not long after becoming the first woman and the first African American to be named "the most powerful person in show business" by *Entertainment Weekly*, Oprah Winfrey, in a deal that landed her $100 million in stocks, licensed her long-running daytime talk show to CBS, the network that also hosted Linda Bloodworth-Thomason's popular sitcoms.[1] That same year, Winfrey, the former Mississippi farm girl and the wealthiest Black woman in the world, announced that she was expanding her multimedia empire to include a magazine, to be published by Hearst. The media industry was banking on *Oprah* viewers to consume her brand in any and all forms, and they were correct: at the turn of the twentieth century, she averaged twenty-two million viewers per week, and her magazine was an instant hit. Critics derided daytime television, but Winfrey's star—and her wealth—rose higher and higher as her fans demonstrated their power as consumers. In 1999, Debbie Stoller, editor of the "third-wave" feminist magazine *Bust*, proclaimed: "I love the women who watch Oprah. They get no respect in our culture, because they have no sexual power and nobody cares about them. But there are so many of them. Who knows what would happen if they all got together!"[2]

Since her meteoric rise to fame in the mid-1980s, Winfrey has generated quite a bit of criticism and scholarship, yet, as Kimberley Springer notes, there are still "unspoken, uninvestigated Oprahs."[3] In this chapter I explore one of those Oprahs: the southern feminist. While feminist scholars occasionally agree with some of the critiques of the overall genre of talk shows as "cheap and trashy" entertainment, they counter that specific dismissals of Winfrey traffic in racism, classism, and sexism.[4] Jane Shattuc asked in 1997, "Are daytime TV talk shows simply sensational commercialism, or could they be a new form of political debate?"[5] Talk shows are feminized spaces rife with lay experts that focus on the opinions of ordinary people, and Winfrey's fan base, 80 percent of whom are women, offers a case study of how this representational privileging of "regular women" and their issues could have radically destabilizing potential in a media landscape driven by and catering to men. As what scholars call a "cultural forum" that overlaps with the public sphere, talk shows by their very nature facilitate the dissemination of a variety of perspectives, "providing an active role for the viewer in debate."[6] Moreover, Winfrey is in control of her own means of production and is as powerful as any of the traditionally dominant white men in the industry.

Indeed, by the mid-1990s, Oprah Winfrey was far and away the most powerful media celebrity in the world. A Black woman from Mississippi with an American bootstraps story, Winfrey became a conduit of widely consumed ideas about contemporary American womanhood at the end of the century through her multimedia approach—hosting a daily television show, acting in and producing films based on novels by Black women, and presiding over a wildly popular televised book club featuring numerous southern and African American women writers. Winfrey's productions represent the nexus of multiple forms of southern feminism and the media platforms—television, film, and literature—examined in the preceding chapters. Although her media conglomerate is based in Chicago, the "southern inflections" of her brand are crucial to her media personality and her overwhelming popularity over the past four decades.[7]

A thorough examination of Winfrey's enormous body of work—her daily talk show from 1986–2011; the various spin-offs of that show as she anointed lifestyle and self-help gurus like Dr. Mehmet Oz and Dr. Phil McGraw; *O Magazine*; her cable station OWN and the various Winfrey shows it airs; her website, Oprah.com; and her podcasts—is beyond my scope here. Instead, in order to examine the southern feminism of Winfrey as a complex individual, celebrity, brand, and influencer, I look at her endorsement, interpretations, and discussions of Black feminist texts as part of her explicit mission to "change the lives" of her viewers. Her choices of texts for her on-air Book Club have enabled Winfrey to expose her largely white audiences to some of the core tenets of radical Black feminism, thus reinserting the "great unspoken," in journalist Kristal Brent Zook's words, of gender politics into popular discussions.[8] Through her televised self-help mission, her promotion of Black feminist fiction, and carefully crafted television episodes and a Hollywood film on that fiction, Winfrey was able to induce empathy without alienating her white viewers and meld the more radical politics of these texts with her own brand of lifestyle feminism. In doing so, Winfrey offered a popular bridge between the contemporary versions of feminism—radical and neoliberal, "second-wave" and "third-wave," white sisterhood and womanism—and this brand of feminism was situated ideologically in the South.

"Girlfriend to the World"
The Oprah Winfrey Show

Winfrey spent her early childhood in the kind of woman-centered Black community that she would later urge her viewers to read about in some of her Book Club choices. Born in 1954, Winfrey lived on her maternal grandmother's farm in Kosciusko, Mississippi, for the first several years of her life. "We were poor—po'," she explained on her show, and she frequently referenced the farm's outhouse to illustrate this poverty.[9] At the age of six, Winfrey moved to Milwaukee, where her mother supported her through welfare and work as a maid. They were so poor, Winfrey has said, that "she collected cockroaches as pets," and she recalls nuns coming to her home to deliver the only Christmas presents she and her stepsiblings received.[10] A victim of neglect, abuse, and molestation in her early teens, Winfrey started getting into trouble, running away, and telling people she had been abandoned so that they would give her money (including, she claims, $100 from Aretha Franklin at one point). In response, her mother sent her south to Nashville to live with her father. After a pregnancy at fourteen that resulted in a stillborn son, Winfrey's father began to impose discipline, and she began to thrive.[11]

An honors student with a gift in oratory, Winfrey won a full scholarship to Tennessee State University to study communications. After a stint at a Nashville radio station, Winfrey moved to local television and then on to Baltimore, where she became the cohost of a local news program and later a daytime show called *People Are Talking*. In 1984, Winfrey got word that producers were looking for an African American woman to host *AM Chicago*, so she sent in a tape.[12] "The unfortunate thing is every single person with the exception of my closest friend Gayle told me you're not gonna make it," she later explained, laughing. "Let's face it, there was nobody who looked like me. I was overweight, and black, and female, and part jeri curl. I don't know another overweight jeri curl person who I can say made it!"¹³ The producers hired her and told her just to be herself, advice that proved to be rewarding: *AM Chicago* outpaced *Donahue*, the nationally syndicated talk show, in local viewership within five months, and within a year it was rebranded as *The Oprah Winfrey Show*.¹⁴

Even as she rapidly stole viewers from Phil Donahue, Winfrey told the *Washington Post* that her real desire was to become known as a great actor. Not long after her move to Chicago, famed producer Quincy Jones suggested her for the role of Sofia in the film version of *The Color Purple* after seeing her show on local television. Citing a longtime "obsession" with the novel and a sense of destiny, Winfrey auditioned, later confessing that she wanted it "more than anything else ever in the world."¹⁵ Besting the Oscar-nominated actor Alfre Woodard, who also auditioned, Winfrey got the part, and her turn as Sofia garnered critical acclaim and award nominations, including the Golden Globe and Oscar for supporting actress.¹⁶

As her Hollywood star rose, Winfrey's show topped the ratings, and she inked a national syndication deal. In 1986, as the host of the most-watched talk show in the nation, Winfrey became the third woman and the first Black person in industry history to take control of her own television productions when she incorporated Harpo Studios. Although Winfrey did not leave her show for Hollywood to pursue her reputed first love of acting, she also did not abandon the craft altogether. On television in Chicago, Winfrey cultivated a persona that she initially modeled after Phil Donahue, the reigning talk-show host in the mid-1980s who pioneered the participation of a mostly female audience. But while Donahue was known for his paternal presence, Winfrey developed her own take on television hosting, and her mediated personality became not just a role but also a moneymaking brand within a decade. Using her journalistic training, her acting skills, and her southern sensibility, Winfrey crafted a host persona that was part girlfriend, part cheerleader, and part guru.¹⁷

Black feminist scholar Kimberley Springer asks of Winfrey, "Where does Oprah the woman end and Oprah the brand begin?"¹⁸ For her part, Winfrey maintains that she is just a regular person, and she often positions herself as equal to her viewers. In the early years of her show, Winfrey moved among her audience and shared the microphone, and she used plural personal pronouns frequently to emphasize this connection. While this was in keeping with the general format of daytime talk shows in the 1980s, in combination with her mediated persona this had the effect of positioning Winfrey as just one of "us." She fed into this by sharing emotions with her viewers; she expressed surprise, confusion, sympathy, happiness, and outrage on cue with her studio audience members, often asking "the question we all have" on their behalf. "In this way," Jennifer Harris and Elwood Watson argue in their edited volume on Winfrey, "she present[ed] herself not as an informed expert but as an informed witness-participant."[19] Early on, Winfrey crafted a very successful parasocial relationship, a kind of "intimacy at a distance" with audience members, viewers, and consumers.[20]

Winfrey's supposedly unscripted self-disclosures at times also positioned her as part of a vast community of American women dealing with similar problems. She famously revealed her childhood sexual abuse on air in 1986 in "what would come to be recognized as a characteristic move" that "collapse[d] the boundaries between the public and the private," according to Harris and Watson.[21] Her set transformed over time into a staged living room wherein Winfrey frequently divulged details of her own personal life, sharing struggles over losing and regaining weight, body image, family tragedies, and sexual violence and trauma. As a major celebrity appearing daily in more and more American homes, as an enormously successful Black businessperson, and as an acclaimed actor with an Oscar nomination, Winfrey continued to hone her winning persona. Her approach became so familiar and successful that scholars gave it a name: "oprahfication," for the "titillating public discussion of the personal, the disclosure of private emotion for mass consumption on national television."[22]

Winfrey entered the world of daytime television on the eve of its most tabloid point. As talk shows proliferated by the end of the 1980s, they competed in their trafficking of the sensational. But Winfrey's Midas touch was a melding of her persona, her style, her choice of topics, and her development of a mission that tapped into the self-help ethos of women's mass media. Scholars have long identified talk shows as the conduit of a form of therapeutic discourse that ostensibly aids guests and viewers in working through emotional problems and serves to publicly promote mental health. Winfrey quickly commanded this kind of talk show therapy. By 1997, just over a decade after the show's national syndication, Beretta E. Smith-Shomade argues, the "mere enunciation" of Winfrey's first name "conjure[d] the sublime example of self-help, authority, and release."[23]

Critics argue that the talk-show-as-therapy model is problematic. Beyond the rather obvious problems of voyeurism and turning to television for mental health resources (especially renowned experts who are only available to the guests during the time it takes to tape the episode), scholars argue that the medium and the format promotes American "self-contained individualism."[24] Yet others contend, and many *Oprah* viewers have attested, that Winfrey's show offers a form of mediated consciousness-raising, of which the therapeutic format is important, as it encourages self-exploration and collective identification on the part of not just the individual guests but also the millions of viewers. Early on, Winfrey cited collective epiphanies, or what she calls "Bing bing!" or "Aha!" moments, as her goal. She used her own reactions as her guide. "You know, I'm just a girl with a microphone," she explained. "When something hits me that what—like, 'Whoa, that was good'—I know that it also affected other people that way."[25]

The Oprah Winfrey Show quickly became a medium for disclosure, bonding, self-exploration, and systemic critique, all in a space dominated by women. Scholars offer mixed reviews of *Oprah*'s feminist potential. As a celebrity who not only hocked products to her viewers but was also a brand herself, Winfrey, according to scholar Cathy Sue Copenhagen, provided a "resistant" space for viewers via both the "multiplicity of female issues" explored on her show and the "democratic forum" for that exploration.[26] As a media personality, Winfrey was not explicitly feminist, and she studiously avoided more controversial topics like reproductive rights. But she did feature other topics of primary concern to contemporary feminists. Sujata Moorti examined the various *Oprah* episodes addressing rape and sexual assault between 1989 and 1991 and found a "protofeminist discursive space" that encouraged women to express their pain, critique violent male sexuality and the legal system, and experience catharsis with the guests. Crucially, at-home viewers did so collectively, with Winfrey and the studio audience together, not just as individuals, even if they were alone in their living rooms. Moorti concludes, "By narrating sexual violence, the discussions on *Oprah* affirm a female experience that has often been repressed and rendered invisible."[27] Winfrey provided a daily parasocial space through which millions were encouraged to see women's personal experiences as shared, significant, and even systemic—all core goals of feminist consciousness-raising groups. Accordingly, Winfrey was lauded by women's organizations: NOW named her a Woman of Achievement in 1986, and in 1989 Gloria Steinem named Winfrey one of *Ms.* magazine's 1988 "women of the year."[28]

In 1991, Winfrey claimed that she and her team deliberately programmed "shows to empower women." While she has been called a "media-friendly feminist," usually derisively, she was also, as Jennifer L. Rexroat argues, America's "foremost de facto feminist" by the 1990s, even if she avoided the f-word herself.[29] The cozy talk show format and Winfrey's "girlfriend to the world" persona were tailor-made for the "I'm not a feminist, but" demographic, women who cited the "second wave" favorably but were unwilling to call themselves feminists.[30] Like Sugarbaker's on *Designing Women*, Winfrey's studio living room could also be seen as a kind of safe, self-contained, public space that privileged women's voices, subjectivity, and systemic critiques, even if the individualized solutions on offer ultimately seem to temper potential for collective feminist action. To be fair, Winfrey never intended to inspire action. Consciousness was what she was after. She explained: "Do I get you to think differently? Do I get you to think at all? Do I get a moment where you go 'Ah, I never thought of it that way before'? That's all I'm looking for."[31]

As Winfrey and her show evolved, this message took shape as an explicit form of neoliberal feminism. In 1996, after a decade at the top of the talk show heap and many Emmy Awards to show for it, Winfrey surveyed the distant field of seventeen contenders that included hosts like Jerry Springer, Montel Williams, and Sally Jesse Raphael, took a hard look at her own show, and decided she did not like what she saw. She deemed tabloid talk shows "the trash pack" and acknowledged her role in the genre. "I don't want to do it anymore," she said in interviews, declaring that "the time has come for this genre of talk shows to move forward."[32] At the time, *Forbes* reported that she was the "highest paid entertainer in the United States," pulling in about $180 million in revenue per year—plenty of money, that is, to completely change her format despite the risk of ceding viewers to the competition.[33]

No stranger to reinvention herself, Winfrey understood the American fascination with "self-creation" years before makeover shows became popular on television. As Winfrey tells her own story, she achieved her status through ingenuity, and in the mid-1990s she accordingly retooled her daily show, dedicating it to helping her viewers improve their own lives. The original goal of the show was, she explained, "to uplift, enlighten, encourage and entertain," but in the mid-1990s the new "mission" became "to use television to transform people's lives, to make viewers see themselves differently, and to bring happiness and a sense of fulfillment into every home."[34] The new goal of self-awareness, empowerment, and improvement—in Winfrey's words, "each individual having his or her own inner revolution"—became its own brand in 1998, when Winfrey introduced the mantra "Change Your Life TV." She explained: "Changing your life ... comes in little moments; it's really about changing the way you think, the way you see your life, the way you see your family, your children, your relationships."[35]

Winfrey made this switch at an interesting time in American feminist history. That summer, *Time* magazine weighed in with yet another story about the "death" of feminism, incongruously featuring Susan B. Anthony,

Betty Friedan, Gloria Steinem, and the contemporary postfeminist television character Ally McBeal on the cover.[36] Of course, feminism was not dead, but it was changing in the late 1990s, as was its relationship to popular culture. Ever the trendsetter, Winfrey harnessed these changes, and the resulting transformation of her show made her the primary conduit of self-empowerment to women viewers nationwide at the perfect historical moment to capture the pop cultural ascendance of neoliberal feminism.

While this version of feminism is most commonly associated with early twenty-first-century "blockbuster" nonfiction texts like Sheryl Sandberg's *Lean In* (2013) and Ann-Marie Slaughter's "Why Women Can't Have It All" (2012), its roots stretch to the Reagan-era backlash and the fracturing of the Women's Liberation Movement.[37] Angie Maxwell and Todd Shields explain that after the 1970s, the movement "lost control of the debate over women's rights as the individual became more powerful than the collective," a shift prompted by the rise of the New Right.[38] Much like Third Way Democratic politics, Stephanie Genz argues, in an attempt to reconsolidate the center left, popular feminism in the 1990s embraced the market logic of neoliberalism, spawning a kind of "free-market feminism" that was "individuated in the extreme."[39] According to neoliberal ideas of gender, each woman is responsible for herself, obscuring structural inequality in favor of an individualized "you go, girl" ethic of personal responsibility and self-actualization, often achieved through consumption.[40]

In addition to the emphasis on women as consumers that is a hallmark of contemporary postfeminism, the micropolitics of developing neoliberal feminism promoted individual empowerment rather than collective activism, with the goal of "internal revolution" rather than structural change. The ascendance of what has been called lifestyle feminism, which, bell hooks explains, rests on "the notion that there could be as many versions of feminism as there were women," combined with the pseudo-feminist ethos of empowerment to offer every woman a feminist style rather than a feminist politics.[41] As a cultural rather than a political phenomenon, lifestyle feminism was disseminated through popular culture instead of organizations, lobbying, or grassroots activism.

If turn-of-the-century lifestyle feminism and neoliberal feminism were placed in a Venn diagram, *The Oprah Winfrey Show* would be at its center. As both a beloved celebrity and a brand, Winfrey became, by the mid-1990s, a de facto feminist "prophet of capital," offering a very effective mix of self-help psychology, spirituality, and consumption. Critics have called this "femvertising," or the hocking of products to women as "empowering," and there is a specific name for the jump in sales of any product Winfrey endorses: the "Oprah Effect."[42]

But Winfrey's race and her southernness are also important parts of this phenomenon. The global logic of neoliberal feminism involves the successful women of the "developed world" helping their less fortunate sisters through international initiatives. The obviously racialized tenets of this kind of feminized global "uplift" smacks of the white saviorism found in the first and second "waves" of American feminism. Like the designing women putting Anthony's girlfriends in 1980s power suits, teaching them proper southern etiquette, and schooling them in business acumen, neoliberal feminism posits that economically successful white women can and should teach impoverished women how to empower themselves, compete economically, join the market, and enjoy the individual fruits of globalization.

This logic was made explicit through several corporate campaigns in the early twentieth century that will be examined in the epilogue, but it is worth noting here that this rhetoric of feminist uplift of exploited sisters in poorer regions—the so-called Global South—also describes historical encounters with "second-wave" feminism in the U.S. South. Janet Allured's work on the Women's Liberation Movement in Louisiana reveals local resentment of national feminist imperialism in the 1970s, culminating in one New Orleanian's 1971 position paper, "To Our Yankee Friends," which proclaimed, "We do not wish to be patronized by your northern arrogance." This "Yankeeism," coming as it did from generally well-meaning northern feminists, echoed African American critiques of "northern white liberals" who believed southerners needed their help with Black community organizing in the Deep South in the early 1960s, and it generally revealed deep-seated prejudices that dismissed the agency and activism of southern women.[43] Regional experiences are an important nexus of intersectional identity in U.S. feminist history, and, more importantly for our purposes here, they are also an important site of new variants of feminism.

As a powerful southern Black woman guiding white women to their more authentic selves, Winfrey both promotes the uplift model of neoliberal feminism and turns its racialized and regional logic on its head. Race and region function in contradictory ways in Winfrey's lifestyle feminism. She often invokes her roots, referring to herself as "a black woman from Mississippi."[44] But, although she credits her move from Milwaukee to Nashville in her early teens as saving her life, the South of her early childhood often appears as backward in Winfrey's recollections, a place she escaped through sheer will and skill.[45] In interviews, in speeches, and on her show,

Winfrey often traffics in the "benighted South."⁴⁶ Scholar John Howard describes a "rare" visit to Mississippi in 1998, when Winfrey took the stage at the Attala County Coliseum. Seated in a rocking chair beneath a banner that read "KOSCIUSKO, MS Welcomes Home Oprah," Winfrey declared to an auditorium full of locals, "Mississippi, Mississippi, Mississippi. There ain't nothin' here but corn. So that means you can do anything."⁴⁷ Although southernness is key to Winfrey's folksy, approachable, "everywoman" persona, her South is a region to be transcended, and this process is possible through self-exploration, transformation, and consumption.

This characterization of the Magnolia State as backward and of Winfrey as its golden child is in keeping with the relationship between neoliberal feminists and the Global South. But Winfrey also troubles this relationship in her frequent shout-outs to strong southern Black women and, increasingly in the late 1990s, references to personal experiences of racism. Scholars have criticized Winfrey for her "raceless" persona and for not using her celebrity to advocate for civil rights. But she has consistently maintained that she is practicing her own brand of racial politics, stating, "I have a great sense of heritage. I feel a strong sense of legacy. But I'm not a flag-waving activist."⁴⁸ Winfrey brought up issues of race on air far more often than critics give her credit for, and certainly more than other television shows of the era, particularly daily talk shows. Within a year of national syndication, she took her show to Forsyth County, Georgia, just north of *Designing Women*'s Atlanta, to challenge the all-white studio audience of locals on their opposition to Black people moving into the county. Winfrey exposed their racism and ignorance by wielding her authority, shutting racists down and then saying to scattered applause, "Black me said that."⁴⁹ Over the years, her shows and interviews were peppered with seemingly casual references to her own encounters with racism, indicating, as Kathryn Lofton notes, the "insider identity" rhetoric through which she establishes solidarity with African American viewers and challenges the prejudices, confusion, and discomfort of white guests.⁵⁰

At the same time, Winfrey has also been critiqued for playing an all-too-familiar role: the mammy. She was tagged with this imagery almost as soon as her show went national. In a 1986 *Washington Post* profile that devotes an inordinate amount of detail to Winfrey's weight, Stephanie Mansfield explained the host's appeal: "If Jane Pauley is the prom queen, Oprah Winfrey is the dorm counselor. . . . People want to hold Barbara Walters' hand. They want to crawl into Winfrey's lap."⁵¹ While some viewers likely responded to Winfrey in this way, this Oprah-as-mammy thesis ignores her agency and specifically Winfrey's control over her own representation. In a direct challenge to the "controlling image" of the mammy, Winfrey performs her ministrations in a house of her own making.[52] Everyone therein works for her, and her flock of millions of adult women viewers hangs on her every word, the opposite of the relationship between the recalcitrant Scarlett and house servant Mammy. Beyond tuning in daily, these viewers purchase the products and books she endorses so faithfully that their consumption influences entire industries. Thus, while Winfrey's persona might tap into racial stereotypes for some viewers, it is also subversive as the story of a wildly successful, southern, Black woman.[53]

As a standard-busting first in so many aspects of her industry, then, Winfrey uniquely represents American neoliberal feminism. Her biography conforms without exaggeration to Algeresque, bootstraps mythology as well as to the individualized "personal responsibility" socioeconomics of the 1990s. She was born into poverty in the Jim Crow South and overcame classism, racism, and sexism through education, tenacity, and natural ability. Yet, because of her "sister sensibility," candidness about her own struggles, and familiarizing use of southern and Black vernacular to translate often-difficult social and psychological concepts, her enormous wealth was not off-putting.[54] Winfrey's status was one to which her audience could aspire, and, significantly, Winfrey herself was there to aid these aspirations. When she deliberately retooled her show in the mid-1990s, she reversed the camera's gaze, setting her sights on her own viewers, helping American women follow suit by "living their best lives."[55]

Winfrey's feminism as it developed in the late 1990s thus exhorted her viewers to focus on the self rather than on structural problems, and she prescribed individual empowerment and consumption rather than collective change and activism. Age-wise, Winfrey is of the "second-wave" generation, but her mid-1990s pivot more closely mirrors some of the developments in the contemporary "third wave," in which activists like Rebecca Walker expanded the notions of what it meant to be a good feminist, exhausted by what they saw as the previous generation's attempts to "constantly measur[e] up to some cohesive fully down-for-the-feminist-cause identity without contradictions and messiness." The rising concept of "choice" in the 1990s may have contradicted the "mainstream ideas of feminism," Walker explains, but they also "push[ed] us to new definitions and understandings of female empowerment and social change."[56]

Likewise, although some scholars dismiss neoliberal feminism as "not feminist enough," or indeed as "a cul-de-sac that reverses into a backlash of right conservatism," this dismissal fails to take into account its important role as a new form of progressive gender politics.[57] Scholars who research reception of pop culture aimed at women tell us, time and again, that rather than simply internalizing the intended message wholesale, readers, viewers, and audience members actively engage with the content of these texts in myriad ways.[58] Oprah Winfrey, the poor Mississippi farm girl who became the richest Black woman in the world by the end of the twentieth century, was a primary source of lifestyle and neoliberal feminism, but fans' reception of this new brand of pop cultural gender politics could foster radical moments. This potential is especially evident in Oprah's Book Club, in which she frequently featured Black feminist texts centered in southern contexts.

"It Will Change the World If Everybody Reads This"
Oprah's Book Club

Any viewer attempting to live her "best life" by consuming all of the products and practicing each of the self-help techniques endorsed by Winfrey on her multiple media platforms by the end of the 1990s could easily end up broke and exhausted.[59] But in 1996 *The Oprah Winfrey Show* offered viewers a comparatively less expensive route to self-improvement: reading along with their favorite host. Prompted by a producer with whom she frequently shared books, Winfrey announced her mission to "get the country reading again" through the development of an on-air book club.[60]

Although critics of television as an educational medium groaned, Winfrey's love of books has deep roots. Quoting Maya Angelou's *I Know Why the Caged Bird Sings* from memory in a 1999 *New York Times* profile, she claimed it had been a revelation to her as a young girl in Mississippi: "I was a colored girl, raised by my grandmother, living in an impoverished town just like her. Maya Angelou grew up to be Maya Angelou. It was my life—it was the possibility for my life."[61] In her paeans to the act of reading, Winfrey frequently cited southern women authors as her inspiration. When *The Color Purple* was published in 1982, she claims that it "hit her like a ton of bricks," and she bought copies for all of her friends.[62] After visiting Winfrey's farmhouse in Indiana, Nobel Prize–winning author Toni Morrison said, "[E]xcept for other writers, I have very seldom seen a home with so many books—all kinds of books, handled and read books. She's a genuine reader, not a decorative one. She's a carnivorous reader."[63] In addition to *The Color Purple*, which Winfrey frequently invoked on her show and in interviews, and works by Toni Morrison, her top ten list includes *To Kill a Mockingbird*, *Their Eyes Were Watching God*, *Jubilee*, and *I Know Why the Caged*

Bird Sings—all works by southern women authors that have, as Cecilia Farr notes, "social justice agendas."[64]

As with Winfrey's television show, there is debate about the feminist value of Oprah's Book Club. Some critics simply dismiss the use of television to promote literature, arguing that the televised Book Club episodes are edited to promote the same self-help, television-as-therapy principles as the show in general, which "places the discussion of books into the context of a women's support group."[65] Others simply lament Winfrey's choice of books as "low-brow."[66] Yet feminist scholars have long challenged this dismissal of women's popular culture, and even those who buy into this distinction must admit that not all of her choices can be called low-brow: the Book Club list between 1996 and 2002 includes works by multiple literary giants like Maya Angelou and Toni Morrison.

It is true that Oprah's Book Club picks generally featured the theme of uplift and were thus an additional medium for her "change your life" mission. As such, according to D. T. Max in the *New York Times*, the Club was "a vast experiment in linked literary imagination and social engineering." Winfrey was upfront about this: "The reason I love books is because they teach us something about ourselves."[67] However, unlike on her daily shows, where audience members were passive viewers, the Book Club episodes, on which a select few were invited to dinner with Winfrey and the author, allowed these viewers an informed voice based on their interpretations of the books. Moreover, these episodes were not singular texts. Oprah's Book Club episodes created a community of women at several levels: the guests chosen by Winfrey (the majority of whom were women), the studio audience, the at-home viewing audience, the local book clubs that formed to read along with Winfrey, and the discussions on Oprah.com. If Winfrey's daily talk show functioned as a parasocial relationship for her viewers, the intertextual Book Club experience offered a real social exchange with the potential for alternative, even radical, feminist messages, albeit mediated and heavily managed by Winfrey herself.[68]

The intimacy of the on-screen Book Club dinners was carefully constructed. For each episode, Winfrey and her staff pored through thousands of viewer letters to choose "what she [found] to be the most compelling responses to each book," and she invited a handful of those readers to the "elegant dinner parties" to discuss the book with each other, Winfrey, and the author.[69] The Book Club branched out from Harpo Studios to different locations for their dinners in certain episodes, but, except for the episode on Toni Morrison's *Paradise*, in which Winfrey brought twenty-two readers to Morrison's classroom at Princeton to discuss the difficult novel, the setting was always such that the Club looked to viewers like a close group of friends. Except for Winfrey and the author, the dinner guests all met each other for the first time on the day of the episode taping, but the format, according to *Oprah* scholars, "mimics" communicative "intimacy" in women's friendships, placing it on the spectrum of supportive same-sex networks that we have seen in other southern feminist texts of this era.[70]

Many of the Book Club episodes offer the usual *Oprah* fare, with novels that feature plucky girls and women who overcome obstacles. Journalist Susan Wise Bauer refers to "Oprah's Misery Index," citing "sufferers who save themselves" as the "recurring theme" of the Club.[71] Winfrey's tried-and-true formula of teletherapy rested on the presence of trauma, or at least internal conflict, to create a platform for self-transformation. The goal of the show was not to titillate voyeurs or viewers but rather to inspire them to see something of themselves in the guests, regardless of the topic. This teletherapeutic strategy of encouraging not just interest or sympathy but also empathy in viewers applied doubly to Oprah's Book Club. While there is a vigorous scholarly debate regarding emotional responses to television viewing, studies consistently show that reading fiction increases empathy levels.[72] The intertextuality of the often-sentimental novels and the talk show geared toward self-transformation provided a unique platform for converting viewers to Winfrey's southern feminism via the Book Club.

Activist critics of consciousness-raising in the 1970s disparaged it as apolitical navel-gazing, and some scholars have argued that Winfrey's patented "confessional" style, her promotion of television as therapy, and her emphasis on individualized self-help might seem a "perversion" of the tactic.[73] The Book Club, however, offered a different kind of space for *Oprah* viewers, one in which women used the novels as points of shared knowledge from which to explore their own experiences, culminating in collective understanding about various aspects of the patriarchal system that counteracted the teletherapeutic emphasis on self-help and individual solutions.[74] Thus, the Book Club offered some readers and dinner guests a feminist community, and at-home viewers did not even have to leave their living rooms to attend.

While some of the criticism of Oprah's Book Club smacks of snobbery about different types of fiction and about television as a medium, it is true that many of the novels Winfrey chose might seem formulaic, featuring major sources of trauma for the primary characters. Many of these too were authored by southern women or were set in the South or both, thus situating the trauma in the context of regional patriarchy.[75] The southern settings thus served as sites of women's experiences writ large. Her invited guests, Winfrey explained in one episode, "all shared a common bond," and her goal was to bring them together in collective consciousness: "It still amazes me that people who are suffering feel that they are alone in the world and no one else has ever experienced whatever pain it is they're feeling at the time." As in any interview on her show, Winfrey encouraged therapeutic storytelling among the guests and, by extension, the viewers at home. "Claim, down to the painful details," Winfrey says to the camera in an episode featuring Anna Quindlen's *Black and Blue*, a novel that explores the terrors of intimate partner violence, and her dinner guests do, often with some tears and hand-holding.[76]

But while the Book Club could raise women's consciousness of the social nature of their gendered experiences, scholar Wendy Parkins points out that the formation of a parasocial community often necessarily eclipses differences.[77] On the Book Club episodes, the staged dinner discussions sometimes avoided race, regardless of its significance in the books. Yet the mere act of encouraging the show's white viewers to read books in which Black characters discuss racialized experiences and racism was a means of fostering awareness of Black feminist ideas, particularly a basic engagement with intersectionality, among Book Club readers. In short, just because Winfrey carefully managed on-air discussions does not mean that readers were not exposed to, challenged by, and possibly changed by difficult concepts through the act of reading.

In a 1992 *New York Times* op-ed, "A Manifesto of Sorts for a Black Feminist Movement," journalist Kristal Brent Zook argued that novelists like Alice Walker, Toni Morrison, and Maya Angelou were perhaps the primary conduits of Black feminist thought to the public, more so than academic texts.[78] Just a few years later, Winfrey became a conduit herself with her Book Club. Through picks like *Song of Solomon*, *The Heart of a Woman*, *Paradise*, *Breath, Eyes, Memory*, and *What Looks Like Crazy on an Ordinary Day*—all novels by African American authors known for their feminist themes and characters chosen for the Book Club in its first two years—Winfrey likely got more white women reading about Black women, their thoughts and feelings about race, and their experiences of systemic inequality than most literature classes in the United States at the time, dominated as they were by the white male canon.[79]

Winfrey's covert promotion of feminism on these episodes was not without precedent, as she frequently hinted at her belief in some fundamental Black feminist tenets throughout the run of her show. Southern foremothers, for instance, are a core part of Winfrey's self-definition. This is both a legacy of the matrilineage of American slavery and a key Black feminist conceptualization of history and praxis.[80] During one visit to Kosciusko, the mayor gave Winfrey the gift of a rutabaga to help her "remember her roots," and, jokes aside, Winfrey frequently and explicitly did. Throughout her tenure on television, Winfrey spoke of the influence of her grandmother, with whom she shared a feather bed during her early childhood in Mississippi. Hattie Mae Lee ran a farm and was strict with her granddaughter. Winfrey cites this discipline as significant to her character development, explaining, "I am what I am because of my grandmother: my strength, my sense of reasoning, everything."[81]

Winfrey also found early support from the community of women at her grandmother's church. She could reportedly read by the age of three, and she gave her first public recitation at age four at Buffalo United Methodist Church. "The sistahs in the front row fanning themselves [used to say] 'Hattie Mae, this child sure can talk,'" she jokes. "'This is the talkingest child.' But that talking paid off."[82] On her infrequent trips to Mississippi, it is these women she visits, aunts and great-aunts and women who remember her as a child reciting scripture in the church on the renamed Oprah Winfrey Road. Her own success, she argues, represents their hard work. "I wouldn't say that I feel an obligation to speak for 'all blacks,'" she said in an interview in 1987, "but I do feel myself as part of a tradition. I carry with me the voices of the women who have gone before me. When I speak for me, I also speak for them."[83] In another interview, she quoted Maya Angelou's "Our Grandmothers" from memory: "I go forth / alone, and stand as ten thousand."[84] Angelou's *I Know Why the Caged Bird Sings* validated Winfrey's existence when she was a teenager, she says, and she calls Angelou a mother figure and one of her "greatest personal teachers," the person she turned to for guidance when tabloids attacked her. Foremothers, she has said, are the "bridges we have crossed over on."[85]

The metaphor of the bridge is a crucial one for Black feminism, as seen in the foundational *This Bridge Called My Back: Writings by Radical Women of Color* (1981). This text focuses on "relationships between women" rather than the traditional feminist focus on those between men and women.[86] This metaphor connotes both oppression and coalition, and *This Bridge Called My Back* was an explicit response to the eclipsing of Black women's experiences and exploitation of their activism by the white-dominated, "second-wave" movement and the male-dominated movement for racial civil rights. The bridge is multifunctional, serving to connect women of color to their foremothers, connect them to each other, and connect feminists across boundaries of race, ethnicity, and class. In the foreword to the second edition of *This Bridge Called My Back*, Toni Cade Bambara writes, "This Bridge can get us there. Can coax us into the habit of listening to each other and learning each other's ways of seeing and being."[87] Calling back to these feminist foremothers, some young women of color in the late 1990s sought to redefine their gender politics across generations, rather than underscoring the generational conflict behind the reigning metaphor of separate feminist "waves." And so when Winfrey refers to these bridges, she both taps into a powerful Black feminist tradition and speaks to the "third-wave multiplicity" of feminism in the 1990s.[88]

The "grounding force" of foremothers for Winfrey goes beyond the living as well. Toni Morrison, one of Winfrey's favorite authors, explains that the "gap between Africa and Afro-America and the gap between the living and the dead does not exist" (a sentiment with which Mudear Lovejoy of *Ugly Ways* would heartily agree).[89] Black feminist theory in general "collaps[es] the boundaries between past, present, and future."[90] In keeping with this, Winfrey insists that the influence of historical Black women has determined the trajectory of her career. In the mid-1990s, looking at the dismal terrain of the tabloid talk shows that dominated daytime television, Winfrey considered quitting. But she explains that one morning over coffee "it just connected": "I am a descendant of slaves and what does that mean? You're an African American woman, you have this show and now you're thinking about giving it up? What would the ancestors say?"[91] More specifically, Winfrey claims that she actively consults her deceased foremothers: "Before I have a big meeting or a decision to make, I go and sit with my ancestors. Literally, I go and sit in my closet and I say their names. I just say their names so that when I walk into the space, I don't walk alone."[92]

Beyond simply paying tribute to the women who came before her, Winfrey offered African American viewers and guests a forum on her television show for speaking about intersectional experiences. bell hooks wrote extensively of how Black women in the 1980s and 1990s resisted "devaluation" through the use of mass media "to offer radically different images" of themselves, images that spoke to both strength and trauma. Citing Audre Lorde, hooks asserts that these forms of self-representation and self-empowerment are crucial to the Black feminist project. Moreover, according to hooks, speaking intersectional trauma—getting it on the record in a society that has worked so hard to silence Black voices—is not a private matter. Rather, it is a necessary component of liberation. Naming trauma is necessary to move forward both personally and politically, hooks argues: "I say remember the pain because I believe true resistance begins with people confronting pain, whether it's theirs or somebody else's, and wanting to do something to change it."[93]

This is the kind of feminist work that undergirds the discussions on several Book Club episodes that focus on works by Black women authors. On the episode featuring Toni Morrison's 1970 novel *The Bluest Eye* (broadcast in April 2000), Winfrey tells viewers that reading the novel would "change the world," and she later included it on her list "25 Books Every Woman Should Read."[94] The novel features eleven-year-old Pecola, a Black girl who "prays for her eyes to turn blue so that she will be as beautiful and as beloved as all the blond, blue-eyed children in America."[95] Book Club readers likely connected Pecola to Winfrey, as her struggles with racist beauty ideals were by this time familiar to her viewers. On different episodes, she confesses to having used a clothespin on her nose as a child (attempting to make it smaller) and to her urgent desire for "the bangs like the little white girls had."[96] On *The Bluest Eye* episode, Winfrey explains that her only photograph of her grandmother, which sits on her desk, is of Hattie Mae holding the white child of her employers in Mississippi. While Hattie Mae often chastised young Oprah, when her grandmother spoke of those white children "there would be this sort of glow inside her." Winfrey says, "When I grew up as a child ain't nobody's eyes were lighting up at all."[97]

Winfrey's self-disclosures combines with the experience of reading Morrison's first novel to force some white viewers to question their own complicity in this system. One of the dinner guests recalls that as a child her mother made her stop being friends with a Black girl, and this memory, combined with the successive experiences of reading *The Bluest Eye* twice and discussing it on the air with a diverse group of women, makes her ask an uncomfortable question: "Did I make that girl wish her eyes were blue?" As Kimberly Chabot Davis notes, this perspective-taking, empathetic response was at the very least "radically unsettling" to the white woman's sense of self and systemic position, and this recurred on several episodes featuring Black authors.[98]

Some of the novels Winfrey chose, and the on-air discussions she led about them, situated the intersectional experiences of Black women firmly in the South. For example, by choosing Lalita Tademy's *Cane River* for the Book Club, Winfrey facilitated her largely white viewership's engagement with the legacy of exploitation of Black women by white men as part and parcel of the sexual economy of slavery. The novel was an interesting choice not just for its subject matter but also because of its author's similarities to Winfrey. As the daughter of generations of Louisianans, Tademy identifies as a member of the southern diaspora. She describes her strong connections to her "southern roots" on the biography page of her website, calling her parents' household in California "Louisiana West" and noting that they maintained "a steady supply of grits, gumbo, cornbread, and collard greens, and a stream of other transplanted southerners eager to share their 'back-home' stories."[99] Also like Winfrey, Tademy battled the various obstacles to Black women's success in sexist, white supremacist, capitalist America, and she beat the odds and won. "For two decades," Tademy explains, "I had hoisted myself upward, hand over hand up the corporate ladder, until I was a vice president for a Fortune 500 high-technology company in Silicon Valley." But, unlike Winfrey, once she had achieved "a coveted position" ("for which I had spent my life preparing," she says), Tademy could not help but look back.[100]

In the author's note at the beginning of *Cane River*, Tademy describes her own journey back to her regional roots. "I found myself secretly thinking about [her great-grandmother] Emily, who she was, how she came to be," she explains. So she did more than look back; she immersed herself in the stories of her maternal ancestors. In the mid-1990s, "driven by a hunger [she] could not name," Tademy quit her job and started traveling to Louisiana to dig through archives, pore over personal papers, work with a genealogist, and interview family members and locals. After two years of research, she began to write by hand the "individual dramas" of the enslaved women in her family tree, from "daughter to mother," all the way to her great-great-great-great grandmother, Suzette, in the 1830s.[101] These handwritten notes became Tademy's first novel, *Cane River*, which Winfrey chose for her Book Club in 2001.

In the afterword, "The Inevitable Telling of *Cane River*," Tademy tells readers that Emily's story, and the story of each of the women in her family, is "a universal story of resilience and strength."[102] This claim that any reader could relate is, of course, classic *Oprah*, and a major general selling point of the Book Club. But *Cane River* is a specific story that details the intersecting oppressions of enslaved women based on archival material, oral histories, and spending lots of time in the Deep South. As she dug into her genealogical research, Tademy kept wanting to go deeper. "I just couldn't keep away from them," she says. Tademy "felt a calling," Winfrey explains on the Book Club episode about *Cane River*, adding, "You know I believe in that."[103]

While Winfrey opens the *Cane River* episode by claiming that its "themes are universal," the novel is about the specific experiences of several generations of Tademy's enslaved foremothers who were sexually exploited by white men in antebellum Louisiana. *Cane River* opens with Suzette getting slapped by her mistress on her ninth birthday in 1834 to teach her "her place," an opening that centers violence against Black women in this story. Suzette's "place" is in the house, serving the family that owns her, but it is also a place of submission to a white man's repeated rapes, which began when she was only thirteen years old. In the dinner discussion, Winfrey underscores not just the physical cruelty of slavery for women but also the emotional trauma; she marvels at the psychological violence in the novel. She explains: "I thought the real horror, aside from the beatings, aside from everything else, is having no choice." Tademy agrees enthusiastically, explaining that the "brutality" was not just physical: "It's of the spiritual and emotional sort and its dominance and what you do with that dominance and what you do to crush spirit."[104]

In the novel and in the Book Club discussion, resistance to the oppressive forces of race, sex, and class is a prevalent theme. In that first scene, the just-slapped young Suzette carefully chooses "Madame's favorite" rosebush and urinates on it as revenge, an act which prompts a "You go, girl" from one of the invited dinner guests. This is patented *Oprah*: the idea that even in slavery women could fight back and improve their own circumstances by virtue of their individual strength and will. Tademy reinforces this message. Frequently relying on the lifestyle-feminist concept of "choice," she says that the women in her family "were victimized, but ... made a choice not to become victims."[105] These choices, according to Tademy, included relationships between white men and enslaved women. Tademy writes of complicated interracial relationships that are violent and exploitive, but such relationships could also be strategic, she argues. The careful shaping and manipulation of white men's emotions and behaviors was a subtle strategy of resistance used by her ancestors across these generations.

Colorism and the prizing of lighter skin thus becomes a means of survival and opportunity in the novel, a theme that Winfrey says she knew was "going to touch a nerve" with her audience.[106] An obvious product of white supremacy—both literally, as lighter skin tones among enslaved populations and free people of color were the product of often-coercive and frequently violent liaisons between white men and Black women, and ideologically, as the variations in tones bred intraracial discrimination—colorism plays a complex role in this novel, as light skin confers both privileges and unique dangers. Tademy explains her own struggle with colorism, a direct product of these women's experiences and constrained choices, in her author's note: "My great-grandmother Emily was color-struck. She barely tolerated being called colored, and never Negro. My mother, the lightest of the grandchildren, with skin white enough to pass if she chose, was a favorite of hers." Tademy writes that she was "unsympathetic" to her great-grandmother's colorism, but she also recognized Emily's strength, her "ability to stare down the defeats of her life and aggressively claim joy as her right, in ways I had never learned to do."[107] And so in *Cane River* colorism is a choice, a brutal but strategic means of survival among enslaved women.

Frequent viewers knew that Winfrey had described her own experiences of colorism on air. In fact, she claims that this kind of discrimination helped to determine her path. She has called herself a "fudgie," explaining, "There are fudgies, gingerbreads, and vanilla creams. In society, as little Negro children, we were taught that the browner you were the tougher time you were gonna have, so a lot of little blacks are born and their parents look at them and say, 'We'll educate her.' That's what they did with me."[108] But Winfrey does not relegate her experiences of colorism to the Jim Crow past, and Tademy's real-life inspiration for *Cane River* does not allow readers and viewers to relegate it to fiction. Rather, Winfrey invites the Black women among her dinner guests to discuss their own experiences.

The present manifestations of colorism are a sore subject, according to Tademy, who expresses surprise on the episode that "the reaction I've gotten is that I really shouldn't have written about that." On the other hand, she says some readers told her that "this explained to them for the first time what some of the origins of that might be. And it brought them a little closer to, if not forgiveness, at least understanding." This prompts one guest to confess, "My own parents were brought together with the idea that they would produce light-skinned children." Dinner guest Stephanie, who struggled with the darker tone of her own skin, explains that the novel for her "conjured up my own family history," specifically "a strong memory" of her grandmother "gently" leaving her at home when she went shopping, "because she could pass and I couldn't." *Cane River* prompted her to see colorism as a dysfunctional tool wielded by Tademy's forebears within an oppressive system: "Immediately ... I [realized] that it was important for survival, for protection, and for equality that you did have to bleach the line." It was, she concludes, a "twisted" and "sad" strategy that mothers took to protect their children. Tademy chimes in that the traumatic context of the history of rape under slavery represented an "opportunity" for women to use this violence to create a better "potential path" for their light-skinned children, who would necessarily be "treated better" according to the illogic of white supremacy.[109]

Even as this discussion serves as a site of bonding between the Black women at the dinner, Winfrey treats *Cane River* as an opportunity to educate her white viewers, explaining that this problem reverberates: "According to our message boards, people are still treated better." She continues: "[O]f all the white people who are reading this book for the first time—and I know I've done a lot of shows over the years on race—it always comes as a shock that there was, first of all, a hierarchy. Because to a lot of people we're just—you're black, you're black, you're just black, everybody's black."[110] Sparked by Tademy's own history and her fictional version of it, Winfrey leads her viewers into a discussion of this touchy aspect of what Saidiya Hartman calls the "afterlife of slavery," or the continuing effects of the institution on Black lives and transatlantic cultures.[111]

In *Cane River*, each generation of women picks up the burden carried by the previous ones, and light skin tone is an important tool of resistance to the complex sexual-racial-economic hierarchies in both enslaved and white communities. "The women of *Cane River* had choices, and they made choices," Tademy explains on *Oprah*, "but they were far closer to survival choices." Even as Tademy's foremothers sacrificed their very bodies to white men to protect their children, they remained determined to improve their lot in the limited confines of enslaved status. Tademy offers an intergenerational network in *Cane River* of women who focus on improving their social situation themselves, in defiance of white supremacy and patriarchy. Tademy argues that these women, through their "choice not to become victims" in the context of overwhelming oppression, "definitely cleared the path" for her.[112]

In this and other Book Club episodes, Winfrey in some ways sublimates her own feminism, relying instead on Black women authors to give voice to it through their novels and on-air discussions. Tademy is adamant about emphasizing the intersections of race, gender, and class that determined her ancestors' experiences and explicit about forcing readers to understand their "interior lives." She explains on the Book Club episode: "One of the things that I did when I was writing the book, I was determined that I wasn't going to give the reader the excuse of saying, 'Well, this is horrific because there was a beating.' And so my mantra when I was writing was 'no whips, no chains,' but I'm going to show you brutality, and it's not brutality of the physical sort." She continues: "One of the things I wanted to do when I wrote the book is I wanted to have it be not something that you were looking and saying, 'This is what a slave's life was like.' I wanted it to be where you felt that you were the person."[113]

Tademy's goal, then, was not simply to induce empathy but also to change the historical perspective of readers and viewers. In keeping with the Black feminist mandate to confront historical trauma in productive ways, Tademy unequivocally cites her "slave roots" as a major "source of strength," and Winfrey emphatically agrees. One of the dinner guests asks Tademy, "[Do you] hear the whispers of your ancestors telling you, 'Well done. Our story has been told'?" Tademy answers that she feels that these women are part of her now. Winfrey replies, "That's interesting, because I've always felt that. I've always felt shored up by my ancestors, even though I don't know their names, and I, you know, say—when I go into a meeting, I bring, you know, Sojourner and Harriet and everybody in that—is sitting in that meeting with me. I feel shored up by them." Relying on the metaphor of grandmothers as "bridges," Winfrey concludes: "[A]s a descendant of slaves myself in this country, I just feel that what has gone on before, what they were able to do ... what they were able to do with nothing, that means the possibilities for our lives today and the lives of our children [are] really boundless and that we need to, as—in the words of James Baldwin—understand that our crowns have been paid for, and we all need to put them on our head and wear [them]."[114]

Even though devoted Book Club participants read 543 pages of Tademy's words about her Louisiana ancestors, Winfrey expertly exerts influence over the message, always getting the final word. When asked by an audience member why she always chooses "books with angst in them," Winfrey replies: "Books are about life. And life is about knowing you can triumph no matter what your circumstances are, you are not a victim. You can triumph. So all the stories I choose, in one way or another, are always ultimately about triumph. You can triumph over your outcomes."[115] The Book Club episodes featuring novels by and about Black women offer an explicitly radical version of feminism that asks Winfrey's viewers to consider the intersectionality of race and gender and to examine their own roles in the white supremacist system. At the same time, Winfrey's feminist framing always firmly positions these texts within neoliberal exhortations of individual uplift and self-transformation.

Winfrey's was a message that sold well. As a media product, Winfrey's late 1990s pivot to lifestyle feminism garnered industry accolades almost immediately, including a Peabody Award and, in 1997, the title "Television Performer of the Year" from TV *Guide*. As part of this turn, the monthly Book Club was enormously successful, earning Winfrey the label "Most Important Person in Books and Media" from *Newsweek* within a year of the Club's first episode. By the end of the century, *The Oprah Winfrey Show* had an average of over five million viewers daily, but the Book Club episodes drew in up to thirteen million viewers by 1999, the midpoint of the six-year first run of the Club. During this initial run, each of Winfrey's picks graced best-seller lists for at least three months, and each went on to sell no fewer than three quarters of a million copies, even those that had been published years before. These astounding sales numbers made Winfrey "the largest seller of books in the contemporary marketplace," achieving what one Scribner executive called the "literary equivalent of inventing penicillin." Many of her authors became millionaires virtually overnight, while the publishing industry made $175 million off the Book Club, phenomena that *People* magazine cheekily called "Touched by an Oprah."[116]

"That Is Where I Come From"
Winfrey's *Beloved*

As her Book Club became an enormous success, Winfrey further capitalized on the intertextual possibilities of her brand of neoliberal Black feminism when she returned to the big screen in 1998. That year, Winfrey's decade-long passion project, a film version of Toni Morrison's novel *Beloved* (1987), was released to theaters nationwide. The Pulitzer Prize–winning novel features the story of a formerly enslaved woman, Sethe, who ran away from a plantation in Kentucky to live with her free mother-in-law, Baby Suggs, in Ohio. When slave catchers catch up with Sethe, she kills her one of her baby daughters rather than see her returned to bondage. Thereafter, Sethe and her family are haunted by the ghost of the murdered baby girl, who later assumes adult human form as Beloved. Through Sethe's harrowing experiences, Morrison leads readers through the Black feminist process of survival, reckoning with the past, and moving forward with the support of a community of women.[117]

Like Tademy, Morrison identified as part of the diaspora rather than as a southerner. In a 1998 interview, she spoke at length of her "complicated notion" of the region, which grew out of her parents' memories—her mother waxing nostalgic about growing up in Alabama and her father condemning his home state of Georgia as "the most racist state in the union."[118] Like Winfrey's mother, Morrison's parents went north as part of the Great Migration, but Morrison herself felt a "sense of community and belonging" when she traveled to the South. In her novels, Black characters, especially the women, often express "ambivalence" about the rural South, bred by Morrison's one-generation-removed experiences, the kind of mixed feelings that track through Winfrey's simultaneous disavowals of Mississippi and shout-outs to the women's community that fostered her there. While Winfrey rarely returns, Morrison's characters often do, so much so that one reviewer wrote, "you know sooner or later she's going to the South." Regional history thus infuses her novels, and there is often a "different sense of the South for men and women," born of "writing about the South" versus "writing in the South," as Carolyn Denard muses in an interview with Morrison.[119] Morrison offers a "reflective South" based on memories and reinterpretations in the vein of folk tale methodology. She explains: "The folk tales are told in such a way that whoever is listening is in it and can shape it and figure it out. It's not over just because it stops. It lingers and it's passed on. It's passed on and somebody else can alter it later."[120]

With Morrison's blessing, this kind of reinterpretation is precisely what Winfrey sought to do with the film version of *Beloved*. Although Oprah's Book Club was booming at this time, drawing hundreds of thousands of readers and millions of viewers each month, and Winfrey chose four other Morrison novels for her viewers to read along with her, she did not put *Beloved* on her official reading list. While it is surely the case that devoted *Oprah* fans were also inspired to read Morrison's novel, Winfrey saved her PR campaign for the film rather than the novel, thus expanding into yet another medium for the potential promotion of her own carefully calibrated version of feminism in the late 1990s. Kristal Brent Zook argued in the *New York Times* that "one could regard Oprah Winfrey's ownership of the film rights" to novels like *Beloved* as part of her "one-woman crusade to bring black feminist thought to popular culture."[121]

By opening with a scene in which the baby ghost wreaks havoc on the family home, prompting Sethe's sons to run away, Winfrey's film introduces itself firmly in the horror genre, and Winfrey, the beloved television host, is at the center of this horror as Sethe.[122] Of paramount concern to Morrison as she wrote *Beloved* was the "recuperation" of the lost "interior lives" of enslaved people. While scholar Markus Nehl sees *Beloved* as one of the first in a series of popular "neo-slave" texts that "counter the erasure of slavery from (white) memory," Morrison's novel does more than shatter silences.[123] In her book on the afterlives of plantations, Jessica Adams argues that violence is often absent in postbellum representations of slavery. Morrison's novel is a direct challenge to this sanitized nostalgia along the lines of what Adams calls the "wounds of returning," which are not a simple "longing for the past" but rather a condition in which "the past itself may return, inflicting new wounds and reopening old ones."[124] Morrison's novel explores this kind of reckoning, and, likewise, Winfrey's film version embraces the continued violence of slavery in later decades, beginning with the first chaotic scene.

While the terrible force of *Beloved* is invisible in the opening pages of the novel, flashbacks make the intersectional traumas of slavery visible and visceral. The film version marks scenes of the past with special lighting and younger actors. When young Sethe, played by Lisa Gay Hamilton, flees with her children on seeing the white men headed into her yard, she is shown from their perspective as they break into the shed. Young Sethe locks eyes defiantly with the camera, challenging both the slave catchers and white viewers to confront the horrors of white supremacy as her infant's blood streams down her dress. Winfrey's familiar voice narrates the flashback, forcing her fans to imagine their revered icon committing these desperate acts. After this scene, Winfrey as Sethe expresses no regret. "I stopped him," she says flatly to Paul D, who was enslaved with her on the plantation years before. "I put my babies where they would be safe."[125]

Scholars argue that the traumas plaguing *Beloved* are not just those of slavery "in general" but also of rape in particular.[126] In the novel, there are numerous references to the sexual violence of slavery. In Winfrey's film *Beloved*, in a graphic flashback to the plantation Sweet Home, the camera takes the perspective of young Sethe as she is sexually assaulted and whipped. Winfrey again narrates the graphic scene, and it ends by lingering on the "tree" of scars on her back, a physical legacy of that attack. This terrorism exists not just in the past or in her memories but also in the present through the "spiteful" presence of the ghost *Beloved*.[127]

As a survival tactic in response to this continuous cycle of pain, the characters in *Beloved* deploy psychological repression as a strategy of resistance. Baby Suggs has lost all memories of her children except for one, while others "work hard to remember as close to nothing as was safe" and spend their days doing the "serious work of beating back the past."[128] *Beloved*, then, was Morrison's, and later Winfrey's, representation of what bell hooks calls "lingering emotional suffering"—historical pain with present repercussions.[129] Although they are difficult to access through traditional historical methodology, the deeper stories of enslaved people are important not just historically but also for the present, Morrison claims: "The struggle to forget, which was important in order to survive, is fruitless, and I want to make it fruitless."[130] Deploying a Black feminist approach to critical memory, *Beloved* forces readers and viewers to confront slavery in the United States not as a past institution but as, hooks argues, "a tragedy of such ongoing magnitude that folks suffer, anguish it today."[131] As Amy, the "whitegirl" who midwifes Sethe's daughter Denver during the escape from Kentucky ("the last thing you'd expect to help," Sethe marvels to Paul D) tells Sethe as she massages her feet, torn from running, "Anything dead coming back to life hurts."[132]

This confrontation with the past runs the gamut of emotions. In the opening pages of the novel, Morrison describes the house as "spiteful" and "full of a baby's venom" that makes its living inhabitants into "victims."[133] Likewise, in Winfrey's *Beloved*, the baby ghost's pain manifests as violent anger in the very first scene. Black feminist theorists have long noted the place of rage in their activism.[134] Brittney Cooper explains that avoidance of anger is both a survival and a resistance strategy; as she puts it, "respectability politics are at their core a rage-management project."[135] As viewers see in the first scene of the film *Beloved*, in which an unseen force upends furniture, slams doors, smashes mirrors, and hurls a dog against the wall, *Beloved*'s rage is destructive, not productive. Morrison explains: "There is a necessity for remembering the horror, but of course there's a necessity for remembering it in a manner in which it can be digested, in a manner in which the memory is not destructive." Writing the novel was, for Morrison, "a way of confronting it and making it possible to remember."[136] The learned behavior of silencing painful memories, represented viscerally in *Beloved* by the bit secured in enslaved peoples' mouths for punishment, prevents reckoning with the past as much as the fear of resurrecting that pain; silence and the suppression of rage go hand in hand. But "interrogating" interior lives, as Winfrey urges her audience to do, is crucial for individual healing and collective resistance. In *Beloved*, for this reckoning to be productive rather than simply retraumatizing, it must involve collectivity: listening to and linking with foremothers, and forging a community of women in the present.[137]

Morrison's *Beloved*, and by extension Winfrey's film version, can thus be seen as forms of resistance themselves, of giving voice to forcibly suppressed historical and emotional truths. Sethe repressed her memories and is forced into a confrontation with the past in the form of her resurrected daughter. This is an especially dangerous process for Sethe because it is done in isolation, which further exacerbates Sethe's suffering in the present. Morrison explains: "And no one speaks, no one tells the story about himself or herself unless forced. They don't want to talk, because they're afraid of it. . . . But when they do say it, and hear it, and look at it, and share it, they are not only one, they're two, and three, and four, you know? The collective sharing of that information heals the individual—and the collective."[138]

And so Sethe is saved in the end by a multigenerational community of women. First, her daughter Denver, exhausted, agoraphobic, and starving, hears the ghost of Baby Suggs urging her to fight back, and she reaches out to the local women who had revered her grandmother. They may have spurned and gossiped about Sethe for years, but when these women hear of the return of the slain baby in the form of Beloved—the very embodiment of past traumas that many of them have worked hard to leave behind—they come together in solidarity. The women meet outside of Sethe's house, gathering in groups of twos and threes, eventually numbering thirty. They surround the gate, waving Bibles and spiritual talismans and singing hymns.[139]

Summoned by this primal keening, the collective song of the intersectional traumas of slavery, Winfrey as Sethe appears with Beloved on the porch. The sound seems to summon the very site of Sethe's foremost trauma: when she sees Denver's white male employer in his wagon on the road beyond the women, she mistakes him for the slave catcher from years before, and she runs to him with a kitchen knife, determined to attack the source of the evil rather than her own beloved this time. Unlike the flashback to Beloved's slaying, Winfrey plays Sethe in this present repeat of the scene, and viewers thus watch her—daytime talk queen, media mogul, the wealthiest Black woman in the world—react to and on the trauma of slavery. Now in the maternal role herself, Denver grabs Sethe, and the women surround her as Beloved screams and disappears. The women have successfully confronted their painful collective history, and, as a sisterhood, they vanquish its embodiment.[140]

Although Winfrey claimed that she stayed true to Morrison's novel—"I just gave you the ending that was in the book," she explained later on her show—there is a crucial difference.[141] As scholar Yvette Christiansë points out, Sethe's experience indicates that recovering memories and confronting the past are not a wholly "positive" experience that renders suppressed peoples visible. Rather, the confrontation is traumatic, and this kind of reckoning does not necessarily heal, or even close, historical wounds.[142] Moreover, in the novel, it is unclear whether the demon Beloved has been banished successfully, and the narrator warns of "roaming loneliness" and of mysterious footprints by the stream near the house in the final chapter. It is an ambiguous ending, and an ominous one, with the narrator cautioning three times that it is "not a story to pass on."[143] After years of terrorism, a collective confrontation with the past frees Sethe, but the narrative does not end there, and it is clear that this kind of reckoning is a process that takes time and requires constant care from the community.

But Winfrey's film does not reference this last chapter. Instead, the final three scenes make an explicitly generational argument, beginning with the youngest generation. Overcoming her fears with some prompting by her deceased grandmother, Denver follows the tried-and-true Winfrey path. She transforms into a newly bold woman with her own opinions who works long hours to support her mother and to gain admission to Oberlin College. The film then turns to the middle generation, represented by Winfrey's Sethe. After Beloved disappears, Sethe, beaten and broken, takes to her bed. When Sethe cries that Beloved, her "best thing," has left her, Paul D reassures her, "You your best thing, Sethe. You are." "Me?" she replies. "Me?"[144] These lines echo Winfrey's daily televised mantra to "remember your spirit," and the scene ends on a hopeful note, indicating that Paul D will help this strong but damaged women to recover.

The final scene of the film refers back to Black foremothers. During the filming of *Beloved*, Winfrey kept close at hand some slavery memorabilia she had collected, especially two framed bills of sale from auctions from the 1840s listing first names and prices. On the set, she told Roger Ebert, she used these documents to prepare for scenes: "I had these in my trailer. Before some scenes, I would light candles and say their names. These are ledgers from plantations. I would say their names and their ages and their prices and this one where they are listed along with the cows and how many plows and how many mules. I would try to call them in. Call them in with a sense of reverence, because I always thought this was bigger than my own little self."[145] Winfrey dedicated scenes to individuals in these documents—"Sue and Bess and Sara"—explaining to director Jonathan Demme that she was not so much acting as "channeling," "open[ing] up and receiv[ing]," feeling the spirits of enslaved forebears "many, many, many times over" as she worked on the film.[146]

Winfrey was thus acutely aware of the burden of history involved in bringing Morrison's narrative to the big screen, and this is evident in the last scene, featuring the spiritual leader Baby Suggs. In a flashback to the clearing in the woods where she leads the community in worship, Baby Suggs tells the rapt crowd, "Love your heart. This. This is the prize. Amen. This the prize."[147] Save an aerial shot of the house, this is the end of the film, leaving the audience with Baby Suggs as a representation of the crucial teachings of the foremothers of Black feminism. Sethe/Winfrey, her own "best thing," will find herself and "remember her spirit." And Denver, supporting her family and bound for Oberlin, represents the uplift mission of neoliberal feminism.[148]

Under Winfrey's care, then, *Beloved* became something different altogether. Reviewers noted the intertextuality of the film—not just the interplay between the movie and the book but also between the movie and the daily talk show. Novelist and film critic Stephen Hunter wrote in the *Washington Post*, "One can see no Oprah in Sethe, no zillionaire's vanity. And that gives great pause, and may be the movie's most powerful statement of possibility: that any Sethe could become an Oprah. It's a lesson to remember."[149] Another critic wrote that, in contrast to the novel, Winfrey's version of Sethe seems "so levelheaded that she could solve problems by talking them over with Oprah."[150] And Winfrey did discuss the "problems" of *Beloved* with her fans. Giving Sethe an additional voice on her television program, as it were, Winfrey did a special episode just on the film, treating it as a text for analysis in the same manner as her chosen novels.

"We asked how you felt about *Beloved* and got the biggest response ever," she proclaims in the opening promo. For the show, she chose seven viewers among the "six thousand or seven thousand" who wrote in to join Winfrey and director Demme for a dinner of "elegant Southern food"—a "meal Sethe would have been proud of"—on a set at Harpo Studios created especially for this purpose. The invited guests had obviously seen the film (the basic prerequisite for an invitation), but they were also frequent viewers of the daytime show, and most of them cite the novel in their reactions to the film as well. As always, Winfrey commanded the discussion of the film and used this interplay between the various media as a platform for her own brand of southern neoliberal feminism.[151]

Regarding the novel *Beloved*, bell hooks discusses the danger that the historical subject matter allows readers to assume the problems of racism are in the past. When the context is antebellum slavery, according to hooks, "readers are not compelled to relate that understanding to concrete contemporary circumstances." In fact, the graphic traumas of slavery may serve to enable readers to "trivialize contemporary pain," thus contributing to the "collective cultural refusal to assume any accountability for the psychological wounding of black people that continues into the present day."[152] Beyond this pitfall of relegating the effects of historical trauma to the past, Saidiya Hartman critiques the "casualness" and "routine display" of scenes of violence against enslaved people, cautioning against a simplistic theory in which such graphic depictions naturally or necessarily induce audience empathy.[153] By presiding over a carefully calibrated dinner conversation about the film, the novel on which it was based, and experiences of white supremacy in the present, Winfrey sought to challenge both receptive deflection and passive viewership. Over the course of the dinner discussion, Winfrey's *Beloved* episode became a site of individualized white consciousness-raising in a manner more explicit than most *Oprah* fare.

In the episode, in contrast to the universalization of personal experiences that is endemic to teletherapy, Winfrey emphasizes that white readers and viewers almost certainly had different relationships and reactions to *Beloved*. The show opens with an exploration of what the film taught some white viewers about their own positions in the white supremacist system. Renee, a southern white woman, had written to Winfrey that she was truly "disturbed" by the film. Winfrey has Renee read aloud portions of her letter, in which she confessed to being raised with "great pride" in her "heritage." She wrote that she was taught that African Americans were subhuman. Reading Morrison's novel, she confessed, didn't touch her, but the visual experience of the film did, changing her pride to shame. "Your movie," she wrote, "taught me that we did not create the animals. We were the animals." The film similarly affected invited guest Audrey: it had made her own family's role in white supremacy real for her, and she wrote to Winfrey that she had been contacted by a man who was a descendant of enslaved people owned by her ancestors. She had in her possession an inventory of the twenty people her family once owned, but when this man wrote to her, her feelings about this document changed. The individuals were embodied, or, as she put it, the "numbers have a name." Ashamed, she explains, "When I saw the tree on Sethe's back, I was shaking." Suddenly, she says at the dinner, "everything, my—my whole ancestry flashed before my eyes." Winfrey reads from a document Audrey brought detailing the whipping of an enslaved man who attempted to escape her ancestors. Even though Audrey had had these documents for years, the film made this history real for her, causing "gut-wrenching guilt."[154]

While there is a danger in viewership of what Hortense Spillers called the "pornotropes" of slavery, particularly sexual violence against Black women, translating into mere voyeurism, there are other pitfalls to the kinds of representation Winfrey crafted as well.[155] Saidiya Hartman worries that representations of the scenes of torture that were characteristic of American slavery tread the "uncertain line between witness and spectator" and often induce not empathy but rather mere "self-reflection." Examining the graphic depictions in abolitionist literature, she asks, "Can the white witness of the spectacle of suffering affirm the materiality of black sentience only by feeling for himself?" Renee's shame and Audrey's trembling while viewing *Beloved* run this risk, as Hartman describes it, of "a too-easy intimacy, the consideration of the self that occurs at the expense of the slaves' suffering, and the violence of the identification."[156]

Winfrey, however, sees the shame of her white guests as productive, something that makes this historical pain real in the present, and, crucially, she sees a reaction that she can guide. Even as they heatedly discuss the film, arguing over interpretations of certain scenes, Winfrey emphasizes that this narrative is not just fiction or, worse, just a good ghost story. She explains the story of Margaret Garner, the enslaved woman whose desperate actions inspired Morrison's novel, repeating emphatically, "This happened. That is what happened." Later in the show, scholar Henry Louis Gates Jr. affirms the significance of the historical inspiration for Morrison's fiction. It's a "heavy thing," he explains, to think in-depth about the very real effects slavery had on its victims.[157]

Even as she reiterates the history, Winfrey makes sure that the episode does not simply dwell in the past. When a guest tries to relegate white supremacy to the antebellum period, she corrects them: "Not just slavery, though. Not just slavery." The Black guests confirm this claim. Jo describes her reaction to the film: "I felt that it was my life. I don't have a slave catcher running after me trying to drag me back, but I still have these fears, and I still have these things that are chasing me. I remember leaving and having $5 in my pocket to raise my two children and—and being in fear. And to look back and see that that was happening then and it—similar circumstances [are] happening to me now." Winfrey manages the discussion so that it weaves evenly between past and present and fiction and reality as a consciousness-raising tool. By the end of the episode, even Brian, who at one point argued that white men were the most discriminated-against group, claims to understand the long legacy of slavery and how its impacts transcended generations: "[S]o ... there are things in society today that I wouldn't have thought about."[158]

Guilt and awareness are critical points in this discussion, but they are not the end goals. Winfrey forces her audience to see not just the realistic aspects of *Beloved* for African Americans but also the productive nature of the empathy engendered by this knowledge. She invites scholar Maxine Mimms to lead the audience through how to think critically about the film. "You really do have to think, 'If I were in her shoes or his shoes, what would I do?'" she tells her dinner companions. "And we've got to decide. How many of us could deal with death or murder in order to be free?" Winfrey repeatedly uses scholars to pose these more abstract questions, and she follows up by personalizing them. When Brian claims that harping on the traumas of slavery will keep Black people down, Winfrey retorts, "I am a descendant of slaves, and I couldn't be prouder of that." Brian responds that she's "an exception," to which Winfrey replies firmly, "No, I'm not." Doing the film, she claims, "empowered her" in new ways because it gave her a true "connection" to history: "Every day, Margaret Garner lived in the psychological space of knowing ... 'When I get home, my children may not be there.' ... And what it takes to do that and not go crazy. ... But somewhere inside her, she says, 'I believe I'm better than this.' ... That is where I come from. ... That is where you come from. That is where we come from."[159]

In her criticism of the "kitsch" response to Morrison's *Beloved*, Sabine Bröck posits that the reading of the novel as a "redemptive" mother-daughter narrative—particularly via the generational savior of Denver—

explains its popularity.[160] This reception potentially applies to Winfrey's personal response to the novel and indeed to her film. Winfrey's rereading of *Beloved* as a redemptive confrontation with the past flattens the original to fit it into her own feminist project, but it is also therefore productive for that project, if not for the more radical Black feminism associated with Morrison's work.

The question then becomes what to do with white people's potentially transformative reactions to her film. Winfrey sees her guests' white guilt as a productive opening into a deeper confrontation with the psychology of white supremacy. When Brian argues that feeling guilty does not foster "healthy peer relationships in America," Winfrey pushes back, pressuring him to see this confrontation with past white violence as useful: "But don't you want to acknowledge—don't you at least—at least now—now you can say, 'I feel somewhat—just something. Something opened inside of me and—and how terrible that was." Brian tries to change the subject, but William, a Black man, takes up Winfrey's cause, arguing that this kind of emotional reckoning can lead to action: "You can't stop there. You can feel it, and I want you to feel it, but we have to begin to effect change in this country at whatever level you—you can effect change." Renee immediately agrees: "Even just passing it on to my daughter, start in my own home." Winfrey, masterfully managing the arc of the discussion, seizes on this: "But if you, one person, Renee, come out of this movie, and you make the decision that you're gonna talk to your children and try to break down that look of righteousness ... that feeling of entitlement and righteousness with your children, then we have already won with this movie."[161] In other words, the guilt-ridden white mother, newly empowered by her engagement with Morrison's novel, Winfrey's film, her fellow discussants, and, of course, Winfrey herself, can teach her own children to break the cycle of white supremacy—an internal revolution rather than a systemic one in accordance with Winfrey's patented neoliberal feminism.

At the end of the episode, in a direct address to the home audience, Winfrey reiterates her mission: "One of the reasons I wanted to do *Beloved* and have talked about it so much is because it was a burning passion for ten years. And I believe it would do exactly what we saw happen in that dinner, allow people to experience and feel the humanity of a time and a people in a way that they hadn't before and just perhaps open their hearts just a little bit wider and start a discussion about who we all are, where we all come from, and what that means to all of us."[162] Doing the film did the same for Winfrey as she hoped for her guests; she reportedly went from an "awareness" of slavery to having "a sense of what slavery felt like."

She later explained that the conversations about "the physicality of slavery" overshadowed its "real legacy," which was "the strength and courage to survive."[163] The film *Beloved* was her attempt at rectifying and deepening American understandings of the past, with the accompanying *Oprah Winfrey Show* episode to help guide interpretations of her feminist take on this history.

However, while Winfrey's earnest "change your life" mission was ratings gold on daytime television, and the *Beloved* episode was watched by millions of faithful viewers, it did not translate quite so successfully to the big screen. *Beloved* was a "very public failure" that earned "less than half of what it cost to make."[164] Winfrey's acting was almost universally praised: *Rolling Stone* gushed over her "pitch-perfect performance" and mused about Oscar buzz, while a *Washington Post* reviewer said simply, "My god, what a blaze of genius she is."[165] But critics also lamented the film's poor translation of what Roger Ebert called "Morrison's labyrinthine structure" and its length of nearly three hours.[166] One later summed up the failure this way: "After ten years of struggling to get the film made, *Beloved* opened and *Bride of Chucky* beat it at the box office." Winfrey was not prepared for this response. "I didn't know what the hell *Bride of Chucky* was," she later confessed.[167] She fell into a depression for several weeks, saying that she "took it personally." "Devastated," "deeply saddened," and wondering why her fans didn't even go to see *Beloved*, she said, "I held a grudge about it for a long time."[168]

Struggling to pull herself together and to soldier on with her daily show, Winfrey took her own advice and consulted one of her self-help gurus, Gary Zukav. He pulled her out of this downward spiral by making her refocus on her intention with the film.[169] Through the *Oprah* episodes that focused on Black feminist texts, including the *Beloved* dinner, Winfrey realized her intention, and in doing so she honed her own version of southern neoliberal feminism. After *Beloved*, she continued with these kinds of texts in her Book Club, pitching them to her devoted audience, which was, unlike the film audience, primed by years of daily viewing to be receptive to her message.

Winfrey consistently claimed that her Book Club was a core part of her mission to change viewers' lives. Of course, exposure to fictionalized experiences of white supremacy does not necessitate understanding, empathy, awareness of privilege, or antiracism. As Kimberly Chabot Davis notes, many critics charge that readers' reactions represent white, middle-class pity, a kind of "emotional catharsis" that "does little to challenge the status quo" and "all too often results in political inertia and complacency." This is aided by Winfrey's universalizing gospel of women's self-help, which results in "a troubling tendency" to "minimize racial difference in their zeal to connect with the characters 'as women.'"[170] Universalizing the historical experiences of Black characters downplays the damage of white supremacy and preempts the psychological reckoning that many Black feminists deem necessary for healing and progress. This kind of apolitical sympathy is not just unhelpful, Davis explains, it is actively obstructionist. According to scholar Lauren Berlant, it is a "privatiz[ation of] the political" that supports hegemonic readings and leads to no "substantial social change."[171]

But, as we have seen, Winfrey carefully inserted her personal experiences and some of the core concepts of Black feminism into the Book Club episodes alongside her neoliberal mission. This intersectional potential is intertextual, via Winfrey's own ancestral and rhetorical relationship with slavery, novels about Black women that address the gendered exploitation of racial slavery, the episodes on which Winfrey discusses these themes with both Black and white guests over dinner, and Winfrey's filmic and televised takes on *Beloved*, Morrison's feminist masterpiece. The *Oprah* episodes featuring texts by Black women about southern Black women offer a more explicitly radical version of feminism that asks Winfrey's viewers to consider the intersectionality of race, gender, and class and to examine their own roles in the white supremacist system. At the same time, Winfrey's feminist framing always firmly positions these texts within neoliberal calls for individual uplift and self-transformation.

"Remember your spirit." "Make the connection." "Live your best life." At the turn of the twenty-first century, Oprah Winfrey was the wealthiest and most famous southern woman on the planet, and she was also the most popular conduit of regional feminism. But it was her own unique brand, an expert blend of her experiences, media savvy, ancestry, and both long-standing and newer forms of American feminism. Winfrey is well known for the promotion of self-help consumerism—Nicole Aschoff includes Winfrey in her analysis of "prophets of capital" on a list with former Facebook COO Sheryl "Lean In" Sandberg and former Microsoft CEO Bill Gates—and the individualized self-improvement associated with neoliberal feminism.[172] But, outside of the academy, Winfrey was also a primary source of Black feminism, even though she never used the self-descriptors "feminist" or "activist," and certainly not "radical," on her show or in interviews. Her racial and gender politics were rooted in her southern past, connecting the historical experiences of Black women in the region to her own extraordinary American success story. "I bring my stuff with me," she told *Newsweek* in 2001. "My history, my past. Mississippi, Nashville. I'm coming with the sistahs in the church.... And then there we all are, sitting up in your meeting, at your table, with the marketing directors."[173] By creating a parasocial, interracial sisterhood of millions, Winfrey offered a complicated form of southern feminism that was alternately both neoliberal and radical, individualized and collective, universal and intersectional. Of the forms of feminism examined herein, Winfrey's was by far the most popular, so much so that it went global and spawned new versions that I examine in the epilogue.

EPILOGUE

"Just a Southern Girl in a Southern World"

SOUTHERN FEMINIST POP CULTURE IN
THE EARLY TWENTY-FIRST CENTURY

At the dawn of the twenty-first century, in a context in which neoconservative politics and the attendant discourse of postfeminism thrived, Ashley Sayeau, writing for *The Nation*, deemed southern feminists to be an "endangered species."[1] Yet, at the same time, regional popular culture remained a vital source of feminist ideas. Indeed, one of the first literary controversies of the century involved a major revision of the white South's treasured *Gone with the Wind*. Publication of Alice Randall's *The Wind Done Gone*, a take on the Old South classic from the perspective of Scarlett O'Hara's enslaved half-sister, was delayed by an injunction from Margaret Mitchell's estate, based on the claim that Randall's novel was copyright infringement and "unabated piracy" of Mitchell's classic narrative. After the U.S. Court of Appeals overturned the injunction, *The Wind Done Gone* enjoyed much critical acclaim. Randall has said that she intended for her novel to be an "antidote," and the world of *The Wind Done Gone*, according to Lisa Schwarzbaum, is "a burlesque" in which enslaved people "are canny and resourceful and really run the place," while "the whites are incompetent weaklings."[2]

Just as *Gone with the Wind* has been dissected and examined, the feminism of *The Wind Done Gone* has generated debate among critics and scholars. Randall's subversion of *Gone with the Wind* meets Toni Morrison's mandate to probe the "interior lives" of enslaved women, giving voice to traumas and triumphs as well as upending racial hierarchies. Scarlett is the Other here, a vapid, needy caricature, while her biracial half-sister Cynara, daughter of Gerald O'Hara and Mammy, is the fully fleshed-out character.[3] The standpoint theory that undergirds this revised version of *Gone with the Wind* positions Randall's text within the Black feminist pop cultural genealogy that includes more famous and celebrated works like *The Color Purple* and *Beloved*. And after six decades of nostalgic celebration of Mitchell's Old South narrative, the popularity of *The Wind Done Gone* at the beginning of the twenty-first century signaled new possibilities for southern feminist popular culture.[4] At the same time, feminist texts emerged about and from the South, trafficking in familiar images of regional feminism, like the traumatized daughter and mother in Callie Khouri's directorial debut *The Divine Secrets of the Ya-Ya Sisterhood* (2002), as well as offering fresh takes, like the "messy," intersectional navigation of racist and sexist stereotypes in the millennial urban South on the BET series *Being Mary Jane*.[5]

Likewise, some of the cultural producers examined in previous chapters continued to evolve along expected trajectories and even diverge into more radical realms in the early twenty-first century.[6] Perhaps not surprisingly, the most famous of them dominated headlines. *Newsweek* deemed the turn of the millennium the "Age of Oprah," and, even then, Winfrey had yet to hit her peak.[7] *O* magazine, a kind of "print version of the talk show," launched in 2000, outsold major competitors, and had a circulation of two million by the following year. Winfrey branched out in other ways too, cofounding Oxygen Media for women, producing the award-winning Broadway musical version of *The Color Purple*, and teaching for a time at Northwestern University's business school with her longtime partner Stedman Graham. In patented *Oprah* fashion, the class included guest speakers like Coretta Scott King, who spoke on "adapting strategies of the civil rights movement to modern business."[8]

All the while, Winfrey's daily show remained the major earner in its genre, and Oprah's Book Club—the biggest book club in the world—continued to boost both book sales and daytime viewership. In June 2000, Winfrey chose a novel about white southern women that challenged readers and viewers to think about the structural and psychological violence of racism and to consider the role of white supremacist patriarchy on a global stage. In *The Poisonwood Bible* (1998), Barbara Kingsolver explores the experiences of the Prices, a Baptist missionary family from Georgia, during their turbulent time in the Congo as it transitioned from colonial rule to independence in the early 1960s. Southern patriarchy serves as a cipher for Western colonialism in this novel, and Kingsolver connects the naïveté of the southern preacher's wife (and the constraints on her) to imperialism, making the personal intensely political.[9] As a Book Club pick, what makes this choice especially interesting is that Winfrey featured it just as she began to get involved in development projects in South Africa. Even as she promoted a novel that heavily criticized U.S. imperialism, Winfrey the millionaire media star was forging her own relationship to the global phenomenon.

Scholars of neoliberal globalization argue that it positions women as both victims in need of rescue and as the ideal capitalist subjects, the "faces of international development." This rhetoric traffics in a kind of "global girl power" that posits that women and girls, if given the appropriate boost, will uplift their families and communities from poverty and join the international market as financially empowered individuals, thus eclipsing questions of structural inequality and social justice in favor of the capitalist economic growth that in fact facilitates those inequities.[10] Many international corporations promote this gendered message. Nike, the founder of the "Girl Effect" campaign in 2004, has been the leader among them, using a familiar "third-wave" rhetoric of empowerment and choice to promote its initiatives. "When one girl finds her power to make different choices that change her life," the Girl Effect website argues, she "inspires others to do so too," igniting "a ripple effect that impacts her family, her community, her country."[11] This rhetoric of individual empowerment as the answer to global structural inequality smartly sidesteps opposition to oppressive structures, offering instead a kind of "free market" gender theory in which each woman and girl, with some corporate philanthropic aid, can achieve equality themselves through participation in the neoliberal economy.[12] Winfrey has been a vocal backer of the Nike campaign, rhetorically and financially, since its inception, and she has even promoted it on her show.

But, perhaps predictably, Winfrey has gone one step further by not just participating in international campaigns but actually starting one herself. At the turn of the twenty-first century, she became "frustrated" by what she called "charity from a distance," in which she would write checks to organizations without feeling that "connection."[13] In 2000, the same year that she featured *The Poisonwood Bible* on her show, Winfrey promised Nelson Mandela, whom she called her "greatest living mentor," that she would build a school in his home country, pledging $10 million to the project.[14] As a first fulfillment of that promise, she and her staff spent three weeks in South Africa—which she called "the single greatest experience of my life"—in 2002, just after she launched the South African edition of O magazine.[15] Over the winter holiday season, Winfrey and her team visited orphanages and schools, where they handed out gifts (school supplies, shoes, clothing, toys, a month's worth of food, and "something most African girls have never seen: Black dolls") to fifty thousand children.[16] "I realized in those moments why I was born, why I'm not married, why I don't have children of my own," she later explained. "Because these are my children." She compared her own experience growing up in poverty to the deprivation she saw in rural South Africa, arguing that with education "you can overcome poverty and despair in your life." "I am living proof of that," she added.[17] Inspired by her trip, Winfrey resolved to do more.

At a star-studded event in 2007, the Oprah Winfrey Leadership Academy for Girls opened in Henley-on-Klip, South Africa, after a $40 million investment from Winfrey with the stated goal of "encourage[ing] each girl to develop her critical thinking and to create the best life possible for her, and then use her life in service to others, no matter her calling." The Academy operates on the same principle as *The Oprah Winfrey Show*: "Do the emotional and spiritual work required to develop authentic power (using your personality to do your soul's work), and you will always be rewarded."[18] Out of 3,500 applicants, Winfrey personally interviewed and chose 152 girls with what she called that "'It' quality."[19] Upon graduation, Winfrey promised, the girls of the inaugural class would "go to the university of their choice anywhere in the world." At graduation four years later, the girls, who called Winfrey "Mom," claimed to be more "ladylike," less "myopic," and in tune with their "greater purpose."[20]

While neoliberal feminism often features middle-class white women as the mentors to working-class women and women of color, in Winfrey's brand, successful Black women were the educators, missionaries, and agents of uplift to the downtrodden women of the world. As with anything Winfrey does, her new mission generated some criticism. In her analysis of the Leadership Academy, Jennifer Harris notes that while many applauded Winfrey's generosity, others critiqued the "excesses"—*Newsweek* called them "Oprahlicious specifications"—of the school, "including china settings and 200-thread-count sheets handpicked by Winfrey, a library with a fireplace, tennis courts, and spacious closets."[21] In *Salon*, Rebecca Traister defended Winfrey and noted the obvious racism in the criticism of the Academy. Americans "don't bat an eye at white heiresses dancing on banquettes," she argued, "but impoverished black girls sleeping on nice-ish sheets?"[22] Winfrey defended her decorating decisions, explaining that the first plans she got from builders looked more like a "chicken coop" than a school: "It was clear that the attitude was, 'These are poor African girls. Why spend all this on them?'"[23] In its emphasis on "gentility and decorum," the Leadership Academy borrows heavily from the model of Miss Porter's, a boarding school for the rich in New England. This historical strategy of "uplift" and respectability politics is a longtime, if controversial, strategy of African American resistance that dovetailed exactly with Winfrey's self-help spirituality.[24] As such, her international philanthropy aimed at underprivileged girls is perhaps the purest distillation of Winfrey's neoliberal feminism, shorn, in this context, of the radical implications seen in the discussions that occasionally graced her Book Club.

But even if it "fulfills an outsider's vision and not a community's," as one critic claims, Winfrey's Leadership Academy is not a superficial intervention in the lives of women abroad.[25] As Harris notes, unlike other celebrity causes in Africa in the late twentieth century, Winfrey's project involves direct, sustained action: she maintains ultimate control of her philanthropic endeavors, and her involvement in the girls' lives lasts many years, from primary schooling through university and, in some cases, beyond. Moreover, although bourgeois uplift through education might be the obvious route to success via the Academy, the idea has some activist backing—Nelson Mandela prompted Winfrey to commit to the project. Harris argues that this connection to a famed freedom fighter who targeted the system of apartheid offered Winfrey the opportunity to "participate vicariously in the civil rights movement" and to help lead this movement in its early twenty-first-century projects.[26]

Winfrey maintains relationships with some of her South African students well into their adulthood. In 2013, she sat down with nine of her "college-age daughters," graduates from the Leadership Academy who were attending universities in the United States, to watch *Life Is But a Dream*, the first video autobiography of pop music superstar Beyoncé. After this group viewing, Winfrey conducted an exclusive interview with the star just hours before the film's debut on HBO. Her girls, Winfrey told Beyoncé, were awed and inspired and had exclaimed after watching, "Mama O, she's just like us!"[27]

At the time, Beyoncé was known for her "girl power" pop songs like "Survivor" and "If I Were a Boy," but, like Winfrey, she had generally taken care to avoid associations with overt feminist politics. In *Life Is But a Dream*, however, Beyoncé removes this mask, making some classic liberal feminist claims. In the scenes featuring her performance of "Run the World (Girls)" at the 2011 Billboard Music Awards, Beyoncé explains: "We have to step up as women and take the lead and reach as high as humanly possible. That's what I'm going to do, and that's my philosophy and what 'Girls' is all about."[28]

Even as she sat down with Winfrey to discuss her deeply personal documentary, Beyoncé was starting to work on her self-titled next album, which would win an NAACP Image Award for Outstanding Album and featured increasingly feminist ideas, lyrics, and imagery. In case this was not clear to all fans, Beyoncé performed at the 2014 MTV Video Music Awards in front of a sky-high "FEMINIST" sign in what *Time* called "the holy grail" of "feminist endorsements."[29] Coupled with the voiceover by Nigerian author Chimamanda Ngozi Adichie reading from her essay "We Should All Be Feminists," Beyoncé put her considerable cultural power into the service of feminism and forced the f-word into the homes of 12.4 million viewers. It reached even more via social media: Twitter analysts determined that two-thirds of tweets about feminism over the following twenty-four hours mentioned Beyoncé. Although it is easy to dismiss social media contributions to discourse, scholars of celebrity feminism argue that these kinds of statements "create a space for public debate."[30] In response to the Video Music Awards (VMA) performance, author Roxane Gay tweeted, "What Bey just did for feminism, on national television, look, for better or worse, that reach is WAY more than anything we've seen." It was a "major moment," according to author Jennifer Pozner, even if it was not followed by visible activism from the star herself.[31]

Celebrity feminism in general generates quite a bit of criticism as "faux feminism," and Beyoncé's especially has come under fire. Not long before the "feminist" VMA performance, bell hooks called the star a "terrorist" who was "colluding in the construction of herself as a slave" and had negative impact on young girls as part of an ongoing, widespread media assault on feminism.[32] Many other Black feminists and scholars, like Brittney Cooper, Feminista Jones, and Tanisha Ford, however, rushed to Beyoncé's defense, arguing that hooks misleadingly "conflated" the star's brand with her personhood, misunderstood Beyoncé's control over her own image, and ignored her reception among Black women audiences.[33] Cooper argues that "[a]fter Beyoncé, feminism was no longer something reserved for Black girls with college degrees or Ph.D.'s."[34] We have seen in interpretations of southern feminist popular culture like *The Color Purple* that audiences are not passive consumers, and likewise they recognize what Beyoncé has done: "seizing" the "master's tools," according to one critic, in order to assert her "right to be a human, a character with many identities, many aspects, attitudes, vulnerabilities, joys, heartbreaks, and realities."[35] The fact that Beyoncé's feminism is riddled with internal contradictions encapsulates its status as celebrity, "fourth-wave," and southern feminism. But her brand also represents an evolution that diverges in some ways from Winfrey's neoliberal feminism and increasingly offers a kind of updated regional radicalism.

Early in this century, Kimberly Springer argued that music is an "untapped" but "accessible educational tool" for feminism, citing artists like Lauryn Hill, India Arie, and Queen Latifah in her proposal for a Black feminist "project fusing music and intellectualism" in the manner of Public Enemy's promotion of Black nationalism in the late 1980s and early 1990s.[36] In her work on Outkast, Regina N. Bradley charts how artists in the region forged "the hip-hop South, a hodgepodge of past, present, and future narrations of blackness."[37] While a thorough analysis of southern feminist music in general, or of Beyoncé's body of work as a kind of Dirty South, "fourth-wave" feminist text in particular, is beyond my scope here, as a final case study I examine how *Lemonade*, her 2016 tour-de-force visual album, taps into, expands, and complicates the southern feminist texts examined herein.

In recent years, Queen Bey's regional and racial identity has merged with her feminist politics in her music. Her Houston roots are well known, and as her work became more "politicized" in the early 2000s, she also began to develop an interest in her Creole maternal family line from New Iberia, Louisiana, using her ancestral status as "practically Cajun royalty" to forge a connection with southern Louisiana, especially New Orleans. Over time, Beyoncé has emphasized her southernness in her work, featuring Houston neighborhoods, plantations, and bayou swamp imagery in her songs and albums.[38]

In February 2016, these themes became explicit as southern politics. The day before she was scheduled to do the halftime show at the Super Bowl, Beyoncé dropped the video for "Formation," the first single from her unreleased new album. Set in post-Katrina New Orleans, the song features the superstar atop an NOPD car in a sea of flooded homes. Surrounded by other Black women, Beyoncé dances amid oil paintings of Black ancestors and, dressed in all white with a parasol, fans herself in an antique-laden parlor, ironically projecting both demureness and defiance. She sings of her father from Alabama and her mother from Louisiana, and, in case audiences miss the southern focus, Beyoncé invited famed New Orleans bounce artist Big Freedia to add to the track. "I like cornbreads and collard greens, bitch," Freedia ad libs in the voiceover. "Oh yeah, you besta believe it." Deemed the twenty-first century's "ambassador of freedom" by NPR, Freedia endorses Beyoncé's vision for the song, explaining that no matter how famous the Houston megastar became, "she still just gon' be a Black southern girl." But that "just" belies the fierceness that both artists believe undergirds the role of the "Black southern girl." Like Beyoncé herself, Freedia "came to slay, bitch," offering the line that then becomes the refrain of the song. "Formation" flashes through traumatic imagery—the flooded city, graffiti that reads "STOP KILLING US," police in riot gear—interspersing it with images of Blackness that are both joyful and rebellious: the church, a New Orleans second line, a small boy dancing in front of the police.[39]

"Formation" thus represents a full embrace of radical racial politics that eclipsed the star's former ambiguity. In her work on women performers, Jayna Brown argues that because they "perform in a culture of surveillance," Black performers "always anticipate a white audience," but, even in texts featuring minstrelesque stereotypes, these artists are "always multiply signifying."[40] While some of Beyoncé's earlier work might be read as more subtle in this regard, "Formation" both shunned and targeted the white gaze. This was explicit enough that it immediately became the subject of a *Saturday Night Live* skit: a few weeks after the Super Bowl, "The Day Beyoncé Turned Black" featured distraught white fans realizing Beyoncé's race for the first time.[41]

Yet while some critics lauded "Formation" as a "black anthem," others saw it as a performative, profiteering masquerade of activism. Alicia Wallace argues that the song "center[ed] Beyoncé" while pretending to focus on New Orleans, appropriating working-class Black trauma to sell the album. Wallace also cites the disconnect between the video's racial politics and its economic argument, claiming that the lines in the song about Beyoncé's enormous wealth, like the references to high fashion, her helicopter, and the "Illuminati," are evidence of "her stamp of approval on the same capitalist system that has oppressed generations of the same black people the song is said to empower." Beyoncé's final line—"Always stay gracious, best revenge is your paper," accompanied by the familiar "pay me" gesture of rubbing the thumbs and fingers together—is for Wallace evidence of the star's retrograde "respectability politics," which called on "black people to remain within the confines of 'good behavior,' work toward a comfortable financial position, and accept it as recompense." Thus, she concludes, "it is unfortunate that people are so starved for relatable and aspirational content that they are prepared to buy in."[42]

Beyoncé's politics, even as they evolve, remain firmly within a capitalist context; she endorses the familiarly aspirational uplift of American entrepreneurialism that is also in keeping with neoliberal feminism. As a gendered message, Beyoncé's lyrics uphold what some call the "Lean In imperative" after Sheryl Sandberg's bestseller *Lean In*. For years the chief operating officer of Facebook, Sandberg argues that it is not simply discriminatory structures that enforce gender inequality. Rather, she claims, women also need to learn to "dismantle the internal barriers holding us back," a process she calls "leaning in." A major mouthpiece of neoliberal feminism, Sandberg prescribes that "each individual's success can make success a little easier for the next," with "success" broadly defined in basic financial terms.⁴³ In "Formation," Beyoncé explains that she has achieved the American dream: "I dream it, I work hard, I grind 'til I own it." This is her success, but it could be her fans' as well: "You just might be a black Bill Gates in the making."⁴⁴ Some critics target the "dissonance" of this capitalist message in an otherwise radical text, but Robin James notes that while this "can be heard as a Black parallel public to white corporate feminism," the "recentering" of this ideology around Black women is significant, if not wholly subversive—something we saw also at the end of *The Color Purple*.⁴⁵

In terms of its economic argument, "Formation" is not revolutionary, but, with the accompanying video images, the message is certainly more complex than general neoliberal self-empowerment. As Beyoncé sings about working hard till she "owns it," the video features an African American man in a bowtie holding up a newspaper featuring Martin Luther King Jr. and emblazoned with the headline "More Than a Dreamer." This is not empty imagery: the day before she released "Formation," Beyoncé and her husband donated $1.5 million to Black Lives Matter. Even as she quietly participated in antiracist philanthropy, Beyoncé sings of a white billionaire while standing atop the flooded NOPD car with her arms spread wide, a stark image that verbally lauds individual success—"I just might be a black Bill Gates in the making"—while visually referencing the violence of structural inequality.⁴⁶

Beyoncé's message is capitalist, yes, but it is also a radical call from the South to Black women to "get in formation." Classic Black feminism is evident in the video's visual references to foremothers, both in the paintings on the walls of the plantation home which "visually do the work of lineage-making," and in the genteel Creole costumes worn by the women in the parlor, a setting that is itself freighted with fraught gendered history.⁴⁷ In *Wounds of Returning*, Jessica Adams takes a tour of Oak Alley plantation in Louisiana guided by a Black woman. This tour guide's role "as surrogate" for the plantation's "white mistresses," Adams argues, "animated a quietly explosive text," making plain "the repressed fact that white power on a plantation was due entirely to the presence of blacks."⁴⁸ In the "Formation" video, Beyoncé quite literally, as Jarvis C. McInnis points out, repurposes the "master's tools" in a takeover of the master's house, a direct challenge to both the brutal history of slavery and to the continued "heavy investment" in plantation culture that persists in the South to the present.⁴⁹

Through carefully gendered imagery, "Formation" offers a Black feminist take on what Saidiya Hartman calls the "afterlife of slavery."⁵⁰ Instead of a whitewashed, Old South narrative, Beyoncé connects the past of enslaved labor to a present in which Black women control the plantation ("work hard 'til I own it") to a revised "plantation future."[51] She thus visually reworks the oppressive geography of the South and the continuing "afterlife of slavery" embodied in the mass commodification of sugar, including the exploitation of labor in factories (which one scholar deems the plantation's "co-conspirator") and the high mortality rates from sugar-related diseases among African Americans. Instead, Beyoncé peoples her plantation exclusively with Black women and girls, revisionary homage to the crucial female labor that "repopulated and nourished" the "sugar plantation machine."[52] Melina Matsoukas, director of the "Formation" video, explains, "[T]his is not a house the slaves are working in, this is a house where the slaves are the masters."[53] According to scholar Patricia Coloma Peñate, Beyoncé's "performance of a historically impossible role for herself within the plantation" offers a rebellious "counter-memory."[54]

But Beyoncé's vision here is not mere fantasy. The groundbreaking work of genealogist Elizabeth Shown Mills details the life of Marie Thérèse Coincoin, who, after being manumitted from slavery in the 1770s, became the "matriarch" of a community of free people of color among the sugar plantations in Louisiana and eventually became the "most propertied, self-made woman on Louisiana's frontier."[55] In addition to a more distant historical model like Coincoin, Beyoncé's Creole ancestry as, in her words, the descendant of "a slave owner who fell in love with and married a slave," inspires her revision of southern history in "Formation."[56]

It's also not just about history. The juxtaposition of the plantation scenes with post-Katrina New Orleans establishes a direct connection between historical systems of oppression. Katherine McKittrick and Clyde Woods explain that although Katrina was a "natural disaster," the devastating effects of the storm were "hierarchically distributed."[57] Jesmyn Ward, one of the foremost American writers of the early twenty-first century and a native of the Gulf Coast, explains the significance of this imagery in "Formation": "She sings to those of us who grew up black in the American South, who swam through Hurricane Katrina, who watched the world sink, who starved for two weeks after the eye passed, who left our dead floating in our houses. She sings to those of us who were displaced, to Las Vegas, to Los Angeles, to Hartford, who lived for months or years or still live in those other places, when the living heart of us is bound so tight with oak and pine we can barely breathe." The southern homeplace, then, maintains historical scars that can open wide to facilitate more wounds, but Black southern popular cultural reappropriation offers a route to redefinition. At the end of the video, when Beyoncé submerges with the police car, sinking it with her body after giving double middle fingers directly to the camera from the front porch of the plantation home, she is saying, according to Ward, "We love this blackness, and if they don't, fuck 'em."[58]

Beyoncé followed the drop of the "Formation" video with a performance of the song at the Super Bowl the next day flanked by a troupe of dancers in Black Panther costumes and a drumline, all of whom were Black women. This reference, as well, has Deep South roots in the 1965 Lowndes County Freedom Organization in Alabama, the precursor to the more famous Black Panther Party that formed in Oakland the following year. As explosive as they were, however, the "Formation" video and televised performance were just a taste; a few months later, Beyoncé released *Lemonade*, the album from which "Formation" was the first single. This album rethinks southern history, centering it on Black women and, in so doing, answering Sherita Johnson's call to reconsider the definition of "the South" in her work on Black women writers in the region. The population of *Lemonade*'s Deep South is not simply the hardworking victims of the racist patriarchy of the plantation. They are also, as Johnson puts it, "productive citizens building communities"—the kind of communities that foment liberation.[59]

In *Lemonade*, which ends with the "Formation" video, Beyoncé co-opts and repurposes not just the Big House, where the likes of Beyoncé's daughter and tennis superstar Serena Williams can be found dancing, but also the entire plantation. She strides through fields and performs "Freedom" in the open air under Spanish-moss-covered trees. "I break chains all by myself," she sings a cappella to an audience of Black women and children. Among the dancers and celebrities like Serena Williams and Zendaya, Beyoncé features the mothers of Michael Brown, Eric Garner, and Trayvon Martin, each holding photographs of their slain children. Together, the women prepare a meal under the stars from vegetables grown in the former kitchen gardens of the quarters of the enslaved, offering, in author Candace Benbow's words, "a meal from Grandma's kitchen, reminding us that we've been here before and everything is going to be alright."[60]

In these scenes, Beyoncé calls on the subversive history of the quarters as a "homeplace" and offers a nourishing take on Alice Walker's mother's garden as the women of *Lemonade* enact the roles of "culture bearers," healers, and resisters.[61] The visual album is about Beyoncé's marriage, but it is also, according to Benbow, a "love letter to sisters."[62] Lindsey Stewart asks, "Might this 'formation' be a tool of imagining community, turning a personal problem into a mighty community struggle?"[63] At the end of *Lemonade*, Brittney Cooper explains, Beyoncé "is calling us into very particular formations—the kinds of collective gatherings that can shift the culture, that can combat white supremacy, and sexism, and homophobia, the kinds of spaces that can use black girl magic to change the world."[64] Liberation, according to *Lemonade*, lies in the love-politics of womanism, and "southern" here is part of a historical trajectory, a "politicized cultural identity" featured in Black women's autobiographical writing in the region that we can read back through Alice Walker to Zora Neale Hurston and beyond.[65]

Of course, critiques of *Lemonade* abound. Many of the complaints are well worn, referencing what some see as Beyoncé's insincere capitalization on feminism. While some scholars target the co-optation of African goddess imagery in *Lemonade*, other critiques are more personal.[66] "Katrina is not your story," New Orleanian Maris Jones wrote in a letter to Beyoncé on the blog *Black Girl Dangerous*.[67] That same day in *Slate*, Shantrelle Lewis argued that the "Formation" video was an "appropriation" of trauma, rather than "advocacy."[68] More specifically, Beyoncé has faced a cascade of lawsuits charging copyright infringement and lack of payment for creative labor from various artists in New Orleans. She has been criticized for using the voices of queer New Orleans performers like Messy Mya and Big Freedia but omitting their images.[69] In 2018, Messy Mya's estate settled a $20 million lawsuit that Beyoncé used their voice without consent, just as New Orleans musical artist and community activist Kimberly Roberts filed a new suit claiming that the superstar violated a contract in her use of video footage Roberts shot during Katrina that appeared in the documentary *Trouble the Water*.[70]

But the album has legions of Black feminist fans. After watching *Lemonade* when it premiered on HBO, Benbow created the *Lemonade* syllabus so that fans could do their homework. *Lemonade* places Beyoncé explicitly in the Black feminist creative tradition, Benbow argues: "It was not a fluke that, when watching *Lemonade*, we could see Zora, Maya, Toni, and June."[71] Regina N. Bradley, perhaps our foremost current scholar of southern music, likewise sees Beyoncé as the heir to a southern Black feminist intellectual tradition stretching back at least to Anna Julia Cooper's *A Voice from the South* (1892).[72] As Beyoncé recites in the film, quoting Warsan Shire's poem "For Women Who Are Difficult to Love," "[t]he past and future merge to meet us here."[73]

And that future is predicated on regional roots. The setting of *Lemonade* is, to quote Riché Richardson, "Beyoncé's South."[74] Kinitra D. Brooks and Kameelah L. Martin explain that "Beyoncé's blueprint for healing" involves first "encouraging" Black women "to go home," to pay homage to foremothers at the sites of their oppression, their communities, and their resistance.[75]

As scholars have noted, the settings of *Lemonade* are very carefully constructed. Destrehan, Louisiana, the setting of the women's communal meal, was the site of the country's largest slave revolt, the German Coast Uprising of 1811. In the uprising, five hundred enslaved people marched toward New Orleans, torching plantations, killing white people, and freeing other enslaved people along the way until they were "brutally put down" and massacred by troops at Destrehan, whereupon their heads were mounted on pikes along dozens of miles of River Road.[76] *Lemonade* links this past to the future, and the South to the nation, through its community of singing, dancing, nourishing, and resisting Black women. After she recites her grandmother-in-law Hattie White's recipe for lemonade and shows footage from Hattie's ninetieth birthday party, Beyoncé explains that the "antidote" is "in your own kitchen," and, contrary to Toni Morrison's warning at the end of *Beloved*, it is "a story to be passed on" between women: "You passed these instructions down to your daughter, who then passed them down to her daughter."[77]

Despite competition in the time slot from the NBA playoffs, *Lemonade* reeled in over three-quarters of a million viewers when it aired on HBO in April 2016, and it was the best-selling album worldwide that year.[78] If Oprah Winfrey was America's "de facto feminist" at the turn of the twenty-first century, Beyoncé assumed that mantle in the 2010s, with a "global platform" that is "incomparable to anything black feminists saw in their generation or since."[79] Beyoncé's feminism owes a clear debt to Winfrey—"You gotta listen when Oprah speaks!" Beyoncé has said of Winfrey's advice to her—but her evolving brand offers a deeply radical, if complicated, kind of southern feminism that *The Oprah Winfrey Show* dared not touch.[80]

Indeed, these developments seem to have influenced Winfrey too. The Oprah Winfrey Network debuted *Queen Sugar* (2016–present) just a few months after Beyoncé released *Lemonade*. The show is set in post-plantation Louisiana and features complex Black women characters who are heirs to the sugarcane fields and the region's harsh history. Like Lalita Tademy's ancestors in *Cane River* and Beyoncé's community of women in *Lemonade*, the female characters on *Queen Sugar*, one of whom is played by Bianca Lawson, Beyoncé's stepsister, redefine this conflicted homeplace as their own—an intersectional process reflected in the title. One reviewer lauds the show's "reinvention" of "feminist TV," citing how Winfrey sneaked this "Black Feminist Masterclass" into viewers' living rooms via OWN, the "channel that is quietly becoming the destination for prestige dramas." The show's influence extends beyond the small screen to social media.[81] One study found that the hashtag "QueenSugarTalks" opened conversations about racial trauma, mental health, and other difficult topics through viewer identification with characters and story lines on the show.[82] Thus, like the early-internet-era chatrooms on Oprah.com, the revolving daily studio audience in Harpo Studios, and the book clubs Winfrey inspired across the globe, OWN's southern feminist programming fosters not just entertainment but also parasocial community creation, self-disclosure, and consciousness-raising.

At the same time, over the course of *Queen Sugar*'s award-winning first few seasons, Winfrey herself was becoming more and more open about her feminist politics. In September 2020, in what she called her "form of protest," Winfrey replaced the image of herself on the front cover of *O* magazine for the first time in its twenty years. Embracing the politics of both Black Lives Matter and #SayHerName, the campaign to address police violence against Black women, the *O* cover that month featured a portrait of Breonna Taylor, the twenty-four-year-old woman who was murdered by Louisville police in March 2020. In her running What I Know for Sure column, Winfrey wrote: "What I know for sure: We can't be silent."[83]

The two most famous American feminists in the second decade of the twenty-first century, then, were Black southern women who have developed and promoted their own evolving brands of gender politics.[84] Each version is enormously popular with audiences, indicating a national appetite for southern feminism. The body of work produced by Winfrey and Beyoncé is the culmination of texts by and about southern women in the 1980s and 1990s that offered feminist models. This pop culture demonstrates how to reckon with the regional gender norms that constricted their mothers, how to form literal and fictive sisterhoods to fight those norms, how to compromise with neoconservative politics and carve a place in the existing order, and how to interweave radical Black feminism with neoliberalism to imagine new futures. As the natural products of this evolution, Winfrey and Beyoncé offer hybrid brands of feminism that are southern in their roots and global in their reach. This hybridity hints at the potential for new variants of feminism in the years to come. In her work on neoliberal feminism, scholar Nancy Fraser hopes that it is a stage in a process that will be followed by an "insurrectionary upsurge."[85] Winfrey and Beyoncé represent two generations and multiple aspects of feminism, and as they each appear to grow more radical in their personae and productions, perhaps this indicates that, as in previous eras, the new feminist revolt will come from the South.

NOTES

Introduction. Wrestling with Scarlett

1. Bartel, *The Complete "Gone with the Wind" Trivia Book*, 161.
2. *The Carol Burnett Show*; Shepard, "CBS Buys *Gone with the Wind*."
3. Pyron, *Southern Daughter*, 459–460; Rutheiser, *Imagineering Atlanta*, 69; Auletta, "The Lost Tycoon"; Nelson, "Ted Turner," 1374; "A Timeline of the Turner Media Empire."
4. Smothers, "Scarlett and Rhett Take Atlanta Again."
5. Rutheiser, *Imagineering Atlanta*, 45; Smothers, "Scarlett and Rhett Take Atlanta Again"; Conroy, "Riding the Wind"; Ripley, *Scarlett*; Gilpin, "Alexandra Ripley, 'Scarlett' Author"; *Scarlett* (miniseries).
6. Jacoby, "New Generation of Women's Publications."
7. Baumgardner and Siegel, *Sisterhood Interrupted*, 105–106, 104; McRobbie, "Postfeminism and Popular Culture," 27–28.
8. Lotz, *Redesigning Women*, 174; Tasker and Negra, introduction, 1.
9. Faludi, *Backlash*, xviii, 76; Dow, *Prime-Time Feminism*, 95; Baumgardner and Richards, *Manifesta*, 93. Note that some scholars differ on the definition of "postfeminism"; U.S. scholars tend to use the one provided herein, while others, particularly in Britain and Australia, define it as a "conceptual shift" to focusing on the issue of difference (Lotz, *Redesigning Women*, 22–23).
10. Barker and McKee, introduction, 11.
11. Rhodes, "Gail Godwin and the Ideal," 59.
12. McPherson, *Reconstructing Dixie*, Kindle location 198.
13. Bobo, "Black Women's Responses," 43–51; Bobo, "Sifting through the Controversy," 332–342; Bobo and Seiter, "Black Feminism and Media Criticism," 286–302; K. Davis, "Oprah's Book Club," 399–419.
14. Tartt, "The Belle and the Lady," 96.
15. Pyron, *Southern Daughter*, 258; *Steel Magnolias*. For an overview of the debate on gender politics within *Gone with the Wind*, see M. Bauer, *A Study of Scarletts*.
16. Richardson, *Emancipation's Daughters*, 26.
17. Hester, "*Steel Magnolias*."
18. Crenshaw, "Demarginalizing the Intersection," 139–167; McDonogh and Hing-Yuk Wong, "Religion and Representation," 41; McPherson, *Reconstructing Dixie*, Kindle location 2193.

19. *Fried Green Tomatoes*; *Something to Talk About*; *Hope Floats*; *Where the Heart Is*; *The Divine Secrets of the Ya-Ya Sisterhood*; Barker and McKee, introduction, 11.
20. McPherson, *Reconstructing Dixie*, Kindle location 2163.
21. Farrell, *Yours in Sisterhood*, 3, 1.
22. Stanonis, *Dixie Emporium*, 5; Cox, introduction to *Dreaming of Dixie*, Kindle, no location; Cox, "The South and Mass Culture," 680; Barker and McKee, introduction, 1, 2.
23. S. Abbott, *Womenfolks*, 84.
24. Gros, "The Wind Done Gone," 139–140.
25. Bone, *The Postsouthern Sense of Place*, 243, 146; Rushing, "No Place for a Feminist," 304; Tate, *A Southern Weave of Women*, 12–13; Gros, "The Wind Done Gone," 139; M. Bauer, *A Study of Scarletts*, 5; Fox-Genovese, "Scarlett O'Hara," 156; Richardson, "Mammy's 'Mules,'" 52–74; Athas, "Why There Are No Southern Writers."
26. Tate, *A Southern Weave of Women*, 7, 74; Gupton, "Un-ruling the Woman," 124.
27. Rushing, "No Place for a Feminist," 293.
28. Stokes, "Constituting Southern Feminists," 98, 99.
29. Allured, *Remapping Second-Wave Feminism*, 5–6; Wilkerson-Freeman, "Stealth in the Political Arsenal," 44–45; Spruill, "Victoria Eslinger, Keller Bumgardner Baron," 397; Giardina, "The Making of a Modern Feminist," 619.
30. Pearson, "Mapping Rhetorical Interventions," 159; Bambara, *The Black Woman*; A. Davis, *Women, Race and Class*; hooks, *Feminism Is for Everybody*; Hull, Scott, and Smith, *All the Women Are White*; Springer, *Still Lifting, Still Climbing*. In chronological order of publication, for some key histories of American feminism that center southern activists, see Evans, *Personal Politics*, 24–82; Anderson-Bricker, "Triple Jeopardy," 49–69; Wilkerson-Freeman, "Stealth in the Political Arsenal"; Stokes, "Constituting Southern Feminists"; Breines, *The Trouble between Us*, 19–50; Keane, "Second-Wave Feminism," 1–56; Rushing, "No Place for a Feminist"; Shockley, *Creating a Progressive Commonwealth*; Giardina, "The Making of a Modern Feminist."
31. Allured, *Remapping Second-Wave Feminism*, 19, 11, 13.
32. Ibid., 105, 3; Giardina, "The Making of a Modern Feminist," 614.
33. Boles and Atkinson, "Ladies," 130, 136.
34. McPherson, *Reconstructing Dixie*, Kindle location 2023.
35. McPherson, *Reconstructing Dixie*, Kindle location, 255.
36. Bennett, "Southern Women Writers," 441–442.
37. Allured, *Remapping Second-Wave Feminism*, 182–197; hooks, *Feminism Is for Everybody*, 5; *Southern Feminist*; Atlanta March Committee letter; Shockley, *Creating a Progressive Commonwealth*, Kindle location 181.
38. V. Taylor, "Sisterhood, Solidarity, and Modern Feminism," 277; Hewitt, "Feminist Frequencies," 659; Hewitt, introduction to *No Permanent Waves*, 4, 5; Evans, "Generations Later, Retelling the Story," 24.
39. Maxwell and Shields, "Toward a New Understanding," 2, 3. For a selection of other scholars who interrogate the "waves" paradigm of feminist history, see, in order of publication date: Sandoval, *Methodology of the Oppressed*; various authors, "Second-Wave Feminism in the United States"; Reger, *Different Wavelengths*; Gilmore, *Feminist Coalitions*; Hoeflinger, "Talking Waves"; Laughlin et al., "Is It Time to Jump Ship?"
40. Springer, "Third Wave Black Feminism?," 1061.

41. I am by no means the first to make this point. See, for instance, Traylor, "Recalling the Black Woman," Kindle location 105; Collins, *Black Feminist Thought*, 139–162; Guy-Sheftall, preface to *Words of Fire*, xiii; De Hart, "Second Wave Feminism(s) and the South," 291; Gluck, "Whose Feminism, Whose History?," 34; Roth, "The Making of the Vanguard Center," 71; Springer, "Third Wave Black Feminism?," 1059, 1061, 1062; Breines, *The Trouble between Us*, 26; Giddings, *When and Where I Enter*, 303–304, 305; Fernandes, "Unsettling 'Third Wave Feminism,'" 103; U. Taylor, "Black Feminisms and Human Agency," 70–71; B. Thompson, "Multiracial Feminism," 39; 7; Maxwell and Shields, "Toward a New Understanding," 6; Allured, *Remapping Second-Wave Feminism*, 90, 99, 100; Farmer, *Remaking Black Power*, 159–192.

42. Hewitt, "Feminist Frequencies," 665.

43. Giardina, "The Making of a Modern Feminist," 611, 612, 622.

44. Gilmore, "The Dynamics of Second-Wave Feminist Activism," 94–117; Allured, *Remapping Second-Wave Feminism*; Shockley, *Creating a Progressive Commonwealth*; Giardina, "The Making of a Modern Feminist," 613; Stokes, "Constituting Southern Feminists," 97; Araiza, "Saying Goodbye to Men," 287; Heying, "I Was Returning to See," 12.

45. Farrell, *Yours in Sisterhood*, 197.

46. Dow, *Prime-Time Feminism*, xix; Bolsterli, *Born in the Delta*, 101; Pollitt and Baumgardner, afterword to *Catching a Wave*, 314; Sowards and Renegar, "Reconceptualizing Rhetorical Activism," 61.

47. Rushing, "No Place for a Feminist," 305, 300. The southern preoccupation with place, particularly questions of regional definitions and distinctiveness, has dominated scholarship about the South and self-representations of the South for many years (Lassiter and Crespino, "Introduction: The End of Southern History," 7). With the twenty-first-century advent of "new southern studies," scholars have interrogated the very idea of regional identity; some argue that there is no "real South" but rather successive representations that create and re-create the region by defining themselves either against or according to an imagined, "authentic," "original" South (Romine, *The Real South*, 12). Whether remotely "authentic" or wholly imagined, these regional images have real-world effects and audiences—they are consumed and engaged with not just by southerners but also by readers and viewers across the nation and the globe (Martyn Bone, "Introduction," 1). For a brief review of this historiographical turn, see Jon Smith, "What the New Southern Studies Does Now."

48. Richardson, *Emancipation's Daughters*, 15, 32–33.

49. Bejarano and Martinez-Ebers, "Latina Mobilization," 165–178; Cha, "Creating a Multiethnic South," 203–225; Odem, "Latin American Immigration," 234–260; Peretz, "Why Atlanta?"

50. Rushing, "No Place for a Feminist," 305, 300.

51. Walker, *The Color Purple*, 208.

Chapter 1. "Keep Living, Daughters"

1. Henry, *Not My Mother's Sister*, 7, 11, 1, 10.
2. B. Bennett, "Making Peace with the Mother," 186, 192.
3. Allison, *Bastard out of Carolina*; Karr, *The Liars' Club*; Wells, *The Divine Secrets*

of the Ya-Ya; Williams, "Between Creation and Devouring," 27–42; Tyler, "Mother-Daughter Myth," 98.

4. Morgan, *Sisterhood Is Powerful*.

5. Lyons, "Playing Dollhouse on a Huge Scale," 146; K. Taylor, "Southern Suffering"; Association for Theatre in Higher Education, "Beth Henley Interview"; Triad Stage, "*Crimes of the Heart* Dramaturgy"; John Griffin Jones, *Mississippi Writers Talking*, 175, 178; Alley Theatre, "In Conversation;" Rosenfeld, "Beth Henley's World;" Henley, *Crimes of the Heart*.

6. Beaufort, "A Play that Proves."

7. Playbill, "Crimes of the Heart"; "Pulitzer Play"; Plunka, *The Plays of Beth Henley*, 3.

8. Lyons, "Playing Dollhouse," 152; Plunka, *The Plays of Beth Henley*, 38, 3; John Griffin Jones, *Mississippi Writers Talking*, 182; Rosenfeld, "Beth Henley's World"; Henley, *Crimes of the Heart*, 37, 11, 67.

9. Auflitsch, "Beth Henley's Early Family Plays," 270; B. Bennett, "Making Peace with the Mother," 186.

10. Seidel, "Gail Godwin and Ellen Glasgow," 287.

11. Fox-Genovese, "Mothers and Daughters," xv–xviii; B. Bennett, "Making Peace with the Mother," 187, 188.

12. Henley, *Crimes of the Heart*, 1.

13. Ibid., 31, 6.

14. Ibid., 72, 31.

15. Plunka, *The Plays of Beth Henley*, 73.

16. Ibid.; Henley, *Crimes of the Heart*, 7, 4, 28, 27, 8, 38.

17. F. King, *Southern Ladies and Gentlemen*, 174.

18. Auflitsch, "Beth Henley's Early Family Plays," 280.

19. Henley, *Crimes of the Heart*, 3, 14, 19, 3, 18; Rosenfeld, "Beth Henley's World of Southern Discomfort"; K. Taylor, "Southern Suffering."

20. F. King, *Southern Ladies and Gentlemen*, 69, 73, 140.

21. Henley, *Crimes of the Heart*, 37, 34, 69, 70.

22. Ibid., 22, 21, 17, 43, 21, 32, 15.

23. Ibid., 25–26, 17, 33.

24. Ibid., 43, 45.

25. Ibid., 15, 18, 5, 26, 6, 112, 65, 67, 77.

26. Ibid., 40, 64, 66–67, 84.

27. Ibid., 20, 23, 64; American Drama Institute, "Expressing 'the Misery and Confusion'"; Plunka, *The Plays of Beth Henley*, 11; Henley, *Crimes of the Heart*, 85, 69.

28. Mohammed, "Females' Journey into Finding," 497; Henley, *Crimes of the Heart*, 95.

29. Caviness, "Female Sexuality in the South," 26.

30. Henley, *Crimes of the Heart*, 100–101, 113, 116.

31. Ibid., 20, 67, 25, 84, 86, 97, 98–99.

32. Ibid., 47–50.

33. Ibid., 89, 48.

34. John Griffin Jones, *Mississippi Writers Talking*, 177.

35. Henley, *Crimes of the Heart*, 49.

36. DeHart, "Second Wave Feminism(s) and the South," 280.

37. McPherson, *Reconstructing Dixie*, Kindle location 2557; Wheeler, *New Women of the New South*, 100–132.

38. McGuire, *At the Dark End of the Street*, Kindle location 1261.
39. Henley, *Crimes of the Heart*, 49, 58, 50, 61.
40. Henley, *Crimes of the Heart*, 119; Caviness, "Female Sexuality in the South," 27.
41. Henley, *Crimes of the Heart*, 119, 120, 121, 124.
42. Rich, "Beth Henley's 'Crimes of the Heart.'"
43. American Drama Institute, "Expressing 'the Misery and Confusion'"; Plunka, *The Plays of Beth Henley*, 13; Playbill, "Crimes of the Heart"; Beaufort, "A Play That Proves."
44. Rich, "Beth Henley's 'Crimes of the Heart.'"
45. B. Bennett, "Making Peace with the Mother," 186, 187; Andreach, *Understanding Beth Henley*, 164.
46. Plunka, *The Plays of Beth Henley*, 42.
47. Lyons, "Playing Dollhouse on a Huge Scale," 148.
48. Ibid., 146.
49. Alley Theatre, "In Conversation with Theresa Rebeck."
50. John Griffin Jones, *Mississippi Writers Talking*, 176–177; Plunka, *The Plays of Beth Henley*, 11.
51. American Drama Institute, "Expressing 'the Misery and Confusion.'"
52. K. Taylor, "Southern Suffering."
53. American Drama Institute, "Expressing 'the Misery and Confusion.'"
54. Gupton, "Un-ruling the Woman," 124.
55. Henley, *Crimes of the Heart*, 29.
56. Gupton, "Un-ruling the Woman," 128.
57. Auflitsch, "Beth Henley's Early Family Plays," 271, 279.
58. Henley, *Crimes of the Heart*, 30.
59. hooks, "Sisterhood: Political Solidarity Between Women," 125; Rosenfeld, "Beth Henley's World."
60. Rosenfeld, "Beth Henley's World"; Lyons, "Playing Dollhouse on a Huge Scale," 158.
61. Ebert, "*Crimes of the Heart*."
62. Rosenfeld, "Beth Henley's World."
63. Canby, "Film: Henley's *Crimes*."
64. Ebert, "*Crimes of the Heart*."
65. Alley Theatre, "In Conversation."
66. Rosenfeld, "Beth Henley's World of Southern Discomfort"; Plunka, *The Plays of Beth Henley*, 23; K. Taylor, "Southern Suffering."
67. K. Taylor, "Southern Suffering."
68. Auflitsch, "Beth Henley's Early Family Plays," 270.
69. Guerra, "Beth Henley," 120.
70. "Author's Bio and Family Photos."
71. Georgia Department of Transportation, "Pleasant Hill Macon"; Wadley, "Tina McElroy Ansa"; "Tina's Bio"; "Voices from the Gaps."
72. Ansa, *Ugly Ways*, Kindle location 769.
73. Ansa, *Ugly Ways*, Kindle location 14; B. Bennett, "Making Peace with the Mother," 194.
74. Ansa, *Ugly Ways*, Kindle locations 694, 461, 1239; Martinson, "Tina McElroy Ansa Interview."

75. Ansa, *Ugly Ways*, Kindle locations 148, 767, 304, 694, 167.
76. Ibid., 767, 694.
77. Ibid., 167, 540, 713, 730, 205, 2071, 721, 264, 785, 1422.
78. Ibid., 195, 205, 2559, 785, 374, 367.
79. Ibid., 167, 148, 855, 74, 802, 809, 2727.
80. Ibid., 318, 148, 103–123, 318, 1037.
81. Ibid., 1514, 231.
82. Ibid., 1514, 231, 1487, 1752, 819, 1743; Auflitsch, "Beth Henley's Early Family Plays," 274.
83. Ansa, *Ugly Ways*, Kindle locations 555, 415, 205.
84. Miller, *Being Ugly*, 3.
85. Ansa, *Ugly Ways*, Kindle location 500.
86. Ibid., 1579, 127, 1560, 1203, 948, 1335, 2894.
87. Ibid., 1615, 1560, 1570, 1615, 1877, 524, 1299.
88. Ibid., 640, 1307, 2117.
89. Ibid., 987, 1307, 2071, 152, 855, 548, 1335.
90. T. Green, "Mother Dear."
91. Martinson, "Tina McElroy Ansa Interview."
92. T. Green, "Mother Dear"; Ansa, *Ugly Ways*, Kindle locations 460, 440, 493, 1839, 1858, 339.
93. Ansa, *Ugly Ways*, Kindle locations 2709, 1385, 2877.
94. Ibid., 3116, 3098, 3249, 3272, 3288.
95. Ibid., 223, 3341.
96. "Tina's Bio"; "Ugly Ways" (*Kirkus*); "Ugly Ways" (*Publishers' Weekly*); Georgia Center for the Book, "Adult Reading List."
97. Whitney, "Tina McElroy Ansa's *Ugly Ways*," ix.
98. T. Green, "Mother Dear;" Whitney, "Tina McElroy Ansa's *Ugly Ways*," 35.
99. Chambers, "Book Review."
100. Collins, *Black Feminist Thought*, 123–129.
101. Ibid., 129.
102. hooks, *Feminist Theory*, 133.
103. Collins, "The Meaning of Motherhood," 43–44.
104. Ibid.; O'Reilly, "Click!"
105. O'Reilly, *Toni Morrison and Motherhood*, 4, 280; Collins, *Black Feminist Thought*, 132; Collins, "Black Women and Motherhood," 149–159; Edwards, "Community Mothering," 80; hooks, *Feminist Theory*, 144; N. Jenkins, "Black Women and the Meaning," 206.
106. Walker, *In Search of Our Mothers' Gardens*, 240.
107. Ibid., 241; E. White, *Alice Walker*, 56. Rebecca Walker is a "third-wave" feminist with personal experience of the maternal conflict between the "waves" of feminism. Her famous rift with her own mother Alice Walker is based, she explains in a book on the subject, on Alice's struggles to reconcile her feminism with her role as a mother (see R. Walker, *Baby Love*).
108. Ansa, *Ugly Ways*, Kindle locations 394, 691, 469, 485, 389, 468.
109. Ibid., 1107, 2189, 2195, 167.
110. T. Green, "Mother Dear"; Whitney, "Tina McElroy Ansa's *Ugly Ways*," 67.
111. Ansa, *Ugly Ways*, Kindle locations 1858, 704.

112. Ibid., 1486, 1480; Surrency, "African Spirituality in the Novels," 59; Whitney, "Tina McElroy Ansa's *Ugly Ways*," 76.
113. Georgia Department of Transportation, "Pleasant Hill Macon"; Jordan, *Broken Silences*, 3.
114. Ansa, *Ugly Ways*, Kindle locations 61, 112, 127, 1486, 1507.
115. Meeks, *Macon's Black Heritage*, 17–18; Jessica Smith and Wooten, "Macon's Racial History"; Georgia Department of Transportation, "Pleasant Hill Macon."
116. Collins, *Black Feminist Thought*, 119–123.
117. Joseph and Lewis, *Common Differences*, 106.
118. Ansa, *Ugly Ways*, Kindle locations 484, 1396.
119. Ibid., 999, 446, 542, 2708.
120. Giardina, "The Making of a Modern Feminist," 619, 620; Cooper, *Beyond Respectability*, 3.
121. Ansa, *Ugly Ways*, Kindle locations 2698, 480, 2698, 1402.
122. Collins, *Fighting Words*, 53.
123. B. Bennett, "Making Peace with the Mother," 194.
124. Ansa, *Ugly Ways*, Kindle locations 194, 448, 2708.
125. B. Bennett, "Making Peace with the Mother," 192.
126. Martinson, "Tina McElroy Ansa Interview."
127. Grooms, "Big Bad Mudear," 654.
128. B. Bennett, "Making Peace with the Mother," 194.
129. Ibid.
130. Ansa, *Ugly Ways*, Kindle location 3103.
131. Auflitsch, "Beth Henley's Early Family Plays," 274.
132. Ansa, *Ugly Ways*, Kindle location 3278.
133. Auflitsch, "Beth Henley's Early Family Plays," 274.
134. B. Bennett, "Making Peace with the Mother," 199.

Chapter 2. "You Get What You Settle For"

1. Schickel, "Gender Bender;" Leo, "Toxic Feminism."
2. Morgan, ed., *Sisterhood Is Powerful*.
3. Dicker, *A History of U.S. Feminisms*, 17.
4. Hewitt, "Beyond the Search for Sisterhood," 315, 316.
5. hooks, "Sisterhood," 127–128.
6. Hollinger, *In the Company of Women*, 4, 7, 8.
7. Ansa, *Ugly Ways*, Kindle locations 469, 1809, 1634, 1688, 675, 1692, 1634.
8. A. Walker, *In Search of Our Mothers' Gardens*, Kindle location 54.
9. Abbandonato, "A View from Elsewhere," 1107; Gates, preface to *Alice Walker*, xi; Watkins, "*The Color Purple*," 17.
10. A. Walker, *In Search of Our Mothers' Gardens*, Kindle location 52; Izgarjan, "Alice Walker's Womanism," 311.
11. Nash, "Practicing Love," 1–24.
12. Lindquist-Dorr, *White Women, Rape, and the Power*, 2.
13. A. Walker, *The Color Purple*, 1, 3–4, 14, 5, 11; Abbandonato, "A View from Elsewhere," 1106; Lindquist-Dorr, *White Women, Rape, and the Power*, 2, 81.
14. A. Walker, *The Color Purple*, 18, 19, 22.

15. Ibid., 33, 36, 22, 35–36.
16. Ibid., 39, 42.
17. Ibid., 66, 71, 73, 84, 86, 89, 93, 94.
18. Ibid., 96, 98, 105, 106, 206, 209, 223; Bobo and Seiter, "Black Feminism and Media Criticism," 288; hooks, "Reading and Resistance," 290.
19. A. Walker, *The Color Purple*, 7, 47, 48, 59, 51, 54, 55.
20. E. White, *Alice Walker*, 57.
21. Byerman, "Walker's Blues," 61; A. Butler, "Quiltmaking," 592.
22. A. Walker, *The Color Purple*, 75.
23. Lorde, "Uses of the Erotic," 53; Griffin, "Textual Healing," 526; Bibler, *Cotton's Queer Relations*, 8.
24. Cooper, *Eloquent Rage*, 20.
25. Griffin, "Textual Healing," 521.
26. A. Walker, *The Color Purple*, 59–60, 77, 79, 80, 81, 119, 152, 126, 75, 52, 82, 118; Abbandonato, "A View from Elsewhere," 1112; McKever-Floyd, "Tell Nobody but God," 427; Musanga, "Toward the Survival," 394.
27. A. Walker, *The Color Purple*, 43–44, 125; hooks, *Sisters of the Yam*, 133.
28. A. Walker, *The Color Purple*, 131, 150.
29. Ibid., 69, 154, 181, 182.
30. A. Walker, *The Color Purple*, 183, 199, 203, 204; Romagnolo, "Naturally Flawed?," 122.
31. A. Walker, *The Color Purple*, 183, 207, 208, 213.
32. Ibid., 218.
33. Wall, "Lettered Bodies and Corporeal Texts," 261.
34. A. Walker, *The Color Purple*, 218, 220–221, 222, 229–230, 252–253, 291; Willis, "Walker's Women," 88.
35. A. Walker, *The Color Purple*, epigraph, 190, 279; Katz, "Show Me How to Do," 185–193.
36. hooks, *Sisters of the Yam*, 163.
37. Nash, "Practicing Love," 2, 3, 8.
38. A. Walker, *Color Purple*, 290, 291, 292, 294, 295; T. Davis, "Walker's Celebration of Self," 31.
39. D. Smith, "*The Color Purple* (Review)," 20.
40. Halberstam, "Imagined Violence/Queer Violence," 189.
41. Henderson, "*The Color Purple*," 79; C. Jenkins, "Queering Black Patriarchy," 986.
42. T. Davis, "Walker's Celebration of Self," 25.
43. T. Davis, *Southscapes*, 11.
44. White, *Alice Walker*, 336–337.
45. Abbandonato, "A View from Elsewhere," 1108.
46. Christopher Lewis, "Cultivating Black Lesbian Shamelessness," 159, 160.
47. José Andres Araiza explains that the "second-wave" feminist newsletter *Goodbye to All That*, which was published in the 1970s in Austin, Texas, advocated for lesbian separatism as "the only true feminism" and was, Araiza argues, "pivotal in jump-starting the modern LGBT civil rights movement" ("Saying Goodbye to Men," 284).
48. hooks, "Reading and Resistance," 285–288; Romagnolo, "Naturally Flawed?," 120; Abbandonato, "A View from Elsewhere," 1110.
49. E. Johnson, *Black. Queer. Southern. Women.*, 20, 6.

50. A. Davis, *Blues Legacies and Black Feminism*, 39, 45.
51. Berlant, "Race, Gender, and Nation," 218, 229.
52. Henderson, "*The Color Purple*," 67.
53. hooks, "Reading and Resistance," 289, 295.
54. C. Jenkins, "Queering Black Patriarchy," 973; Berlant, "Race, Gender, and Nation," 227; Lorde, "The Master's Tools," 110–113.
55. Jacqueline Jones, "Fact and Fiction," 663.
56. McKittrick and Woods, "No One Knows the Mysteries," 5.
57. Bone, *The Postsouthern Sense of Place*, 1, 30–31.
58. McKittrick, *Demonic Grounds*, x, xii, 143; Jacqueline Jones, "Fact and Fiction," 663–664.
59. Roosevelt, "Message to the Conference."
60. E. White, *Alice Walker*, 24, 27; Cobb, *The Selling of the South*, 1; R. Gray, "Inventing Communities, Imagining Places," xv; M. Holmes, "From Euphoria to Cataclysm," 313; University of Missouri School of Law, "Lynchings by State and Race"; National Association for the Advancement of Colored People, "History of Lynchings;" McAleer, "Great Indignation," 49; Greene, "Fear and Loathing in Mississippi," 85–106.
61. Jacqueline Jones, "Fact and Fiction," 655.
62. A. Walker, *The Same River Twice*, 263, 266, 18, 55, 50, 35; *The Color Purple* (film).
63. A. Walker, *The Same River Twice*, 154, 157, 53, 54, 143, 155–156, 144, 35, 219, 219, 160.
64. M. Wallace, "Blues for Mr. Spielberg."
65. *The Color Purple* (film); A. Walker, *The Same River Twice*, 21.
66. *Tony Brown's Journal*, "Purple Rage;" Bobo, "Sifting through the Controversy," 332, 337.
67. Romagnolo, "Naturally Flawed?," 118.
68. Deborah McDowell, "Reading Family Matters," in *Changing Our Own Words: Essays on Criticism, Theory, and Writing by Black Women* (New Brunswick: Rutgers University Press, 1989), 78, quoted in C. Jenkins, "Queering Black Patriarchy," 969–970.
69. Shipp, "Blacks in Heated Debate"; Bobo, "Black Women's Responses," 43; C. Jenkins, "Queering Black Patriarchy," 970, 969, 972; Bobo, "Sifting through the Controversy," 337, 338; Gates, preface to *Alice Walker*, xi. Crenshaw addresses these "divided loyalties" regarding black male violence against black women in "Mapping the Margins." It should be noted that Black men did not universally condemn *The Color Purple*. Scholar Calvin Hernton lauded Walker, asserting, "Black women writers are telling it like it is, and often not telling all of it" (quoted in E. White, *Alice Walker*, 437).
70. A. Walker, *The Color Purple*, afterword, n.p.
71. Musanga, "Toward the Survival," 391, 394.
72. A. Walker, "In These Dissenting Times," 15.
73. hooks, *Reel to Real*, 213.
74. Ricks, "Normalized Chaos," 344, 347.
75. E. White, *Alice Walker*, 59.
76. A. Walker, "Women," 19.
77. A. Walker, *In Search of Our Mothers' Gardens*, 378–379; C. Robinson, "The Evolution of Alice Walker," 304, 305; T. Davis, "Walker's Celebration of Self," 26; Henderson, "*The Color Purple*," 67; Washington, "An Essay on Alice Walker," 39; Izgarjan, "Alice Walker's Womanism," 305, 309.

78. E. White, *Alice Walker*, 400–401, 7, 10, 423–424.
79. A. Walker, *The Same River Twice*, 162, 29, 29, 161, 163, 202, 203, 35, 203.
80. A. Walker, *The Same River Twice*, 215, 214.
81. hooks, *Reel to Real*, 2; Walker, *The Same River Twice*, 282, 40–41.
82. Quoted in Bobo, "Black Women's Responses."
83. hooks, *Reel to Real*, 53, 207, 205, 208, 209; hooks, *Yearning*, 4.
84. Bobo and Seiter, "Black Feminism and Media Criticism," 291; hooks, *Reel to Real*, 209; Dolan, *The Feminist Spectator as Critic*, 2; Dow, *Prime-Time Feminism*, 2–3, 4, 12; H. Gray, *Watching Race*, 91; Smith-Shomade, *Shaded Lives*, 4.
85. Bobo and Seiter, "Black Feminism and Media Criticism," 291, 300; Bobo, "Sifting through the Controversy," 335, 336.
86. hooks, *Sisters of the Yam*, 25, 26.
87. E. White, *Alice Walker*, 430.
88. *Tony Brown's Journal*, "Purple Rage."
89. Shipp, "Blacks in Heated Debate."
90. A. Walker, *The Same River Twice*, 41.
91. Ibid., 285, 250, 256; Bobo, "Sifting through the Controversy"; 335, 336; Bobo and Seiter, "Black Feminism and Media Criticism," 291, 300.
92. Hooks, *Reel to Real*, 53, 197, 210.
93. Shipp, "Blacks in Heated Debate."
94. Griffin, "Textual Healing," 110.
95. Weller, "The Ride of a Lifetime;" Ulven, "Together We Came"; "The Dialogue"; "Makers."
96. "Makers"; *On Story*, "Thelma and Louise."
97. "Makers"; "The Dialogue"; Mahiana, "Callie Khouri."
98. Bielby and Bielby, "Women and Men in Film," 255; Hollinger, *In the Company of Women*, 2–3.
99. Bielby and Bielby, "Women and Men in Film," 249.
100. Bielby and Bielby, "Women and Men in Film," 255; Eraso, "*Thelma & Louise*," 63; Laderman, "What a Trip," 43; Greenberg, "*Thelma and Louise*'s Exuberant Polysemy," 20; Rohter, "The Third Woman."
101. Weller, "The Ride of a Lifetime."
102. "Makers."
103. "The Dialogue"; Weller, "The Ride of a Lifetime"; "Makers"; Schickel, "Gender Bender"; Hollinger, *In the Company of Women*, 116, 117; Greenberg, "*Thelma and Louise*'s Exuberant Polysemy," 20; A. Thompson, "Geena Davis, Callie Khouri."
104. Lipsitz, "*Thelma & Louise*."
105. *On Story*, "Thelma and Louise"; *Thelma & Louise*.
106. F. King, *Southern Ladies and Gentlemen*, 45–46.
107. *Thelma & Louise*.
108. Ibid.; Weller, "The Ride of a Lifetime"; *On Story*, "Thelma and Louise."
109. Cobb, *The Selling of the South*, 228–253. Cobb notes that Arkansas ranked at bottom of pollution controls nationally during this time (ibid., 238).
110. Braudy, "Satire into Myth," 29.
111. Eraso, "*Thelma & Louise*," 67.
112. *Thelma & Louise*.
113. Putnam, "The Bearer of the Gaze," 295.

114. *Thelma & Louise.*
115. Putnam, "The Bearer of the Gaze," 295.
116. Althouse, "*Thelma and Louise*," 767; alh, "*Thelma and Louise*," 2.
117. *Thelma & Louise.*
118. *Thelma & Louise*; Hart, "Til Death Do Us Part," 433.
119. *Thelma & Louise.*
120. *Thelma & Louise*; Lechner, *The South of the Mind*, 164; Coulthard, "Killing Bill," 168.
121. Schickel, "Gender Bender."
122. Hollinger, *In the Company of Women*, 120.
123. *Thelma & Louise*; Hollinger, *In the Company of Women*, 130; Putnam, "The Bearer of the Gaze," 295; Schickel, "Gender Bender"; Turan, "Smooth Ride"; Leo, "Toxic Feminism."
124. *Thelma & Louise.*
125. *Thelma & Louise*; Schickel, "Gender Bender"; Hart, "Til Death Do Us Part," 433; Greenberg et al., "The Many Faces," 28.
126. *Thelma & Louise*; Putnam, "The Bearer of the Gaze," 293; Laderman, "What a Trip," 41; Kinder, "*Thelma and Louise* and *Messidor*," 30.
127. Putnam, "The Bearer of the Gaze," 301; Carlson, "Is This What Feminism Is."
128. "Personal Quotes."
129. Schickel, "Gender Bender."
130. Ibid.
131. Ibid.; A. Johnson, "Baccantes at Large," 22.
132. Hollinger, *In the Company of Women*, 122.
133. Paige, "Wanted Dead or Alive"; Higonnet, "Suicide," 103.
134. "Personal Quotes."
135. Berlant, *The Female Complaint*, 114.
136. A. Johnson, "Baccantes at Large," 23.
137. Paige, "Wanted Dead or Alive"; Hart, "Til Death Do Us Part," 431, 440.
138. Hollinger, *In the Company of Women*, 124.
139. Kinder, "*Thelma and Louise* and *Messidor*," 30.
140. Diane Glancy, "Columbus Meets Thelma and Louise," 13.
141. Weller, "The Ride of a Lifetime."
142. Schickel, "Gender Bender."
143. Hollinger, *In the Company of Women*, 117; Carlson, "Is This What Feminism Is."
144. Kaplan, "Rebel Citizenship," 2.
145. K. Smith, "As a Feminist Film."
146. Schickel, "Gender Bender."
147. Ibid.
148. Williams, "What Makes a Woman Wander," 28.
149. Hart, "Til Death Do Us Part," 436.
150. Chumo, "*Thelma and Louise* as Screwball Comedy," 24.
151. Laderman, "What a Trip," 53; Williams, "What Makes a Woman Wander," 28.
152. Lipsitz, "*Thelma & Louise.*"
153. alh, "*Thelma and Louise*," 2.
154. Halberstam, "Imagined Violence/Queer Violence," 190–191.
155. Russell, "I'm Not Gonna Hurt You."

156. Halberstam, "Imagined Violence/Queer Violence," 187, 191.
157. Althouse, *"Thelma and Louise,"* 770, 771.
158. Russell, "I'm Not Gonna Hurt You"; Hollinger, *In the Company of Women*, 119; "Makers." For examples of critics who ignored Harlan's clear pre-rape predatory signals, see Carr, *"Thelma and Louise"*; Kroll, "Back on the Road Again"; Mason, "The Movie *Thelma and Louise"*; Brian Johnson, "Feminist Fast Lane."
159. *On Story*, *"Thelma and Louise."*
160. Schickel, "Gender Bender"; Bielby and Bielby, "Women and Men in Film," 249.
161. Putnam, "The Bearer of the Gaze," 296.
162. Schickel, "Gender Bender."
163. A. Thompson, "Geena Davis, Callie Khouri."
164. Hollinger, *In the Company of Women*, 124.
165. Henry, *Not My Mother's Sister*, 17.
166. Berlant, *The Queen of America*, 222–223, 227.
167. R. Walker, "Becoming the Third Wave," 41.
168. Ibid.
169. "*Thelma & Louise*: Awards"; "*Thelma & Louise* Wins Original Screenplay." The film was also nominated in the following categories: Best Actress in a Leading Role (Davis), Best Actress in a Leading Role (Sarandon), Best Director (Scott), Best Cinematography, and Best Film Editing.

Chapter 3. "The Business of Being a Woman"

1. Baumgardner and Siegel, *Sisterhood Interrupted*, 111, 117; Evans, *Tidal Wave*, 226; Spruill, *Divided We Stand,* 322; Sapiro and Conover, "The Variable Gender Basis," 519.
2. Rottenberg, "How Neoliberalism Colonised Feminism."
3. Woods, "Sittin' on Top of the World," 47.
4. Miller, *"Designing Women,"* Kindle location 970; Rottenberg, "The Rise of Neoliberal Feminism," 419; Alterman, *The Cause*, 365; Takiff, *A Complicated Man*, 92–93; Velasco, *Centrist Rhetoric*, 32; Bronner, "Resisting the Right," 271.
5. Genz, "Third Way/ve," 335.
6. Dow, *Prime-Time Feminism*, xxv; Stanonis, *Dixie Emporium*, 5; Patterson, "Road Kill."
7. Sanguinette, "The South Rises Again"; Rochlin, "Prime Time of Bloodworth-Thomason"; "Meet the 2013 Tribeca Filmmaker"; Stocks, "A Conversation with Linda Bloodworth-Thomason."
8. Waxman, "Hollywood Friend Comes Back"; Park, "When Not Battling Delta Burke"; Proffitt, "Linda Bloodworth-Thomason."
9. Bloodworth-Thomason, *"Designing Women* Creator."
10. Bianculli, *Teleliteracy*, 5; Hinrichsen, Caison, and Rountree, "Introduction: The Televisual South," Kindle locations 93, 99.
11. Dow, *Prime-Time Feminism*, 86.
12. Corry, "ABC's *After the Sexual Revolution*;" Faludi, *Backlash*, 97, 1.
13. J. Butler, "Redesigning Discourse," 13; Gunther, "CBS and the Steel Magnolia."
14. Proffitt, "Linda Bloodworth-Thomason."
15. Sanguinette, "The South Rises Again."
16. Rochlin, "The Prime Time of Bloodworth-Thomason."

17. Brennan, "*Designing Women* Back."
18. Sanguinette, "The South Rises Again."
19. McPherson, *Reconstructing Dixie*, Kindle location 2390.
20. "Bloodworth-Thomason, Linda (Joyce)"; "Bloodworth-Thomason to Teach Course"; "Villa Marre."
21. Cobb, *Redefining Southern Culture*, 144, 145.
22. M. Hobson, *Legend of the Black Mecca*, 1, 3, 4.
23. Baldwin, *Evidence of Things Not Seen*, 11, 4.
24. Ibid., 77; K. Kruse, *White Flight*, 4, 8, 6; Bone, *Postsouthern Sense of Place*, 140; Rutheiser, *Imagineering Atlanta*, 3.
25. K. Kruse, *White Flight*, 261; Carter, *George Wallace to Newt Gingrich*, 95; Georgia Archives, "Skyline—Empire City;" Rutheiser, *Imagineering Atlanta*, 4.
26. Bloodworth-Thomason, "*Designing Women* Creator on Clinton."
27. Rochlin, "The Prime Time of Bloodworth-Thomason."
28. Allured, "Louisiana, the American South," 391; McPherson, *Reconstructing Dixie*, Kindle location 2388.
29. Dow, *Prime-Time Feminism*, 104–106, 108. Sarah Wilkerson-Freeman coined the phrase "stealth feminism" (Wilkerson-Freeman, "Stealth in the Political Arsenal," 122), and Dow refers to discussion of "women's issues" in *Designing Women* (Dow, *Prime-Time Feminism*, 108).
30. McPherson, *Reconstructing Dixie*, Kindle location 2422; "Designing Women," Emmys.com; Rochlin, "The Prime Time of Linda Bloodworth-Thomason."
31. *Designing Women*, "Designing Women."
32. Brennan, "*Designing Women* Back."
33. McPherson, *Reconstructing Dixie*, Kindle location, 2432, 2334.
34. Ibid., Kindle location 304.
35. *Designing Women*, "And Justice for Paul"; *Designing Women*, "The IT Men"; *Designing Women*, "Nashville Bound"; *Designing Women*, "I'll Be Home for Christmas"; *Designing Women*, "Reese's Friend"; *Designing Women*, "Heart Attacks"; *Designing Women*, "Second Time Around"; *Designing Women*, "New Year's Daze"; Rutheiser, *Imagineering Atlanta*, 53.
36. *Designing Women*, "Reese's Friend"; *Designing Women*, "A Big Affair"; *Designing Women*, "The IT Men"; *Designing Women*, "High Rollers."
37. Applebome, *Dixie Rising*, 186; Cunningham, *American Politics*, 12; Cobb, *Away Down South*, 68.
38. *Designing Women*, "But They're Really Great Curtains."
39. Rutheiser, *Imagineering Atlanta*, 51; Cobb, *The Selling of the South*, 94.
40. Baldwin, *Evidence of Things Not Seen*, 2.
41. *Designing Women*, "Nightmare from *Hee Haw*."
42. Lechner, *The South of the Mind*, 111–112.
43. Fraser, "Feminism, Capitalism," 6.
44. Bernstein, "Pulling Itself Out."
45. Dow, *Prime-Time Feminism*, 104; Brennan, "*Designing Women* Back."
46. "Meet the 2013 Tribeca Filmmaker #27"; "Bloodworth-Thomason to Teach Course."
47. *Designing Women*, "Killing All the Right People." Later that year, Bloodworth-Thomason sued the hospital where her mother received the transfusion and settled,

and she succeeded in getting the American Red Cross and the Centers for Disease Control to adopt blood screening methods that could have prevented her mother's death (Gordon, "TV Producer's Mother Died").

48. *Designing Women*, "Suzanne Goes Looking."
49. See Dow, *Prime-Time Feminism*, for lengthy discussions of feminist sitcoms and dramas in the 1970s.
50. Faludi, *Backlash*, ix, 99–102; *Designing Women*, "Mary Jo's First Date"; *Designing Women*, "Manhunt"; *Designing Women*, "Mary Jo's Dad Dates Charlene"; *Designing Women*, "Of Human Bondage"; *Designing Women*, "Reservations for Eight."
51. *Designing Women*, "Design House"; *Designing Women*, "Great Expectations"; *Designing Women*, "Grand Slam, Thank You Ma'am"; *Designing Women*, "Hardhats and Lovers"; *Designing Women*, "Strange Case of Clarence and Anita."
52. *Designing Women*, "Strange Case of Clarence and Anita."
53. B. Carter, "Television Gets on the Bandwagon."
54. *Designing Women*, "Strange Case of Clarence and Anita."
55. J. Butler, "Redesigning Discourse," 21; Faludi, *Backlash*, xii; Entman, "Framing," 55.
56. *Designing Women*, "Strange Case of Clarence and Anita."
57. Sullivan and Goldzwig, "Women's Reality," 240; Berlant, "The Queen of America," 568; J. Butler, "Redesigning Discourse," 21; Lubiano, "Black Ladies, Welfare Queens."
58. *Designing Women*, "Bachelor Suite."
59. *Designing Women*, "Stand and Fight"; Dow, *Prime-Time Feminism*, 122.
60. *Designing Women*, "The Rowdy Girls"; Miller, "*Designing Women*," Kindle location 1101.
61. McPherson, *Reconstructing Dixie*, Kindle location 667.
62. *Designing Women*, "Design House"; *Designing Women*, "Anthony Jr."; *Designing Women*, "The Rowdy Girls"; *Designing Women*, "The Candidate"; *Designing Women*, "And Justice for Paul"; *Designing Women*, "Perky's Visit"; *Designing Women*, "Old Spouses Never Die Part 1."
63. *Designing Women*, "Fools Rush In"; *Designing Women*, "The Bachelor Auction"; *Designing Women*, "Howard the Date"; *Designing Women*, "Oh, What a Feeling"; *Designing Women*, "Foreign Affairs"; McPherson, *Reconstructing Dixie*, Kindle location 2481; Dow, *Prime-Time Feminism*, 107.
64. "Classic U.S. Sitcom *Designing Women*"; Kovalchik, "12 Perfectly Arranged Facts"; Stein, "The 'Designing Women' Revival"; Dow, *Prime-Time Feminism*, 106.
65. *Designing Women*, "First Day of the Last"; *Designing Women*, "Anthony and Vanessa"; *Designing Women*, "Viva Las Vegas"; *Designing Women*, "Fools Rush In."
66. Cornwall, Gideon, and Wilson, "Reclaiming Feminism," 1–2.
67. Gaston, *The New South Creed*, 5, 11.
68. Wheeler, *New Women*, xv; Cox, *Dixie's Daughters*, 1; Case, "The Historical Ideology," 628.
69. *Designing Women*, "A Big Affair."
70. *Designing Women*, "Stranded."
71. *Designing Women*, "Getting Married and Eating Dirt."
72. Schmidt, "Southern Practice of Eating Dirt"; Isenberg, *White Trash*, 135.
73. M. Hobson, *The Legend of the Black Mecca*, 5, 1, 170; McPherson, *Reconstructing Dixie*, Kindle location 2496: Rutheiser, *Imagineering Atlanta*, 63.

74. McPherson, *Reconstructing Dixie*, Kindle location 2095.
75. Rutheiser, *Imagineering Atlanta*, 53.
76. Mitchell, *Gone with the Wind*, 656–657, 973; Bone, *Postsouthern Sense of Place*, 146.
77. "Turner Acquires"; Rutheiser, *Imagineering Atlanta*, 69.
78. "TNT Takes Its First Step"; *Designing Women*, "Old Spouses Never Die Part 1"; *Designing Women*, "Cruising."
79. Miller, "*Designing Women*," Kindle location 1186; McPherson, *Reconstructing Dixie*, Kindle location 880.
80. Rutheiser, *Imagineering Atlanta*, 40–41.
81. McPherson, *Reconstructing Dixie*, Kindle location 2095.
82. *Designing Women*, "Gone with the Whim, Part 1;" *Designing Women*, "Gone with the Whim, Part 2."
83. *Designing Women*, "Gone with the Whim, Part 1;" *Designing Women*, "Gone with the Whim, Part 2;" Miller, "*Designing Women*," Kindle location 1017.
84. Romine, *The Real South*, 17.
85. *Designing Women*, "Gone with the Whim, Part 2."
86. Rutheiser, *Imagineering Atlanta*, 3; *Designing Women*, "Strange Case of Clarence and Anita." Sullivan and Goldzwig also note the potential allusion to *Thelma and Louise* ("Women's Reality," 237).
87. *Designing Women*, "On the Road Again."
88. Park, "When Not Battling Delta Burke."
89. Gunther, "CBS and the Steel Magnolia."
90. Du Brow, "CBS Aims to Divide, Conquer"; Park, "When Not Battling Delta Burke"; Gunther, "CBS and the Steel Magnolia"; Rochlin, "Prime Time of Bloodworth-Thomason"; Proffitt, "Linda Bloodworth-Thomason"; Sanguinette, "The South Rises Again."
91. Bloodworth-Thomason, "*Designing Women* Creator"; Abbott, "A Long and Winding Road," 12, 1, 4; Hale, "The Making of the New Democrats," 221, 223; Carter, *From George Wallace to Newt Gingrich*, 102; Gillon, *The Pact*, 81, 94.
92. Isenberg, *White Trash*, 300.
93. Miller, "*Designing Women*," Kindle location 1205.
94. Takiff, *A Complicated Man*, 123.
95. Alterman, *The Cause*, 363; *Frontline*, "Interview with John Brummett."
96. *Frontline*, "Interview with Danny Thomason."
97. Clinton quoted in P. Abbott, "A Long and Winding Road," 12; *Frontline*, "Interview with Shirley Abbott."
98. S. Holmes, "The 1992 Campaign"; *Frontline*, "Interview with Danny Thomason."
99. *Frontline*, "Interview with Martha Sexton"; *Frontline*, "Interview with Ron Addington"; Alterman, *The Cause*, 363.
100. Bruck, "Hillary the Pol"; *Frontline*, "Interview with Sara Ehrman."
101. Safire, "Macho Feminism, R.I.P."; Z. Eisenstein, "Sexual Politics of the New Right," 567–569.
102. Gillon, *The Pact*, 72, 73.
103. P. Green, "Cultural Rage," 40; G. Robinson, "One Eye on the Mirror"; Bruck, "Hillary the Pol"; Gillon, *The Pact*, 80.
104. Bruck, "Hillary the Pol."
105. Gillon, *The Pact*, 80.

106. Wilkerson-Freeman, "Stealth in the Political Arsenal," 79, 78.
107. *American Experience*, "Clinton"; Gillon, *The Pact*, 75, 82.
108. "Bill Clinton on the Johnny Carson Show."
109. Golshan, "Bill Clinton's First Major Appearance."
110. M. White, "Son of the Sixties," 103.
111. Applebome, *Dixie Rising*, 46; K. Kruse, *White Flight*, 245, 246; MacLean, "Neo-Confederacy versus the New Deal," 308–330.
112. Gillon, *The Pact*, 98.
113. Applebome, *Dixie Rising*, 44; Cunningham, *American Politics*, 78; Gillon, *The Pact*, 98; P. Abbott, "A Long and Winding Road," 9.
114. Spruill, "Feminism, Anti-Feminism, and the Rise," 52.
115. Page, "Newt on Ditches."
116. Applebome, *Dixie Rising*, 44, 45.
117. Ibid.; Rutheiser, *Imagineering Atlanta*, 99; MacLean, "Neo-Confederacy versus the New Deal," 308, 309, 316; Applebome, *Dixie Rising*, 25.
118. Barry Goldwater in 1960, quoted in Maxwell and Shields, *The Long Southern Strategy*, 19.
119. Parry-Giles, *Hillary Clinton in the News*, 31.
120. Baumgardner and Siegel, *Sisterhood Interrupted*, 129; Evans, *Tidal Wave*, 215; A. Davis, afterword to *To Be Real*, 279.
121. Sapiro and Conover, "The Variable Gender Basis," 519, 497; Sulfaro, "Affective Evaluations of First Ladies," 489.
122. E. J. Dionne, Jr., "Democrats Hear Emotional Please"; Shepard, "Clinton a Hit."
123. Gates, "Hating Hillary"; Alterman, *The Cause*, 363–364, 365; Gillon, *The Pact*, 95; Parry-Giles, *Hillary Clinton*, 31, 40, 37; Draper, "How Hillary Became 'Hillary.'"
124. Carter, *From George Wallace to Newt Gingrich*, 89; Maurer, "Media Feeding Frenzies," 67.
125. Mahaffey, "In Defense of Another," 383; M. Kruse, "The TV Interview that Haunts."
126. Goodman, "Hillary Breaking Ground."
127. M. Brown, "Feminism and Cultural Politics," 255.
128. Parry-Giles, *Hillary Clinton*, 8.
129. Sheehy, "What Hillary Wants."
130. Draper, "How Hillary Became 'Hillary.'"
131. Parry-Giles, *Hillary Clinton*, 33; N. King, *Hillary: Her True Story*, 174; M. Kruse, "The TV Interview that Haunts"; Bruck, "Hillary the Pol."
132. Bloodworth-Thomason, "*Designing Women* Creator."
133. Lundsford, "Arkansas Memories Project"; N. King, *Hillary: Her True Story*, 178; "Woman behind *Man From Hope*"; Rochlin, "Prime Time of Bloodworth-Thomason."
134. Parry-Giles and Parry-Giles, *Constructing Clinton*, 35; *The Man from Hope*.
135. Timmerman, "1992 Presidential Campaign Films," 366; *The Man from Hope*.
136. Alterman, *The Cause*, 363; Abbott, "A Long and Winding Road," 6; Timmerman, "1992 Presidential Campaign Films," 367, 368, 364; Parry-Giles and Parry-Giles, *Constructing Clinton*, 37; *The Man from Hope*.
137. Maurer, "Media Feeding Frenzies," 70; Parry-Giles and Parry-Giles, *Constructing Clinton*, 37, 36, 39.
138. *The Man from Hope*.

139. Bruck, "Hillary the Pol"; *Frontline*, "Interview with Patty Criner"; *The Man from Hope*.
140. *The Man from Hope*; Parry-Giles and Parry-Giles, *Constructing Clinton*, 26.
141. Bloodworth-Thomason, "Woman behind *Man from Hope*."
142. Rochlin, "Prime Time of Bloodworth-Thomason;" Bloodworth-Thomason, "*Designing Women* Creator;" Parry-Giles and Parry-Giles, *Constructing Clinton*, 31.
143. Proffitt, "Linda Bloodworth-Thomason."
144. *Designing Women*, "The Odyssey."
145. Proffitt, "Linda Bloodworth-Thomason."
146. Dowd, "Clinton's Best Friends."
147. Waxman, "Hollywood Friend."
148. Ibid.; "Harry Z. Thomason"; Bloodworth-Thomason, "*Designing Women* Creator."
149. *Women of the House*, "Miss Sugarbaker Goes to Washington"; *Women of the House*, "Guess Who's Sleeping in Lincoln's Bed"; *Women of the House*, "You Talk Too Much"; *Women of the House*, "Women in Film."
150. Black, "The Newest Southern Politics," 591; K. Kruse, *White Flight*, 263; Applebome, *Dixie Rising*, 91; Cunningham, *American Politics*, 244.

Chapter 4. "Change Your Life Television"

1. "Oprah Winfrey Named Most Powerful."
2. De Moraes, "In CBS Deal"; Canedy, "The Media Business"; Kuczynski, "Winfrey Breaks New Ground"; Maffeo, "'Bust'-ing Out All Over."
3. Springer, "Delineating the Contours," xi.
4. Livingstone and Lunt, *Talk on Television*, 2.
5. Shattuc, *The Talking Cure*, 85, 2–3.
6. Livingstone and Lunt, *Talk on Television*, 30.
7. Hinrichsen, Caison, and Rountree, "Introduction: The Televisual South," Kindle location 228.
8. Zook, "A Manifesto of Sorts."
9. *The Oprah Winfrey Show Twentieth Anniversary Collection*, "The Interviews."
10. *The Oprah Winfrey Show Twentieth Anniversary Collection*, "Christmas Kindness."
11. Van Meter, "Looking for Oprah," 10; Howard, "Beginnings with Oprah," 9; Mansfield, "And Now, Heeeeeeeere's Oprah!"
12. "Oprah Winfrey's Official Biography"; "Oprah Winfrey: Biography."
13. *The Oprah Winfrey Show Twentieth Anniversary Collection*, "The Beginning."
14. Marion, "When Oprah Was Ours"; Rothe, *Popular Trauma Culture*, 56; Decker, "Saint Oprah," 170.
15. *The Oprah Winfrey Show Twentieth Anniversary Collection*, "The Beginning"; *The Oprah Winfrey Show Twentieth Anniversary Collection*, "Surrender."
16. E. White, *Alice Walker*, 404; Mansfield, "And Now, Heeeeeeeere's Oprah!"; "Oprah Winfrey's Official Biography"; Ebert, "*The Color Purple*."
17. *The Oprah Winfrey Show Twentieth Anniversary Collection*, "The Beginning"; "Oprah Winfrey's Official Biography"; Moorti, "Cathartic Confessions or Emancipatory Texts?," 85; J. Harris and Watson, "Introduction," 5.

18. Springer, "Delineating the Contours," xi.
19. Copenhagen, "The Death of Postfeminism," 11, 29; Shattuc, *The Talking Cure*, 95–96; Harris and Watson, "Introduction," 5.
20. Livingstone and Lunt, *Talk on Television*, 169; Harris and Watson, "Introduction," 3; Haag, "Oprah Winfrey," 115–121.
21. "13 Shocking Oprah Show Moments; Harris and Watson, "Introduction," 6.
22. Hall, "The 'Oprahfication' of Literacy," 651; Moorti, "Cathartic Confessions or Emancipatory Texts?," 87; Rothe, *Popular Trauma Culture*, 57; Farr, *Reading Oprah*, 53.
23. Farrell, *Yours in Sisterhood*, 21, 61; Yang, "TV Talk Show Therapy," 469–491; Smith-Shomade, "You'd Better Recognize," 112.
24. Peck, "Talking about Racism," 108–109; Dow, *Prime-Time Feminism*, xxi; Kozol, "Fracturing Domesticity," 664.
25. Shattuc, *The Talking Cure*, 128; *The Oprah Winfrey Show Twentieth Anniversary Collection*, "Aha!;" *The Oprah Winfrey Show Twentieth Anniversary Collection*, "Stranger Danger."
26. Copenhagen, "The Death of Postfeminism," 8–9.
27. Moorti, "Cathartic Confessions or Emancipatory Texts?," 83, 89.
28. Copenhagen, "The Death of Postfeminism," 1, 2, 34; Lofton, *Oprah*, 1; Masciarotte, "C'mon Girl," 89; Smith-Shomade, "You'd Better Recognize," 119; Rexroat, "I'm Everywoman," 22.
29. Copenhagen, "The Death of Postfeminism," 36; Rexroat, "I'm Everywoman," 19.
30. Zucker, "Disavowing Social Identities," 423–435; Masciagno, *Rethinking Feminist Identification*; Heywood and Drake, *Third Wave Agenda*, 1.
31. Livingstone and Lunt, *Talk on Television*, 43; Travis, "'It Will Change the World,'" 1024; *The Oprah Winfrey Show Twentieth Anniversary Collection*, "Authentic Power."
32. Travis, "It Will Change the World," 1026.
33. Moorti, "Cathartic Confessions or Emancipatory Texts?," 85.
34. R. Thompson, foreword to *The Oprah Phenomenon*, vii, viii; Lofton, *Oprah*, 4.
35. Lofton, *Oprah*, 4; Parkins, "Oprah Winfrey's Change Your Life TV," 145.
36. Lotz, *Redesigning Women*, 3; Baumgardner and Siegel, *Sisterhood Interrupted*, 125; *Time*, June 29, 1998, cover, https://content.time.com/time/covers/0,16641,19980629,00.html.
37. V. Taylor, "Sisterhood, Solidarity, and Modern Feminism," 1, 204; Mann, *Micro-Politics*, 1; Rottenberg, "The Rise of Neoliberal Feminism," 418; Fraser, "Feminism, Capitalism," 114, 110.
38. Maxwell and Shields, "Toward a New Understanding," 2.
39. Genz, "Third Way/ve," 36.
40. Calkin, "Feminism, Interrupted?," 298; H. Eisenstein, "Feminism Seduced," 414; McRobbie, "Feminism, the Family," 119; Prugl, "Neoliberalising Feminism," 614–631; Rottenberg, "The Rise of Neoliberal Feminism," 420, 425, 424.
41. Tasker and Negra, introduction to "Interrogating Feminism," 8; Genz, "Third Way/ve," 333; Groeneveld, "Be a Feminist," 179–190; hooks, *Feminism Is for Everybody*, 5, 6.
42. Aschoff, *The New Prophets of Capital*, 10; Windels et al., "Selling Feminism," 18; Lofton, *Oprah*, 23; Winch, *Girlfriends and Postfeminist Sisterhood*, 2.
43. Allured, *Remapping Second-Wave Feminism*, 1, 2.

44. Van Meter, "Oprah Winfrey Is on a Roll."
45. Blyth, "Oprah Winfrey Believes."
46. Tindall, "The Benighted South," 281–294.
47. Howard, "Beginnings with Oprah," 7.
48. Rexroat, "I'm Everywoman," 25.
49. Cloud, "Hegemony or Concordance?," 115–137; Peck, "Talking about Racism," 12; *The Oprah Winfrey Show Twentieth Anniversary Collection*, "The Headlines: Forsyth County."
50. Lofton, *Oprah*, 127.
51. Mansfield, "And Now, Heeeeeeeere's Oprah!"
52. Collins, *Black Feminist Thought*, 69.
53. T. Johnson, "It's Personal"; Crowley, *Feminism's New Age*, 139; Collins, *Black Sexual Politics*, 142–143; Stanley, "The Specter of Oprah Winfrey," 40–41; Howard, "Beginnings with Oprah," 3.
54. Crowley, *Feminism's New Age*, 134.
55. *The Oprah Winfrey Show Twentieth Anniversary Collection*, "A Private Tour of Oprah's Home"; "Your Best Life."
56. Maxwell and Shields, "Toward a New Understanding," 8; R. Walker, "Being Real," xxx, xxxi, xxxvi–xxxvii.
57. Genz, "Third Way/ve," 335.
58. Bobo, "Black Women's Responses"; Bobo, "Sifting through the Controversy"; Bobo and Seiter, "Black Feminism and Media Criticism"; K. Davis, "Oprah's Book Club"; Modleski, *Loving with a Vengeance*; Radway, *Reading the Romance*; Dow, *Prime-Time Feminism*, 2–4; Livingstone and Lunt, *Talk on Television*, 39; Lofton, *Oprah*, 179; Hall, "The 'Oprahfication' of Literacy," 655.
59. Okrant, *Living Oprah*.
60. Decker, "Saint Oprah," 171–172.
61. Max, "The Oprah Effect."
62. Hall, "The 'Oprahfication' of Literacy," 649.
63. Farr, *Reading Oprah*, 31.
64. Ibid., 31, 32.
65. Decker, "Saint Oprah," 173
66. Hall, "The 'Oprahfication' of Literacy," 655.
67. Max, "The Oprah Effect."
68. Farr, *Reading Oprah*, 58; Hartley, *Reading Groups Book*, 4.
69. Max, "The Oprah Effect"; Hall, "The 'Oprahfication of Literacy," 652.
70. Hall, "The 'Oprahfication' of Literacy," 656; Frith, Raisborough, and Klein, "C'mon Girlfriend," 476.
71. S. Bauer, "Oprah's Misery Index."
72. K. Davis, "Oprah's Book Club," 400; Lofton, *Oprah*, 16; Rothe, *Popular Trauma Culture*, 52, 97; Appel, "Fictional Narratives," 62–83; Bal and Veltkamp, "How Does Fiction Reading Influence Empathy?"; Gerbner et al., "Living with Television," 17–40; Hogan, "Fictions and Feelings," 184–195; D. Johnson, "Transportation into a Story," 150–155; Keen, *Empathy and the Novel*.
73. Farrell, *Yours in Sisterhood*, 64; Copenhagen, "The Death of Postfeminism," 20.
74. Copenhagen, "The Death of Postfeminism," 20.
75. These include Anna Quindlen's *Black and Blue* (1998), which is set in Florida

and is about intimate partner violence; Kaye Gibbons's *Ellen Foster* (1987), which features the traumas of child molestation and parental suicide; Sheri Reynolds's *The Rapture of Canaan* (1995), which centers on a religious cult featuring sexism and torture for perceived sins; Billie Letts's *Where the Heart Is* (1995), which examines poverty and homelessness; Breena Clark's *River, Cross My Heart* (2000), which explores grief after the accidental death of a child in Washington, D.C.; and Pearl Cleage's *What Looks Like Crazy on an Ordinary Day* (1997), in which the main character leaves Atlanta after being diagnosed with HIV.

76. *The Oprah Winfrey Show*, "Oprah's Book Club," *Black and Blue*, May 22, 1998.

77. Parkins, "Winfrey's Change Your Life TV," 154.

78. Zook, "A Manifesto of Sorts."

79. Morrison, *Song of Solomon*; *The Oprah Winfrey Show*, "How'd They Do That"; Angelou, *The Heart of a Woman*; Morrison, *Paradise*; *The Oprah Winfrey Show*, "Oprah's Book Club: Toni Morrison;" Danticat, *Breath, Eyes, Memory*; Cleage, *What Looks Like Crazy on an Ordinary Day*; *The Oprah Winfrey Show*, "Oprah's Book Club: Things Every Woman Should Know."

80. Spillers, "Mama's Baby, Papa's Maybe," 65–66; Hartman, *Lose Your Mother*, 76–77.

81. *The Oprah Winfrey Show Twentieth Anniversary Collection*, "Maya Angelou"; Plasa, *Icon Critical Guides*, 33; Lindsey, "Love Letter to Black Feminism," 4; Howard, "Beginnings with Oprah," 4, 5.

82. Howard, "Beginnings with Oprah," 7.

83. Rexroat, "I'm Everywoman,'" 25.

84. Harris, "What Is Africa to Me?," 299.

85. *The Oprah Winfrey Show Twentieth Anniversary Collection*, "The Beginning"; Howard, "Beginnings with Oprah," 5.

86. Moraga, "Refugees of a World," n.p.

87. Hinton, "Sturdy Black Bridges," 64; Fernandes, "Unsettling 'Third Wave Feminism,'" 98; Bambara, "Foreword," vii.

88. *The Oprah Winfrey Show Twentieth Anniversary Collection*, "The Headlines: The Little Rock Nine"; "Oprah's Mother, Vernita Lee"; Baumgardner and Siegel, *Sisterhood Interrupted*, 143, 142.

89. Morrison quoted in Plasa, *Icon Critical Guides*, 33.

90. Lindsey, "A Love Letter to Black Feminism," 4.

91. Rexroat, "I'm Everywoman," 26.

92. J. Harris, "What Is Africa to Me?," 299.

93. hooks, *Sisters of the Yam*; hooks, *Yearning*, 215.

94. Haber and Hart, "25 Books Every Woman Should Read"; Travis, "It Will Change the World," 1035; *The Oprah Winfrey Show Twentieth Anniversary Collection*, "Do Your Eyes Light Up?"

95. "*The Bluest Eye*: About the Book."

96. Howard, "Beginnings with Oprah," 9; "Oprah's Hair through the Years."

97. Tornabene, "Here's Oprah"; *The Oprah Winfrey Show Twentieth Anniversary Collection*, "Do Your Eyes Light Up?"

98. *The Oprah Winfrey Show Twentieth Anniversary Collection*, "Do Your Eyes Light Up?"; K. Davis, "Oprah's Book Club," 409.

99. "Biography."

100. Tademy, *Cane River*, xi.
101. Ibid., xi, xii, xv.
102. Ibid., 536.
103. *The Oprah Winfrey Show*, "Oprah's Book Club: *Cane River*."
104. Ibid.
105. Ibid.
106. Ibid.
107. Tademy, *Cane River*, x.
108. Mansfield, "And Now, Heeeeeeeere's Oprah!"
109. *The Oprah Winfrey Show*, "Oprah's Book Club: *Cane River*."
110. Ibid.
111. Hartman, *Scenes of Subjection*, 6.
112. *The Oprah Winfrey Show*, "Oprah's Book Club: *Cane River*."
113. Ibid.
114. Ibid.
115. Lofton, *Oprah*, 180; *The Oprah Winfrey Show*, "Anne Murray and Her Daughters."
116. "Oprah Winfrey's Official Biography"; Kay, "My Mom and Oprah Winfrey," 53; Max, "The Oprah Effect"; R. Butler, Cowan, and Nilsson, "From Obscurity to Bestseller," 23, 24; Hall, "The 'Oprahfication' of Literacy," 647; Decker, "Saint Oprah," 172; Lofton, *Oprah*, 148; Copenhagen, "The Death of Postfeminism," 23; Farr, *Reading Oprah*, 18.
117. Morrison, *Beloved*.
118. Denard, "Blacks, Modernism, and the South," 1. Fred Hobson deems Morrison a southerner "by legacy if not by birth" (*The Southern Writer*, 93), and Linda Tate notes "how inextricably tied she and her African American characters are to their knotty roots in the South" ("A Second Southern Renaissance," 491).
119. Denard, "Blacks, Modernism, and the South," 2, 4, 3, 7, 10.
120. Darling, "In the Realm of Responsibility," 5–6.
121. Zook, "A Manifesto of Sorts."
122. *Beloved* (film).
123. Nehl, *Transnational Black Dialogues*, 12.
124. Adams, *Wounds of Returning*, 5, 2.
125. *Beloved* (film).
126. Plasa, *Icon Critical Guides*, 72,
127. Ibid., 78; *Beloved* (film); Morrison, *Beloved*, 107–108, 62, 256, 119, 235, 251.
128. Morrison, *Beloved*, 5, 72, 113, 218, 6, 73, 36, 42.
129. hooks, *Yearning*, 216.
130. Plasa, *Icon Critical Guides*, 37.
131. Hinrichsen et al., "Introduction," Kindle location 212; hooks, *Yearning*, 216.
132. Morrison, *Beloved*, 42, 35.
133. Ibid., 5, 3.
134. *A Place of Rage*; Plasa, *Icon Critical Guides*, 23, 25.
135. Cooper, *Eloquent Rage*, 150.
136. Plasa, *Icon Critical Guides*, 33.
137. Morrison, *Beloved*, 171, 58, 71, 203; Plasa, *Icon Critical Guides*, 55; hooks, *Killing Rage, Ending Racism*, 140, 142.

138. Plasa, *Icon Critical Guides*, 33.
139. *Beloved* (film); Morrison, *Beloved*, 240, 256.
140. Morrison, *Beloved*, 257, 259; Plasa, *Icon Critical Guides*, 77; *Beloved* (film).
141. *The Oprah Winfrey Show*, "*Beloved* Dinner with Oprah."
142. Christiansë, *Toni Morrison*, 46; Nehl, *Transnational Black Dialogues*, 57.
143. Morrison, *Beloved*, 267, 273.
144. *Beloved* (film).
145. Roger Ebert, "Winfrey Confronts the Strength."
146. Ibid.; Stodghill, "Daring to Go There."
147. *Beloved* (film).
148. Rothe, *Popular Trauma Culture*, 63.
149. Hunter, "Beloved."
150. Maslin, "No Peace."
151. *The Oprah Winfrey Show*, "*Beloved* Dinner with Oprah."
152. hooks, *Killing Rage*, 141.
153. Hartman, *Scenes of Subjection*, 3.
154. *The Oprah Winfrey Show*, "*Beloved* Dinner with Oprah."
155. Spillers, "Mama's Baby, Papa's Maybe," 67.
156. Hartman, *Scenes of Subjection*, 4, 19, 20.
157. *The Oprah Winfrey Show*, "*Beloved* Dinner with Oprah."
158. Ibid.
159. Ibid.
160. Bröck, "Postmodern Mediations and *Beloved*'s Testimony," 39, 36.
161. *The Oprah Winfrey Show*, "*Beloved* Dinner with Oprah."
162. Ibid.
163. Stodghill, "Daring to Go There."
164. Zillman, "Oprah Winfrey *Beloved* Movie Failure"; Clemetson, "It's Constant Work."
165. Travers, "*Beloved*"; Hunter, "Beloved."
166. Ebert, "*Beloved*."
167. Radish, "Oprah Winfrey Talks Her Career."
168. Clemetson, "It's Constant Work."
169. Radish, "Oprah Winfrey Talks Her Career."
170. K. Davis, "Oprah's Book Club," 400, 407, 404.
171. Berlant, "The Subject of True Feeling," 54.
172. Lofton, *Oprah*, 7; Aschoff, *The New Prophets of Capital*, 10; Rothe, *Popular Trauma Culture*, 52.
173. Clemetson, "It's Constant Work."

Epilogue. "Just a Southern Girl in a Southern World"

1. Sayeau, "Southern Ms."
2. "*The Wind Done Gone*"; Schur, "*The Wind Done Gone* Controversy," 5–33; Schwarzbaum, "*The Wind Done Gone*."
3. Randall, *The Wind Done Gone*," 135, 84.
4. Gros, "*The Wind Done Gone*," 145; Argall, "A Rib from My Chest," 231.
5. *The Divine Secrets of the Ya-Ya Sisterhood*; M. Harris, "How *Being Mary Jane* Chal-

lenges Stereotypes"; Siebler, "Black Feminists in Serialized Dramas," 152; Nealy, "Refining the Angry Black Woman"; F. Harris and Coleman, "Trending Topics," 1; Rossie, *Being Mary Jane and Postfeminism*," 25–41.

6. Ansa, *Taking After Mudear*; *The Divine Secrets of the Ya-Ya Sisterhood*; Bloodworth-Thomason, *Liberating Paris*; Tademy, *Red River*; Tademy, *Citizens Creek*.

7. "Age of Oprah."

8. "The Color Purple"; Clemetson et al., "Oprah on Oprah."

9. Kingsolver, *The Poisonwood Bible*.

10. Calkin, "Feminism, Interrupted?," 658, 662, 654.

11. "Imagine the World"; "Our Story"; "The Girl Effect."

12. Ghadery, "#MeToo," 257–259; Sands, "How Oprah Winfrey Is Empowering Girls."

13. Samuels, "Oprah Goes to School."

14. *The Oprah Winfrey Show Twentieth Anniversary Collection*, "Christmas Kindness."

15. Lofton, *Oprah*, 5.

16. *The Oprah Winfrey Show Twentieth Anniversary Collection*, "Oprah's 50th Birthday Bash."

17. *The Oprah Winfrey Show Twentieth Anniversary Collection*, "Christmas Kindness."

18. J. Harris, "What Is Africa to Me?," 293; Winfrey, "What I Know for Sure."

19. Samuels, "Oprah Goes to School."

20. J. Harris, "What Is Africa to Me?," 293; Palumbo, "Meet the Graduates."

21. J. Harris, "What Is Africa to Me?," 294; Samuels, "Oprah Goes to School."

22. Traister, "What Oprah Can't Forget."

23. Samuels, "Oprah Goes to School."

24. J. Harris, "What Is Africa to Me?," 297; Cooper, *Beyond Respectability*, 15.

25. J. Harris, "What Is Africa to Me?," 302.

26. Ibid., 301, 302.

27. *Oprah's Next Chapter*, "Beyoncé"; *Oprah's Super Soul Conversations*, "Beyoncé."

28. Cooper, *Eloquent Rage*, 26; *Life Is But a Dream*.

29. J. Bennett, "How to Reclaim the F-Word."

30. Lilburn et al., "Celebrity Feminism as Synthesis," 243.

31. J. Bennett, "How to Reclaim the F-Word."

32. hooks, "Dig Deep: Beyond *Lean In*"; McRobbie, *The Aftermath of Feminism*; "hooks: Beyoncé Is a Terrorist"; J. King, "Is Beyoncé a Terrorist?"

33. J. King, "Is Beyoncé a Terrorist?"; Brooks and Martin, "Introduction: Beyoncé's *Lemonade* Lexicon," 1.

34. Cooper, *Eloquent Rage*, 30.

35. Ghansah, "How Sweet It Is."

36. Springer, "Third Wave Black Feminism?," 1077.

37. Bradley, *Chronicling Stankonia*, 6.

38. Brooks, "Suga Mama, Politicized"; Steptoe, "Beyoncé's Western South Serenade," 186–187; Beyoncé, "No Angel"; Beyoncé, "Déjà Vu."

39. Beyoncé, "Formation"; Scott Lewis, "It's Not Just a Lyric"; Fenstertock, "Big Freedia"; "Big Freedia"; "What Beyoncé Told Freedia."

40. J. Brown, *Babylon Girls*, 15.

41. *Saturday Night Live*, "The Day Beyoncé Turned Black."

42. A. Wallace, "A Critical View of Beyoncé's 'Formation,'" 191, 192, 194, 195.
43. Sandberg, "Why I Want Women to Lean In."
44. Beyoncé, "Formation."
45. T. Harris, "'Formation' and the Black-Ass Truth," 155; James, "How Not to Listen," 69.
46. Beyoncé, "Formation"; "Tidal to Donate $1.5 Million."
47. Ford, "Beysthetics," 197.
48. Adams, *Wounds of Returning*, 70.
49. McInnis, "Black Women's Geographies," 763; Bradley, *Chronicling Stankonia*, 64.
50. Hartman, *Lose Your Mother*, 6.
51. McKittrick, "Plantation Futures," 4, 5, 6; McInnis, "Black Women's Geographies," 759; Richardson, *Emancipation's Daughters*, 231.
52. Spillers, "Mama's Baby, Papa's Maybe," 67; McInnis, "Black Women's Geographies," 741; Muhammad, "The Sugar That Saturates"; Follett, "Rise and Fall of Sugar," 61–90; McInnis, "Black Women's Geographies," 746.
53. Sisson, "Beyoncé's 'Formation.'"
54. Peñate, "Beyoncé's Diaspora Heritage," 118, 120.
55. Mills, "Demythicizing History," 402; Mills, "Laying a Legend to Rest," 177.
56. "Beyoncé in Her Own Words"; McInnis, "Black Women's Geographies," 764.
57. McKittrick and Woods, "Introduction," 2.
58. Ward, "In Beyoncé's 'Formation'"; Stack, *Call to Home*, xv; T. Johnson, *Black Women in New South*, 127; McFadden, "Beyoncé's 'Formation' Reclaims Black America."
59. "Beyoncé Live at Super Bowl 2016"; S. Johnson, *Black Women in New South*, 6.
60. Beyoncé, *Lemonade*; Tinsley, *Beyoncé in Formation*, Kindle location 1817; Benbow, foreword to *The Lemonade Reader*, xxi.
61. A. Davis, *Women, Race and Class*, 39; Battle-Baptiste, "In This Here Place," 235; Brooks and Martin, "Introduction: Beyoncé's *Lemonade* Lexicon," 2.
62. Benbow, foreword to *The Lemonade Reader*, xxi.
63. Stewart, "Something Akin to Freedom," 27.
64. Cooper, *Eloquent Rage*, 218.
65. Nash, "Practicing Love," 1–24; S. Johnson, *Black Women in New South*, 97.
66. For a discussion of Beyoncé's use of African goddess imagery, see Finley and Willis, "Some Shit Is Just for Us," 17–18; Melanie Jones, "The Slay Factor," 98–110; Tsang, "Signifying Waters," 123–132.
67. Maris Jones, "Dear Beyoncé."
68. Shantrelle Lewis, "'Formation' Exploits New Orleans' Trauma."
69. Birgitta Johnson, "She Gave You *Lemonade*," 236; Gipson, "From Destiny's Child to Coachella," 150; Highsmith, "Beyoncé Reborn," 142; Steptoe, "Beyoncé's Western South Serenade," 189.
70. Andrews, "Lawsuit Charges Beyoncé with Appropriation"; Simoneaux, "As Messy Mya Lawsuit Settles." Roberts's lawsuit was dismissed (U.S. Eastern District of Louisiana, *Kimberly Roberts v. Prettybird Pictures*).
71. Benbow, foreword to *The Lemonade Reader*, xxi.
72. Bradley, afterword to *The Lemonade Reader*, 250.
73. Beyoncé, *Lemonade*.
74. Richardson, *Emancipation's Daughters*, 221.

75. Brooks and Martin, "Introduction: Beyoncé's *Lemonade* Lexicon," 3.
76. Simmons, "Landscapes, Memories, and History"; Fessenden, "How a Nearly Successful Slave Revolt"; Steptoe, "Beyoncé's Western South Serenade," 188; Buman, "Historiographical Examinations," 318–337.
77. Beyoncé, *Lemonade*; Gipson, "From Destiny's Child to Coachella," 146, 148.
78. Josephs, "Beyoncé's *Lemonade* Premiere"; Parisi, "Beyoncé's *Lemonade*."
79. Brooks and Martin, "Introduction: Beyoncé's *Lemonade* Lexicon," 1.
80. *Oprah's Super Soul Conversations*, "Beyoncé."
81. Bowman, "*Queen Sugar* Is Reinventing"; Philips, "*Queen Sugar* Is a Black Feminist."
82. Francis and Finn, "A Theoretically-Based Analysis," 1104–1112.
83. "Oprah Says 26 Billboards"; Couric, "Why Oprah Gave Up Her Magazine Cover."
84. Richardson, *Emancipation's Daughters*, 221.
85. Fraser, "Feminism, Capitalism," 4.

BIBLIOGRAPHY

Abbandonato, Linda. "'A View from Elsewhere': Subversive Sexuality and the Rewriting of the Heroine's Story in *The Color Purple*." *PMLA* 106, no. 5 (October 1991): 1106–1115.
Abbott, Phillip. "A Long and Winding Road: Bill Clinton and the 1960s." *Rhetoric and Public Affairs* 9, no. 1 (Spring 2006): 1–20.
Abbott, Shirley. *Womenfolks: Growing Up Down South*. Boston: Ticknor and Fields, 1983.
Adams, Jessica. *Wounds of Returning: Race, Memory, and Property on the Postslavery Plantation*. Chapel Hill: University of North Carolina Press, 2007.
"Age of Oprah." *Newsweek*, January 8, 2001, cover.
alh. "*Thelma and Louise*." *off our backs* 21, no. 8 (August/September 1991): 2.
Alley Theatre. "In Conversation with Theresa Rebeck and Beth Henley." https://web.archive.org/web/20200804204606/https://www.alleytheatre.org/crimes.
Allison, Dorothy. *Bastard out of Carolina*. New York: Dutton, 1992.
Allured, Janet. "Louisiana, the American South, and the Birth of Second-Wave Feminism." *Louisiana History* 54, no. 4 (Fall 2013): 389–432.
Allured, Janet. *Remapping Second-Wave Feminism: The Long Women's Rights Movement in Louisiana*. Athens: University of Georgia Press, 2016.
Alterman, Eric. *The Cause: The Fight for American Liberalism from Franklin Roosevelt to Barack Obama*. New York: Penguin, 2012.
Althouse, Ann. "*Thelma and Louise*: Do Rape Shield Rules Matter?" *Loyola of Los Angeles Law Review* 757 (1992): 757–772.
American Drama Institute. "Expressing 'the Misery and Confusion Truthfully': An Interview with Beth Henley." Free Library, 2005. https://www.thefreelibrary.com/Expressing+%22the+misery+and+confusion+truthfully%22%3A+an+interview+with . . .-a0126556706.
American Experience. "Clinton." PBS, May 7, 2012. https://www.pbs.org/video/american-experience-clinton.
Anderson-Bricker, Kristin. "'Triple Jeopardy': Black Women and the Growth of Feminist Consciousness in SNCC, 1964–1975." In *Still Lifting, Still Climbing: Contemporary African American Women's Activism*, edited by Kimberley Springer, 49–69. New York: New York University Press, 1999.
Andreach, Robert. *Understanding Beth Henley*. Columbia: University of South Carolina Press, 2006.

Andrews, Travis M. "Lawsuit Charges Beyoncé with Appropriation." *Valley News* (West Lebanon, NH), February 8, 2017. https://www.vnews.com/Beyonce-is-being-sued-for-sampling-New-Orleans-culture-in—Lemonade—7986112.
Angelou, Maya. *The Heart of a Woman*. New York: Random House, 1981.
Ansa, Tina McElroy. *Taking After Mudear*. St. Simons Island, Ga.: DownSouth Press, 2007.
Ansa, Tina McElroy. *Ugly Ways*. New York: Houghton Mifflin Harcourt, 1993. Kindle.
Appel, Mark. "Fictional Narratives Cultivate Just-World Beliefs." *Journal of Communication* 58, no. 1 (2008): 62–83.
Applebome, Peter. *Dixie Rising: How the South Is Shaping American Values, Politics, and Culture*. New York: Times Books, 1996.
Araiza, Jose Andres. "Saying Goodbye to Men: Southern Feminists Publishing News While Challenging Patriarchy." *Journal of Communication Inquiry* 38, no. 4 (2014): 273–290.
Argall, Nicole. "A Rib from My Chest: Cynara's Journey as an Africana Womanist." *CLA Journal* 47, no. 2 (December 2033): 231–243.
Aschoff, Nicole. *The New Prophets of Capital*. New York: Verso, 2015.
Association for Theatre in Higher Education. "Beth Henley Interview." YouTube, 2010. https://www.youtube.com/watch?v=tKjLHGFxmcw.
Athas, Daphne. "Why There Are No Southern Writers." In *Women Writers of the Contemporary South*, edited by Peggy Whitman Prenshaw, 295–308. Oxford: University Press of Mississippi, 1984.
Atlanta March Committee. "Letter," March 9, 1987. Folder 2, box 2, "Southern Feminist 1982–1989," *Southern Feminist* Collection, David M. Rubenstein Rare Book and Manuscript Library, Duke University.
Auflitsch, Susanne. "Beth Henley's Early Family Plays: Dysfunctional Parenting, the South, and Feminism." *American Studies* 46, no. 2 (2001): 267–280.
Auletta, Ken. "The Lost Tycoon." *New Yorker*, April 16, 2001. https://www.newyorker.com/magazine/2001/04/23/the-lost-tycoon.
"Author's Bio and Family Photos." Tina McElroy Ansa. http://www.tinamcelroyansa.com/bio.html.
Bal, P. Mattijs, and Martijn Veltkamp. "How Does Fiction Reading Influence Empathy?" *PLOS ONE*, no. 1 (2013). https://journals.plos.org/plosone/article?id=10.1371/journal.pone.0055341.
Baldwin, James. *The Evidence of Things Not Seen*. New York: Owl Books, 1985.
Bambara, Toni Cade, ed. *The Black Woman: An Anthology*. New York: New American Library, 1970.
Bambara, Toni Cade. Foreword to *This Bridge Called My Back: Writings by Radical Women of Color*, edited by Cherríe Moraga and Gloria Anzaldúa, xl–xliii. Watertown, Mass.: Persephone Press, 1981.
Barker, Deborah, and Kathryn McKee. Introduction to *American Cinema and the Southern Imaginary*, 1–23. Athens: University of Georgia Press, 2011.
Bartel, Pauline. *The Complete "Gone with the Wind" Trivia Book: The Movie and More*. Lanham: Taylor Trade Publishing, 1989.
Battle-Baptiste, Whitney. "'In This Here Place': Interpreting Enslaved Homeplaces." In *Archaeology of Atlantic Africa and the African Diaspora*, edited by Akinwumi

Ogundiran and Toyin Falola, 233–248. Bloomington: Indiana University Press, 2007.

Bauer, Margaret Donovan. *A Study of Scarletts: Scarlett O'Hara and Her Literary Daughters*. Columbia: University of South Carolina Press, 2014.

Bauer, Susan Wise. "Oprah's Misery Index." *Christianity Today*, December 7, 1998. https://www.christianitytoday.com/ct/1998/december7/8te070.html.

Baumgardner, Jennifer, and Amy Richards. *Manifesta: Young Women, Feminism, and the Future*. New York: Farrar, Straus and Giroux, 2000.

Baumgardner, Jennifer, and Deborah Siegel. *Sisterhood Interrupted: From Radical Women to Grrls Gone Wild*. New York: Palgrave, 2007.

Beaufort, John. "A Play That Proves There's No Explaining Awards." *Christian Science Monitor*, November 9, 1981. https://www.csmonitor.com/1981/1109/110901.html.

Bejarano, Christina E., and Valerie Martinez-Ebers. "Latina Mobilization: A Strategy for Increasing the Political Participation of Latino Families." In *The Legacy of Second-Wave Feminism in American Politics*, edited by Angie Maxwell and Todd Shields, 165–178. New York: Palgrave, 2018.

Beloved. Directed by Jonathan Demme. Harpo Films and Touchstone Pictures, 1998.

Benbow, Candace. Foreword to *The Lemonade Reader*, edited by Kinitra D. Brooks and Kameelah L. Martin, xx–xxii. New York: Routledge, 2019.

Bennett, Barbara. "Making Peace with the Mother." In *The World Is Our Home: Society and Culture in Contemporary Southern Writing*, edited by Jeffery J. and Nancy Summer Folks, 186–200. Lexington: University of Kentucky Press, 2000.

Bennett, Barbara. "Southern Women Writers and the Women's Movement." In *The History of Southern Women's Literature*, edited by Carolyn Perry and Mary Louise Weaks, 439–446. Baton Rouge: Louisiana State University Press, 2002.

Bennett, Jessica. "How to Reclaim the F-Word? Just Call Beyoncé." *Time*, August 26, 2014. https://time.com/3181644/beyonce-reclaim-feminism-pop-star.

Berlant, Lauren. *The Female Complaint: The Unfinished Business of Sentimentality in American Culture*. Durham: Duke University Press, 2008.

Berlant, Lauren. *The Queen of American Goes to Washington City: Essays on Sex and Citizenship*. Durham: Duke University Press, 1997.

Berlant, Lauren. "Race, Gender, and Nation in *The Color Purple*." In *Alice Walker: Critical Perspectives Past and Present*, edited by Henry Louis Gates Jr., 211–238. New York: Amistad, 1993.

Berlant, Lauren. "The Subject of True Feeling: Pain, Privacy, and Politics." In *Cultural Pluralism, Politics, and the Law*, edited by Austin Stuart and Thomas Kearns, 49–84. Ann Arbor: University of Michigan Press, 1999.

Bernstein, Fred A. "Pulling Itself Out of the Ratings Heap, *Designing Women* Becomes TV's Trashy New Smash." *People*, April 20, 1987. https://people.com/archive/pulling-itself-out-of-the-ratings-waste-heap-designing-women-becomes-tvs-trashy-new-smash-vol-27-no-16.

Beyoncé. "Déjà Vu (MTV Video Version)." 2006. https://www.youtube.com/watch?v=RQ9BWndKEgs.

Beyoncé. "Formation (Official Video)." 2016. https://www.youtube.com/watch?v=WDZJPJV__bQ&list=PLUZ_BcQNQ4DOa4eDvd7OA9kyWFgRt-3zb&index=42&t=0s.

Beyoncé. "No Angel (Video)." 2013. https://www.youtube.com/watch?v
=d7PPjEB2QZQ.
"Beyoncé in Her Own Words: Her Life, Her Body, Her Heritage." *Vogue*, August 6, 2018. https://www.vogue.com/article/beyonce-september-issue-2018.
"Beyoncé Live at Super Bowl 2016." YouTube. https://www.youtube.com/watch?v
=3hZFz3bHUAg.
Bianculli, David. *Teleliteracy: Taking Television Seriously*. Syracuse: Syracuse University Press, 2000.
Bibler, Michael P. *Cotton's Queer Relations: Same-Sex Intimacy and the Literature of the Southern Plantation, 1936–1968*. Charlottesville: University of Virginia Press, 2009.
Bielby, Denise B., and William T. Bielby. "Women and Men in Film: Gender Inequality among Writers in a Culture Industry." *Gender and Society* 10, no. 3 (June 1996): 248–270.
"Big Freedia: Getting the 'Formation' Call from Beyoncé." YouTube. https://www
.youtube.com/watch?v=ZYHAuc3nhDU.
"Bill Clinton on the Johnny Carson Show 1988" [*The Tonight Show with Johnny Carson*, season 27, episode 69, July 28, 1988]. https://www.youtube.com/watch?v
=TfcKQcGg_sM.
"Biography." Lalita Tademy. http://www.lalitatademy.com/biography.
Black, Earl. "The Newest Southern Politics." *Journal of Politics* 60, no. 3 (August 1998): 591–612.
Bloodworth-Thomason, Linda. "*Designing Women* Creator on Bill Clinton and Her New Documentary: 'I Believe in Honest Propaganda." *Hollywood Reporter*, November 19, 2013. https://www.hollywoodreporter.com/news/linda
-bloodworth-thomason-bill-clinton-657625.
Bloodworth-Thomason, Linda. *Liberating Paris*. New York: William Morrow, 2000.
"Bloodworth-Thomason, Linda (Joyce) 1947–." Encyclopedia.com. https://www
.encyclopedia.com/arts/educational-magazines/bloodworth-thomason-linda
-joyce-1947.
"Bloodworth-Thomason to Teach Course." *University of Arkansas News*, November 7, 2006. https://news.uark.edu/articles/9184/bloodworth-thomason-to-teach
-course.
"*The Bluest Eye*: About the Book." Oprah.com. http://www.oprah.com/oprahsbook
club/the-bluest-eye-by-toni-morrison.
Blyth, Amber. "Oprah Winfrey Believes If She Didn't Leave the Neighborhood Where She Lived with Her Mom in Milwaukee, She Could Have Lost Her Life." *Fabiosa*, November 27, 2019. https://fabiosa.com/dvgfen-ctentlfs-rsafr-aumgr
-pbnns-oprah-winfrey-believes-if-she-didn-t-leave-the-neighborhood-where-she
-lived-with-mom-in-milwaukee-she-could-have-lost-her-life.
Bobo, Jacqueline. "Black Women's Responses to *The Color Purple*." *Jump Cut* 33 (1988). https://www.ejumpcut.org/archive/onlinessays/JC33folder
/ClPurpleBobo.html.
Bobo, Jacqueline. "Sifting through the Controversy: Reading *The Color Purple*." *Callaloo* 39 (Spring 1989): 332–342.
Bobo, Jacqueline, and Ellen Seiter. "Black Feminism and Media Criticism: The *Women of Brewster Place*." *Screen* 32, no. 3 (1991): 286–302.

Boles, Jacqueline, and Maxine P. Atkinson. "Ladies: South by Northwest." In *Southern Women*, edited by Caroline M. Dillman, 127–138. New York: Routledge, 1988.
Bolsterli, Margaret Jones. *Born in the Delta: Reflections on the Making of a Southern White Sensibility*. Knoxville: University of Tennessee Press, 1991.
Bone, Martyn. "Introduction: Old/New/Post/Real/Global/No South: Paradigms and Scales." In *Creating and Consuming the American South*, edited by Martyn Bone, Brian Ward, and William A. Link, 1–26. Gainesville: University Press of Florida, 2015.
Bone, Martyn. *The Postsouthern Sense of Place in Contemporary Fiction*. Baton Rouge: Louisiana State University Press, 2005.
Bowman, Sabienna. "*Queen Sugar* Is Reinventing Feminist TV." *Bustle*, February 11, 2017. https://www.bustle.com/p/why-queen-sugar-is-the-show-feminists-should-be-paying-attention-to-37342.
Bradley, Regina N. Afterword to *The Lemonade Reader*, edited by Kinitra D. Brooks and Kameelah L. Martin, 250–252. New York: Routledge, 2019.
Bradley, Regina N. *Chronicling Stankonia: The Rise of the Hip-Hop South*. Chapel Hill: University of North Carolina Press, 2021.
Braudy, Leo. "Satire into Myth." *Film Quarterly* 45, no. 2 (Winter 1991–1992): 28–29.
Breines, Winifred. *The Trouble between Us: An Uneasy History of Black and White Women in the Feminist Movement*. New York: Oxford, 2006.
Brennan, Patricia. "*Designing Women* Back by Popular Demand." *Washington Post*, February 1, 1987. https://www.washingtonpost.com/archive/lifestyle/tv/1987/02/01/designing-women-back-by-popular-demand/772444a8-f8b5-40eb-b0a9-4b8c50107652.
Bröck, Sabine. "Postmodern Mediations and Beloved's Testimony: Memory Is Not Innocent." *American Studies* 43, no. 1 (1998), 33–49.
Bronner, Stephen Eric. "Resisting the Right: Challenging the Neoconservative Agenda." In *Confronting the New Conservatism: The Rise of the Right in America*, edited by Michael J. Thompson, 269–284. New York University Press, 2007.
Brooks, Daphne A. "Suga Mama, Politicized." *Nation*, November 30, 2006. https://www.thenation.com/article/archive/suga-mama-politicized.
Brooks, Kinitra D., and Kameelah L. Martin. "Introduction: Beyoncé's Lemonade Lexicon: Black Feminism and Spirituality in Theory and Practice." In *The Lemonade Reader*, edited by Kinitra D. Brooks and Kameelah L. Martin, 1–4. New York: Routledge, 2019.
Brown, Jayna. *Babylon Girls: Black Women Performers and the Shaping of the Modern*. Durham: Duke University Press, 2008.
Brown, Mary Ellen. "Feminism and Cultural Politics: Television Audiences and Hillary Rodham Clinton." *Political Communication* 14, no. 2 (1997): 255–270.
Bruck, Connie. "Hillary the Pol." *New Yorker*, May 23, 1994. https://www.newyorker.com/magazine/1994/05/30/hillary-the-pol.
Buman, Nathan A. "Historiographical Examinations of the 1811 Slave Insurrection." *Louisiana History* 53, no. 3 (Summer 2012): 318–337.
Butler, Alana. "Quiltmaking among African American Women as a Pedagogy of Care, Empowerment, and Sisterhood." *Gender and Education* 31, no. 5 (2019): 590–603.

Butler, Jeremy. "Redesigning Discourse: Feminism, the Sitcom, and Designing Women." *Journal of Film and Video* 45, no. 1 (Spring 1993): 13–26.

Butler, Richard J., Benjamin W. Cowan, and Sebastian Nilsson. "From Obscurity to Bestseller: Examining the Impact of Oprah Book Club Selections." *Publishing Research Quarterly* 20 (Winter 2005): 23–34.

Byerman, Keith. "Walker's Blues." In *Alice Walker: Modern Critical Views*, edited by Harold Bloom, 59–66. New York: Chelsea House, 1989.

Calkin, Sydney. "Feminism, Interrupted? Gender and Development in the Era of 'Smart Economics.'" *Progress in Development Studies* 15, no. 4 (2015): 295–307.

"Callie Khouri." Southern Belle Fest, October 11, 2013. Accessed December 17, 2022. https://web.archive.org/web/20161102032928/http://southernbellefest.com/callie-khouri.

Canby, Vincent. "Film: Henley's *Crimes of the Heart*." *New York Times*, December 12, 1986. https://www.nytimes.com/1986/12/12/movies/film-henley-s-crimes-of-the-heart.html.

Canedy, Dana. "The Media Business: Oprah Winfrey and Hearst to Start a Magazine." *New York Times*, July 9, 1999. https://www.nytimes.com/1999/07/09/business/the-media-business-oprah-winfrey-and-hearst-to-start-magazine.html.

Carlson, Margaret. "Is This What Feminism Is All About?" *Time*, June 24, 1991. https://content.time.com/time/subscriber/article/0,33009,973242,00.html.

The Carol Burnett Show. Season 10, episode 8, November 13, 1976. YouTube. https://www.youtube.com/watch?v=-8wVvGQ0P4Y.

Carr, Jay. "*Thelma & Louise*: Buddies with Heart." *Boston Globe*, May 24, 1991.

Carter, Bill. "Television Gets on the Bandwagon of the Thomas-Hill Contretemps." *New York Times*, November 4, 1991. https://www.nytimes.com/1991/11/04/news/television-gets-on-the-bandwagon-of-the-thomas-hill-contretemps.html.

Carter, Dan. *From George Wallace to Newt Gingrich: Race in the Conservative Counterrevolution, 1963–1994*. Louisiana State University Press, 1996.

Case, Sarah H. "The Historical Ideology of Mildred Lewis Rutherford: A Confederate Historian's New South Creed." *Journal of Southern History* 68, no. 3 (2002): 599–628.

Caviness, Alison Ruth. "Female Sexuality in the South: The Contemporary Southern Belle in the Works of Beth Henley, Fannie Flagg, and Alice Walker." MA thesis, University of Virginia, 2005.

Cha, Frank. "Creating a Multiethnic South: Vietnamese American Cultural and Economic Visibility before and after Hurricane Katrina." In *Creating and Consuming the American South*, edited by Martyn Bone, Brian Ward, and William A. Link, 203–225. Gainesville: University Press of Florida, 2015.

Chambers, Veronica. "Book Review: The Things That Drive You Crazy Can Make You Whole: *Ugly Ways* by Tina McElroy Ansa." *Los Angeles Times*, August 24, 1993. https://www.latimes.com/archives/la-xpm-1993-08-24-vw-27318-story.html.

Chopin, Kate. *The Awakening*. New York: Bantam, 1899.

Christiansë, Yvettte. *Toni Morrison: An Ethical Poetics*. New York: Fordham University Press, 2013.

Chumo, Peter. "*Thelma & Louise* as Screwball Comedy." *Film Quarterly* 45, no. 2 (Winter 1991–1992): 24.

Clark, Breena. *River, Cross My Heart*. New York: Little, Brown, 1999.

"Classic U.S. Sitcom *Designing Women* Being Rebooted." MSN.com, August 14, 2018.

Accessed December 18, 2022. https://web.archive.org/web/20180815013852
/https://www.msn.com/en-nz/entertainment/news/classic-us-sitcom-designing
-women-being-rebooted/ar-BBLWlSh.
Cleage, Pearl. *What Looks Like Crazy on an Ordinary Day*. New York: Avon, 1997.
Clemetson, Lynette. "It's Constant Work." *Newsweek*, January 8, 2001, 44–45.
Clemetson, Lynette, Joan Raymond, Bret Begun, Ana Figueroa, and Julie Halpert. "Oprah on Oprah." *Newsweek*, January 8, 2001, 38–47.
Cloud, Dana L. "Hegemony or Concordance? The Rhetoric of Oprah's Rags-to-Riches Biography." *Critical Studies in Mass Communication* 13, no. 2 (1996): 115–137.
Cobb, James C. *Away Down South: A History of Southern Identity*. New York: Oxford University Press, 2007.
Cobb, James C. *Redefining Southern Culture: Mind and Identity in the Modern South*. Athens: University of Georgia Press, 1999.
Cobb, James C. *The Selling of the South: The Southern Crusade for Industrial Development*. Baton Rouge: Louisiana State University Press, 1982.
Collins, Patricia Hill. *Black Feminist Thought: Knowledge, Consciousness, and the Politics of Empowerment*. New York: Routledge, 1990.
Collins, Patricia Hill. *Black Sexual Politics*. New York: Routledge, 2004.
Collins, Patricia Hill. "Black Women and Motherhood." In *Motherhood and Space: Configurations of the Maternal Through Politics, Home, and the Body*, edited by S. Hardy and C. Wiedmer, 149–159. Palgrave, 2005.
Collins, Patricia Hill. *Fighting Words: Black Women and the Search for Justice*. Minneapolis: University of Minnesota Press, 1998.
Collins, Patricia Hill. "The Meaning of Motherhood in Black Culture and Black Mother-Daughter Relationships." In *Double-Stitch: Black Women Write about Mothers and Daughters*, edited by Beverly Guy-Sheftall, Jacqueline Jones Royster, Janet Sims-Wood, Miriam DeCosta-Willis, and Lucille P. Fultz, 42–60. Boston: Beacon Press, 1991.
The Color Purple. Directed by Steven Spielberg. Amblin Entertainment, 1986.
"The Color Purple." New York Theatre Guide com. September 22, 2017. https://www.newyorktheatreguide.com/reviews/the-color-purple-0.
Conroy, Sarah Booth. "Riding the Wind: Scarlett Revisited." *Washington Post*, September 25, 1991. https://www.washingtonpost.com/archive/lifestyle/1991/09/25/riding-the-wind-scarlett-revisited/3e04e8fb-2b5d-4151-8a59-838a916d9702.
Cooper, Brittney C. *Beyond Respectability: The Intellectual Thought of Race Women*. Champaign: University of Illinois Press, 2017.
Cooper, Brittney C. *Eloquent Rage: A Black Feminist Discovers Her Superpower*. New York: St. Martin's, 2018.
Copenhagen, Cathy Sue. "The Death of Postfeminism: Oprah and the Riot Grrrls Talk Back." PhD thesis, Montana State University, 2002.
Cornwall, Andrea, Jasmine Gideon, and Kalpana Wilson. "Reclaiming Feminism: Gender and Neoliberalism." IDS *Bulletin* 39, no. 6 (December 2008): 1–9.
Corry, John. "ABC's *After the Sexual Revolution*." *New York Times*, July 30, 1986. https://www.nytimes.com/1986/07/30/arts/abc-s-after-the-sexual-revolution.html.
Coulthard, Lisa. "Killing Bill: Rethinking Feminism and Film Violence." In *Interrogating Postfeminism: Gender and the Politics of Popular Culture*, edited by Diane Negra and Yvonne Tasker, 153–175. Durham: Duke University Press, 2007.

Couric, Katie. "Why Oprah Gave Up Her Magazine Cover for Breonna Taylor." KatieCouricMedia.com, August 11, 2020. https://katiecouric.com/news/gayle-king-on-why-oprah-gave-up-her-magazine-cover-for-breonna-taylor.
Cox, Karen L. *Dixie's Daughters: The United Daughters of the Confederacy and the Preservation of Confederate Culture*. Gainesville: University Press of Florida, 2003.
Cox, Karen L. *Dreaming of Dixie: How the South Was Created in Mass Culture*. Chapel Hill: University of North Carolina Press, 2011. Kindle.
Cox, Karen L. "The South and Mass Culture." *Journal of Southern History* 75, no. 3 (August 2009): 677–690.
Crenshaw, Kimberlé. "Demarginalizing the Intersection of Race and Sex: A Black Feminist Critique of Antidiscrimination Doctrine, Feminist Theory and Antiracist Politics." *University of Chicago Legal Forum* 1 (1989): 139–167.
Crenshaw, Kimberlé. "Mapping the Margins: Intersectionality, Identity Politics, and Violence against Women of Color." *Stanford Law Review* 43, no. 6 (July 1991): 1241–1299.
Crowley, Karlyn. *Feminism's New Age: Gender, Appropriation, and the Afterlife of Essentialism*. Albany: State University of New York Press, 2011.
Cunningham, Sean. *American Politics in the Postwar Sunbelt*. Cambridge: Cambridge University Press, 2014.
Danticat, Edwidge. *Breath, Eyes, Memory*. New York: Soho Press, 1994.
Darling, Marsha. "In the Realm of Responsibility: A Conversation with Toni Morrison." *Women's Review of Books* 5 (March 1988): 5–6.
Davis, Angela Y. Afterword to *To Be Real: Telling the Truth and Changing the Face of Feminism*, edited by Rebecca Walker, 279–284. New York: Anchor Books, 1995.
Davis, Angela Y. *Blues Legacies and Black Feminism: Gertrude "Ma" Rainey, Bessie Smith, and Billie Holiday*. New York: Vintage, 1998.
Davis, Angela Y. *Women, Race and Class*. New York: Random House, 1981.
Davis, Kimberley Chabot. "Oprah's Book Club and the Politics of Cross-Racial Empathy." *International Journal of Cultural Studies* 7, no. 4 (2004): 399–419.
Davis, Thadious M. *Southscapes: Geographies of Race, Region, and Literature*. Chapel Hill: University of North Carolina Press, 2014.
Davis, Thadious M. "Walker's Celebration of Self in Southern Generations." In *Alice Walker: Modern Critical Views*, edited by Harold Bloom, 25–37. New York: Chelsea House, 1989.
Decker, Jeffrey Louis. "Saint Oprah." *Modern Fiction Studies* 52, no. 1 (Spring 2006): 169–178.
DeHart, Jane Sherron. "Second Wave Feminism(s) and the South: The Difference that Differences Make." In *Women of the American South: A Multicultural Reader*, edited by Christie Anne Farnham, 273–302. New York: New York University Press, 1997.
De Moraes, Lisa. "In CBS Deal, Oprah Gets a Wheel of Fortune." *Washington Post*, April 2, 1999. https://www.washingtonpost.com/archive/lifestyle/1999/04/02/in-cbs-deal-oprah-gets-a-wheel-fortune-100-million/6edbc7ee-9362-416e-94e1-0139ba72844e.
Denard, Carolyn. "Blacks, Modernism, and the American South: An Interview with Toni Morrison." *Studies in the Literary Imagination* 31, no. 2 (1998), 1–16.

"Designing Women." Television Academy. https://www.emmys.com/shows/designing-women.
Designing Women. "And Justice for Paul." Season 1, episode 15, February 15, 1987.
Designing Women. "Anthony and Vanessa." Season 4, episode 18, February 5, 1990.
Designing Women. "Anthony Jr." Season 2, episode 3, September 28, 1987.
Designing Women. "The Bachelor Auction." Season 5, episode 5, October 22, 1990;
Designing Women. "Bachelor Suite." Season 1, episode 22, May 11, 1987.
Designing Women. "A Big Affair." Season 1, episode 3, October 20, 1986.
Designing Women. "But They're Really Great Curtains." Season 3, episode 7, January 2, 1989.
Designing Women. "The Candidate." Season 3, episode 2, November 21, 1988.
Designing Women. "Cruising." Season 2, episode 8, November 16, 1987.
Designing Women. "Design House." Season 1, episode 6, November 17, 1986.
Designing Women. "Designing Women." Season 1, episode 1, September 29, 1986.
Designing Women. "First Day of the Last Decade of the Twentieth Century, Part 2." Season 4, episode 14, January 1, 1990.
Designing Women. "Fools Rush In." Season 7, episode 7, November 13, 1992.
Designing Women. "Foreign Affairs." Season 4, episode 23, April 3, 1990.
Designing Women. "Getting Married and Eating Dirt." Season 3, episode 4. December 5, 1988.
Designing Women. "Gone With the Whim, Part 1." Season 7, episode 21, May 24, 1993.
Designing Women. "Gone With the Whim, Part 2." season 7, episode 22, May 24, 1993.
Designing Women. "Grand Slam, Thank You Ma'am." Season 1, episode 21, May 4, 1987.
Designing Women. "Great Expectations." Season 2, episode 13, January 4, 1988.
Designing Women. "Hardhats and Lovers." Season 3, episode 6, December 19, 1988.
Designing Women. "Heart Attacks." Season 2, episode 7, November 9, 1987.
Designing Women. "High Rollers." Season 2, episode 18. February 8, 1988.
Designing Women. "Howard the Date." Season 2, episode 11, December 14, 1987.
Designing Women. "I'll Be Home for Christmas." Season 2, episode 12, December 21, 1987.
Designing Women. "The IT Men." Season 1, episode 9, December 4, 1986.
Designing Women. "Killing All the Right People." Season 2, episode 4, October 5, 1987.
Designing Women. "Manhunt." Season 4, episode 10, December 4, 1989.
Designing Women. "Mary Jo's Dad Dates Charlene." Designing Women. Season 1, episode 19. April 6, 1987.
Designing Women. "Mary Jo's First Date." Season 1, episode 5, November 3, 1986.
Designing Women. "Nashville Bound." Season 1, episode 17, March 16, 1987.
Designing Women. "New Year's Daze." Season 1, episode 11, January 1, 1987.
Designing Women. "Nightmare from Hee Haw." Season 4, episode 4, October 16, 1989.
Designing Women. "The Odyssey." Season 7, episode 12, January 15, 1993.
Designing Women. "Oh, What a Feeling." Season 4, episode 17, January 29, 1990.
Designing Women. "Of Human Bondage." Season 7, episode 1. September 25, 1992.
Designing Women. "Old Spouses Never Die Part 1." Season 1, episode 12, February 1, 1987.
Designing Women. "On the Road Again." Season 7, episode 4, October 23, 1992.

Designing Women. "Perky's Visit." Season 1, episode 7, November 24, 1986.
Designing Women. "Reese's Friend." Season 1, episode 16, February 22, 1987.
Designing Women. "Reservations for Eight." Season 2, episode 22, March 28, 1988.
Designing Women. "The Rowdy Girls." Season 4, episode 6, October 30, 1989.
Designing Women. "Second Time Around." Season 2, episode 14, January 11, 1988.
Designing Women. "Stand and Fight." Season 3, episode 20, May 8, 1989.
Designing Women. "Stranded." Season 2, episode 10, December 7, 1987.
Designing Women. "The Strange Case of Clarence and Anita." Season 6, episode 8, November 4, 1991.
Designing Women. "Suzanne Goes Looking for a Friend." Season 4, episode 24, April 9, 1990.
Designing Women. "Viva Las Vegas." Season 7, episode 6, November 6, 1992.
"The Dialogue: Callie Khouri Interview, Part 1." YouTube. https://m.youtube.com/watch?v=sd_4jAMdxl4.
Dicker, Rory C. *A History of U.S. Feminisms.* New York: Seal Press, 2016.
Dionne, E. J. "Democrats Hear Emotional Pleas." *Washington Post,* July 15, 1992. https://www.washingtonpost.com/archive/politics/1992/07/15/democrats-hear-emotional-pleas/5da4851f-9ee1-4337-99e1-8296bdb80a2d.
The Divine Secrets of the Ya-Ya Sisterhood. Directed by Callie Khouri. All Girl Productions, 2002.
Dolan, Jill. *The Feminist Spectator as Critic.* Ann Arbor: University of Michigan Press, 2012.
Dow, Bonnie J. *Prime-Time Feminism: Television, Media Culture, and the Women's Movement since 1970.* Philadelphia: University of Pennsylvania Press, 1996.
Dowd, Maureen. "Clinton's Best Friends Find It a Tough Role." *New York Times,* May 27, 1993. https://www.nytimes.com/1993/05/27/us/clinton-s-best-friends-find-it-a-tough-role.html.
Du Brow, Rick. "CBS Aims to Divide, Conquer." *Los Angeles Times,* May 22, 1992. http://articles.latimes.com/1992-05-22/entertainment/ca-364_1_designing-women.
Draper, Robert. "How Hillary Became 'Hillary.'" *New York Times Magazine.* October 11, 2016. https://www.nytimes.com/2016/10/16/magazine/how-hillary-clinton-became-hillary.html.
Ebert, Roger. "*Crimes of the Heart.*" RogerEbert.com, December 12, 1986. https://www.rogerebert.com/reviews/crimes-of-the-heart-1986.
Ebert, Roger. "*The Color Purple.*" RogerEbert.com, December 20, 1985. https://www.rogerebert.com/reviews/the-color-purple-1985.
Ebert, Roger. "Winfrey Confronts the Strength and the Spirits in 'Beloved.'" RogerEbert.com, October 11, 1998. https://www.rogerebert.com/interviews/winfrey-confronts-the-strength-and-the-spirits-of-beloved.
Edwards, Arlene. "Community Mothering: The Relationship between Mothering and the Community Work of Black Women." *Journal of the Motherhood Initiative* 2, no. 2 (2000): 87–100.
Eisenstein, Hester. "Feminism Seduced: Globalisation and the Uses of Gender." *Australian Feminist Studies* 25 (2010): 413–431.
Eisenstein, Zillah R. "The Sexual Politics of the New Right: Understanding the 'Crisis of Liberalism' for the 1980s." *Signs* 7, no. 3 (Spring 1982): 567–588.

Entman, Robert M. "Framing: Toward a Clarification of a Fractured Paradigm." *Journal of Communication* 43, no. 4 (Autumn 1993): 51–58.
Eraso, Carmen Indurain. "*Thelma & Louise*: 'Easy Riders' in a Male Genre." *Atlantis* 23, no. 1 (June 2001): 63–73.
Evans, Sara M. "Generations Later, Retelling the Story." In *The Legacy of Second-Wave Feminism in American Politics*, edited by Angie Maxwell and Todd Shields, 19–38. New York: Palgrave, 2018.
Evans, Sara [M.]. *Personal Politics: The Roots of Women's Liberation in the Civil Rights Movement and the New Left*. New York: Vintage, 1979.
Evans, Sara M. *Tidal Wave: How Women Changed America at Century's End*. New York: Free Press, 2003.
Faludi, Susan. *Backlash: The Undeclared War against American Women*. New York: Crown, 1991.
Farmer, Ashley D. *Remaking Black Power: How Black Women Transformed an Era*. Chapel Hill: University of North Carolina Press, 2017, 159–192.
Farr, Cecilia Konchar. *Reading Oprah: How Oprah's Book Club Changed the Way America Reads*. Albany: State University of New York Press, 2005.
Farrell, Amy Erdman. *Yours in Sisterhood:* Ms. *Magazine and the Promise of Popular Feminism*. Chapel Hill: University of North Carolina Press, 1998.
Fensterstock, Alison. "Big Freedia in the 21st Century Ambassador of Freedom." NPR, October 30, 2018. https://www.npr.org/2018/10/30/655851421/big-freedia-is-the-21st-centurys-ambassador-of-freedom?t=1609323659196.
Fernandes, Leela. "Unsettling 'Third Wave Feminism': Feminist Waves, Intersectionality, and Identity Politics in Retrospect." In *No Permanent Waves: Recasting Histories of U.S. Feminism*, edited by Nancy Hewitt, 98–119. New Brunswick, N.J.: Rutgers University Press, 2010.
Fessenden, Marissa. "How a Nearly Successful Slave Revolt Was Intentionally Lost to History." *Smithsonian*, January 8, 2016. https://www.smithsonianmag.com/smart-news/its-anniversary-1811-louisiana-slave-revolt-180957760.
Finley, Cheryl, and Deborah Willis. "Some Shit Is Just for Us." In *The Lemonade Reader*, edited by Kinitra D. Brooks and Kameelah L. Martin, 17–18. New York: Routledge, 2019.
Follett, Richard. "The Rise and Fall of American Sugar." In *Plantation Kingdom: The American South and Its Commodities*, edited by Richard Follett, Sven Beckert, Peter Coclanis, and Barbara Hahn, 61–90. Baltimore: Johns Hopkins University Press, 2016.
Ford, Tanisha C. "Beysthetics: 'Formation' and the Politics of Style." In *The Lemonade Reader*, edited by Kinitra D. Brooks and Kameelah L. Martin, 192–201. New York: Routledge, 2019.
Fox-Genovese, Elizabeth. "Mothers and Daughters: The Tie That Binds." In *Southern Mothers: Fact and Fictions in Southern Women's Writing*, edited by Nagueyalti Warren and Sally Wolff, xv–xviii. Baton Rouge: Louisiana State University Press, 1999.
Fox-Genovese, Elizabeth. "Scarlett O'Hara: The Southern Lady as 'New Woman.'" In *Half Sisters of History: Southern Women and the American Past*, edited by Catherine Clinton, 154–179. Durham: Duke University Press, 1994.
Francis, Diane B., and LeChrista Finn. "A Theoretically-Based Analysis of Twitter

Conversations about Trauma and Mental Health: Examining Responses to Storylines on the Television Show *Queen Sugar*." *Health* 37, no. 9 (2022): 1104–1112.
Fraser, Nancy. "Feminism, Capitalism, and the Cunning of History." *New Left Review* 56 (March/April 2009): 97–117.
Fried Green Tomatoes. Directed by Jon Avnet. Universal Pictures, 1991.
Frith, Hannah, Jayne Raisborough, and Orly Klein. "C'mon Girlfriend: Sisterhood, Sexuality, and the Space of the Benign in Makeover TV." *International Journal of Cultural Studies* 13, no. 5 (2010): 471–489.
Frontline. "Stories of Bill: Interview with Danny Thomason." May 11, 1996. https://www.pbs.org/wgbh/pages/frontline/shows/choice/bill/thomason.html.
Frontline. "Stories of Bill: Interview with John Brummett." May 11, 1996. https://www.pbs.org/wgbh/pages/frontline/shows/choice/bill/brummett.html.
Frontline. "Stories of Bill: Interview with Martha Sexton." June 11, 1996. https://www.pbs.org/wgbh/pages/frontline/shows/choice/bill/sexton.html.
Frontline. "Stories of Bill: Interview with Patty Criner." May 13, 1996. https://www.pbs.org/wgbh/pages/frontline/shows/choice/bill/criner.html.
Frontline. "Stories of Bill: Interview with Ron Addington." No date. https://www.pbs.org/wgbh/pages/frontline/shows/choice/bill/addington.html.
Frontline. "Stories of Bill: Interview with Sara Ehrman." June 15, 1996. https://www.pbs.org/wgbh/pages/frontline/shows/choice/bill/ehrman.html.
Frontline. "Stories of Bill: Interview with Shirley Abbott." May 28, 1996. https://www.pbs.org/wgbh/pages/frontline/shows/choice/bill/abbott.html.
Gaston, Paul M. *The New South Creed: A Study in Southern Mythmaking*. New York: Knopf, 1970.
Gates, Henry Louis, Jr. "Hating Hillary." *New Yorker*, February 18, 1996. https://www.newyorker.com/magazine/1996/02/26/hating-hillary.
Gates, Henry Louis, Jr. Preface to *Alice Walker: Critical Perspectives Past and Present*, ix–xiii. New York: Amistad, 1993.
Gaunt, Kyra. "Beyoncé's *Lemonade* and the Black Swan Effect." In *The Lemonade Reader*, edited by Kinitra D. Brooks and Kameelah L. Martin, 215–233. New York: Routledge, 2019.
Genz, Stephanie. "Third Way/ve: The Politics of Postfeminism." *Feminist Theory* 7, no. 3 (2006): 333–353.
Georgia Archives. "Skyline—Empire City of the South—Atlanta." Georgia Archives Virtual Vault. https://vault.georgiaarchives.org/digital/collection/postcard/id/1654.
Georgia Center for the Book. "Adult Reading List: Books All Georgians Should Read." http://www.georgiacenterforthebook.org/Read-Georgia-Books.
Georgia Department of Transportation. "Pleasant Hill Macon: Tina McElroy Ansa." YouTube, November 1, 2016. https://www.youtube.com/watch?v=ymbHBhsrqbI.
Gerbner, George, Larry Gross, Michael Morgan, and Nancy Signorielli. "Living with Television: The Dynamics of the Cultivation Process." In *Perspectives on Media Effects*, edited by Jennings Bryant and Dolk Zillmann, 17–40. New York: Routledge, 1986.
Ghadery, Farnush. "#MeToo—Has the 'Sisterhood' Finally Become Global or Just Another Product of Neoliberal Feminism?" *Transnational Legal Theory* 10, no. 2 (2019), 252–274.

Ghansah, Rachel Kaadzi. "How Sweet It Is to Be Loved by You: The Beyhive." NPR, March 17, 2014. https://www.npr.org/sections/therecord/2014/03/17/258155902/how-sweet-it-is-to-be-loved-by-you-the-beyhive?t=1605620298963.

Giardina, Carol. "The Making of a Modern Feminist Vanguard, 1964–1973: Southern Women Whose Leadership Shaped the Movement and the Nation—A Synthetic Analysis." *Journal of Southern History* 85, no. 3 (August 2019): 611–652.

Gibbons, Kaye. *Ellen Foster*. New York: Vintage, 1997.

Giddings, Paula J. *When and Where I Enter: The Impact of Black Women on Race and Sex*, 2nd ed. New York: William Morrow, 2007.

Gillon, Steven M. *The Pact: Bill Clinton, Newt Gingrich, and the Rivalry That Defined a Generation*. New York: Oxford, 2008.

Gilmore, Stephanie, "The Dynamics of Second-Wave Feminist Activism in Memphis, 1971–1982: Rethinking the Liberal/Radical Divide." *NWSA Journal* 15, no. 1 (Spring 2003): 94–117.

Gilmore, Stephanie, editor. *Feminist Coalitions: Historical Perspectives on Second-Wave Feminism in the United States*. Champaign: University of Illinois Press, 2008.

Gilpin, Kenneth N. "Alexandra Ripley, 'Scarlett' Author, Dies at 70." *New York Times*, January 27, 2004. https://www.nytimes.com/2004/01/27/arts/alexandra-ripley-scarlett-author-dies-at-70.html.

Gipson, L. Michael. "From Destiny's Child to Coachella." In *The Lemonade Reader*, edited by Kinitra D. Brooks and Kameelah L. Martin, 144–154. New York: Routledge, 2019.

"The Girl Effect: I Dare You to See I Am the Answer." YouTube, May 22, 2008. https://www.youtube.com/watch?v=-Vq2mfF8puE.

Glancy, Diane. "Columbus Meets Thelma and Louise and the Ocean Is Still Bigger Than Any of Us Thought." *Women's Review of Books* 9, nos. 10–11 (July 1992): 13.

Gluck, Sherna Berger. "Whose Feminism, Whose History? Reflections on Excavating the History of (the) U.S Women's Movement(s)." In *Community Activism and Feminist Politics: Organizing Across Race, Class, and Gender*, edited by Nancy A. Naples, 31–56. New York: Routledge, 1998.

Golshan, Tara. "Bill Clinton's First Major Appearance at a Convention Almost Destroyed His Career." *Vox*, July 26, 2016. https://www.vox.com/2016/7/26/12285312/bill-clinton-dnc-1988-speaker-late-night.

Gone with the Wind. Directed by Victor Fleming and George Cukor. Selznick International Pictures, Metro-Goldwyn Mayer, 1939.

Goodman, Ellen. "Hillary Breaking Ground on Front Line." *Pensacola News Journal*, July 19, 1992.

Gordon, Marcy. "TV Producer's Mother Died of AIDS from Transfusion." *AP News*, May 14, 1994. https://www.apnews.com/ce1efe9e1cfcb210adc1eff70e9172e8.

"Governor's Mansion." *Encyclopedia of Arkansas*. http://www.encyclopediaofarkansas.net/entries/governors-mansion-5028.

Gray, Herman S. *Watching Race: Television and the Struggle for Blackness*. Minneapolis: University of Minnesota Press, 2004.

Gray, Richard. "Inventing Communities, Imagining Places: Some Thoughts on Southern Self-Fashioning." In *South to a New Place: Region, Literature, Culture*, edited by Suzanne W. Suzanne and Sharon Monteith, xiii–xxiii. Baton Rouge: Louisiana State University Press, 2002.

Green, Philip. "Cultural Rage and the Right-Wing Intellectuals." In *Confronting the New Conservatism: The Rise of the Right in America*, edited by Michael J. Thompson, 31–55. New York: New York University Press, 2007.
Green, Tara T. "Mother Dear: The Motivations of Tina Ansa's Mudear." *Griot: The Journal of African American Studies*, Spring 2002. https://libres.uncg.edu/ir/uncg/f/T_Green_Mother_2002.pdf.
Greenberg, Harvey R. "*Thelma & Louise*'s Exuberant Polysemy." *Film Quarterly* 45, no. 2 (Winter, 1991–1992): 20–21.
Greene, Kate. "Fear and Loathing in Mississippi: The Attack on Camp Sister Spirit." *Journal of Lesbian Studies* 7, no. 2 (2003): 85–106.
Griffin, Farrah Jasmine. "Textual Healing: Claiming Black Women's Bodies, the Erotic and Resistance in Contemporary Novels of Slavery." *Callaloo* 19, no. 2 (Spring 1996): 519–536.
Groeneveld, Elizabeth. "'Be a Feminist or Just Dress Like One': *BUST*, Fashion, and Feminism as Lifestyle." *Journal of Gender Studies* 18, no. 2 (June 2009): 179–190.
Grooms, Anthony. "Big Bad Mudear." *Callaloo* 17, no. 2 (Spring 1994): 653–654.
Gros, Emmeline "*The Wind Done Gone* or Rewriting Gone Wrong: Retelling Southern Social, Racial, and Gender Norms through Parody." *South Atlantic Review* 80, no. 3–4 (2016): 135–160.
Guerra, Jonnie. "Beth Henley: Female Quest and the Family Play Tradition." In *Making a Spectacle: Feminist Essays on Contemporary Women's Theatre*, edited by Lynda Hart, 118–130. Ann Arbor: University of Michigan Press, 1989.
Gunther, Marc. "CBS and the Steel Magnolia." *New York Times*, March 3, 1991. https://www.nytimes.com/1991/03/03/arts/television-cbs-and-the-steel-magnolia.html.
Gupton, Janet L. "Un-ruling the Woman: Comedy and the Plays of Beth Henley and Rebecca Gilman." In *Southern Women Playwrights: New Essays in Literary History and Criticism*, edited by Robert L. McDonald and Linda Rohrer Paige, 124–139. Tuscaloosa: University of Alabama Press, 2002.
Guy-Sheftall, Beverly. Preface to *Words of Fire: An Anthology of African American Feminist Thought*, xiii–xx. New York: New Press, 1995.
Haag, L. L. "Oprah Winfrey: The Construction of Intimacy in the Talk-Show Setting." *Journal of Popular Culture* 26 (1993): 115–121.
Haber, Leigh, and Michelle Hart. "25 Books Every Woman Should Read." Oprah.com. https://www.oprah.com/inspiration/25-books-all-women-should-read-in-their-lifetime.
Halberstam, Judith. "Imagined Violence/Queer Violence: Representation, Rage, and Resistance." *Social Text* 37 (Winter 1993): 187–201.
Hale, Jon F. "The Making of the New Democrats." *Political Science Quarterly* 110, no. 2 (1995): 207–232.
Hall, Mark. "The 'Oprahfication' of Literacy: Reading 'Oprah's Book Club.'" *College English* 65, no. 6 (July 2003): 646–667.
Harris, Felicia L., and Loren Saxton Coleman. "Trending Topics: A Cultural Analysis of Being Mary Jane and Black Women's Engagement on Twitter." *Black Scholar* 48, no. 1 (2018): 43–55.
Harris, Jennifer. "'What Is Africa to Me?' The Oprah Winfrey Leadership Academy." In *The Oprah Phenomenon*, edited by Jennifer Harris and Elwood Watson, 293–308. Lexington: University Press of Kentucky, 2007.

Harris, Jennifer, and Elwood Watson. "Introduction: Oprah Winfrey as Subject and Spectacle." In *The Oprah Phenomenon*, edited by Jennifer Harris and Elwood Watson, 1–31. Lexington: University Press of Kentucky, 2007.
Harris, Marquita. "How *Being Mary Jane* Challenges Stereotypes about Black Women on TV." *Refinery29.com*. February 15, 2017. https://www.refinery29.com/en-us/2017/02/140778/being-mary-jane-black-women-stereotypes.
Harris, Tamara Winfrey. "'Formation' and the Black-Ass Truth about Beyoncé and Capitalism." In *The Lemonade Reader*, edited by Kinitra D. Brooks and Kameelah L. Martin, 155–157. New York: Routledge, 2019.
"Harry Z. Thomason (1940–)" *Encyclopedia of Arkansas*. http://www.encyclopediaofarkansas.net/encyclopedia/entry-detail.aspx?entryID=2759.
Hart, Lynda. "Til Death Do Us Part: Impossible Spaces in *Thelma and Louise*." *Journal of the History of Sexuality* 4, no. 3 (January 1994): 430–446.
Hartley, Jenny. *Reading Groups Book*. New York: Oxford, 2002.
Hartman, Saidiya V. *Lose Your Mother: A Journey along the Atlantic Slave Route*. New York: MacMillan, 2008.
Hartman, Saidiya V. *Scenes of Subjection: Terror, Slavery, and Self-Making in Nineteenth-Century America*. New York: Oxford University Press, 1997.
Henderson, Mae G. "*The Color Purple*: Revisions and Redefinitions." In *Alice Walker: Modern Critical Views*, edited by Harold Bloom, 67–80. New York: Chelsea House, 1989.
Henley, Beth. *Crimes of the Heart*. New York: Penguin, 1981.
Henry, Astrid. *Not My Mother's Sister: Generational Conflict and Third-Wave Feminism*. Bloomington: Indiana University Press, 2004.
Hester. "*Steel Magnolias*." *A Young Person's Guide to Feminist Films*, April 17, 2017. Accessed December 18, 2022. https://yafeministfilmsblog.wordpress.com/2017/04/17/steel-magnolias.
Hewitt, Nancy. "Beyond the Search for Sisterhood: American Women's History in the 1980s." *Social History* 10, no. 3 (October 1995): 299–321.
Hewitt, Nancy. "Feminist Frequencies: Regenerating the Wave Metaphor." *Feminist Studies* 38, no. 3 (Fall 2012): 658–680.
Hewitt, Nancy A. Introduction to *No Permanent Waves: Recasting Histories of U.S. Feminism*, edited by Nancy A. Hewitt, 1–12. New Brunswick, N.J.: Rutgers University Press, 2010.
Heying, Sarah. "'I Was Returning to See if the Ghosts Were Still Astirring': Southern Lesbian Reflexivity as a Social Movement in *Feminary* (1979–1982)." *Journal of Lesbian Studies* 26, no. 1 (2022): 12–26.
Heywood, Leslie, and Jennifer Drake. *Third Wave Agenda: Being Feminist, Doing Feminism*. Minneapolis: University of Minnesota Press, 1997.
Highsmith, Lauren V. "Beyoncé Reborn: *Lemonade* as Spiritual Enlightenment." In *The Lemonade Reader*, edited by Kinitra D. Brooks and Kameelah L. Martin, 133–143. New York: Routledge, 2019.
Higonnet, Margaret. "Suicide: Representations of the Feminine in the Nineteenth Century." *Poetics Today* 6, nos. 1–2 (1985): 103–118.
Hine, Darlene Clark. "Rape and the Inner Lives of Black Women in the Middle West." *Signs* 14, no. 4 (Summer 1989): 912–920.
Hinrichsen, Lisa, Gina Caison, and Stephanie Rountree. "Introduction: The Tele-

visual South." In *Small-Screen Souths: Region, Identity, and the Cultural Politics of Television*, edited by Lisa Hinrichsen, Gina Caison, and Stephanie Rountree, Kindle location 82–510. Baton Rouge: Louisiana State University Press, 2017. Kindle.

Hinton, KaaVonia. "'Sturdy Black Bridges': Discussing Race, Class, and Gender." *English Journal* 94, no. 2 (November 2004): 60–64.

Hobson, Fred. *The Southern Writer in the Postmodern World*. Athens: University of Georgia Press, 1991.

Hobson, Maurice J. *The Legend of the Black Mecca: Politics and Class in the Making of Modern Atlanta*. Chapel Hill: University of North Carolina Press, 2019.

Hoeflinger, Emily. "Talking Waves: Structures of Feminist Movements and the Potential of a Wave Economy." *Third Space* 8, no. 1 (Summer 2008). https://journals.lib.sfu.ca/index.php/thirdspace/article/view/hoeflinger/3232.

Hogan, Patrick. "Fictions and Feelings: On the Place of Literature in the Study of Emotion." *Emotion Review* 2, no. 2 (2010): 184–195.

Hollinger, Karen. *In the Company of Women: Contemporary Female Friendship Films*. Minneapolis: University of Minnesota Press, 1998.

Holmes, Michael S. "From Euphoria to Cataclysm: Georgia Confronts the Great Depression." *Georgia Historical Quarterly* 58, no. 3 (Fall 1974): 313–330.

Holmes, Steven A. "The 1992 Campaign: Candidate's Record; Race Relations in Arkansas Reflect Gains for Clinton, but Raise Questions." *New York Times*, April 3, 1992. https://www.nytimes.com/1992/04/03/us/1992-campaign-candidate-s-record-race-relations-arkansas-reflect-gains-for.html.

hooks, bell. *Ain't I a Woman: Black Women and Feminism*. Boston: South End Press, 1981.

hooks, bell. "Beyoncé Is a Terrorist." DailyMotion, n.d. https://www.dailymotion.com/video/x2dz23u.

hooks, bell. "Dig Deep: Beyond *Lean In*." *Feminist Wire*. October 28, 2013. https://thefeministwire.com/2013/10/17973/.

hooks, bell. *Feminism Is for Everybody: Passionate Politics*. New York: Pluto, 2000.

hooks, bell. *Feminist Theory: From Margin to Center*. Boston: South End Press, 1984.

hooks, bell. *Killing Rage, Ending Racism*. New York: Penguin, 1995.

hooks, bell. "Reading and Resistance: *The Color Purple*." In *Alice Walker: Critical Perspectives Past and Present*, edited by Henry Louis Gates Jr., 284–295. New York: Amistad, 1993.

hooks, bell. *Reel to Real: Race, Sex, and Class at the Movies*. New York: Routledge, 1996.

hooks, bell. "Sisterhood: Political Solidarity between Women." *Feminist Review* 23 (Summer 1986): 125–138.

hooks, bell. *Sisters of the Yam: Black Women and Self-Recovery*. New York: Routledge, 2015.

hooks, bell. *Yearning: Race, Gender, and Cultural Politics*. New York: Routledge, 2015.

Hope Floats. Directed by Forest Whitaker. Twentieth Century Fox, 1998.

Howard, John. "Beginnings with Oprah." In *Stories of Oprah: The Oprahfication of American Culture*, edited by Trystan T. Cotton and Kimberly Springer, 3–18. Columbia: University Press of Missouri, 2010.

Hull, Akasha (Gloria T.), Patricia Bell Scott, and Barbara Smith, eds. *All the Women*

Are White, All the Men Are Black, but Some of Us Are Brave: Black Women's Studies. New York: Feminist Press, 1982.

Hunter, Stephen. "'Beloved': The Haunting Truth." *Washington Post,* October 16, 1998. https://www.washingtonpost.com/wp-srv/style/longterm/movies/videos/belovedhunter.htm.

"Imagine the World if Six Million Girls Unlocked Their Power?" Girl Effect. https://www.girleffect.org.

Isenberg, Nancy. *White Trash: The 400-Year-Old Untold History of Class in America.* New York: Viking, 2016.

Izgarjan, Aleksandra. "Alice Walker's Womanism: Perspectives Past and Present." *Gender Studies* 11, no. 1 (January 2012): 304–315.

Jacoby, Tamar. "New Generation of Women's Publications." *New York Times,* March 3, 1986. https://www.nytimes.com/1986/03/03/style/new-generation-of-women-s-publications.html.

James, Robin. "How Not to Listen to *Lemonade*: Music Criticism and Epistemic Violence." In *The Lemonade Reader,* edited by Kinitra D. Brooks and Kameelah L. Martin, 69–76. New York: Routledge, 2019.

Jenkins, Candice Marie. "Queering Black Patriarchy: The Salvific Wish and Masculine Possibility in Alice Walker's *The Color Purple.*" *Modern Fiction Studies* 48, no. 4 (2002): 969–1000.

Jenkins, Nina. "Black Women and the Meaning of Motherhood." In *Redefining Motherhood: Changing Identities and Patterns,* edited by Sharon Abbey and Andrea O'Reilly, 201–213. Toronto: Second Story Press, 1998.

Johnson, Albert. "Baccantes at Large." *Film Quarterly* 45, no. 2 (Winter 1991–1992): 22–23.

Johnson, Birgitta. "She Gave You *Lemonade,* Stop Trying to Say It's Tang." In *The Lemonade Reader,* edited by Kinitra D. Brooks and Kameelah L. Martin 234–235. New York: Routledge, 2019.

Johnson, Brian D. "Feminist Fast Lane." *MacLean's,* May 27, 1991.

Johnson, Dan. "Transportation into a Story Increases Empathy, Prosocial Behavior, and Perceptual Bias toward Fearful Expressions." *Personality and Individual Differences* 52, no. 2 (2012): 150–155.

Johnson, E. Patrick. *Black. Queer. Southern. Women.: An Oral History.* Chapel Hill: University of North Carolina Press, 2018.

Johnson, Sherita L. *Black Women in New South Literature and Culture.* New York: Routledge, 2010.

Johnson, Tammy. "It's Personal: Race and Oprah." *Colorlines,* December 15, 2001. https://www.colorlines.com/articles/its-personal-race-and-oprah.

Jones, Jacqueline. "Fact and Fiction in Alice Walker's *The Color Purple.*" *Georgia Historical Quarterly* 72, no. 4 (Winter 1988): 653–669.

Jones, John Griffin. *Mississippi Writers Talking: Interviews with Eudora Welty, Shelby Foote, Elizabeth Spencer, Barry Hannah, and Beth Henley.* Oxford: University Press of Mississippi, 1982.

Jones, Maris. "Dear Beyoncé: Katrina Is Not Your Story." *Black Girl Dangerous,* February 10, 2016. https://www.bgdblog.org/2016/02/dear-beyonce-katrina-is-not-your-story.

Jones, Melanie C. "The Slay Factor: Beyoncé Unleashing the Black Feminine Divine in a Blaze of Glory." In *The Lemonade Reader*, edited by Kinitra D. Brooks and Kameelah L. Martin, 98–110. New York: Routledge, 2019.
Jordan, Shirley. *Broken Silences: Interviews with Black and White Women Writers*. New Brunswick, N.J.: Rutgers University Press, 1995.
Joseph, Gloria, and Jill Lewis. *Common Differences: Conflicts in Black and White Feminist Perspectives*. New York: Doubleday, 1981.
Josephs, Brian. "Beyoncé's *Lemonade* Premiere Pulls Solid Ratings for HBO." *Spin*, April 26, 2016. https://www.spin.com/2016/04/beyonce-lemonade-ratings-hbo.
Kaplan, Michael. "Rebel Citizenship and the Cunning of the Liberal Imaginary in *Thelma & Louise*." *Communication and Critical/Cultural Studies* 5, no. 1 (2008): 1–23.
Karr, Mary. *The Liars' Club*. New York: Viking, 1995.
Katz, Tamar. "Show Me How to Do Like You: Didacticism and Epistolary Form in *The Color Purple*." In *Alice Walker: Modern Critical Views*, edited by Harold Bloom, 185–193. New York: Chelsea House, 1989.
Kay, Linda. "My Mom and Oprah Winfrey: Her Appeal to White Women." In *The Oprah Phenomenon*, edited by Jennifer Harris and Elwood Watson, 51–64. Lexington: University Press of Kentucky, 2007.
Keane, Katarina. "Second-Wave Feminism in the American South, 1965–1980." PhD diss., University of Maryland, 2009.
Keen, Suzanne. *Empathy and the Novel*. New York: Oxford University Press, 2007.
Kinder, Marsha. "*Thelma & Louise* and *Messidor* as Feminist Road Movies." *Film Quarterly* 45, no. 2 (Winter 1991–1992): 30.
King, Florence. *Southern Ladies and Gentlemen*. New York: Bantam Books, 1975.
King, Jamilah. "Is Beyoncé a Terrorist: Black Feminist Scholars Debate bell hooks." *Colorlines*, May 9, 2014. https://www.colorlines.com/articles/beyonce-terrorist-black-feminist-scholars-debate-bell-hooks.
King, Norman. *Hillary: Her True Story*. New York: Birch Lane Press, 1993.
Kingsolver, Barbara. *The Poisonwood Bible*. HarperCollins, 1998.
Kovalchik, Kara. "12 Perfectly Arranged Facts about *Designing Women*." *Mental Floss*, March 7, 2016. https://www.mentalfloss.com/article/76665/12-perfectly-arranged-facts-about-designing-women.
Kozol, Wendy. "Fracturing Domesticity: Media, Nationalism, and the Question of Feminist Influence." *Signs*, Spring 1995, 646–667.
Kroll, Jack. "Back on the Road Again." *Newsweek*, May 27, 1991, 61–62.
Kruse, Kevin. *White Flight: Atlanta and the Making of Modern Conservatism*. Princeton, N.J.: Princeton University Press, 2007.
Kruse, Michael. "The TV Interview That Haunts Hillary Clinton." *Politico Magazine*, September 26, 2016. https://www.politico.com/magazine/story/2016/09/hillary-clinton-2016-60-minutes-1992-214275.
Kuczynski, Alex. "Winfrey Breaks New Ground with Magazine." *New York Times*, April 3, 2000. https://www.nytimes.com/2000/04/03/business/winfrey-breaks-new-ground-with-magazine.html.
Laderman, David. "What a Trip: The Road Film and American Culture." *Journal of Film and Video* 48, nos. 1–2 (Spring/Summer 1996): 41–57.
Lassiter, Matthew D., and Joseph Crespino. "Introduction: The End of Southern His-

tory." In *The Myth of Southern Exceptionalism*, 3–24. New York: Oxford University Press, 2010.
Laughlin, Kathleen A., Julie Gallagher, Dorothy Sue Cobble, Eileen Boris, Premilla Nadasen, Stephanie Gilmore, and Leandra Zarnow. "Is It Time to Jump Ship? Historians Rethink the Waves Metaphor." *Feminist Formations* 22, no. 1 (Summer 2010): 76–135.
Lechner, Zachary J. *The South of the Mind: American Imaginings of White Southernness, 1960–1980*. Athens: University of Georgia Press, 2018.
Lemonade. Directed by Melina Matsoukas. Parkwood Entertainment, 2016.
Leo, John. "Toxic Feminism on the Big Screen." *U.S. News and World Report*, June 20, 1991.
Letts, Billie. *Where the Heart Is*. London: Sceptre, 1995.
Lewis, Christopher S. "Cultivating Black Lesbian Shamelessness: Alice Walker's *The Color Purple*." *Rocky Mountain Review* 66, no. 2 (2012): 158–175.
Lewis, Scott. "It's Not Just a Lyric—Beyoncé's Roots Are Hardcore Cajun and Creole." 107 JAMS, February 10, 2016. https://107jamz.com/its-not-just-a-lyric-beyonces-roots-are-hardcore-cajuncreole.
Lewis, Shantrelle. "'Formation' Exploits New Orleans' Trauma." *Slate*, February 10, 2016. https://slate.com/human-interest/2016/02/beyonces-formation-exploits-new-orleans-trauma.html.
Life Is but a Dream. Directed by Beyoncé Knowles. ICM Partners, 2013.
Lilburn, Sandra, Susan Magarey, and Susan Sheridan. "Celebrity Feminism as Synthesis: Germaine Greer, *The Female Eunuch* and the Australian Print Media," *Continuum* 14, no. 3 (2000): 335–348.
Lindquist-Dorr, Lisa. *White Women, Rape, and the Power of Race in Virginia, 1900–1960*. Chapel Hill: University of North Carolina Press, 2004.
Lindsey, Treva B. "A Love Letter to Black Feminism." *Black Scholar* 45, no. 4 (2015): 1–6.
Lipsitz, Raina. "'Thelma & Louise': The Great Film about Women." *Atlantic*, August 31, 2011. https://www.theatlantic.com/entertainment/archive/2011/08/thelma-louise-the-last-great-film-about-women/244336.
Livingstone, Sonia, and Peter Lunt. *Talk on Television: Audience Participation and Public Debate*. New York: Routledge, 1994.
Lofton, Kathryn. *Oprah: The Gospel of an Icon*. Berkeley: University of California Press, 2011.
Lorde, Audre. "The Master's Tools Will Never Dismantle the Master's House." In *SisterOutsider: Essays and Speeches*, by Audre Lorde, 110–113. New York: Crossing Press, 1984.
Lorde, Audre. "Uses of the Erotic: The Erotic and Power." In *SisterOutsider: Essays and Speeches*, 53–59. New York: Crossing Press, 1984.
Lotz, Amanda D. *Redesigning Women: Television after the Network Era*. Champaign: University of Illinois Press, 2006.
Lubiano, Wahneema. "Black Ladies, Welfare Queens, and State Minstrels: Ideological War by Narrative Means." In *Race-ing Justice, En-gendering Power: Essays on Anita Hill, Clarence Thomas, and the Social Construction of Reality*, edited by Toni Morrison, 323–363. New York: Penguin, 1992.

Lundsford, Scott. "Arkansas Memories Project: Harry Thomason." Pryor Center for Arkansas Oral and Visual History, October 17, 2014. http://pryorcenter.uark.edu/interview.php?thisProject=Arkansas%20Memories&thisProfileURL=THOMASON-Harry&displayName=Harry%20Thomason&thisInterviewee=476.

Lyons, Bonnie. "Playing Dollhouse on a Huge Scale: An Interview with Beth Henley." In *The Muse upon My Shoulder: Discussions of the Creative Process*, edited by Sylvia Skaggs McTague, 145–159. Teaneck, N.J.: Fairleigh Dickinson University Press, 2004.

MacLean, Nancy. "Neo-Confederacy versus the New Deal: The Regional Utopia of the Modern American Right." In *The Myth of Southern Exceptionalism*, edited by Matthew Lassiter and Joseph Crespino, 308–330. New York: Oxford University Press, 2010.

Maffeo, Lois. "'Bust'-ing Out All Over: The Tits and Twats Revolution." *Stranger*, September 23, 1999. https://www.thestranger.com/seattle/bust-ing-out-all-over/Content?oid=2091.

Mahaffey, Jerome Dean. "In Defense of Another: The Role of Hillary Rodham Clinton and *60 Minutes* in the Gennifer Flowers Scandal." *White House Studies* 7, no. 4 (2001): 373–388.

Mahiana, Ana Maria. "Callie Khouri: Scripting *Thelma & Louise*." Scraps from the Loft, January 2, 2017. https://scrapsfromtheloft.com/2017/01/02/callie-khouri-scripting-thelma-louise.

"Makers: Callie Khouri, Oscar Winner, Writer, Producer." *Yahoo!life*, September 16, 2013. https://www.yahoo.com/lifestyle/callie-khouri-oscar-winning-writer-205230981.html.

The Man from Hope. Directed by Linda Bloodworth-Thomason. Clinton Library, 1992. YouTube. https://m.youtube.com/watch?v=MrujaQDlN28.

Mann, Patricia S. *Micro-Politics: Agency in a Postfeminist Era*. Minneapolis: University of Minnesota Press, 1994.

Mansfield, Stephanie. "And Now, Heeeeeeeere's Oprah!" *Washington Post*, October 21, 1986. https://www.washingtonpost.com/archive/lifestyle/1986/10/21/and-now-heeeeeeeeres-oprah/24ca6df5-45b2-47da-8d90-d8a61ede0330.

Marion, Jane. "When Oprah Was Ours." *Baltimore Magazine*, May 2011. https://www.baltimoremagazine.com/section/community/when-oprah-was-ours.

Martinson, Connie. "Tina McElroy Ansa Interview." *Connie Martinson Talks Books*. Drucker Institute, October 1993. https://calisphere.org/item/fa80524dd54f528b71f4464c369161d2.

Masciagno, Patricia S. *Rethinking Feminist Identification: The Case for de Facto Feminism*. Westport: Praeger, 1997.

Masciarotte, Gloria-Jean. "C'mon Girl: Oprah Winfrey and the Discourse of Feminine Talk." *Genders* 11 (January 1991): 81–110.

Maslin, Janet. "No Peace from a Brutal Legacy." *New York Times*, October 16, 1998. https://www.nytimes.com/1998/10/16/movies/film-review-no-peace-from-a-brutal-legacy.html.

Mason, M. S. "The Movie *Thelma & Louise* Isn't Just about Trashing Men." *Christian Science Monitor*, July 1, 1991.

Maurer, Paul J. "Media Feeding Frenzies: Press Behavior during Two Clinton Scandals." *Presidential Studies Quarterly* 29, no. 1 (March 1999): 65–79.

Max, D. T. "The Oprah Effect." *New York Times*, December 26, 1999. https://www.nytimes.com/1999/12/26/magazine/the-oprah-effect.html.

Maxwell, Angie, and Todd Shields. *The Long Southern Strategy: How Chasing White Voters in the South Changed American Politics*. New York: Oxford University Press, 2019.

Maxwell, Angie, and Todd Shields. "Toward a New Understanding of Second-Wave Feminism." In *The Legacy of Second-Wave Feminism in American Politics*, 1–18. New York: Palgrave, 2018.

McAleer, Scott. "Great Indignation: A Study of Racial Violence in Thomas County, Georgia, 1930." *Georgia Historical Quarterly* 87, no. 1 (Spring 2003): 48–87.

McDonogh, Gary W., and Cindy Hing-Yuk Wong. "Religion and Representation in the Filmic South." In *Images of the South: Constructing a Regional Culture on Film and Video*, edited by Karl G. Heider, 24–54. Athens: University of Georgia Press, 1993.

McFadden, Syreeta. "Beyoncé's 'Formation' Reclaims Black America's Narrative from the Margins." *Guardian*, February 8, 2016. https://www.theguardian.com/commentisfree/2016/feb/08/beyonce-formation-black-american-narrative-the-margins.

McGuire, Danielle L. *At the Dark End of the Street: Black Women, Rape, and Resistance—A New History of the Civil Rights Movement*. New York: Penguin, 2010. Kindle.

McInnis, Jarvis C. "Black Women's Geographies and the Afterlives of the Sugar Plantation." *American Literary History* 31, no. 4 (Winter 2019): 771–774.

McKern, Sharon. *Redneck Mothers, Good Ol' Girls, and Other Southern Belles: A Celebration of the Women of Dixie*. New York: Viking, 1979.

McKever-Floyd, Preston. "'Tell Nobody but God': The Theme of Transformation in *The Color Purple*." *CrossCurrents* 57, no. 3 (2007): 426–433.

McKittrick, Katherine. *Demonic Grounds: Black Women and the Cartographies of Struggle*. Minneapolis: University of Minnesota Press, 2006.

McKittrick, Katherine. "Plantation Futures." *Small Axe* 17, no. 3 (November 2013): 1–15.

McKittrick, Katherine, and Clyde Woods. "Introduction: No One Knows the Mysteries at the Bottom of the Ocean." In *Black Geographies and the Politics of Place*, 1–14. Boston: South End Press, 2007.

McPherson, Tara. *Reconstructing Dixie: Race, Gender, and Nostalgia in the Imagined South*. Durham: Duke University Press. Kindle.

McRobbie, Angela. *The Aftermath of Feminism: Gender, Culture, and Social Change*. New York: Sage, 2009.

McRobbie, Angela. "Feminism, the Family, and the New 'Mediated' Maternalism." *New Formations* 80 (2013): 119–137.

McRobbie, Angela. "Postfeminism and Popular Culture." *Feminist Media Studies* 4, no. 3 (2004): 255–264.

McRobbie, Angela. "Postfeminism and Popular Culture: Bridget Jones and the New Gender Regime." In *Interrogating Postfeminism: Gender and the Politics of Popular Culture*, edited by Diane Negra and Yvonne Tasker, 27–40. Durham: Duke University Press, 2007.

Meeks, Catherine. *Macon's Black Heritage: The Untold Story*. Macon, Ga.: Tubman African American Museum, 1997.

"Meet the 2013 Tribeca Filmmaker #27: Linda Bloodworth-Thomason Fights for Marriage Equality in *Bridegroom*." *Indiewire*, April 13, 2013. https://www.indiewire.com/2013/04/meet-the-2013-tribeca-filmmaker-27-born-into-activism-linda-bloodworth-thomason-fights-for-marriage-equality-in-bridegroom-39476.

Miller, Monica Carol. *Being Ugly: Southern Women Writers and Social Rebellion*. Baton Rouge: Louisiana State University Press, 2017.

Miller, Monica Carol. "*Designing Women* and Its Postsouthern, Postfeminist Legacy." In *Small-Screen Souths: Region, Identity, and the Cultural Politics of Television*, edited by Lisa Hinrichsen, Gina Caison, and Stephanie Rountree, Kindle location 926–1277. Louisiana State University Press, 2017. Kindle.

Mills, Elizabeth Shown. "Demythicizing History: Marie Thérèse Coincoin, Tourism, and the National Historic Landmarks Program." *Louisiana History* 53, no. 4 (Fall 2012): 402–437.

Mills, Elizabeth Shown. *Isle of Canes*. Provo: Ancestry, 2006.

Mills, Elizabeth Shown. "Laying a Legend to Rest: Marie Thérèse Coincoin and Archaeological Sites 16NA785 and 16NA789." *Louisiana History* 62, no. 2 (Spring 2021): 177–224.

Mitchell, Margaret. *Gone with the Wind*. New York: MacMillan, 1936.

Modleski, Tania. *Loving with a Vengeance: Mass-Produced Fantasies for Women*. London: Methuen, 1982.

Mohammed, Marwa G. "Females' Journey into Finding the Self in Beth Henley's *Crimes of the Heart*." *Journal of College of Languages* (2014): 495–509.

Moorti, Sujata. "Cathartic Confessions or Emancipatory Texts? Rape Narrative on *The Oprah Winfrey Show*." *Social Text*, no. 57 (Winter 1998): 83–102.

Moraga, Cherríe. "Refugees of a World on Fire: Preface to the Second Edition." In *This Bridge Called My Back: Writings by Radical Women of Color*, edited by Cherríe Moraga and Gloria Anzaldúa, n.p. 2nd ed. New York: Kitchen Table Press, 1983.

Moraga, Cherríe, and Gloria Anzaldúa, editors. *This Bridge Called My Back: Writings by Radical Women of Color*. 2nd ed. New York: Kitchen Table Press, 1983.

Morgan, Robin, ed. *Sisterhood Is Powerful: An Anthology of Writings from the Women's Liberation Movement*. New York: Random House, 1970.

Morrison, Toni. *Beloved*. New York: Penguin, 1987.

Morrison, Toni. *Paradise*. New York: Knopf, 1997.

Morrison, Toni. "The Site of Memory." In *Inventing the Truth: The Art and Craft of Memoir*, 2nd ed., edited by William Zinsser, 83–102. New York: Houghton Mifflin, 1995.

Morrison, Toni. *Song of Solomon*. New York: Knopf, 1977.

Muhammad, Khalil Gibran. "The Sugar That Saturates the American Diet Has a Barbaric History as the 'White Gold' That Fueled Slavery." *New York Times*, August 14, 2019. https://www.nytimes.com/interactive/2019/08/14/magazine/sugar-slave-trade-slavery.html.

Musanga, Terrence. "Toward the Survival and the Wholeness of the African American Community: A Womanist Reading of Alice Walker's *The Color Purple*." *Journal of Black Studies* 50, no. 4 (2019): 388–400.

Nash, Jennifer C. "Practicing Love: Black Feminism, Love-Politics, and Postintersectionality." *Meridians* 11, no. 2 (2011), 1–24.

National Association for the Advancement of Colored People. "History of Lynchings." https://www.naacp.org/history-of-lynchings.

Nealy, Aliya. "Refining the Angry Black Woman: *Being Mary Jane* and Black Feminist Rage." *Medium*, April 29, 2015. https://medium.com/@Aliya_Nealy/redefining-the-angry-black-woman-being-mary-jane-and-black-feminist-rage-3b48614f26b5.

Nehl, Markus. *Transnational Black Dialogues: Re-imagining Slavery in the Twenty-First Century*. New York: Columbia University Press, 2016.

Nelson, Murry R., editor. "Ted Turner." In *American Sports 4*, 1374. Westport: Greenwood, 2013.

Odem, Mary E. "Latin American Immigration and the New Multiethnic South." In *The Myth of Southern Exceptionalism*, edited by Matthew Lassiter and Joseph Crespino, 234–260. New York: Oxford, 2010.

Okrant, Robyn. *Living Oprah: My One-Year Experiment to Walk the Walk of the Queen of Talk*. New York: Center Street, 2010.

On Story. "*Thelma and Louise*: A Conversation with Callie Khouri." Season 4, episode 6. May 24, 2014. https://www.pbs.org/video/-story-thelma-and-louise-conversation-callie-khouri.

"Oprah Says 26 Billboards Are 'My Form of Protest.'" *Oprah*, August 10, 2020. https://www.oprahmag.com/life/a33515050/breonna-taylor-billboards-oprah-magazine-louisville.

"Oprah's Hair through the Years." Oprah.com. http://www.oprah.com/oprahshow/oprahs-hairstyles.

"Oprah's Mother, Vernita Lee, on Motherhood, Her Milwaukee History." WISN 12 News. https://www.youtube.com/watch?v=vc5y2qxpKDY.

Oprah's Next Chapter. "Beyoncé." February 16, 2013.

Oprah's Super Soul Conversations. "Beyoncé." September 15, 2020. https://podcasts.apple.com/us/podcast/beyoncé/id1264843400?i=1000491408241.

"Oprah Winfrey: Biography." *TV Guide*. https://www.tvguide.com/celebrities/oprah-winfrey/bio/168611.

"Oprah Winfrey Named Most Powerful Person in Entertainment Industry." *Jet*, November 9, 1998. https://web.archive.org/web/20081208223131/http://findarticles.com/p/articles/mi_m1355/is_n24_v94/ai_2125735.

The Oprah Winfrey Show. "Anne Murray and Her Daughters/Oprah's Book Club: *River, Cross My Heart*." November 10, 1999.

The Oprah Winfrey Show. "*Beloved* Dinner with Oprah." October 30, 1998.

The Oprah Winfrey Show. "How'd They Do That/Book Club: *Song of Solomon*." November 18, 1996.

The Oprah Winfrey Show. "Oprah Opens Up about Her Abusive Childhood." October 20, 2010. http://www.oprah.com/own-oprahshow/oprah-opens-up-about-her-abusive-childhood-video.

The Oprah Winfrey Show. "Oprah's Book Club: *Black and Blue*." May 22, 1998.

The Oprah Winfrey Show. "Oprah's Book Club: *Cane River*." September 24, 2001.

The Oprah Winfrey Show. "Oprah's Book Club: Things Every Woman Should Know." October 28, 1998.

The Oprah Winfrey Show. "Oprah's Book Club: Toni Morrison." March 6, 1998.

The Oprah Winfrey Show Twentieth Anniversary Collection. "Aha!" Disc 2. 2006.

The Oprah Winfrey Show Twentieth Anniversary Collection. "Authentic Power." Disc 2. 2006.
The Oprah Winfrey Show Twentieth Anniversary Collection. "The Beginning." Disc 1. 2006.
The Oprah Winfrey Show Twentieth Anniversary Collection. "Christmas Kindness." Disc 6. 2006.
The Oprah Winfrey Show Twentieth Anniversary Collection. "Do Your Eyes Light Up?" Disc 2. 2006.
The Oprah Winfrey Show Twentieth Anniversary Collection. "The Headlines: Forsyth County, 1987." Disc 4. 2006.
The Oprah Winfrey Show Twentieth Anniversary Collection. "The Headlines: The Little Rock Nine, 1996." Disc 4. 2006.
The Oprah Winfrey Show Twentieth Anniversary Collection. "The Interviews." Disc 3. 2006.
The Oprah Winfrey Show Twentieth Anniversary Collection. "Maya Angelou." Disc 2. 2006.
The Oprah Winfrey Show Twentieth Anniversary Collection. "Oprah's 50th Birthday Bash." Disc 6. 2006.
The Oprah Winfrey Show Twentieth Anniversary Collection. "A Private Tour of Oprah's Home." Disc 2. 2006.
The Oprah Winfrey Show Twentieth Anniversary Collection. "Surrender." Disc 2. 2006.
The Oprah Winfrey Show Twentieth Anniversary Collection. "Stranger Danger." Disc 2. 2006.
"Oprah Winfrey's Official Biography." Oprah.com. http://www.oprah.com/pressroom/oprah-winfreys-official-biography.
O'Reilly, Andrea. *Toni Morrison and Motherhood: A Politics of the Heart.* Albany: State University of New York Press, 2004.O'Reilly, Jane. "Click! The Housewife's Moment of Truth." *Ms.*, Spring 1972. https://msmagazine.com/2021/03/04/from-the-vault-click-the-housewifes-moment-of-truth-ms-magazine-spring-1972.
"Our Story." Girl Effect. https://www.girleffect.org/who-we-are/our-story.
Page, Clarence. "Newt on Ditches and Dirty Britches." *Chicago Tribune*, January 22, 1995. https://www.chicagotribune.com/news/ct-xpm-1995-01-22-9501210248-story.html.
Paige, Linda Rohrer. "Wanted Dead or Alive: The Female Outlaw and Callie Khouri's *Thelma and Louise.*" *American Studies Journal* no. 50 (2007). http://www.asjournal.org/50-2007/the-%20female-outlaw-and-callie-khouris-thelma-and-louise.
Palumbo, Stephanie. "Meet the Graduates of the Oprah Winfrey Leadership Academy for Girls." Oprah.com. http://www.oprah.com/spirit/oprah-winfrey-leadership-academy-for-girls-graduation-photos/all.
Parisi, Paula. "Beyoncé's *Lemonade* Was the World's Best-Selling Album in 2016." *Variety*, April 25, 2017. https://variety.com/2017/music/news/beyonce-lemonade-drake-one-dance-best-selling-2016-1202395667.
Park, Jeannie. "When Not Battling Delta Burke, Linda Bloodworth-Thomason and Harry Thomason Are Redesigning CBS." *People*, January 28, 1991. https://people.com/archive/when-not-battling-delta-burke-linda-bloodworth-thomason-and-harry-thomason-are-redesigning-cbs-vol-35-no-3.

Parkins, Wendy. "Oprah Winfrey's Change Your Life TV and the Spiritual Everyday." *Continuum* 15, no. 2 (2001): 145–157.
Parry-Giles, Shawn J. *Hillary Clinton in the News: Gender and Authenticity in American Politics*. Champaign: University of Illinois Press, 2014.
Parry-Giles, Shawn J., and Trevor Parry-Giles. *Constructing Clinton: Hyperreality and Presidential Image-Making in Postmodern Politics*. Frankfurt: Peter Lang, 2002.
Patterson, Troy. "Road Kill." *Slate*, March 26, 2008. http://www.slate.com/articles/arts/television/2008/03/road_kill.html.
Pearson, Kyra. "Mapping Rhetorical Interventions in 'National' Feminist Histories: Second Wave Feminism and 'Ain't I a Woman.'" *Communication Studies* 50, no. 2 (1999): 158–173.
Peck, Janice. "Talking about Racism: Framing a Popular Discourse of Race on Oprah Winfrey." *Cultural Critique* no. 27 (Spring, 1994): 89–126.
Peñate, Patricia Coloma. "Beyoncé's Diaspora Heritage and Ancestry in Louisiana." In *The Lemonade Reader*, edited by Kinitra D. Brooks and Kameelah L. Martin, 111–122. New York: Routledge, 2019.
Peretz, Tal. "Why Atlanta? A Case Study of How Place Produces Intersectional Social Movement Groups." *Gender, Place and Culture* 27, no. 10 (2020): 1438–1459.
"Personal Quotes." In "Callie Khouri Biography." IMDB.com. https://www.imdb.com/name/nm0451884/bio?ref_=nm_dyk_qu#quotes.
Philips, Carmen. "*Queen Sugar* Is a Black Feminist Masterclass That's Coming Back to Your TV TONIGHT." *Autostraddle*, June 20, 2017. https://www.autostraddle.com/queen-sugar-season-1-review-a-black-feminist-masterclass-thats-coming-back-to-your-tv-tonight-383435.
A Place of Rage. Directed by Pratibha Parmar. 1991.
Plasa, Carl. *Icon Critical Guides: Toni Morrison, 'Beloved.'* London: Icon Books, 1998.
Playbill. "Crimes of the Heart." https://www.playbill.com/production/crimes-of-the-heart-john-golden-theatre-vault-0000008401.
Plunka, Gene A. *The Plays of Beth Henley: A Critical Study*. Jefferson, N.C.: McFarland, 2005.
Pollitt, Katha, and Jennifer Baumgardner. Afterword to *Catching a Wave: Reclaiming Feminism for the 21st Century*, edited by Rory Dicker and Alison Piepmeier, 309–319. Boston: Northeastern University Press, 2003.
Proffitt, Steve. "Linda Bloodworth-Thomason: A Key to That Hollywood-Arkansas Connection." *Los Angeles Times*, November 22, 1992. http://articles.latimes.com/1992-11-22/opinion/op-2043_1_linda-bloodworth-thomason.
Prugl, Elisabeth. "Neoliberalising Feminism." *New Political Economy* 20 (2015): 614–631.
"Pulitzer Play: Comedy of Three Sisters." *New York Times*, April 14, 1981. https://www.nytimes.com/1981/04/14/theater/pulitzer-play-comedy-of-3-sisters.html.
Putnam, Ann. "The Bearer of the Gaze in Ridley Scott's *Thelma and Louise*." *Western American Literature* 27, no. 4 (Winter 1993): 291–302.
Pyron, Darden Asbury. *Southern Daughter: The Life of Margaret Mitchell*. New York: Oxford University Press, 1991.
Quindlen, Anna. *Black and Blue*. New York: Random House, 1998.

Radish, Christina. "Oprah Winfrey Talks Her Career, how *The Color Purple* Changed Her Life, *The Butler*, Refusing to Do *Prisoners*, and more at SBIFF." *Collider*, February 7, 2014. https://collider.com/oprah-winfrey-the-butler-color-purple-interview.

Radway, Janice. *Reading the Romance*. Chapel Hill: University of North Carolina Press, 1984.

Randall, Alice. *The Wind Done Gone*. New York: Houghton Mifflin, 2001.

Reger, Jo, editor. *Different Wavelengths: Studies of Contemporary Women's Movement*. New York: Routledge, 2005.

Rexroat, Jennifer. "'I'm Everywoman': Oprah Winfrey and Feminist Identification." In *Stories of Oprah: The Oprahfication of American Culture*, edited by Trystan T. Cotton and Kimberly Springer, 19–32. Columbia: University Press of Missouri, 2010.

Reynolds, Sheri. *Rapture of Canaan*. New York: Penguin, 1995.

Rhodes, Carolyn. "Gail Godwin and the Ideal of Southern Womanhood." In *Women Writers of the Contemporary South*, edited by Peggy Whitman Prenshaw, 55–66. Oxford: University Press of Mississippi, 1984.

Rich, Frank. "Beth Henley's 'Crimes of the Heart.'" *New York Times*, November 5, 1981. https://www.nytimes.com/1981/11/05/theater/the-theater-beth-henley-s-crimes-of-the-heart.html.

Richardson, Riché. *Emancipation's Daughters: Reimagining Black Femininity and the National Body*. Durham: Duke University Press, 2021.

Richardson, Riché. "Mammy's 'Mules' and the Rules of Marriage in *Gone with the Wind*." In *American Cinema and the Southern Imaginary*, edited by Deborah Barker and Kathryn McKee, 52–74. Athens: University of Georgia Press, 2011.

Ricks, Shawn Arango. "Normalized Chaos: Black Feminism, Womanism, and the (Re)Definition of Trauma and Healing." *Meridians* 16, no. 2 (2018): 343–350.

Ripley, Alexandra. *Scarlett: The Sequel to Margaret Mitchell's 'Gone with the Wind.'* New York: Grand Central Publishing, 1991.

Robinson, Cynthia Cole. "The Evolution of Alice Walker." *Women's Studies* 38, no. 3 (2009): 293–311.

Robinson, Gaile. "One Eye on the Mirror, the Other on the Ballot Box." *Los Angeles Times*. June 19, 1992. http://articles.latimes.com/1992-06-19/news/vw-693_1_hillary-clinton.

Rochlin, Margy. "The Prime Time of Linda Bloodworth-Thomason: With Her Husband, Harry, the Unflappable Producer Has Become CBS's Comedy Franchise." *Los Angeles Times*, September 27, 1992. https://www.latimes.com/archives/la-xpm-1992-09-27-tm-66-story.html.

Rohter, Larry. "The Third Woman of *Thelma and Louise*." *New York Times*, June 5, 1991. https://www.nytimes.com/1991/06/05/movies/the-third-woman-of-thelma-and-louise.html.

Romagnolo, Catherine. "Naturally Flawed? Gender, Race, and the Unnatural in *The Color Purple*." *Storyworlds* 8, no. 2 (2016): 113–133.

Romine, Scott. *The Real South: Southern Narrative in the Age of Cultural Reproduction*. Baton Rouge: Louisiana State University Press, 2008.

Roosevelt, Franklin D. "Message to the Conference on Economic Conditions of the South." July 4, 1938. https://www.presidency.ucsb.edu/documents/message-the-conference-economic-conditions-the-south.

Rosenfeld, Megan. "Beth Henley's World of Southern Discomfort." *Washington Post*. December 12, 1986. https://www.washingtonpost.com/archive/lifestyle/1986/12/12/beth-henleys-world-of-southern-discomfort/f81b42e6-b5a9-40e7-90d7-83286dad061f.

Rossie, Amanda. "*Being Mary Jane* and Postfeminism's Problem with Race." In *Emergent Feminisms: Complicating a Postfeminist Media Culture*, edited by Jessalynn Keller and Maureen E. Ryan, 25–41. Routledge, 2018.

Roth, Benita. "The Making of the Vanguard Center: Black Feminist Emergence in the 1960s and 1970s." In *Still Lifting, Still Climbing: African American Women's Contemporary Activism*, edited by Kimberly Springer, 70–90. New York University Press, 1999.

Rothe, Anne. *Popular Trauma Culture: Selling the Pain of Others in the Mass Media*. New Brunswick, N.J.: Rutgers University Press, 2011.

Rottenberg, Catherine. "How Neoliberalism Colonised Feminism—and What You Can Do about It." *Conversation*, May 23, 2018. https://theconversation.com/how-neoliberalism-colonised-feminism-and-what-you-can-do-about-it-94856.

Rottenberg, Catherine. "The Rise of Neoliberal Feminism." *Cultural Studies* 28, no. 3 (2014): 418–437.

Rushing, Wanda. "No Place for a Feminist: Intersectionality and the Problem South." *Gender and Society* 31, no. 3 (June, 2017): 293–309.

Russell, David. "'I'm Not Gonna Hurt You': Legal Penetrations in *Thelma and Louise*." *Americana* 1, no. 1 (Spring 2002). http://www.americanpopularculture.com/journal/articles/spring_2002/russell.htm.

Rutheiser, Charles. *Imagineering Atlanta: The Politics of Place in the City of Dreams*. New York: Verso, 1996.

Safire, William. "Macho Feminism, R.I.P." *New York Times*, January 27, 1992. https://www.nytimes.com/1992/01/27/opinion/essay-macho-feminism-rip.html.

Samuels, Allison. "Oprah Goes to School." *Newsweek*, January 7, 2007. https://www.newsweek.com/oprah-goes-school-98521.

Sandberg, Sheryl. "Why I Want Women to Lean In." *Time*, March 7, 2013. https://ideas.time.com/2013/03/07/why-i-want-women-to-lean-in.

Sandoval, Chela. *Methodology of the Oppressed*. Minneapolis: University of Minnesota Press, 2000.

Sands, Nicole. "How Oprah Winfrey Is Empowering Girls and Women around the World." *People*, November 4, 2016. https://people.com/human-interest/oprah-winfrey-people-25-women-changing-the-world-with-new-normal-for-women.

Sanguinette, Marsha. "The South Rises Again with Humor Thanks to Bloodworth-Thomason." *Deseret News*, November 27, 1990. https://www.deseret.com/1990/11/27/18893491/the-south-rises-again-with-humor-thanks-to-bloodworth-thomason.

Sapiro, Virginia, and Pamela Johnston Conover. "The Variable Gender Basis of Electoral Politics: Gender and Context in the 1992 U.S. Election." *British Journal of Political Science* 27, no. 4 (October 1997): 497–523.

Saturday Night Live. "The Day Beyoncé Turned Black" skit, "Melissa McCarthy" episode. Season 41, episode 13, February 13, 2016.

Sayeau, Ashley. "Southern Ms." *Nation*, November 18, 2004. https://www.thenation.com/article/archive/southern-ms.

Scarlett (television miniseries). Directed by Jon Erman. RHI Entertainment, 1994.
Schickel, Richard. "Gender Bender over *Thelma & Louise*." *Time*, June 24, 1991. https://content.time.com/time/subscriber/article/0,33009,973234,00.html.
Schmidt, William E. "Southern Practice of Eating Dirt Shows Signs of Waning." *New York Times*, February 13, 1984. https://www.nytimes.com/1984/02/13/us/southern-practice-of-eating-dirt-shows-signs-of-waning.html.
Schur, Richard. "*The Wind Done Gone* Controversy: American Studies, Copyright Law, and the Imaginary Domain." *American Studies* 44, no. 1–2 (Spring/Summer 2003): 5–33.
Schwarzbaum, Lisa. "*The Wind Done Gone*: Alice Randall Retells *Gone with the Wind* from the African American Perspective." *Entertainment Weekly*, May 18, 2001. https://ew.com/article/2001/05/18/wind-done-gone-alice-randall-retells-gone-wind-african-american-perspective.
Seidel, Kathryn Lee. "Gail Godwin and Ellen Glasgow: Southern Mothers and Daughter." *Tulsa Studies in Women's Literature* 10, no. 2 (Autumn 1991): 287–294.
Shattuc, Jane M. *The Talking Cure: TV Talk Shows and Women*. New York: Taylor & Francis, 1997.
Sheehy, Gail. "What Hillary Wants." *Vanity Fair*, May 1992. https://www.vanityfair.com/news/1992/05/hillary-clinton-first-lady-presidency.
Shepard, Richard F. "CBS Buys *Gone with the Wind* for TV for $35 Million." *New York Times*, April 6, 1978. https://www.nytimes.com/1978/04/06/archives/cbs-buys-gone-with-the-wind-for-tv-for-35-million-seventh-on-rental.html.
Shepard, Robert. "Clinton a Hit with Women's Caucus." UPI. July 14, 1992. https://www.upi.com/Archives/1992/07/14/Clinton-a-hit-with-womens-caucus/9548711086400.
Shipp, E. R. "Blacks in Heated Debate over *The Color Purple*." *New York Times*, January 27, 1976. https://www.nytimes.com/1986/01/27/us/blacks-in-heated-debate-over-the-color-purple.html.
Shockley, Megan Taylor. *Creating a Progressive Commonwealth: Women Activists, Feminism, and the Politics of Social Change in Virginia, 1970s–2000s*. Baton Rouge: Louisiana State University Press, 2018. Kindle.
Siebler, Kay. "Black Feminists in Serialized Dramas: The Gender/Sex/Sexuality/Race Politics of *Being Mary Jane* and *Scandal*." *Journal of Popular Film and Television* 47, no. 3 (2019): 152–162.
Simmons, Lakisha Michelle. "Landscapes, Memories, and History in Beyoncé's *Lemonade*." *UNC Press Blog*, April 28, 2016. https://uncpressblog.com/2016/04/28/lakisha-simmons-beyonces-lemonade.
Simoneaux, Marie. "As Messy Mya Lawsuit Settles, Another New Orleans Artist Sues Beyoncé." *Nola.com*, February 26, 2018. https://www.nola.com/news/crime_police/article_e603cf1f-9bcc-5618-9425-7be498df1356.html.
Sisson, Patrick. "Beyoncé's 'Formation': How a Historic Pasadena Went Southern Gothic for This Year's Biggest Video." *Curbed*, February 9, 2016. https://archive.curbed.com/2016/2/9/10953432/beyonce-formation-music-video-production-design.
Smith, Dinitia. "*The Color Purple* (Review)." In *Alice Walker: Critical Perspectives Past and Present*, edited by Henry Louis Gates Jr., 19–21. New York: Amistad, 1993.

Smith, Jessica, and Nicholas Wooten. "John Oliver Killen's *Youngblood*: Macon's Racial History." https://libraries.mercer.edu/api/dspace_previews/warc/file_52827/macons-racial-history.

Smith, Jon. "What the New Southern Studies Does Now." *Journal of American Studies* 49, no. 4 (November 2015): 861–870.

Smith, Kyle. "As a Feminist Film, *Thelma & Louise* Fails Miserably." *New York Post*, April 7, 2016. https://nypost.com/2016/04/07/as-a-feminist-film-thelma-louise-fails-miserably.

Smith-Shomade, Beretta E. *Shaded Lives: African American Women and Television*. New Brunswick, N.J.: Rutgers University Press, 2002.

Smith-Shomade, Beretta E. "You'd Better Recognize: Oprah the Iconic and Television Talk." In *Feminist Television Criticism: A Reader*, 2nd ed., edited by Charlotte Brunsdon and Lynn Spigel. Maidenhead, England: Open University Press, 2008.

Smothers, Ronald. "Scarlett and Rhett Take Atlanta Again." *New York Times*, December 16, 1989. https://www.nytimes.com/1989/12/16/us/scarlett-and-rhett-take-atlanta-again.html.

Something to Talk About. Directed by Lasse Holström. Warner Brothers, 1995.

Southern Feminist 3, no. 1 (January/February 1986), 3, Folder 3, Southern Feminist Collection, David M. Rubenstein Rare Book and Manuscript Library, Duke University, Durham, North Carolina.

Sowards, Stacey K., and Valerie R. Renegar. "Reconceptualizing Rhetorical Activism in Contemporary Feminist Contexts." *Howard Journal of Communications* 17, no. 1 (2006): 57–74.

Spillers, Hortense. "Mama's Baby, Papa's Maybe: An American Grammar Book." *Diacritics* 17, no. 2 (Summer 1987): 64–81.

Springer, Kimberly. "Delineating the Contours of the Oprah Culture Industry." In *Stories of Oprah: The Oprahfication of American Culture*, edited by Trystan T. Cotton and Kimberly Springer, vii–xix. Jackson: University Press of Mississippi, 2010.

Springer, Kimberly, ed. *Still Lifting, Still Climbing: Contemporary African American Women's Activism*. New York: New York University Press, 1999.

Springer, Kimberly. "Third Wave Black Feminism?" *Signs* 27, no. 4 (Summer 2002): 1059–1082.

Spruill, Marjorie J. *Divided We Stand: The Battle over Women's Rights and Family Values That Polarized American Politics*. New York: Oxford University Press, 2017.

Spruill, Marjorie J. "Feminism, Anti-Feminism, and the Rise of a New Southern Strategy in the 1980s." In *The Legacy of Second-Wave Feminism in American Politics*, edited by Angie Maxwell and Todd Shields, 39–70. New York: Palgrave, 2018.

Spruill, Marjorie Julian. "Victoria Eslinger, Keller Bumgardner Baron, Mary Heriot, Tootsie Holland, and Pat Callair: Champions of Women's Rights in South Carolina." In *South Carolina Women: Their Lives and Times*, vol. 3, edited by Marjorie Julian Spruill, Valinda W. Littlefield, and Joan Marie Johnson, 373–408. Athens: University of Georgia Press, 2012. Kindle.

Stack, Carol B. *Call to Home*. New York: Hachette, 1996.

Stanley, Tashia L. "The Specter of Oprah Winfrey: Critical Black Female Spectatorship." In *The Oprah Phenomenon*, edited by Jennifer Harris and Elwood Watson, 35–50. Lexington: University Press of Kentucky, 2007.

Stanonis, Anthony. *Dixie Emporium: Tourism, Foodways, and Consumer Culture in the American South*. Athens: University of Georgia Press, 2008.
Steel Magnolias. Directed by Kenny Leon. Lifetime Movie Network, 2012.
Steel Magnolias. Directed by Herbert Ross. Tristar Pictures, 1989.
Stein, Megan. "The 'Designing Women' Revival Is Happening and We Couldn't Be More Excited." *Country Living*, September 16, 2018. https://www.countryliving.com/life/entertainment/a22737164/designing-women-revival.
Steptoe, Tyina. "Beyoncé's Western South Serenade." In *The Lemonade Reader*, edited by Kinitra D. Brooks and Kameelah L. Martin, 183–191. New York: Routledge, 2019.
Stevens, Dana. "*Thelma & Louise.*" *Slate*, February 15, 2011. https://slate.com/culture/2011/02/thelma-louise-alternate-ending-why-it-would-have-ruined-the-film.html.
Stewart, Lindsey. "Something Akin to Freedom: Sexual Love, Political Agency, and Lemonade." In *The Lemonade Reader*, edited by Kinitra D. Brooks and Kameelah L. Martin, 19–30. New York: Routledge, 2019.
Stocks, Joey. "A Conversation with Linda Bloodworth-Thomason." Dramatists' Guild, October 19, 2017. https://www.dramatistsguild.com/a-conversation-with-linda-bloodworth-thomason.
Stodghill, Ron. "Daring to Go There." *Time*, June 24, 2001. http://content.time.com/time/magazine/article/0,9171,140092,00.html.
Stokes, Ashli Quesinberry. "Constituting Southern Feminists: Women's Liberation Newspapers in the South." *Southern Communication Journal* 70, no. 2 (2005): 91–108.
Sulfaro, Valerie A. "Affective Evaluations of First Ladies: A Comparison of Hillary Clinton and Laura Bush." *Presidential Studies Quarterly* 37, no. 3 (September 2007): 486–514.
Sullivan, Patricia A., and Steven R. Goldzwig. "'Women's Reality' and the Untold Story: *Designing Women* and the Revisioning of the Thomas-Hill Hearings." In *Outsiders Looking In: A Communication Perspective on the Hill-Thomas Hearings*, edited by Paul Siegel, 229–247. New York: Hampton Press, 1996.
Surrency, Jeneen K. "African Spirituality in the Novels of Tina McElroy Ansa." PhD diss., University of Florida, 2011.
Tademy, Lalita. *Cane River*. New York: Grand Central Publishing, 2001.
Tademy, Lalita. *Citizens Creek*. New York: Atria Books, 2015.
Tademy, Lalita. *Red River*. New York: Grand Central Publishing, 2007.
Takiff, Michael. *A Complicated Man: The Life of Bill Clinton as Told by Those Who Know Him*. New Haven: Yale University Press, 2010.
Tartt, Donna. "The Belle and the Lady: An Investigation into Enduring Southern Stereotypes." *Oxford American* 26 (1999): 94–105.
Tasker, Yvonne, and Diane Negra. Introduction to *Interrogating Postfeminism: Gender and the Politics of Popular Culture*, 1–26. Durham: Duke University Press, 2007.
Tate, Linda. "A Second Southern Renaissance." In *The History of Southern Women's Literature*, edited by Carolyn Perry and Mary Louise Weaks, 491–497. Baton Rouge: Louisiana State University Press, 2002.
Tate, Linda. *A Southern Weave of Women: Fiction of the Contemporary South*. Athens: University of Georgia Press, 1996.

Taylor, Kate. "Southern Suffering, with a Dose of Sugar." *New York Sun*. January 11, 2008. https://www.nysun.com/arts/southern-suffering-with-a-dose-of-sugar/69359.

Taylor, Ula. "Black Feminisms and Human Agency." In *No Permanent Waves: Recasting Histories of U.S. Feminism*, edited by Nancy Hewitt, 61–76. New Brunswick, N.J.: Rutgers University Press, 2010.

Taylor, Verta. "Sisterhood, Solidarity, and Modern Feminism." *Gender and Society* 3, no. 2 (June 1989): 277–286.

Thelma & Louise. Directed by Ridley Scott. Pathé Entertainment, 1991.

"*Thelma & Louise*: Awards." IMDB. https://www.imdb.com/title/tt0103074/awards.

"*Thelma & Louise* Trailer." YouTube. https://www.youtube.com/watch?v=PRr0HY9MPZ0.

"*Thelma & Louise* Wins Original Screenplay: 1992 Oscars." YouTube. https://m.youtube.com/watch?v=29ePCxCBZ14.

"13 Shocking *Oprah Show* Moments." Oprah.com. https://www.oprah.com/own-where-are-they-now/the-oprah-shows-most-shocking-moments_1.

Thompson, Anne. "Geena Davis, Callie Khouri, and Mimi Polk Gitlin Talk *Thelma & Louise* at 20." *Indie Wire*, August 21, 2015. https://www.indiewire.com/2011/08/geena-davis-callie-khouri-and-mimi-polk-gitlin-talk-thelma-louise-at-20-184944.

Thompson, Becky. "Multiracial Feminism: Recasting the Chronology of Second-Wave Feminism." In *No Permanent Waves*, edited by Nancy Hewitt, 39–60. New Brunswick, N.J.: Rutgers University Press, 2010.

Thompson, Robert. Foreword to *The Oprah Phenomenon*, edited by Jennifer Harris and Elwood Watson, vii–viii. Lexington: University Press of Kentucky, 2007.

"Tidal to Donate $1.5 Million to Black Lives Matter." *Billboard*, February 5, 2016. https://www.billboard.com/articles/news/6867174/tidal-donating-15-million-black-lives-matter-social-nonprofit-groups.

"A Timeline of the Turner Media Empire." *Atlanta Journal Constitution*, March 4, 2019. https://www.ajc.com/business/turner-broadcasting-timeline/Oa63C3Of3MhiFoZaSNUz3K.

Timmerman, David M. "1992 Presidential Campaign Films: The Contrasting Narratives of George Bush and Bill Clinton." *Presidential Studies Quarterly* 26, no. 2 (Spring 1996): 364–373.

"Tina's Bio." Tina McElroy Ansa. https://tinamcelroyansa.com/tinas-bio.

Tindall, George B. "The Benighted South: Origins of a Modern Image." *Virginia Quarterly Review* 40, no. 2 (Spring 1964): 281–294.

Tinsley, Omise'eke. *Beyoncé in Formation: Remixing Black Feminism*. Austin: University of Texas Press, 2018. Kindle.

"TNT Takes Its First Step." *Broadcasting*, October 3, 1988. https://www.americanradiohistory.com/hd2/IDX-Business/Magazines/Archive-BC-IDX/88-OCR/BC-1988-10-03-OCR-Page-0044.pdf.

Tony Brown's Journal. "Purple Rage." 1986.

Tornabene, Lyn. "Here's Oprah." *Woman's Day*, October 1, 1986, 56.

Traister, Rebecca. "What Oprah Can't Forget." *Salon*, January 13, 2007. https://www.salon.com/2007/01/13/oprah_school.

Travers, Peter. "*Beloved*." *Rolling Stone*, October 16, 1998. https://www.rollingstone.com/movies/movie-reviews/beloved-99790.

Travis, Trysh. "'It Will Change the World If Everybody Reads This Book': New Thought Religion and Oprah's Book Club." *American Quarterly* 59, no. 3 (September 2007): 1017–1041.

Traylor, Eleanor. "Re-Calling the Black Woman." In *The Black Woman*, edited by Toni Cade Bambara, Kindle location 58–180. New York: New American Library, 1970. Kindle.

Triad Stage. "*Crimes of the Heart* Dramaturgy: Beth Henley." https://sites.google.com/site/crimesoftheheartdramaturgy/beth-henley.

Tsang, Martin L. "Signifying Waters: The Magnetic and Poetic Magic of Oshún as Reflected in Beyoncé's *Lemonade*." In *The Lemonade Reader*, edited by Kinitra D. Brooks and Kameelah L. Martin, 123–132. New York: Routledge, 2019.

Turan, Kenneth. "Smooth Ride for *Thelma & Louise*." *Los Angeles Times*, May 24, 1991. https://www.latimes.com/archives/la-xpm-1991-05-24-ca-2303-story.html.

"Turner Acquires 'Gone with the Wind.'" *New York Times*, August 14, 1987. https://www.nytimes.com/1987/08/14/arts/turner-acquires-gone-with-the-wind.html.

Tyler, Lisa. "Mother-Daughter Myth and the Marriage of Death in *Steel Magnolias*." *Literature/Film Quarterly* 22, no. 2 (1994): 98–104.

Ulven, Allison. "Together We Came: Callie Khouri." Arab American Institute, June 11 2018. https://www.aaiusa.org/together_we_came_callie_khouri.

University of Missouri School of Law. "Lynchings by State and Race, 1882–1968." http://law2.umkc.edu/faculty/projects/ftrials/shipp/lynchingsstate.html.

"*Ugly Ways*." *Kirkus Reviews*, July 26, 1993. https://www.kirkusreviews.com/book-reviews/tina-mcelroy-ansa/ugly-ways.

"*Ugly Ways*." *Publishers' Weekly*, https://www.publishersweekly.com/9780151925537.

U.S. Eastern District of Louisiana. *Kimberly Roberts v. Prettybird Pictures, Inc., Order of Dismissal*. July 31, 2018. https://pacer.uscourts.gov.

Van Meter, Jonathan. "Looking for Oprah." *Oxford American* 26 (Spring 1999). https://main.oxfordamerican.org/magazine/itemlist/category/125-issue-26-spring-1999-southern-women-double-issue.

Van Meter, Jonathan. "Oprah Winfrey Is on a Roll (Again)." *Vogue*, August 15, 2017. https://www.vogue.com/article/oprah-winfrey-vogue-september-issue-2017.

Velasco, Antonio de. *Centrist Rhetoric: The Production of Political Transcendence in the Clinton Presidency*. New York: Lexington Books, 2010.

"Villa Marre." *Encyclopedia of Arkansas*. http://www.encyclopediaofarkansas.net/encyclopedia/entry-detail.aspx?entryID=2108.

"Voices from the Gaps: Tina McElroy Ansa." University of Minnesota, 2009. https://conservancy.umn.edu/bitstream/handle/11299/166076/Ansa,%20Tina%20McElroy.pdf;sequence=1.

Wadley, Ted. "Tina McElroy Ansa." *New Georgia Encyclopedia*. https://www.georgiaencyclopedia.org/articles/arts-culture/tina-mcelroy-ansa-b-1949.

Walker, Alice. *The Color Purple*. New York: Simon & Schuster, 1982.

Walker, Alice. *In Search of Our Mothers' Gardens: Womanist Prose*. New York: Harcourt, Brace, Jovanovich, 1983. Kindle.

Walker, Alice. "In These Dissenting Times." In *Revolutionary Petunias and Other Poems*, 15. London: Women's Press, 1988.

Walker, Alice. *The Same River Twice: Honoring the Difficult*. New York: Scribner, 1996.

Walker, Alice. "Women." In *Revolutionary Petunias and Other Poems*, 19. London: Women's Press, 1988.
Walker, Rebecca. *Baby Love: Choosing Motherhood after a Lifetime of Ambivalence*. London: Profile Books, 2007.
Walker, Rebecca. "Becoming the Third Wave." *Ms.*, January/February 1992, 41.
Walker, Rebecca. "Being Real: An Introduction." In *To Be Real: Telling the Truth and Changing the Face of Feminism*, edited by Rebecca Walker, xxix–xl. New York: Anchor Books, 1995.
Wall, Wendy. "Lettered Bodies and Corporeal Texts." In *Alice Walker: Critical Perspectives Past and Present*, edited by Henry Louis Gates Jr., 261–274. New York: Amistad, 1993.
Wallace, Alicia. "A Critical View of Beyoncé's 'Formation.'" *Black Camera* 9, no. 1 (Fall 2017): 189–196.
Wallace, Michele. "Blues for Mr. Spielberg." *Village Voice*, March 18, 1986, 21–24, 26. CineFiles, University of California Berkeley Art Museum and Pacific Film Archive. https://webapps.cspace.berkeley.edu/cinefiles/imageserver/blobs/b1640b27-26d5-4a06-8478/content/linked_pdf.
Ward, Jesmyn. "In Beyoncé's 'Formation,' A Glorification of 'Bama' Blackness." NPR, February 10, 2016. https://www.npr.org/sections/codeswitch/2016/02/10/466178725/in-beyonc-s-formation-a-song-for-the-bama?t=1605443187741.
Washington, Mary Helen. "As Essay on Alice Walker." In *Alice Walker: Critical Perspectives Past and Present*, edited by Henry Louis Gates Jr., 37–49. New York: Amistad, 1993.
Watkins, Mel. "*The Color Purple*." In *Alice Walker: Critical Perspectives Past and Present*, edited by Henry Louis Gates Jr., 16–18. New York: Amistad, 1993.
Waxman, Sharon. "Hollywood Friend Comes Back into the Picture." *Washington Post*, January 29, 1998. https://www.washingtonpost.com/wp-srv/politics/special/clinton/stories/thomason012998.htm?.
Weller, Sheila. "The Ride of a Lifetime." *Vanity Fair*, February 11, 2012. https://www.vanityfair.com/news/2011/03/the-making-of-thelma-and-louise-201103.
Wells, Rebecca. *The Divine Secrets of the Ya-Ya Sisterhood*. New York: Harper Collins, 1996.
"What Beyoncé Told Freedia about 'Formation' Before It Dropped." *Fuse*, November 10, 2016. https://www.youtube.com/watch?v=PSvxJheVsOY.
Wheeler, Marjorie Spruill. *New Women of the New South: The Leaders of the Woman Suffrage Movement in the Southern States*. New York: Oxford University Press, 1993.
Where the Heart Is. Directed by Matt Williams. Twentieth Century Fox, 2000.
White, Evelyn C. *Alice Walker: A Life*. New York: Norton, 2004.
White, Mark. "Son of the Sixties: The Controversial Image of Bill Clinton." *History* 103, no. 254 (2018): 100–123.
Whitney, Melissa Sue Romweber. "Tina McElroy Ansa's *Ugly Ways* and *Taking after Mudear*: Mother-Daughter Psychological Diasporas." MA thesis, University of Texas at San Antonio, 2009.
Wilkerson-Freeman, Sarah. "Stealth in the Political Arsenal of Southern Women: A Retrospective for the Millennium." In *Southern Women at the Millennium: A Historical Perspective*, edited by Melissa Walker, Jeanette R. Dunn, and Joe P. Dunn, 42–82. Columbia: University of Missouri Press, 2003.

Williams, Keira V. "'Between Creation and Devouring': Southern Women Writers and the Politics of Motherhood." *Southern Cultures* 21, no. 2 (Summer 2015): 27–42.
Williams, Linda. "What Makes a Woman Wander." *Film Quarterly* 25, no. 2 (Winter 1991–1992): 27.
Willis, Susan. "Walker's Women." In *Alice Walker: Modern Critical Views*, edited by Harold Bloom, 81–95. New York: Chelsea House, 1989.
Winch, Alison. *Girlfriends and Postfeminist Sisterhood*. London: Palgrave MacMillan, 2013.
"The Wind Done Gone." *Publishers Weekly*, n.d. https://www.publishersweekly.com/978-0-618-13309-3.
Windels, Kasey, Sara Champlin, Summer Shelton, Yvette Sterbenk, and Maddison Poteet. "Selling Feminism: How Female Empowerment Campaigns Employ Postfeminist Discourse." *Journal of Advertising* 49 (2019): 18–33.
Winfrey, Oprah. "What I Know for Sure: Life's Greatest Work." *Oprah*, n.d. https://www.oprah.com/omagazine/oprah-on-opening-her-leadership-academy.
Wolfe, Margaret Ripley. *Daughters of Canaan: A Saga of Southern Women*. Lexington: University Press of Kentucky, 1995.
"The Woman behind *The Man from Hope*." *New York Times*, September 17, 2017. https://www.nytimes.com/2017/09/17/opinion/man-from-hope-clinton.html.
Women of the House. "Guess Who's Sleeping in Lincoln's Bed." Season 1, episode 3, January 9, 1995.
Women of the House. "Miss Sugarbaker Goes to Washington." Season 1, episodes 1–2, January 4, 1995.
Women of the House. "Women in Film." Season 1, episode 10, August 25, 1995.
Women of the House. "You Talk Too Much." Season 1, episode 6, January 25, 1995.
Woods, Clyde. "'Sittin' on Top of the World': The Challenge of Blues and Hip-Hop Geography." In *Black Geographies and the Politics of Place*, edited by Katherine McKittrick and Clyde Woods, 46–81. Boston: South End Press, 2007.
Yang, Xiaoping. "TV Talk Show Therapy as a Distinct Genre of Discourse." *Discourse Studies* 10, no. 4 (2008): 469–491.
"Your Best Life." *Oprah Magazine*, n.d. Accessed December 22, 2022. https://web.archive.org/web/20190330212819/https://www.oprahmag.com/life.
Zillman, Claire. "Oprah Winfrey *Beloved* Movie Failure." *Fortune*, August 15, 2017. https://fortune.com/2017/08/15/oprah-winfrey-movie-failure-advice.
Zook, Kristal Brent. "A Manifesto of Sorts for a Black Feminist Movement." *New York Times*, November 12, 1995. https://www.nytimes.com/1995/11/12/magazine/a-manifesto-of-sorts-for-a-black-feminist-movement.html.
Zucker, Alyssa N. "Disavowing Social Identities: What It Means When Women Say, 'I'm Not a Feminist, But.'" *Psychology of Women Quarterly* 28 (2004): 423–435.

INDEX

Academy Awards (Oscars), 31, 83, 85, 87, 126, 156
Adichie, Chimamanda Ngozi, 164
Angelou, Maya, 134, 135, 137, 138
Ansa, Tina McElroy: *Taking After Mudear*, 195n6; *Ugly Ways*, 13, 16, 32–51, 54, 55, 139
Anthony, Susan B., 129
Armey, Dick, 121

backlash, 2–3, 10, 79, 98
Being Mary Jane (television show), 160
"belle" stereotype, 72, 89; in *Crimes of the Heart*, 19, 20, 23; on *Designing Women*, 105, 106; in *Gone with the Wind*, 2, 3, 4, 6–7
Beloved (Morrison), 146–150
Big Freedia, 165, 170
Black feminism: 5, 49, 55, 68, 167; in *Beloved*, 146–149, 155; "bridge" metaphor, 138–139; foremothers, 43, 67–68, 137–139, 149, 151, 167, 170; lesbianism, 59, 63–64, 66, 71; in literature: 137–138, 140, 156; motherhood, 41–44, 46; music, 164, 165, 170, 171; role of rage, 59, 71, 85, 107, 148–149; sisterhood, 53, 59; socialism, 64; trauma and memory, 139, 144, 147–150, 152, 157; in *Ugly Ways*, 49, 50; in *The Wind Done Gone*, 159–160; Oprah Winfrey, 124–125, 139–140, 146–147, 156–157. See also womanism
Black Lives Matter, 167
Bloodworth-Thomason, Linda, 88–90, 109, 112, 115, 120, 121–122; *Designing Women*, 90–108, 119–122; *The Man from Hope*, 116–119; *Women of the House*, 120–121
Bluest Eye, The (Morrison), 140
Bosia, Akosua, 68

Burke, Delta, 91
Burnett, Carol, 1
Bush, George H. W., 88, 99, 103
Bush, George W., 121
Bust magazine, 123

Cane River (Tademy), 141–145
Carter, Dixie, 91, 94
Carter, Rosalynn, 107
celebrity feminism, 163, 164
Chicks, the (formerly the Dixie Chicks), 12
Chopin, Kate, 7
civil rights movement, 44, 91, 117 160, 163; backlash against, 88, 92, 105, 109, 112–113; role of women, 8–9, 11, 25, 138; Alice Walker and, 55, 65–66, 68
Clark, Breena, 192n75
Cleage, Pearl, 192n75
Clinton, Bill, 88–89, 91, 108–116, 120, 121; *The Man from Hope*, 116–119
Clinton, Chelsea, 111, 118, 119
Clinton, Hillary Rodham, 88, 91; as first lady of Arkansas 110–112; during 1992 campaign, 114–115, 116, 118, 119, 120
Clinton, Roger, 110, 117, 118
Coincoin, Marie Thérése, 168
colorism, 142–143
Color Purple, The: film: 66–71, 81, 83, 84, 126; novel, 13–14, 53–66, 78, 126, 160, 167; play, 160
consciousness raising, 12; in *The Color Purple*, 55, 59, 60, 71; on *Designing Women*, 93; on *The Oprah Winfrey Show*, 127–128, 136–137, 152, 154; in *Thelma & Louise*, 52, 78, 81; in *Ugly Ways*, 42, 44
Crimes of the Heart (Henley), 16–32, 33, 36, 37, 44, 50–51

233

Dallas (television show), 10
Davis, Geena, 73, 85
Delay, Tom, 121
Demme, Jonathan, 151, 152
Designing Women (television show), 90–108, 119–122. *See also* Bloodworth-Thomason, Linda
Divine Secrets of the Ya-Ya Sisterhood, The: Khouri film, 160; Wells novel, 15
Donahue, Phil, 69, 126
Dukes of Hazzard, The (television show), 10, 76

Elliott, Missy, 12
Emmy Awards, 89, 93, 97, 129
Equal Rights Amendment, 7

Flowers, Gennifer, 114
"fourth-wave" feminism, 164–165
Friedan, Betty, 130

Garner, Margaret, 153, 154
Gates, Bill, 157, 167
German Coast Uprising, 171
Gibbons, Kaye, 192n75
Gingrich, Newt, 112–113, 121
Girl Effect (Nike campaign), 161
Glasgow, Ellen, 7
Global South, 131, 132
Goldberg, Whoopi, 66, 69
Golden Girls, The (television show), 97
Gone with the Wind: on *Designing Women*, 90, 105–107, 120; feminism in, 3; Mitchell novel, 6–7; 1970s–1980s film revival, 1–3, 5, 9–10; racism, 4–5

Henley, Beth: 16; *Crimes of the Heart*, 16–32, 33, 36, 37, 44, 50–51
Hill, Anita, 84, 87, 99, 120
HIV-AIDS, 97, 192n75
Hurston, Zora Neale, 7, 170

In Search of Our Mothers' Gardens (A. Walker), 43–43, 54
intimate partner violence: in *The Color Purple*, 61, 67, 70–71; in *Crimes of the Heart*, 10, 21, 24; on *Designing Women*, 100; in *The Man from Hope*, 118; on *The Oprah Winfrey Show*, 137
Ivins, Molly, 107

Jones, Quincy, 126
Joplin, Janis, 7

Keaton, Diane, 31
Kelley, Virginia, 110, 118
Kennedy, John F., 117
Kennedy, Robert, 117
Khouri, Callie, 72–73; *The Divine Secrets of the Ya-Ya Sisterhood*, 160; *Thelma & Louise*, 52–54, 72–86, 87, 100, 107–108
King, Martin Luther, Jr., 117, 167
Kingsolver, Barbara, 160–161
Knowles, Beyoncé, 13, 163–172

labor unionism, 95
"lady" stereotype, 6, 9; in *Crimes of the Heart*, 19, 30, 31; on *Designing Women*, 92–93, 101, 105, 106; in *Gone with the Wind*, 7, 9
Lange, Jessica, 31
Lee, Spike, 67
Letts, Billie, 192n75
LGBTQ+ rights, 10, 180n47
lifestyle feminism, 46, 122, 125, 130, 134, 142
Lost Cause, 1, 6–7, 10, 13, 20, 106
lynching, 60, 65
Lynn, Loretta, 12

"mammy" stereotype, 48, 56, 132–133, 160
Mandela, Nelson, 161, 163
Man from Hope, The (Bloodworth-Thomason film), 116–119. *See also* Clinton, Bill
Mary Tyler Moore Show, The (television show), 10, 98
*M*A*S*H* (television show), 89, 90
McCullers, Carson, 7, 16
Messy Mya, 170
#MeToo, 73
Mitchell, Margaret, 1, 4, 7, 105. *See also Gone with the Wind*
Morrison, Toni, 134, 135, 137, 139; *Beloved*, 146–150; *The Bluest Eye*, 140; *Paradise*, 135

National Book Award, 53, 55, 71, 139
neoconservatism, 13, 88, 89, 90, 159, 172; "family values," 111; gender, 94, 112, 114, 121; race, 92
neoliberal feminism, 41, 130–131, 161, 166–167; on *Designing Women*, 88, 96, 100, 103, 122; Beyoncé Knowles, 166–167; in *Ugly*

Ways, 44, 46, 50; Oprah Winfrey, 129–134, 145, 151, 152, 157, 161–163
New Democrats, 88; Bill Clinton, 89, 91, 107, 112, 116, 119; on *Designing Women*, 94, 103
New South Creed, 103
new southern studies, 104, 175n47

O'Connor, Flannery, 7, 16, 28, 83
O'Hara, Scarlett. See *Gone with the Wind*
One Day at a Time (television show), 10, 89

Paradise (Morrison), 135
Parton, Dolly, 12
Poisonwood Bible, The (Kingsolver), 160–161
postfeminism, 2–3, 88, 129–130, 159
Potts, Annie, 91, 94
Pulitzer Prize, 16, 28, 44, 53, 55, 71, 146

Queen Sugar (television show), 171

Rainey, Gertrude "Ma," 7
Randall, Alice, 159–160
rape: in *Beloved*, 148, 153; in *Cane River*, 141–142, 143; in *The Color Purple*, 55–56, 61, 65, 67; in *Crimes of the Heart*, 24–26, 30; on *Designing Women*, 100, 107; on *The Oprah Winfrey Show*, 128; in *Thelma & Louise*, 75–76, 77, 82–83
Reagan, Nancy, 111
Reagan, Ronald, 10, 88, 94, 97, 103, 130
respectability politics, 46, 47–48, 63, 149, 162–163, 166
Revolutionary Petunias (A. Walker), 67–68
Reynolds, Sheri, 192n75
Richards, Ann, 107, 116, 121
Ripley, Margaret, 2
Roberts, Kimberly, 170

Sandberg, Sheryl, 130, 157, 166–167
Sarandon, Susan, 74, 79, 82, 85
Scott, Ridley, 73, 77, 83
"second-wave" feminism, 54, 89, 128–129, 138; backlash against, 79, 98, 130; motherhood, 42, 50; sisterhood, 52–53; in South, 8–9, 11, 29, 44, 50, 131; "waves" model, 10–11
Simone, Nina, 7
sisterhood, 30, 52–54, 85, 87; in *The Color Purple*, 58, 62, 64; neoliberal feminism,

122; race, 8, 55; "second wave," 16, 17, 50, 95; in *Thelma & Louise*, 73, 79, 80, 83; "third wave," 15
Slaughter, Ann-Marie, 130
slavery: "afterlife of slavery," 144, 147, 148, 154, 167–170; in *Beloved*, 147–149, 151, 155–156; in *Gone with the Wind*, 4, 106, 107; violence against women in, 67, 140, 141–144, 147, 152, 153
Smart, Jean, 91
Smith, Bessie, 7
Smith, Lillian, 7
southern gothic, 16–17, 28, 31, 32, 83
Southern Strategy, 92, 113, 121
Spacek, Sissy, 31
Spielberg, Steven, 66, 69
Steel Magnolias (film), 3, 4–6, 72, 94, 104, 105
Steinem, Gloria, 53, 128, 130
suicide, 192n75; in *Crimes of the Heart*, 18, 26, 27, 31, 49, 50; in *Thelma & Louise*, 79, 80

Tademy, Lalita, 140–141; *Cane River*, 141–145; other novels, 195n6
Taking After Mudear (Ansa), 195n6
talk shows, 124, 126–127, 129, 132, 139; teletherapy, 127–128, 136, 152. See also Winfrey, Oprah
Thelma & Louise (Khouri film), 52–54, 72–86, 87, 100, 107–108
"third-wave" feminism, 85, 87, 88, 114, 133, 161; generational conflict, 15–16, 17, 44, 178n107; "waves" model, 10–11; Oprah Winfrey, 123, 125, 139
Third Way: feminism, 86, 88–89, 95, 100, 103–104, 107, 121; politics 88–89, 109, 119, 120, 130
Thomas, Clarence, 84–85, 87, 98–99, 107
Thomason, Danny, 109, 110
Thomason, Harry, 88, 89, 108, 109, 112, 116
Till, Emmett, 26
TLC, 12
Tonight Show with Johnny Carson, The (television show), 112
Turner, Ted, 2, 106

Ugly Ways (Ansa), 13, 16, 32–51, 54, 55, 139

violence, 52, 54, 75, 76, 81–83, 147; lynching, 60, 65. See also intimate partner violence; rape

Walker, Alice, 137, 170, 178n107; *In Search of Our Mothers' Gardens*, 42–43, 54; *Revolutionary Petunias*, 67–68. See also *Color Purple, The*
Walker, Rebecca, 85, 87, 114, 133, 178n107
Wells, Rebecca, 15
Welty, Eudora, 7, 16, 28
Whatever Happened to Baby Jane (drama), 99, 100, 107
Williams, Serena, 169
Williams, Tennessee, 16, 19

Wind Done Gone, The (Randall), 159–160
Winfrey, Oprah, 6, 13, 123–126, 160, 171–172; *Beloved* (film), 146–156; Book Club, 134–146, 156–157; Leadership Academy, 161–163; *The Oprah Winfrey Show*, 12, 126–134
womanism, 54–55, 59, 62, 64, 69, 170
Women of the House (television show), 120–121. *See also* Bloodworth-Thomason, Linda
Wonder, Stevie, 61
Wynette, Tammy, 114, 115

www.ingramcontent.com/pod-product-compliance
Lightning Source LLC
Chambersburg PA
CBHW031745230426
43669CB00007B/488